PENSIONS

PENSIONS

James A. Hamilton
Actuary—Vice President, The Wyatt Company

Dorrance C. Bronson
Actuary—Vice President, The Wyatt Company

McGRAW-HILL BOOK COMPANY, INC.
New York   Toronto   London   1958

PENSIONS

The Authors

JAMES A. HAMILTON

Born, September 12, 1906, Kingston, Ontario, Canada. B.A., Queens University, 1927; M.A., Pennsylvania State University, 1930; M.S., University of Chicago, 1932. Instructor in Mathematics, Pennsylvania State University, 1928–1933. Conducted courses in Actuarial Science for Metropolitan Life Insurance Company, 1933–1939, and for Actuaries Club of New York, 1939–1942; Lecturer, Insurance Society of New York, 1938–1939. Research Assistant, Metropolitan Life, 1939–1942. Major and Actuary, Life Section, Contract Insurance Branch, Department of Finance, U.S. Army, 1942–1945. Vice President and Treasurer, The Wyatt Company since 1946. Fellow, Society of Actuaries; Member, Fraternal Actuarial Society.

DORRANCE C. BRONSON

Born, December 30, 1899, Lowville, New York. A.B., University of Michigan, 1924. Employed in Life Actuarial Department, and Assistant Actuary, Group Actuarial Department, Travelers Insurance Company, 1924–1937. Assistant Actuary, Office of the Actuary, Social Security Administration, 1937–1944. Vice President and Actuary, The Wyatt Company, 1946 to date. Fellow, Society of Actuaries; Associate, Institute of Actuaries (Great Britain); Member, Fraternal Actuarial Association. Member of, or on staff of, sundry committees studying retirement plans, social insurance, and employee benefits. Coauthor, "Employee Retirement Plans," 1945. Author, "Concepts of Actuarial Soundness in Pension Plans," 1957. Has written numerous papers and addresses on actuarial subjects.

Preface

In recent years pension plans have become a vital element in the economy of the United States. The emphasis on adequate provision for old age, the huge sums of money that are being set aside currently to meet future benefit payments, the place of pensions in labor negotiations, the relation of private plans to social security legislation, and the growing interest of governmental agencies in the supervision of these plans all bear witness to the importance of the pension movement.

This book reviews the reasons for the great interest in private pension plans and presents and discusses the designing, funding, and financing of these plans, and the special problems of public and quasi-public retirement systems. It avoids both the highly technical actuarial aspects of pensions and the too-elementary approach. For college students, for employees of insurers and trust companies, for persons covered by these plans, and for the organizations—corporate, union, and public—charged with the responsibilities of administering pension plans, it is hoped that this book will serve as a definitive text and reference. Although there is some repetition verging on duplication, it is believed that this will make the book more useful and readable than would the adoption of the alternative procedure of including many cross references.

The book has been slowly put together over a long period of time, as the requirements of the authors' consulting work would permit, and attempting to keep it up to date to reflect the rapid developments in the pension field has been a difficult matter. Only with the valued assistance of our associates has this been possible. We are indebted to several of our colleagues for their assistance and particularly to Mrs.

Ruth Kundin, who edited the complete manuscript; Miss Elvira Del Signore, who was in charge of the deciphering of our dictation and notoriously poor handwriting, and Mr. John Forsyth, who prepared the chapter treating with pension plans in Canada. We also wish to register our appreciation for the comments made by Mr. Joseph Crimmins and Mr. George Shugart, both of whom read the manuscript and offered many helpful suggestions.

JAMES A. HAMILTON
DORRANCE C. BRONSON

Contents

Funding the Pension Plan; Employee Contributions; Provisions to Protect the Employee; Provisions to Protect the Employer; Provisions to Protect the Insurer or Trustee

CHAPTER 1

The Place of a Pension Plan
in an Employee-welfare Program

Definition and Character. A *pension plan* is a program for providing regular payments to retired employees for life. Normally, it involves accumulation of funds in a systematic manner during the employees' working years and subsequent distribution of those funds during the period when the employees can no longer be carried on the payroll because of old age or serious disability. In the past a *pension* was a gratuity or bounty given by an employer, but the term is currently used to denote any form of periodical retirement benefit.[1]

In practice, the employee often contributes substantially toward the cost of a pension plan, and even in those cases where the employer pays the entire cost the pension is considered not as a gift but as a convenient means of fulfilling the employer's responsibilities toward his old and loyal employees, whether the resulting pension is viewed as a reward, as continued payroll, as a charge for human depreciation, as a distribution of deferred pay, as organized savings, as a social service, as a business economy, as a union commitment, or as a pay-

[1] The terms *pension* and *pension plan* are used throughout this book, although the connotation of *pension* is sometimes taken as the "charity" or "paternalism" concept of old-age benefits, a rather obsolete viewpoint today. The term *pension* is more immediately meaningful and easier to use than an expression obtained from combining such a word as "retirement," "superannuation," or "old age" with "plan," "system," "scheme," or "program." Also the word *pensioner* is more definite than recently coined words, such as "retirant" and "retiree," in that *pensioner* connotes one to whom a pension is being paid whereas the other expressions may refer to any retired person.

ment under any other philosophy of pensions that the employer may profess.

Reasons for Pension Plans. Regardless of his theory of pensions, an employer does seem to have a definite responsibility to employees who grow old in his service; practically, he cannot discharge super-annuated employees who have not saved sufficiently for old age with-out taking steps to aid them. Public opinion in recent years has so emphasized this responsibility that an employer's reputation in a com-munity and his chances of securing and retaining desirable employees will suffer if he does not make some definite provision for aged and incapacitated employees with long periods of service. Employees, often through labor organizations, have brought pressure on many concerns to install pension plans and other welfare programs.

An adequate pension plan permits an employer to replace older employees at the time when their efficiency has begun to decline. Retention of employees beyond the time when their effectiveness has definitely deteriorated constitutes a drag on the smooth operation of the entire organization. Retirement of older employees provides oppor-tunities for promotion among the younger, more vigorous employees. This keeps avenues of advancement open and improves employee morale and efficiency. Maintenance of a young and progressive organ-ization is facilitated.

Funding a Pension Program. Business and other enterprises are dependent on the efficient use of men and machines. Since men and machines both are subject to depreciation with age, provision for their orderly replacement upon obsolescence is a necessary cost of doing business. It has been advanced that just as depreciation reserves are accumulated to provide for replacing machines and other physical properties, so yearly contributions to a pension plan made during an employee's active service will make possible his replacement upon reaching retirement age.[2] This concept of a pension liability which accrues during, rather than at the end of, the employee's working years has led to the adoption of formalized pension plans many years before most employees are ready to retire. Yearly contributions are

---

[2] This analogy was expressed by the 1949 Steel Industry Board (a fact-finding board) and influenced its findings in favor of noncontributory pensions; however, the coupling of men with machines has had its severe critics.

placed in a reserve fund—with an insurance company or a trustee—and invested at interest to become available for pension payments following the retirement of the employee. The procedure of spreading pension costs over certain periods of time and the resulting accumulation of a fund from which payments may subsequently be made is termed *funding* a pension plan. To the extent that the money required for the benefit is set aside before retirement takes place the procedure is termed *advance funding*.

In the past, various procedures have been followed in making pensions available to retired employees. Before the time when advance-funding methods became popular, most pensions in this country were provided without specific funding procedures. In some cases the employer would make a formal agreement to provide a retiring employee with a predetermined life pension and would pay the designated amounts out of current operating revenues during the employee's retirement. In other cases the employer would grant whatever pension, if any, he believed was necessary when the employee retired, depending on the individual circumstances (this latter is frequently termed an *informal pension method*). The realization that relatively large pension payments may be required at times in the future when the employer is not in a suitable financial position to make them and the failure of some employers to make them have greatly increased the relative prevalence of the funded plan under which the estimated cost of the pensions is met, in part or in full, before the employee's retirement.

Financing a Pension Plan. Closely allied to the matter of funding a pension is its financing. There are two principal mediums widely used for the investment of the amounts contributed under a formal pension plan established on the principles of advance-funding techniques. These are the life-insurance company and the bank or trust company (or in some cases individual trustees). In most instances the financing agency selected not only is charged with the responsibility of investing the funds contributed under the plan and of paying benefits to the designated recipient but also assists with the administration of the plan to some degree.

Occasionally neither of these financing mediums will be selected, but rather the employer will operate the pension plan on a pay-as-you-go basis, making pension disbursements from current income.

This type of arrangement is now infrequently found; from the stand-point of the pensioners it is a hazardous one with little in the way of guarantee of future benefits. On rare occasions the pension plan will be financed through the creation and accumulation of a special reserve account on the employer's books. Since the employer has ready access to the funds, this does not constitute an arm's-length transaction, and he is not permitted to deduct from his taxable income any amounts so set aside before they are paid out to the employees.

In some situations both of the main types of financing are used concurrently, sometimes with certain classes of employees covered under a plan financed through an insurer and with other classes under a trust-fund plan. In other instances, one method will be used to provide the basic retirement benefit, but for some employees—for ex-ample, the higher-paid personnel—the basic benefit will be supple-mented by benefits provided under a separate plan which sometimes utilizes the other financing medium.

In still other instances, especially in the case of large pension plans, a split-funding approach is adopted under which both types of financing are used for a single plan, with part of the contributions channeled into a trust fund and the balance contributed under an insurance-company group-annuity contract.

A Pension Plan as Part of an Integrated Welfare Program. Funda-mentally, the purpose of a pension plan is to provide retirement payments to aged employees; it may also provide other benefits, such as payments in event of death, of serious long-term disability, or of termination of employment. These collateral benefits, however, do not give complete and adequate protection against all the hazards con-fronting an employee. Other welfare needs, such as those for indemnity or expense payments during unexpected or prolonged sickness and hospitalization and for payment of doctors' or surgeons' bills are direct and immediate. Even when a pension plan provides some death benefit, it may be insufficient to care satisfactorily for the employee's dependents. Many employers feel that a well-rounded welfare program must provide basic death benefits, accident-and-sickness benefits, and hospital-and-surgical benefits; frequently, these benefits, and some-times others—such as the recently popular major medical benefits—are provided through a program of group insurance to which the employee usually makes substantial contributions. The Blue Cross and Blue Shield programs, for hospitalization and surgical expense, respectively, are frequently adopted. Combining these "current-risk" benefits with a pension plan goes far toward completing a well-rounded welfare program, since the pension plan provides old-age protection during the employee's declining years. A pension plan carries commitments far into the future and is a most important element in the employer's welfare scheme. The benefits and contributions under the pension plan should be carefully integrated with those applicable to the balance of the welfare program so that substantial benefits may be provided for the several contingencies and so that the contributions required of both employer and employee may be paid without undue sacrifice.

Established Businesses Safest for Pension Plans. Frequently the cost of a pension plan is 5 to 15 per cent of the payroll of the employees covered by the plan, and the employer usually contributes all or most of this cost; it is rare that an employee is called upon to contribute to an industrial pension fund more than 5 per cent of his earnings. The pension plan is the most expensive constituent of the welfare program, often costing more than all the other benefits combined. In return, a pension plan, if properly understood by the employees, should prove to be the most satisfactory part of a welfare program in creating better employee-employer feeling. Irrevocable employer contributions of the magnitude required for pensions are usually regarded as definite and indisputable manifestations of the employer's good will and cooperation.

Because a pension plan is essentially a long-range savings program, one upon which employees will base their hopes for their future and around which they can build their personal financial plans, it should be designed on a permanent basis, and restrictive changes and modifications should be made only after careful consideration and as a last resort. The element of a pension plan that is most subject to uncertain appraisal at the time of its adoption is the ability of the employer to maintain his intended scale of contributions. Curtailment of contributions makes modification of the pension plan inevitable and jeopardizes its success. It should be recognized, when a plan is adopted, that unexpected business reverses, depressions, or other mis-

fortunes may make it at times very difficult for the employer to pay
the contributions and that it may be necessary to draw upon surplus
to keep the plan in operation or to suspend contributions temporarily. Before finally deciding to adopt a plan and also before determining the scale of his contributions, the employer should have in
mind conservative long-range forecasts of his probable earnings available for pension contributions, together with an analysis of the effects
of making contributions from surplus for a limited period of adverse
business conditions. Since a pension plan entails very substantial costs
to the employer, since those costs are justified only if the plan fulfills
the purpose for which it was created, and since a reduction in the
benefits provided by a plan almost inevitably brings employee dissatisfaction, the employer should carefully review his business prospects
before considering its adoption, unless his organization is a well-
established, stable one with good prospects of being able to continue
the plan into the indefinite future. In some instances, temporary
conditions or expediency, such as war conditions of unusual industrial
activity, union demands, short-term tax advantages, or competition
in the labor market, have resulted in disregard of this principle.

Employees' Aid in Planning the Pension Program. A pension
plan should augment the personal thrift programs of employees, but
in some instances the pension plan and social-security benefits will be
practically the only bulwark an employee has against a dependent
old age. The benefits provided by the plan, the amount of contributions required of them, and the administration of the plan are of
paramount interest to employees. Only if the plan fits their needs and
their ability to make contributions, if required, will it be acceptable
to them and beneficial to the employer.

A pension plan drawn up entirely by an employer and presented
on a take-it-or-leave-it basis will rarely be satisfactory. This is particularly true where the employees are asked to contribute or are offered
a plan superimposed on a noncontributory plan and requiring substantial employee contributions. The design of those parts of the
retirement program that most directly affect the employees (types of
benefits, amounts of benefits, scale of contributions, and certain administrative details) is equally a matter of common sense and technical

detail. During the time when the provisions of the plan are being developed, cooperation in the design of the plan by representatives of the employees at management or lower levels, sometimes as a delegated committee, oftentimes is sought. A better mutual understanding of the problems should result, and employees will take greater interest in a plan they have helped to devise.

Just as unilateral action on the part of the employer may result in a poorly designed plan that does not function properly or in a plan that a labor union refuses to accept, so may a plan that is installed solely in response to, and on the terms of, a demand on the part of union or other employee groups turn out to meet only part of the retirement problem. It may ignore basic funding principles, is likely to be overliberal in the amount of proposed benefits, may ignore sound protection in the administrative provisions, and, in general, may tend to take an optimistic and unscientific view of the costs and long-range commitments that the employer is asked to accept. This may result in an impossible burden for the employer to bear in his competitive position, with a future result of deficiencies in the fund and ultimate disappointment and frustration among pensioners and employees looking forward to a pension. A plan designed solely to accommodate employee demands is likely to give inadequate consideration to the importance of making available suitable and effective retirement benefits for the employees compensated on a salaried basis and particularly the executive-employee group of a company—the individuals on whom the major responsibility rests for the continuation of the company's business in an efficient and profitable manner and, therefore, the ones among whom it is most important that timely retirements take place.

Private Pensions Only Part of Full Program. The inclusion of a pension plan within an employer's welfare program is logical, practicable, and increasingly common. Such a welfare program itself is a sort of middle layer in the total system of monetary security against the personal hazards of life. The basic layer comprises what government must or may do to prevent abject want where earning capacity is lacking, lost, or suspended; this is the field of benefits to meet presumptive need—old-age and survivors and disability insurance, unemployment insurance, workmen's compensation, state temporary-disability benefits, old-age assistance, aid to dependent children, aid to the blind, and public assistance generally, augmented in many instances by public and private charity.

The top layer of the general system of security is typically American; it lies in the many avenues of individual thrift. Home ownership, bank savings, investments, government bonds, life insurance, annuities, and many other methods characteristic of today's sacrifice for tomorrow's wants have long had a prominent place in our democratic philosophy.

The cooperative effort of individual employers and their employees toward organized pensions is a natural intermediate step between the statutory benefits basic to presumptive need and the heterogeneous and frequently rather speculative measures for security taken by the individual. This text deals mainly with this middle layer of protection; but, in doing so, it is necessary to refer frequently to the governmental basic layer, a résumé of which is given in Chapter 2.

The Social Security and
Railroad Retirement Acts—
Their Relation to Private Pension Plans

Background. In the past, few workers have been able to look forward to a degree of financial independence after retirement comparable to that enjoyed during the period when they were gainfully employed. This situation may have been the result of illness, educational deficiencies, inability to find steady work, failure to adjust to changing times, or other circumstances over which little or no control could be exercised. It has been estimated (with not very good documentation) that as recently as 20 years ago one-fourth to one-third of American men and women over age sixty-five had to rely chiefly on relief or family assistance for support.

Dependency became more pronounced toward the end of the nineteenth century and during the early twentieth century by reason of changes in the economic and social system that had been taking place over a considerable period of time. In the days when the family unit was more cohesive and self-sufficient than at present and when nonmechanical agriculture engaged the activities of a much greater part of the population, the duties of individuals as they became older could be made to conform to the diminution in their activity. The result was that such individuals continued to perform functions of only gradually diminishing economic value. To some extent there was, and still is, a tendency to transfer older employees of business organizations to lighter duties with decreasing responsibility; but as industrialization became more widespread, as improvements in health conditions permitted more employees to reach an advanced age, and particularly as more and more emphasis was placed on efficiency and skill in industry, opportunities for the employment of aged and impaired employees decreased. To put it somewhat differently, the time was approaching when there would not be enough routine guard and night-watchman jobs to accommodate the growing number of super-annuated employees.

A continuously decreasing birth rate (up to World War II) showed a similar effect in enlarging the proportion of the aged, and other influences were improvements in medical science, public health, and related fields of endeavor. Still another element that contributed to the natural aging of the population was the curtailment in the rate of immigration, which restricted one source of supply of younger people. Gradually it became evident that some measure of nationwide protection against economic and social insecurity in old age was essential.

Social Security Act. In June, 1934, in recognition of these conditions, the President appointed the Committee on Economic Security to study the problem of economic dependency and to recommend appropriate federal legislation. This study culminated in the Social Security Act, which became law on August 14, 1935.[1]

Old-age-and-survivors-and-disability-insurance Benefits. The Social Security Act provides a first floor of protection against many forms of economic and social insecurity. It includes provision for unemployment compensation, for public assistance to stated needy groups, certain public-welfare services, and old-age and survivors insurance. From the standpoint of pensions, the last of these items—which was enlarged in 1956 to include disability-insurance benefits—is of particular interest.

The *old-age-benefit* plan embodied in the Social Security Act became effective in its original form on January 1, 1937. Benefit payments, which were to commence not earlier than 1942, were related to total eligible wages earned by an employee in covered employment from the time he was first eligible for coverage under the act until he

---

[1] Certain provisions of the act did not become effective until later.

attained the retirement age of sixty-five.[2] A pension credit was allocated to each insured on the basis of his earnings in much the same manner as it is customary to allocate pension credits under many private pension plans. This idea of individual equities was carried over into the original Social Security Act from private insurance, together with the concept of the accumulation of large reserve funds to meet the pension payments. The monthly pension payable to insured persons who satisfied the conditions of eligibility was as follows:

1. ½ per cent of the first $3,000 of total eligible earnings (all years combined; limit $3,000 per year) subsequent to December 31, 1936, but prior to age sixty-five, plus

2. $\frac{1}{12}$ per cent of the next $42,000 of such earnings, plus

3. $\frac{1}{24}$ per cent of all the remaining eligible earnings in excess of $45,000, subject to a maximum retirement income of $85 per month

It soon became evident that this original formula relating benefits to aggregate eligible compensation did not provide a suitable benefit for those who reached age sixty-five in the early years following passage of the act. In addition, it did not provide benefits to members of the family other than the retired worker himself. The act was accordingly amended in 1939 to substitute *old-age and survivors insurance* [3] for *old-age benefits*. Under the new plan the old-age-insurance benefit was based on average wages [4] instead of on total accumulated wages. The *primary insurance benefit* for the retired worker was 40 per cent of his first $50 of average monthly wages plus 10 per cent of the next $200, all increased by 1 per cent for each year of coverage. This amendment meant greatly increased benefit payments for those retiring in the early years of the plan's operation before they had had the opportunity to accumulate any appreciable amount of total wages.

---

[2] Covered employment was generally limited to industrial wage earners and other employees of corporate enterprises. Other types of employees were excluded from coverage, including farm laborers; self-employed persons; domestic servants; professional people, such as doctors, lawyers, and accountants; employees of federal, state, and local governments; employees of charitable, religious, and other non-profit organizations; and other small groups. Eligible wages earned in covered employment were credited up to a limit of $3,000 received from any one employer in any one calendar year.

[3] Often referred to as OASI.

[4] Limited to the stated maximum.

The new plan recognized that the economic unit to be protected was the family and provided for additional benefits to be paid to dependents of the retired worker. The plan went further than providing old-age benefits and extended coverage to the dependents of eligible workers who died before reaching the retirement age. Covered employees became eligible for benefits as early as 1940 under the amended act, and pensions greatly increased over those originally contemplated were made effective after shorter periods of coverage.

These changes, effective in 1939, continued, with minor amendments, until August, 1950, when, after several different proposals had been considered by Congress, a new law was passed which retained the alleged—and challenged—philosophy inherent in the preceding measure that the system is truly contributory insurance. Under the 1950 law the *primary insurance amount* for the retired worker was 50 per cent of the first $100 of average monthly wage plus 15 per cent of the next $200.[5]

A further increase in the OASI benefits was enacted in 1952, first payments on the new basis being for the month of September, 1952, and extending to those already in receipt of benefits as well as to future beneficiaries. This change brought the primary insurance amount to 55 per cent of the first $100 plus 15 per cent of the next $200; the already retired employees received increases through a "conversion table."

Up to 1954 there had been three substantial increases in the OASI benefits enacted by Congress, and the wage ceiling was raised from $3,000 a year to $3,600 a year by the 1950 law. In 1954 Congress passed a fourth substantial increase in benefits and again raised the wage ceiling, this time to $4,200 a year. In 1956 fundamental amendments were enacted; coverage was again broadened to bring in the military and a larger group of the self-employed; younger retirement ages for women were introduced; and an income benefit became available (starting in July, 1957) for severe and prolonged cases of disability. A brief résumé of the benefits under the law as amended through 1956 follows (referred to now as OASDI, with the addition of disability benefits).

[5] The 1 per cent increment was discarded, while the eligible annual covered wage was increased to $3,600.

The Primary Insurance Amount. The *primary insurance amount* at age sixty-five under the Social Security Act is a monthly income to the insured which is determined by the following formula:

1. 55 per cent of the first $110 of average monthly earnings in covered employment, plus

2. 20 per cent of the excess, if any, of average monthly earnings over $110 (but never more than $240 in excess of $110, i.e., a maximum benefit of $108.50 a month)

The minimum pension is $30 per month.

For example, if an individual was covered [6] under old-age and survivors insurance from January 1, 1954, to January 1, 1985, at which time he attained his sixty-fifth birthday, and if his earnings over this period aggregated $115,320, his average monthly wage would be $310 ($115,320 ÷ 372), and his primary insurance amount would be:

1. 55 per cent of $110...................................	$ 60.50 per month
2. 20 per cent of ($310 − $110), or 20 per cent of $200......	40.00 per month
Total..	$100.50 per month

The primary insurance amount for a retiring female employee may commence in a reduced amount as early as age sixty-two. If she so elects, the amount commencing at that age would be 80 per cent of her regular primary amount computed on her *average wage up to* age sixty-two. She may increase this 80 per cent by $\frac{5}{9}$ per cent of the primary amount for each month she delays making the election, so that 100 per cent is reached if she defers commencement until age sixty-five. Once she makes the election for reduced early benefit, it is fixed at that level for life.

Commencing on July 1, 1957, the regularly computed primary insurance amount is payable as a *disability-insurance benefit,* subject to certain conditions:

1. Total and permanent disability (by a rather strict definition)

2. Fully and currently insured status at time of disability

3. Minimum duration of disability 6 months

[6] That is, was working in an employment covered by the terms of the act; this coverage now comprises nearly 100 per cent of employment compensated by wages or salary.

4. Insured has attained age fifty (but the disability may have commenced before age fifty)

The initial finding of disability is made by the state rehabilitation agencies, and continuation of disability benefits is conditioned on the insured's acceptance of rehabilitation efforts on his behalf. Supplementary benefits (see below) are not payable in conjunction with disability benefits until the disabled worker reaches age sixty-five and enters upon the old-age roll.

Supplementary Benefits. The Internal Revenue Service, in adopting its integration formula,[7] assumed that the old-age-insurance benefits paid under the act will average 150 per cent of the primary insurance amount, because of benefit payments to the insured's wife and/or his dependent children. For example, a wife will receive 50 per cent of her husband's primary insurance amount commencing when she is sixty-five, or, if she is younger, if she has a dependent child, providing her husband is then receiving the primary insurance amount. She need not wait until age sixty-five but may at age sixty-two reduce her benefit to 75 per cent of that otherwise due at age sixty-five (i.e., a reduction to $37\frac{1}{2}$ per cent of the husband's benefit instead of 50 per cent). If her election occurs after age sixty-two and before age sixty-five a graded amount applies. If the husband is not receiving old-age-insurance benefits, the wife's benefit will not commence until his does, although she may have already attained age sixty-five (or age sixty-two) or have a child in her care.[8] If the insured is receiving old-age benefits, a benefit to a child is also payable during its dependency under age eighteen, or older if the child is disabled. The maximum monthly benefit payable to a family for one wage earner is $200.

Other supplementary benefits under the old-age-survivors-and-disability-insurance title of the act are payable to survivors of a qualified deceased wage earner or deceased retired wage earner. Monthly benefits are payable to certain survivors—to a widow, if, or when, she has attained age sixty-two (without reduction, unlike wives and female employees), to a widow under sixty-two if she has a child of the deceased

---

[7] See Chap. 5, pp. 92, 93.

[8] If she is entitled by her own wage record, she will receive her primary insurance amount (reduced at age sixty-two, or in full at age sixty-five) even if her husband does not.

in her care, to a child or children of the deceased with or without the widow, and, if none of these monthly benefits is immediately payable, to one or both parents of the deceased wage earner if the father is over sixty-five or the mother over sixty-two, and if they were chiefly dependent upon the wage earner at the time of his death. Monthly widow's benefits cease upon a widow's remarriage and are suspended if she earns income in excess of the allowable maximums stated in the law. Monthly benefits for the children cease upon marriage or on the attainment of age eighteen (unless they are disabled), whichever is earlier; if they receive income in excess of the maximum allowable under the law, their benefits may be suspended. A lump-sum death benefit equal to three times the primary insurance amount (but with a $255 maximum) will be paid upon the death of any insured or retired worker, but this does not prevent the payment of other benefits to his survivors.

Although $200 is the limit of the total amount of OASDI monthly income that may be received for one wage earner, the maximum monthly payment is further restricted to an amount not in excess of 80 per cent of the average monthly wage.

The percentage of the primary insurance amount that is payable under various circumstances is shown in Table 2-1.

For example, an insured person retires upon attaining age sixty-five with a wife aged fifty and two dependent children aged ten and fifteen respectively; there would be payable 250 per cent (maximum $200 a month) of the primary insurance amount for the 3 years until the older child reached age eighteen (assuming that this child does not lose its dependency status by working or marrying in the meantime); 200 per cent for the next 5 years, until the second child attains age eighteen; 100 per cent for the following 4 to 7 years until the wife attains age sixty-two and elects the benefit commencement, when the benefit is increased to 137½ per cent of the primary amount, or until election is made later, when it reaches 150 per cent if commencement of wife's portion is deferred until she reaches age sixty-five. At the death of the retired wage earner, the pension payable, if any, would be determined by applying the appropriate percentage indicated by the right-hand portion of Table 2-1 to the primary insurance amount.

TABLE 2-1. OLD-AGE-AND-SURVIVORS-AND-DISABILITY-INSURANCE BENEFITS
AS PERCENTAGES OF PRIMARY INSURANCE AMOUNT

If wage earner is alive, retired and age 65, or age 50 and disabled		If wage earner is dead	
Recipients *	Per cent of primary amount	Recipients *	Per cent of primary amount
Wage earner alone (or with wife under 65 and no children)..	100	Widow with: 1 child.............	150
		2 children..........	200
With wife aged 62 (or over)...............	137½ to 150	3 children..........	250
		4 or more children...	Etc.†
With wife, any age, and 1 or more children..	150 plus 50 per child †	Widow over 62 with no children.........	75
No wife and 1 or more children...........	100 plus 50 per child †	Full orphans: 1 child.............	75
		2 children..........	125
		3 children..........	175
		4 or more children...	Etc.†

* Children in the above table are unmarried dependent children not yet aged eighteen (unless disabled).

† To a maximum monthly amount of $200 in all, or to the greater of (1) 80 per cent of average monthly wage or (2) 1½ times primary insurance amount if the greater of (1) and (2) is less than $200.

The minimum payment under any circumstances is $30 per month (or $24 for a female worker retiring at age sixty-two), even though application of the 50 or 75 per cent factors to the primary amount would produce less.

Eligibility. A number of requirements must be met to satisfy the conditions of eligibility. For example, wages to be counted must have been received for employment in a covered occupation in 1937 or subsequent thereto, wages after 1954 in excess of $4,200 in any one year are not counted (for the period 1937 to 1950 wages in excess of $3,000 and for 1951 to 1954 wages in excess of $3,600), and wages in any quarter to be included for counting *covered time* must have aggregated at least $50 (there are special rules for self-employed and farm wages), although there is no minimum for computing average earnings.

To determine a primary insurance amount, a person may measure his covered wages against time elapsed since 1936 or since 1950, whichever basis will produce an insured status; or in the case of newly covered persons, the period after 1954 (and now 1956) may be used for a temporary period. The use of 1950 is the new start contained in the 1950 amendments and under which 6 quarters after 1950 are necessary. For insured status, a person must have been in covered employment in 40 calendar quarters since 1936 or in at least half of the quarters following 1936 or attainment of age twenty-one, if later—or, under the new start, after 1950 (or, for a temporary period, under special rules in the 1956 amendments)—computed up to the quarter in which he became sixty-five or died if death occurred before sixty-five.

Eligibility for survivors benefits always exists if the deceased at the time of his retirement or death had 40 quarters of coverage or met the requirement of the half-the-possible-quarters rule mentioned in the preceding paragraph. If this requirement is not met and a deceased nonretired worker leaves unmarried children under age eighteen, benefits are payable (to the children and to the widow if alive and qualified) if the deceased worked in at least 6 calendar quarters of the last 13 quarters preceding his death.

The 1954 and 1956 legislation effected an important change in the determination of average monthly wage for benefit purposes and also introduced a new feature with respect to severe and prolonged disability. Concerning the first point, in determining his average monthly wage an employee is now permitted to drop out—from both numerator and denominator—the 5 years of lowest earnings. Not only does this privilege provide, in effect, a new start after 1954 and 1956 (since, for example, the 5 years after 1952 and before 1958 may be dropped out) but it serves to increase the average monthly wage for use in future years for practically all covered employees now earning less than $4,200.

The second feature is the *disability freeze*. An employee with at least 20 quarters of coverage out of the preceding 40 quarters and with at least 6 quarters out of the last 13 quarters who incurs a serious disability of indefinite duration will have the period of time of such disability (after the first 6 months thereof) ignored both in the computation of his average monthly wage and with respect to any loss of insured status otherwise possible. This provision is fully retroactive in establishing the start of the disability for any applications filed within a given time.

The disability freeze seems an appropriate provision, since to penalize the permanently and totally disabled worker because of his disability appears unjust. With the advent of the disability-insurance benefit in the 1956 legislation, it appears that now the chief function of the disability freeze will operate before age fifty.

In the original act numerous classes of wage earners were not covered—for example, self-employed business and professional men, farm workers, domestic servants, fishermen, casual workers, governmental employees, employees of charitable or nonprofit educational institutions, employees of other nonprofit organizations, and the employees covered under the Railroad Retirement Act. Through the 1950 to 1956 amendments, however, most of these exclusions are removed, although a few classes of professional employment continue to be excluded, as well as certain irregular farm and domestic labor. Also governmental employees are not directly included, but for nonfederal public employees it is possible to obtain OASDI coverage by a state-federal compact; nonprofit organizations are excluded but are given the option of voluntary inclusion.

Scope of Coverage. The primary purpose of a national old-age-pension system is to provide a measure of security to the greatest number of employees of the greatest number of employers where such security is clearly desirable and where the benefits can be provided within the bounds of fiscal and administrative reason. From a purely administrative viewpoint, it would be possible to grant everyone a pension upon the attainment of a certain retirement age if benefits were made available without the collection of payroll taxes. When a plan is adopted that requires the payment of payroll taxes, it has seemed necessary to set conditions for the groups of persons who are to be covered and for the amount and nature of their benefits. Hence the Social Security Act, before the 1954 amendments, excluded such employee groups as farm workers or household servants because of the difficulty of collecting and crediting the specific payroll taxes that would be required for individuals in these groups. Because many farm workers' employment is seasonal and usually only a part of the remuneration is in the form of cash, it is difficult to obtain an index of the real income earned by these workers; servants tend to change employers frequently or to have many part-time jobs at one time. The 1954 amendments brought most of these workers within the coverage of the act by requiring the payment of taxes by any one employer who pays $100 or more in cash wages to an agricultural employee during a calendar year or who pays any domestic worker in a private home $50 or more in cash wages during a calendar quarter. The 1956 amendments widened the coverage even more.

The amendments have thus brought under the provisions of the act most workers who were previously excluded from coverage simply because of administrative reasons. Long strides have been taken toward the ultimate goal of complete coverage, which many consider necessary to ensure equitable operation of the plan.

There is, however, no unanimity of opinion on the validity of the administrative reasons for any exclusions. The many seemingly capricious lines of demarcation for who is covered and who is not and the manner in which those conversant with the law may secure coverage, together with the anomalies in certain voluntary features of the act, may well provide further compelling reasons for the enactment of a complete coverage program in some future year, with some flat uniform minimum benefit to all, regardless of covered employment or average monthly wage.

Once the classes that are to be covered have been determined, it is important that a national system makes the plan compulsory for all workers falling into those classes. Without this element of compulsion, selection would be exercised against the program by many employees; e.g., those in ill health would seek coverage for the death benefits involved, and those nearest retirement age would join up for the retirement benefits.

Financing. The old-age-and-survivors-insurance plan as embodied in the 1956 revised Social Security Act calls for contributions in the form of payroll taxes on wages up to $4,200 per annum per covered employee. Originally, employer and employee were each to pay 1 per cent of wages through 1939, 1½ per cent for 1940 to 1942, 2 per cent for 1943 to 1945, 2½ per cent for 1946 to 1948, and 3 per cent thereafter. Congress repeatedly froze the tax rate at 1 per cent for each year from 1940 to 1946, and in 1947 froze the rate again at 1 per cent through 1949. A factor contributing to these actions was uncertainty whether a reserve or a pay-as-you-go basis of financing is the more appropriate. The war and its fiscal problems did not help to resolve this uncertainty.

While a 1½ per cent tax rate went into effect on January 1, 1950, the 1950 amendments set up a new schedule of taxes, keeping the 1½ per cent rate in effect through 1953, raising it to 2 per cent for 1954 to 1959, to 2½ per cent for 1960 to 1964, to 3 per cent for the next 5 years, and finally to 3¼ per cent for 1970 and thereafter. In 1954 the scheduled 2 per cent rate took effect, and the tax schedule was modified somewhat by the 1954 amendments, which set the rate for 1970 to 1974 at 3½ per cent and for 1975 and thereafter at 4 per cent. The 1956 amendments added ¼ per cent to these rates all along the line, starting with 1957; this increase was for the new disability-insurance benefit and goes into a separate account under the trust fund.

The self-employed are subject to 1½ times these rates, representing a compromise between the total employee-and-employer rate of tax and the single rate. It was contended in the actuarial studies made on the basis of this tax schedule that this system of tax rates might well make the program self-supporting; only the future, including the action taken by Congress when these tax increases are due to occur, will determine whether this will prove out.

Not only are the benefits provided through the Social Security Act of vital interest to an employer because they establish a basic amount of pension which he may supplement, but also the taxes that are collected to pay for the old-age-and-survivors-and-disability-insurance pensions are also of considerable importance. If ultimately the employer will be required to contribute greatly increased rates of payroll tax, he may be correspondingly hampered in finding funds for his private employee-retirement plan.

Funding Considerations. Private retirement systems operate most effectively under an insurance-company, trust-company, or other savings arrangement for the creation of a reserve fund into which periodical contributions are made. These contributions, improved at interest, provide at retirement the amounts necessary to pay the pension liabilities that mature in the future. Some plans provide for the payment of a year's pensions out of income received in the same year, but these plans are dangerous actuarially and only appropriate, if at all, for permanent institutions with a long history of stabilized revenue-producing power. Nearly all formal private plans call for the accumulation of contributions from the employer or from the employer and employee jointly in order to provide the ensuing payments during retirement.

In the case of a national system, the necessity or indeed the desirability of such accruals is not apparent. The government, through its ability to impose taxes, has ultimate access to the resources of the nation. It can provide pensions for a generation of retired employees entirely through taxation of the current generation of active employees and employers without the establishment and accrual of a large reserve fund. Authorities who favor such a pay-as-you-go system point to the fact that in the first 13 operating years (through 1949) of the Social Security Act (during which time only 1 per cent of eligible payroll was collected from employees and 1 per cent from employers) reserves accumulated to over 11 billion dollars. Other authorities, leaning more to the procedure followed for private pension plans, point out that even in 1957 the reserve (some 22 billion dollars) falls short of meeting the actuarial liability for even those already drawing benefits and hold that an adequate reserve fund should be accumulated under a national system to care for the estimated payments that will ultimately be required for each group of covered employees as they reach retirement age. This procedure, by reason of the increased contributions required in the early years, would call for substantially increased social-security-tax collections now with less likely increase in tax rates in later years.

Much, both confused and lucid, has been written attempting to show that the accumulation of the reserve fund is a mere fiction, in that such money coming into the Treasury, if evidenced by the issuance of government bonds, will be immediately spent by the government for current expenses or public works with the result that no reserve fund will actually exist. It is claimed that the benefits paid in any year must, in effect, be met by that year's income from both social-security tax and other taxes. The critics of this position hold that if the social-security-tax income is used to purchase outstanding federal-government obligations or if it is expended by the government as it is collected, leaving a certificate of indebtedness in the fund, it reduces the current tax burden or borrowing needs in other directions. According to this latter point of view, it is entirely proper to consider the federal-old-age-insurance Trust Fund as a partial reserve fund in the usual sense. The weight of opinion is that, per se, there is a true invested reserve fund present in this method, but this does not mean that holding this opinion implies endorsement of the full-actuarial-reserve method.[9]

In 1939, Congress, in amending the original Social Security Act, apparently abandoned the full-actuarial-reserve method of funding previously implied and provided that the Trust Fund was to represent only a partial or contingency reserve. The amended act, hearings on it, and committee reports were interpreted to mean that the Trust Fund should not normally exceed three times the greatest annual disbursements to be required in the ensuing 5-year period. But because the war and the subsequent high level of business activity increased the amount of taxable payroll and also deferred the retirement of many persons who normally would have retired at age sixty-five, the Trust Fund came to greatly exceed this three-times amount, even though tax rates were repeatedly frozen at 1 per cent.

The new schedule of tax rates (exclusive of the special $\frac{1}{4}$ per cent disability tax of 1956) included in the 1954 amendments carries the implication of an accumulation of a very large reserve fund in order that interest on the securities, augmented by the current contributions

[9] For example, in its report to the Senate Committee on Finance, April, 1948, the Advisory Council on Social Security stated in Recommendation 22: "Unlike private insurance, a social-insurance scheme backed by the taxing power of the Government does not need full reserves sufficient to cover all liabilities."

of future years, might meet the benefits requirements without federal subsidy.

One argument presented by the proponents of freezing the tax rate at 1 per cent each for employer and employee was that the accumulation of a large reserve fund would tempt legislators to increase benefits and extend coverage in an unsound manner. The counterargument is that keeping the rate low gives a false sense of small costs, which can be an even greater lever for liberalization.

The Railroad Retirement Act. A retirement act for railroad employees, embodying both benefit provisions and taxing provisions, was enacted in 1934 but was found by the United States Supreme Court to be unconstitutional in a test suit brought by the carriers. Substitute measures were enacted in 1935, one of which provided for benefits, the other for taxes. Although litigation against this legislation was started, certain annuities were granted to employees who retired while it was in effect. Before the litigation was settled, the 1935 act was superseded by the Railroad Retirement Act of 1937, which, as several times amended, is in effect at the present time. The constitutionality of the 1937 act has never been brought to a test in the courts.

The Railroad Retirement Act of 1937 became effective on June 24, 1937. It covers the employees of most railroads, express companies, and sleeping-car companies that are subject to Part I of the Interstate Commerce Act. It also covers the employees of certain subsidiaries owned or controlled by such companies, of certain railroad associations, and of most railroad labor organizations. Until 1951, the employment subject to this act was not subject to the Social Security Act, although employees could accumulate credits for both types of covered employment. Legislation in 1951 in effect put railroad employees under the OASI coverage as far as death, retirement, or termination of railroad service are concerned during the first 10 years of railroad employment, after which they revert to the railroad act. The Railroad Retirement Act is particularly notable because it represents the first instance where the government has sponsored, by legislation, a special retirement plan for employees of a special class of private corporations.

Many significant changes in the law have been made since its enactment, the most important being the amendments of 1946, 1947, 1951, 1954, and 1956. Because of the complexity of the act and its involved history since 1937, it is not possible to cover adequately all its phases in this text. It will suffice to describe without great detail the provisions for benefits and contributions as they exist at the present time (December 31, 1957).

Old-age and Family Benefits. Old-age benefits under the act normally commence at age sixty-five upon retirement from railroad employment. Subject to having 30 years or more of credited railroad service, the benefits may commence as early as age sixty, in full for women but in reduced amount for men. Several different eligibility conditions for disability benefits are provided. Subject to 20 years of railroad service, a disability benefit is payable in case an employee becomes permanently disabled for work in his regular occupation. If an employee is sixty or over and becomes so disabled, the benefit is available without regard to years of service. When the disability is sufficiently severe permanently to prevent any regular employment (railroad or otherwise), benefits are available if the disabled person has either 10 years of railroad service or is sixty or over.

Several forms of family benefits are provided upon the death of a covered employee, designed to parallel most of those of the Social Security Act. Monthly benefit payments are furnished to widows or dependent widowers aged sixty (reduced from sixty-five in 1954) or over, to younger widows with children under eighteen, to children of such widows or to orphan children, and to elderly (aged sixty) dependent parents; also, there are two types of lump-sum death benefits: (1) a lump sum where no survivor is eligible for monthly benefits and (2) any excess of employee's contribution, with allowance for interest, over all monthly benefits received before death. The extra benefit for a wife who is sixty-five or over while the retired husband is alive, or for his child, of the same type as granted in the Social Security Act, is now also found in the railroad list of benefits, having been included by the 1951 legislation.

The old-age benefits provided by the act are based on the unit-benefit principle, i.e., a specified benefit component for each year of credited service. The employee's average monthly compensation during his period of railroad service [10] is the base for the unit benefit. This unit is determined as 3.04 per cent of the first $50 of average monthly wage, plus 2.28 per cent of the next $100, plus 1.52 per cent of the next $200. These rates include the 10 per cent increase of 1956. The total monthly benefit is this unit benefit multiplied by the years of railroad service credited to the employee at the time of retirement for age or disability.

The family benefits, except for that of the wife, are not, as are those of the Social Security Act, determined as a direct proportion of the employee's old age unit benefit. However, the Railroad Retirement Act resembles the Social Security Act in that it adopts the flat-percentage concept for survivor's benefits.[11]

The explanation of the benefits given above applies only to employees who die or retire with 10 or more years of railroad service. The amendments to the act of 1951 made a very important change from the prior law in that until an employee has 10 years of railroad service he is covered, in effect, for social-security benefits instead of railroad benefits, even though during that period he pays his contributions (as does the carrier) according to the railroad-retirement contribution rates described below. This is a considerable step in the direction of a complete coordination of the two acts.

Financing. The plan is financed by joint contributions from the carriers, other subject employers, and covered employees. The contribution rates have been changed from time to time and are necessarily set at a substantially higher level than the tax rates in connection with the Social Security Act. The number of old-age beneficiaries of the Railroad Retirement Act started out at a fairly high level, the plan having taken over most of the existing list of pensioners on the rolls of the carriers at the inception of the act. This is in contrast to

[10] Here the average is based on railroad compensation divided by the period of railroad service only, while under the Social Security Act covered wages are divided by the total time elapsed since age twenty-one (or since 1936 or 1950 by the new start) regardless of gaps in employment subject to that act, although the lowest 5 years of earnings may be omitted.

[11] For an outline of the family benefits, see Robert J. Myers and John A. MacDougall, "The Railroad Retirement Act in 1954," *Social Security Bulletin,* February, 1955.

the situation under the Social Security Act, where there is a consider-able deferment of any heavy pension roll. Recent actuarial valuations of the railroad system have indicated the necessity of a level contribu-tion of at least some 12 or 13 per cent of covered payroll (up to $4,200) and estimates of the cost after the 10 per cent increase in retirement benefits enacted in 1956 go to over 15 per cent. The present payroll tax schedule calls for $6\frac{1}{4}$ per cent from each party—the employer and the employee—and for each year hereafter. This rate is obviously in-adequate.

Supplementing Retirement Benefits under a National System. A program of old-age pensions as provided by the Social Security Act is still compatible with arrangements to provide supplementary benefits, either through individual initiative or through the medium of private employer-employee retirement plans. This idea has been well ex-pressed in the following statement by the social-security committees of three well-known insurance organizations: [12]

There should be neither conflict nor confusion between Social Security, properly defined, and that type of security which comes from the exercise of personal industry and thrift. While the one represents the basic protection which can safely be provided through government programs set up by so-ciety at large, the other gives the individual the right and the opportunity to raise himself and his family to such level of security as his industry and thrift dictate. They complement each other rather than conflict with each other.

If Social Security benefits ever become accepted as a satisfactory standard of individual security, the "will to work" will be weakened or destroyed. And if this happens, not only will the system of Social Security fall of its own weight but it will undermine the very foundation of a sound overall economy. It is not easy to determine the point above which the size and scope of benefits under a Social Security plan will interfere with the incentive to work and produce. The claims for ever larger benefits will be many and appealing. Only public prudence and a deep sense of statesmanship on the part of our political leaders will protect both Social Security itself and the vigor of our economy.

[12] From a statement by the social-security committees of the American Life Con-vention, the Life Insurance Association of America, and the National Association of Life Underwriters.

It may be questioned whether the system set up by the Railroad Retirement Act (sometimes called *class legislation*) is properly included in the term *social security*. It is more akin to a *staff pension plan* carried on under government aegis. Supporting this idea is the contention, thus far supported in fact, that the employees and employers fully support the system by their contributions, that is, without charge to the government. Many feel that this is only temporizing and that in due course of time, unless full coordination with the Social Security Act takes place, the federal government will have to step in with subsidies from general revenue. As long as a separate system such as this exists, the larger social-security program cannot function at its best.

CHAPTER 3

Types of Benefits

RETIREMENT BENEFITS

The fundamental objective of a pension plan is to provide a life income for each employee covered by the plan, payable monthly, annually, or at other regular intervals and commencing upon his retirement. This payment is expressed in various terms, such as *pension, retirement benefit, annuity,* and *retirement income.* Regardless of its name, since it is based on the traditional life-annuity principle, it is most useful for the purpose of this chapter to call it an *annuity.* It should be borne in mind that this term is perfectly general, applies to any regular series of payments, and does not necessarily imply the existence of a formal annuity contract, such as those sold by life-insurance companies.

The annuity payments of a pension plan are usually constant in amount, but it is possible to provide different amounts of income at different periods, corresponding to changing needs. For example, a pension plan may provide an annuity as long as either the retired employee or his wife is alive, but with a larger income during their joint lifetime than after the first death. Again, if the pension plan provides for retirement before commencement of OASDI benefits, it may be felt desirable to arrange for a larger annuity before the social-security benefit is available and a smaller annuity thereafter, so that the income from the pension plan and later from the continued pension and social-security plan will be approximately level throughout the entire period after retirement.[1]

---

[1] We are omitting here all reference to *variable annuities,* which are discussed as a separate topic in Chap. 9.

Pure Life Annuity. The simplest form of annuity is the *pure life annuity,* also called *straight life annuity* and sometimes just *life annuity,* under which payments, once begun, continue throughout the balance of the lifetime of the *annuitant* (the recipient of the annuity benefits) and cease immediately upon his death with no further payments to anyone. The pure life annuity of a given amount is the least expensive among the various types of life annuities in use for pensions.

A group of annuitants, all of the same age and all starting to receive identical life annuities will, except by coincidence, receive different numbers of payments and differing total returns corresponding to the length of time each one lives. This disparity is characteristic of a life annuity, which has its being because of the impossibility of knowing in advance how long any particular annuitant will live; however, it is possible to predict within reasonable limits of error the number of deaths each year among a large group of annuitants. On the basis of such a prediction it is not difficult to determine the amount needed at retirement, on the average, to provide the pure-life-annuity payments.

Refund Life Annuity. To avoid the appearance of forfeiture which arises under a pure life annuity when the death of the annuitant occurs soon after the commencement of the annuity and long before the aggregate annuity payments have equaled the original cost or a predetermined part of the cost of the annuity, *refund life annuities* are issued. They provide for additional payments to a beneficiary in the event that the annuitant dies before receiving a predetermined number of payments or amount of benefit. Since for any annuitant a refund annuity always provides for at least as many payments as does a pure life annuity and in the cases of early death requires additional payments to a beneficiary, it is a more expensive form. Refund life annuities are of several types, as described below.

Cash Refund. The *cash-refund life annuity* provides for payment in one sum to the beneficiary, upon the death of the annuitant, of the excess, if any, of the total initial value or purchase price of the annuity over the total amount of the payments made to the annuitant up to the time of his death. Thus at least the total value or purchase price will be paid back either to the annuitant or to the annuitant and his beneficiary.

Installment Refund. The *installment-refund life annuity* provides for continuation of the annuity payments to a beneficiary upon the death of the annuitant, until the total of the annuity payments to both of them has equaled the total original value or purchase price. Frequently the beneficiary has the option of obtaining the commuted value of such residual payments in a lump sum. The installment-refund annuity is slightly less expensive than the cash-refund annuity, since any funds for a beneficiary are kept at interest for a period of time after the annuitant dies.

Modified Refund. A *modified-refund annuity,* of either the cash-refund or the installment-refund type, provides for the return of only a predetermined part of the value or purchase price which is in excess of annuity payments received before the annuitant's death. The return may be in the form of a lump sum or installments to the annuitant's beneficiary. An illustration of the modified-refund type is a life annuity for an employee purchased by means of joint employer and employee contributions, with provision that the annuity payments will not be less than the total of the employee's contributions.

Life Annuity with Term Certain. The *life annuity with term certain* provides payments for a specified period (such as 5, 10, or 20 years) and thereafter for the lifetime of the annuitant. For example, if the annuitant dies after receiving 92 monthly payments under a life annuity with a 10-year-certain provision, his beneficiary will receive identical monthly payments for the next 28 months (perhaps with the right to commute into one sum). The cost of this form of annuity increases with an increase in the length of the term-certain period selected. Given any particular refund type of annuity, it is possible to select term-certain periods that will produce values or purchase prices either higher or lower than that for the refund annuity. Sometimes this type of annuity is described as a life annuity with an n-year certain and continuous period, e.g., life annuity with 10-year certain and continuous.

Joint-and-survivor Annuity. Under a *joint-and-survivor annuity,* annuity payments are made as long as any one of a designated group of persons remains alive. In a pension plan, a joint-and-survivor annuity is frequently made available to a retiring employee with a wife or other dependent, in which case the employee and his wife or other dependent comprise the designated group. Usually this annuity is provided as an option that the employee may elect ahead of retirement date; frequently the election must be made not less than a specified number of years, such as 3 or 5, before retirement date. The amount of each annuity payment is smaller than the annuitant would otherwise receive if this option were not in effect, because annuity payments will be continued to the beneficiary if he or she should survive the annuitant. Annuity payments are made during the joint lifetime of the employee and his beneficiary and are then continued during the remaining lifetime of the survivor. It is possible to provide for a specified income during their joint lifetime and a reduced income after the first death, or to provide for a reduction only if the principal annuitant dies first. The age and sex of the nominated contingent annuitant will have a decided influence on the cost; or, stated otherwise, the sex and age of the contingent annuitant will decidedly affect the amount of benefit provided by a given sum available for this purpose.[2]

Annuity Certain. A series of periodic payments for a specified length of time only is an *annuity certain,* since a predetermined number of payments is made regardless of the death or survival of any life or group of lives. The amount of each payment is determined solely by the initial investment (principal amount), and the interest assumed to be earned on that investment. Such an annuity is not satisfactory in a pension plan because payments cease with the expiration of the specified period, at which time the entire principal amount with interest has been disbursed, even though the annuitant may still be living.

Annuity Forms Used in Pension Plans. A pension plan usually specifies one form of annuity as the normal or basic annuity that will be provided unless some other type is chosen. Usually the income under any of the optional annuity forms is in an amount that is

[2] That part of the joint-and-survivor annuity that falls due to the survivor of two lives is a *reversionary annuity* to the survivor. In general, a reversionary annuity calls for payment to a designated person commencing upon the death of another designated person. See Chap. 15 for an illustration of the reduced benefit payable.

determined actuarially to have the same present value at date of retirement as has the normal annuity. For the same cost, the income provided by a refund option or a joint-and-survivor option is less than that provided by a pure-life-annuity option. A particular type of annuity may not suit the needs of all employees. An employee without dependents, for instance, might choose the pure life annuity as providing the largest income, while a married employee might prefer a reduced joint-and-survivor annuity or one of the refund-annuity types.

Many pension plans specify the pure life annuity, and many a refund annuity (either cash or installment), as the normal annuity form. Since a pure life annuity provides the largest income, it is frequently adopted as the normal annuity form in pension plans where the employer pays the entire cost. When the employee contributes toward the cost of the pension, a refund annuity providing for a minimum total of payments at least equal to the total of the employee's contributions (the modified-cash-refund life annuity), with or without interest, is usually the normal annuity.

The Early-retirement Option. Many pension plans permit retirement, in some cases only with the employer's consent, a few years earlier than the normal age specified in the plan. The amount of each annuity payment will be lower in this case than if the employee retires at the normal retirement age, because there will usually be fewer payments made into the fund to provide his annuity and also because it will be necessary to pay his pension over a longer period. If such retirement is not caused by permanent and total disability and occurs before age sixty-five, and hence before the annuitant becomes eligible to receive full social-security benefits for age (females can now get a reduced benefit at sixty-two), the amount that is available for retirement benefits may be utilized to provide a twofold benefit consisting of a temporary life annuity to age sixty-five in an amount approximating the social-security benefits to be received after age sixty-five plus a life annuity of a level amount from the earlier retirement age. The temporary annuity ceases when the social-security benefits begin at age sixty-five, and thus the retired employee is permitted to receive an approximately level income throughout his retirement period (successive increases in OASI benefits have caused this leveled-out payment to prove irregular instead).

WITHDRAWAL BENEFITS

Funded pension plans presuppose the accumulation of a reserve fund from the periodic contributions made by or for the participating employees. These contributions may be made entirely by the employer or jointly by employer and employee, but only rarely by employee alone. The rate (or rates) of contribution is such that as retirements occur there will be on hand or available under a firm commitment a sufficient accumulation of funds to provide the respective pensions.

Return of Employee's Contributions. Pension plans that provide for contributions by the employee do not usually take account of anticipated withdrawals in determining the employee's contribution rate but instead provide that the employee's contributions will be refunded to him upon withdrawal from the plan, as will occur if he resigns or is discharged before retirement. Short of a compulsory plan (e.g., social security) this is a necessary provision, because few employees would participate in a pension plan if their accumulations were forfeited upon withdrawal, especially since the withdrawal might be involuntary, as in the case of a discharge. From the standpoint of broader social considerations, too, forfeiture of an employee's contributions upon withdrawal from a pension plan would not be desirable because it would take away from him part of his savings for old age.

The refund frequently includes interest on the employee's contributions, usually at not more than the rate used in making the actuarial valuation under the pension plan. Paying this interest increases the cost of the plan but makes it more acceptable to employees who are accustomed to receiving interest on their savings. In lieu of receiving the refund in cash, the employee is often given the option of leaving his contributions with the pension plan and at retirement age receiving the pension provided by them. This option is socially desirable since it permits the employee to build up at least some retirement benefit even though he changes jobs, but it adds to the administrative cost of the pension plan in that it necessitates keeping records on former employees scattered far and wide. Where the employee is entitled only to the accumulation of his own contributions, he usually chooses the cash payment rather than the deferred-annuity option when he withdraws from the plan.

Application of Employer's Contributions. When a pension plan is established, a decision must be made whether a withdrawing employee is to be permitted any share of the funds arising from the employer's contributions. If the plan provides that the funds arising out of the employer's contributions made on behalf of an employee will become his equity, either in total or in part, upon termination of employment, the plan is said to provide for *vesting*. The provision for vesting may permit a cash payment to the employee, but more frequently, and especially where the amount involved is substantial, a benefit is provided in the form of a deferred paid-up pension with payments commencing at the normal retirement date set by the plan, usually conditioned on the employee's accepting the same type of benefit with respect to his own contributions.

There are good grounds for providing in a pension plan that withdrawing employees may retain, in the form of a paid-up annuity rather than in cash, at least a part of the employer's contributions already made in their behalf. Vesting rights are given on the theory that a pension plan is to some extent a recognition of service performed and that each year's service should be rewarded by a contingent interest in the employer's contributions. Methods of funding whereby contributions are made each year toward a benefit related to the employee's salary for that year (and hence related to the service rendered in that year) make it appear that the complete pension is provided bit by bit over the employee's entire working life and that on withdrawal the employee should be entitled to the partial pension already credited. Society is best served when the employee is not too heavily penalized for changing jobs but rather is permitted to collect pension credits from all his employers so that upon his retirement he will have an adequate pension even though it comes from several sources, including social-security benefits.

On the other hand, the inclusion of any substantial degree of vesting in a plan increases the cost. Where the rate of the employer's contributions is not based on estimated withdrawals, the reversions from withdrawals as they occur may be used to reduce the employer's current outlay or to provide additional annuities for the remaining employees.[3]

Furthermore, one of the purposes of a pension plan is to hold employees, and vesting may be in conflict with this purpose. When the vesting provision permits a cash payment based on the accumulated value of all or part of the employer's contributions, the payment is practically a termination-wage settlement. If permitted indiscriminately, this method is likely to have the disadvantage of encouraging the withdrawal of employees who are temporarily embarrassed financially. The payment of a withdrawal value in cash may be more justified when the withdrawal is involuntary, although this also defeats the purpose of old-age protection. Certain industries whose employment is not stabilized may adopt such an arrangement to provide a severance payment when business necessity requires termination of employment.

During World War II, and also during the Korean War, the method of vesting employer contributions in cash upon an employee's termination of employment had a quality somewhat different from a mere reflection of pension credits. The wage- and salary-stabilization laws, which held down the compensation of employees in these periods of labor scarcity, induced employers to seek a method of circumventing the pay ceilings by establishing a pension or profit-sharing plan that would accumulate a fund for the employee to secure later on. Also, there were certain tax advantages that made employer contributions to such a plan more attractive to the employee than a current increase in his direct compensation. To a somewhat lesser degree, this latter point will undoubtedly continue to be an advantage arising out of a funded pension plan.

Since the inclusion of vesting rights in a pension plan may indirectly increase the employer's cost substantially, this privilege is often restricted to those employees who have given a minimum amount of service to the employer. Most of the pension plans that provide for vesting rights require some minimum period either of employment or of participation in the pension plan before vesting takes place; in addition, an age requirement is often included. A pension plan may

[3] This latter treatment, however, may be contrary to Internal Revenue Service regulations.

provide, for example, that the employer's contributions will vest only in those withdrawing employees who have had at least 10 years' service and have attained age forty-five. Vesting rights are sometimes still further restricted by provision for only partial vesting of the employer's equity after a minimum period of service, with full vesting later. For instance, such a provision might vest 50 per cent of the employer's equity after 10 years' service and 100 per cent after 20 or more years' service. Sometimes a graded scale of vesting is adopted; for example, 10 per cent of the employer's portion of the accrued benefit might be vested for each year commencing with the fifth year, with 100 per cent vesting after the fourteenth year.

In the past some form of vesting has been much more frequently found in contributory than in noncontributory plans and more often in plans for salaried employees than in wage-employee plans. Many recently negotiated union settlements call for a vesting provision to be included in noncontributory pension plans covering wage employees.

DEATH BENEFITS

Pension plans are adopted primarily to provide a retirement income for superannuated employees. However, as in the case of withdrawals, it frequently appears desirable to include benefits payable when employees die before retirement or a short time after retirement. If the pension plan provides for employee contributions, provision is made for at least a death benefit based on those contributions. Whether any additional death benefit will be paid, based on the employer's contributions, is a matter for decision when the pension plan is drawn up. Of course, if a cash-withdrawal benefit is to be included, a death benefit of at least equal amount is needed to prevent an anomalous situation; without such death benefit, employees in ill health might resign in anticipation of impending death and thereby procure as a withdrawal benefit what would be tantamount to a death benefit. A death benefit based on the employer's contributions can add considerably to the employer's cost, and its inclusion in a plan will be largely determined by the employer's willingness and ability to contribute sufficiently under the plan to provide a death benefit as well as an adequate retirement benefit. In making a decision, consideration should be given to the amount of death benefits provided elsewhere by group insurance or some other welfare program. A death benefit is sometimes included in a pension plan in order to supplement group-life-insurance benefits.

Return of Employee's Contributions upon Death before Retirement. With some rare exceptions, pension plans that require employee contributions provide for payment to the employee's beneficiary or his estate, upon the death of the employee before retirement, of an amount at least equal to the sum of the employee's contributions. The reason for this provision is similar to that for refunding the employee's contributions upon withdrawal: it avoids any appearance of forfeiture of the employee's money. The death benefit frequently includes interest on the employee's contributions, with a consequent increase in the cost of the pension plan. Normally, if the employee's contributions alone are refunded upon withdrawal, at least equal treatment is accorded in event of death; if interest is added to the contributions upon withdrawal, it is also added in event of death. The withdrawal benefit is frequently smaller than the death benefit, but a withdrawal benefit larger than the death benefit would be incongruous.

Certain types of pension plans provide for a death benefit before retirement in the form of life insurance rather than a benefit based directly on contributions. For example, pension plans based on individual policies or group-permanent contracts frequently provide $1,000 insurance for each $10 of monthly retirement annuity.[4]

Return of Employee's Contributions upon Death after Retirement. A refund annuity is usually specified as the normal annuity form in pension plans providing for employee contributions. The refund is frequently the sum of the employee's contributions, without interest or with interest to date of retirement, less part or all of the annuity benefits paid up to the time of his death.

Death Benefits Based on Employer's Contributions. For the employer who wishes to include in the pension plan a death benefit based on the employer's contributions and payable to the employee's beneficiary or estate, there are two different basic methods, either of which may be used:

1. Payment of a death benefit, related to the accumulated amount

[4] See Chap. 9.

of the employer's contributions (and, if contributory, employee contributions) with or without interest

2. Payment of a specified amount of death benefit which commonly will bear a fixed relationship to the amount of annuity being purchased for the employee

The death benefit in a group-annuity plan normally is a return of the employee's own contributions and therefore conforms to the first method above. The joint-and-survivor option or a widow's benefit, based on part or all of both the employee's and the employer's contributions also falls under this method. Where some sort of special insurance arrangement is required in order to provide a fixed sum at the employee's death, as under 2 above, the individual-insurance-annuity-policy plan or a group-permanent-insurance policy is usually adopted,[5] although occasionally trust-fund plans also make provision for a death benefit of a specified amount, such as 1 year's salary.

DISABILITY BENEFITS

An employee may have to cease work because of physical or mental disability long before he would normally retire by reason of age. Hence, a pension plan may logically provide for an annuity upon permanent disability as well as for an annuity upon superannuation. In fact, it is probable that an employee's need for a pension is greater when permanent and complete retirement is occasioned by disability than when it is caused by old age, for disability is relatively unexpected and rarely prepared for. Also, disability occurring before retirement age may come at the time when an employee's family responsibilities are still great and his opportunities for saving have been few. Finally, disability may necessitate expensive medical treatment.

Temporary disability usually may be adequately provided for by means of accident and sickness insurance frequently included in an employer's welfare program, usually through the medium of group-insurance contracts or by a continuation-of-pay program under which the employer continues during temporary disability part or all of an employee's regular compensation. Several states now require statutory

[5] See Chap. 9.

benefits for temporary disability. To supplement this welfare program it is often considered desirable to include in a pension plan an income benefit payable during permanent and total disability. The size of this benefit, for reasons discussed later,[6] must be modest in relation to the regular compensation of the disabled employee. For the average wage earner an ideal benefit would approximately reproduce the pay the employee was receiving before disablement, reduced by the amount of any disability benefits received under OASDI or workmen's-compensation laws or from other sources. However, this ideal benefit can seldom be even approximated without high cost.

Disability Benefits in Current Pension Plans. While many of the pension plans now in effect do not make provision for disability benefits, an increasing proportion of the plans currently going into effect or being amended do provide for such benefits. Most plans treat a withdrawal because of disability just as any other withdrawal would be treated or as a reduced-annuity early-retirement case. There are three principal reasons for failure to provide satisfactory disability protection:

1. *The cost of the benefit.* A disability-income provision adds appreciably to the cost of a pension plan. Many employers feel that their obligation to their employees increases in proportion to the service rendered by those employees and that, since old-age retirement comes only after many years of service while disability may occur after short periods of service, the financial burden of providing adequate old-age benefits is all they can and should assume.

2. *Difficulty of securing a disability benefit in an insured plan.* For many years most insurers did not underwrite disability-retirement benefits because of the unfavorable experience they had in the period 1925 to 1935. During that period disability claims under ordinary- and group-life-insurance contracts so far exceeded those anticipated that the premiums charged for the benefit proved utterly inadequate, and the insurers sustained heavy losses. More recently some insurers are permitting the inclusion of disability benefits in their plans.

3. *Difficulty of administration.* Total-and-permanent disability, unlike old age or death, is difficult to define precisely, and recoveries from disability adjudged "permanent" are not uncommon. For this reason

[6] See pp. 133, 134.

insurers which generally issued life-insurance policies with a disability-income benefit before 1932 have attempted to simplify administration of the benefit by defining *permanent disability* as total disability that has persisted for a period of 3, 4, or 6 months. This definition has had the unfortunate result of bringing many temporary disabilities within the total-and-permanent-disability class and has increased administrative difficulties by necessitating constant reexamination of claims in order that recoveries may be discovered and benefits discontinued.

It is still feasible, however, to include a disability-income benefit, payable only in event of total and permanent disability, in certain pension plans. By not regarding a disability as being permanent merely by reason of such disability's having persisted for a specified time, it may be practicable to provide modest disability benefits. The employer with intimate knowledge of his employees is in an especially favorable position to judge the merits of a claim and to determine the true extent of disability. The disability-income benefit in some recently established pension plans is, therefore, limited to those employees who, after a period of incapacity such as 6 months, are in the judgment of a physician totally incapable, mentally or physically, of further performance of substantially gainful employment, with the probability that such incapacity will be permanent. In other recent plans, particularly some of those sponsored by organized labor, a disability of permanent type that prevents an employee who has the requisite years of service and/or age from performing his customary duties or other duties offered by the employer entitles him to a disability pension. This latter type is more difficult to administer than the former and will prove more costly.

The withdrawal benefit, providing for return of the employee's contributions, is available upon retirement for disability, but this is not a true disability benefit since it amounts to utilization of a savings deposit. Particularly if disability occurs soon after the employee's entry into the pension plan, the amount of the deposit available upon withdrawal will be small and totally inadequate to support him for any length of time. Under most retirement plans the employer's contributions are not available in event of withdrawal because of disability, because the employer's contribution is usually discounted for death losses and hence could only be available to employees withdrawing in good health. Otherwise disabled persons could withdraw and receive the employer's contributions in contemplation of death, in which event it would develop that the amount of discount allowed for death among healthy lives had proved far too great.

By making use of the provision, contained in most pension plans issued by insurers, that permits optional early retirement within the 10 years before the normal retirement age specified in the plan, it is possible to provide to employees disabled in the 10-year period a disability income of a smaller amount than the pension which otherwise would have been credited for payment from normal retirement age. The employer can supplement this reduced income resulting from early retirement by purchasing additional annuities from the insurer or otherwise, such as making up the balance on a pay-as-you-go basis. The premiums charged for annuities by the insurer would probably presuppose issuance to healthy lives only, for whom, on the average, annuity payments would continue for a longer period of time than to disabled lives of the same age and sex. Thus the employer would pay a higher price for these supplemental annuities than their probable duration justifies.

One type of disability benefit usually available under individual-policy insured pension plans provides for waiver of premium and hence waiver of contributions by employer and employee during the employee's total disability (after, usually, some waiting period). Such a benefit has the effect of assuring the employee of full retirement benefits when he reaches retirement age without the necessity of contributions from either employer or employee during disablement but makes no provision for the payment of a pension to him until he reaches normal retirement age. This type of benefit is still generally written by insurers in their individual policies because it does not provide the incentive for malingering that is present under a disability-income benefit; it has not been a source of excessive claims. This arrangement is somewhat similar to the disability-freeze provision in the 1954 social-security amendments, which preserves the full benefit "earned" before disability until the normal retirement age. The problems encountered when a disability-annuity benefit is included in a trust-fund plan are not so complex as is the case with an insured type of plan, because the trust-fund plan does not contain the guarantees regarding payment of benefits found in the insured plans and because the question of preservation of equity among plans, as exemplified by the underwriting rules of the insurer, does not arise under the trust-fund plan.

Age and Service Requirements. Because the employer usually feels that the benefits under a pension plan should bear a relation to the period of an employee's service, it is customary, where disability is covered, to include a service requirement, such as 10 or 15 years, and frequently an age condition as well, such as fifty, before an employee will be eligible for a benefit. In addition to the definition of what constitutes disability, it is also usual to specify in the plan what medical requirements are to be followed and whether retirement for disability will be requested by the employee or the employer.[7]

With respect to disability-retirement pensions payable after June, 1957, regardless of type of plan or funding medium, consideration will have to be given to the 1956 amendments of the Social Security Act.[8] Now that disability benefits after age fifty will be available as monthly-income payments under the OASDI program, framers of private pension plans will have to consider the same sort of coordination problems between any disability-pension provisions the plan may contain and the OASDI disability benefits—that is, to work out a meshing of the two along one of the lines used for harmonizing the two old-age benefits. In general, this would seem to present certain alternative fundamental approaches: (1) of the *addition type,* with the plan's disability payment independent of the federal disability amount (the meshing being accomplished through the predetermined-benefit formula) and (2) of the *offset type,* with the plan's disability benefit reduced by part or all of the federal disability payment. In general, it would seem that for a given plan the basis used for the old-age benefits could be made applicable to the disability. There are, however, especially in the offset method, numerous troublesome details to be worked out.

[7] A fuller discussion of these restrictions is included in Chap. 4.
[8] See résumé of the act in Chap. 2.

MISCELLANEOUS BENEFITS

In this chapter the principal benefits found in pension plans have been described. There are occasional plans, or proposals for plans, that contain unusual features, often actuarially anomalous for the purposes of cost determination. For example, a few plans provide that the pension fund will pay 1 year's salary in the event of death—a feature unrelated to the pension or to the contributions for the pension. A few recently negotiated plans include provision for a death benefit to pensioners, although no death benefit is provided to non-retired employees from the pension plan. Still other pension plans (including some negotiated plans) provide that the pension benefit will be continued for a specified period, such as 1 year, after the pensioner dies. One argument sometimes presented as favoring the inclusion of such a benefit in the pension plan (rather than the more logical utilization of a life-insurance contract) is that the cost is not taxable to the employee while the cost of a paid-up life-insurance benefit, becoming effective upon the retirement of the employee, might be deemed to be income constructively received by him upon his retirement and as such taxable to him.

Sometimes temporary-sickness payments, or even medical and hospital costs, are proposed to be paid from the pension plan. A pension plan is a long-range commitment, and these current-risk types of benefits should generally be handled by arrangements separate and apart from the pension fund.

In some instances the employer may feel that the pension formula of the plan does less for a particular employee than is the employee's due. Instead of trying to force some additional benefit out of the fund, such as by changing the formula to meet a particular case, it would seem better for the employer to supplement the regular pensions in these special cases (the fewer the better) by making direct payment outside the pension plan proper.

CHAPTER 4

Basic Provisions of a Pension Plan

The basic provisions of a pension plan define eligibility, state the conditions that an eligible employee must satisfy in order to participate in the plan, state the benefits provided, and establish procedures for administering the plan. These basic provisions may be classified as follows:

1. Requirements for employee participation
2. Requirements for receipt of retirement benefits
3. Statement of retirement benefits
4. Statement of subsidiary benefits
5. Provisions for meeting the cost
6. Administrative provisions
   a. To protect the employee
   b. To protect the employer
   c. To protect the insurer or trustee

Eligibility requirements, participation requirements, amounts of benefits, and administrative provisions must be set out in considerable detail. With due regard for the objectives of the plan, these provisions should be kept as simple and straightforward as possible in order that the employees may understand exactly the benefits to which they are entitled, when and under what conditions they are to receive those benefits, and what, if anything, they themselves must pay toward the cost of providing the benefits. The simpler and clearer the provisions of the plan, the less chance there is for misinterpretation and misunderstanding on the part of either employer or employee and of all others having any connection with the plan's administration.

The type of pension plan (group annuity, group permanent, individual-policy pension trust, or noninsured trust fund) will determine certain administrative provisions and partially influence the kinds of benefits and methods of contribution, but all types of plans must have a foundation or background of basic definitions, statements of benefits, and administrative provisions. Sometimes there is a tendency to utilize too many and too complicated benefits and unnecessary administrative provisions. While each pension plan must be more or less custom-built, the tailoring to fit a specific situation should follow certain recognized patterns, and, regardless of the type of plan, the use of certain conventional provisions is advisable.

The basic provisions discussed in this chapter are dealt with in a general way, on the assumption of free choice of provisions in designing the plan. With respect to some of the features discussed, certain rather definite patterns have developed in the field of *noncontributory plans* (under which the employer pays all the costs without employee contributions) formulated through the processes of collective bargaining between labor unions and employers. No attempt is made to qualify the provisions explained herein by reference to these patterns. This will be done in Chapter 14, which deals with the more specialized subject of negotiated plans.

Eligibility for Participation. While many noncontributory pension plans are designed to cover all regular full-time employees, it is not always necessary or desirable to include all employees as members (or participants) in a pension plan. Since the Social Security Act provides benefits for covered employees based on the first $4,200 of their annual earnings, an employer may wish to limit benefits under his plan to employees who are paid over $4,200. Again, younger employees recently hired, those paid on an hourly basis, or those doing certain types of work may be subject to such a high rate of turnover that very few will remain to reach retirement age. Their inclusion in the pension plan might entail needless administrative expense and be contrary to the plan's basic purpose.

Participation in a pension plan is, therefore, frequently limited to those employees who meet certain eligibility requirements and, in the case of contributory plans, who elect to subscribe thereto. These requirements normally fall into four classes:

1. Minimum-service requirements
2. Minimum- and maximum-age requirements
3. Minimum-salary or wage requirements
4. Requirements based on occupation or class of employment

One or more of these requirements may be used to determine eligibility for participation in a specific plan. In the past, a few pension plans have limited participation to male employees, presumably on the assumption that few females continued in employment to reach retirement age. Today such a requirement is almost never used and would probably be considered discriminatory under the Internal Revenue Code,[1] although a higher minimum age for eligibility of women than for that of men is permissible. It also seems permissible to require a longer waiting period for eligibility for female employees than for male employees.

Minimum-service Requirements. A requirement that provides for participation by only those employees who have worked for the employer for some minimum period of time is designed to eliminate floaters and other employees subject to rapid turnover, whose inclusion in the plan would create extra administrative expense without providing them with worthwhile benefits. The length of the waiting period depends on the particular situation of the employer, but for plans that must meet the requirements of the Internal Revenue Code it should not be longer than 5 years. A 1-year waiting period, which is quite common, may be desirable for a stable organization with a small turnover, while a 3-to-5-year period would be more suitable for an organization that is experiencing an unusual temporary expansion.

In a few instances, concerns not wishing to penalize the permanent employee by requiring a relatively long eligibility period have designed their plans with, say, a 5-year waiting period but with coverage made retroactive to the end of the first year of employment when the 5-year period has been completed, although this course carries with it a continuing indeterminate cost element, sometimes deemed objectionable, with respect to the retroactive service credits.

[1] The Internal Revenue Service imposes a number of criteria that a pension plan must satisfy if the employer's contributions toward the plan, the income on the fund, and the benefits payable from the plan are to receive favorable tax treatment. These criteria are discussed in Chap. 5.

A minimum-service requirement for participation is found much less frequently in noncontributory plans than in contributory plans and rarely occurs in negotiated plans, although in these plans it is not unusual to find that eligibility to receive a pension at retirement may require a minimum period of service, such as 10 years.

Minimum- and Maximum-age Requirements. A minimum-age requirement may be included in a pension plan for much the same reason that a service requirement is made. It eliminates from participation the younger employees, among whom much of the personnel turnover normally occurs. This is particularly true of the younger women employees, many of whom resign after a few years to be married. In addition, a pension plan, which by its nature provides for the payment of benefits far in the future, does not have great appeal for younger workers and hence fails to impress its importance on the young group. Notwithstanding these logical reasons for including a minimum-age requirement, many plans do not include such a requirement, probably because it is felt that the pension plan may exert some slight influence toward the retention of the more promising of the younger employees and because any appearance of discriminating among employees merely because of age is avoided. Age thirty is commonly used when a minimum age is specified.

Decision on either or both points—minimum service or minimum age—is important and necessary mainly in the case of contributory plans, where employees and employer jointly bear the cost, although some noncontributory plans, where the cost is borne entirely by the employer, adopt these minimums in determining credited service for benefit purposes.

A maximum age of becoming employed, such as fifty, fifty-five, or sixty, is sometimes used in determining the employees eligible to become participants. There are two reasons for this limitation. In the first place, the amount of pension that can justifiably be provided over a short period of employment is meager, since pension plans, by their very nature, assume a retirement income built up over a large portion of the worker's employed lifetime. In the second place, the cost of providing a given amount of pension increases rapidly with the age of entry of the employee into the plan, and many employers feel that the cost of providing pensions for employees who are hired at an advanced age is prohibitive for the services rendered. In practice, a substantial number of plans do not have a maximum-age-of-hire requirement. The hiring practices of the employer, the fact that a definite retirement age is normally specified in all plans, and limiting benefits for short service periods may perhaps obviate the need for a maximum-age requirement.

Careful consideration must be given to those employees who are near or beyond the retirement age when a plan is first adopted. Many of these employees have given many years of service to the employer and, in the interest of the morale and efficiency of the organization, should be retired when they reach or have already passed normal retirement age. In the plans that include these oldest employees, the employer usually pays the entire cost of a pension based on some or all of the employee's period of service before the inception of the plan. The cost of providing pensions for these aged employees is substantial; hence most employers amortize this cost over a period of several years. Sometimes, probably too often, an employer is advised or decides on his own initiative to exclude entirely from the plan individuals above a certain age, such as fifty-five, sixty, or sixty-five, regardless of their length of service. This decision is usually based on the high costs for these individuals when expressed as lump sums or as premiums or contributions to be met before retirement age. Actually these necessarily high costs may be thinned out by meeting them over longer periods of time. Another reason frequently cited is that the Internal Revenue Service will not always allow current tax deductibility on the high costs for these lives. This is not a wholly valid reason, because the contributions made by the employer for these older employees, if not tax-deductible in one year, may be carried over and treated as tax-deductible in later years. One philosophy of pensions is that when the employer has money to spend for retirement benefits he could not do better than to apply it first toward meeting his immediate pension problem by providing for the retirement of the present aged and near-aged in his employ and that, therefore, these older lives should not be excluded from the formal pension plan. The alternative, it is argued, is to keep them on the payroll as "hidden pensioners" or to treat them variously on a discretionary basis by special grants without reserve backing, a practice that gives them less security than that offered to the younger group. Such practice may also lessen the value of the pension plan in solving personnel problems, since dissatisfied pensioners are poor advertising.

Minimum-pay Requirements. The Social Security Act provides for covered employees old-age benefits based on their first $4,200 of annual pay (previously $3,600, and before that $3,000). A substantial number of the pension plans adopted since about 1940 have been designed to supplement this provision by limiting participation to employees earning over $3,000 or $3,600 yearly, pensions being based only on pay in excess of those amounts. Some plans that had used $3,000 previously changed to $3,600 when the social-security limit was increased; other plans did not make the change, retaining the $3,000 figure. A similar situation arose when the limit was increased to $4,200. The use of a minimum-pay requirement reduces materially the aggregate pension cost to the employer since it eliminates a large proportion of the payroll. For pension plans to meet the requirements of the Internal Revenue Code, a minimum-pay requirement may be used if certain limitations on size of benefits are observed, that is, if they satisfy the social-security integration rules. Many employers who installed pension plans several years ago restricted the membership in the plan by imposing a $3,000 minimum-salary requirement, only to find some years later that a large proportion of their employees had become eligible because the inflationary trend greatly increased compensation levels.

Several factors should be considered before it is decided whether or not to use a minimum-pay requirement. In groups composed largely of permanent, salaried employees, a $4,200 dividing line may appear artificial and discriminatory to the employees. This impression would be especially likely under an hourly-rate pension plan. It may engender ill will and impair employee morale.

Many of the objections to the minimum-pay plan can be avoided by including all pay groups but providing a lower rate of pension for those earning less than the minimum. This *bent-formula method* has come into greater use in recent years than has the total exclusion from the plan of employees earning less than some fixed amount, such as $4,200 a year.

Requirements Based on Class of Employment. Participation in a pension plan may be limited to the more valuable and longer-service employees by basing eligibility upon class of employment. In doing so it is important to adopt requirements that the Internal Revenue Service will not consider discriminatory. Categories of eligibility frequently used in current pension plans, and generally satisfactory to the Service, include the following:

Full-time employees
Regular employees
Salaried employees
Regular (or full-time) salaried employees
Hourly-rate employees
Union employees

Individuals operating in the form of a proprietorship or a partnership may not participate in pension plans that are subject to Internal Revenue Service approval, although their employees may participate in plans established on their behalf. Employees of corporations who are also stockholders may freely be permitted to participate if their stockholdings are small; if they own a substantial proportion of the stock, they may participate but run the risk of having the Internal Revenue Service request limitations on benefits in order to prevent discrimination. Directors are usually excluded unless they are actively engaged as officers or employees.

Another type of limitation may exclude specified occupational groups, such as salesmen, straight-commission employees, or employees of certain departments, plants, or subsidiary organizations. Exclusions based entirely on occupational status are comparatively rare. Exclusions of this type may need to be satisfactorily explained by the employer before the Internal Revenue Service will approve the plan.

The adoption of proper eligibility requirements is extremely important, since those requirements may influence the employees' acceptance of, or enthusiasm for, the pension plan and hence may determine whether the plan is to be a success or a failure. In addition, the cost of the plan is affected by the number of covered employees and their earnings. Employment data should normally be analyzed in accordance with the groupings suggested by each of the four common eligibility requirements. From such an analysis may be determined the wisdom and cost of including or omitting certain groups of employees from participation.

Frequently in recent years groups of union employees have negotiated with employers for pension plans applicable only to the employees who are within the particular collective-bargaining group. Often where two or more unions operate within the same company, separate plans—though perhaps identical—are set up with one union's membership under one plan and another union's membership under another. On the other hand, and more frequently, several unions will agree to subscribe to a common plan for all the employer's hourly-rate employees or, sometimes, even to a plan covering all employees, salaried as well as hourly.

Eligibility for Pensions. In addition to eligibility requirements for membership, there are requirements (usually based on age or a combination of age and service) for receipt of retirement benefits. A definitely stated age at which retirement will normally take place is generally adopted in order to formalize a pension plan and to permit the development of a definite benefit and an actuarial estimate of costs. A specific retirement age protects the employer by providing for retirement of his employees before they become inefficient but not before they have reached a reasonably advanced age. At the same time a definite retirement age gives the employee a feeling of security and permits him to arrange his financial affairs to best advantage in anticipation of his forthcoming retirement. Some flexibility in retirement age is, however, usually provided by permitting optional retirement during the 5 or 10 years immediately preceding *normal* retirement age (generally at an actuarially reduced rate of pension, although in some plans without reduction and in others at an increased rate of pension if the early retirements are in the interest of the employer). Under certain prescribed conditions retirement may usually be postponed beyond the normal retirement age.

A service requirement for retirement may be utilized in conjunction with an age requirement but is rarely used by itself. Its use is based on the theory that a pension should be a reward for, and bear some relation to, service rendered and that a pension proportional to only a few years' service would not only be costly (because of the advanced age at which the service is rendered) but also often too small to have practical value.

Normal Retirement Age. Most industrial pension plans provide for normal retirement at age sixty-five. This provision conforms with the

Social Security Act, under which age sixty-five is the earliest age at which the full amount of old-age primary-insurance payments are available.

The higher the retirement age, the lower the cost of providing a given pension. The adoption of age sixty-five for normal retirement in most cases permits an adequate pension without excessive cost to either employer or employee. In practice, some employers who have adopted sixty-five as their normal retirement age provide for retiring specified classes of employees at a lower age. For instance, women are sometimes retired at sixty, though this increases the pension cost considerably, particularly since females live on the average several years longer than males.[2] A number of airline operators have provided for normal retirement of pilots at sixty. In a few instances, truck operators have provided for retirement of drivers at sixty. Companies with operations in tropical areas sometimes permit employees in those areas to retire at an earlier age than employees in domestic operations. The United Mine Workers' welfare plan contemplates retirement at age sixty. The Internal Revenue Service, in granting approval to the minimum-pay plans using a normal retirement age below age sixty-five, has required special tests for integration with social-security benefits to make sure that the use of the lower age does not result in discrimination in favor of the higher-paid or executive employee.

Service Requirements for Retirement. Many pension plans adopted before 1930 contained a minimum-service requirement, usually in conjunction with a normal retirement age. For example, retirement would take place at sixty-five if the employee had 20 years of service; otherwise retirement would be at seventy. Frequently, retirement was voluntary at fifty-five or sixty if the employee had some specified amount of service, such as 20 or 30 years. Occasionally a plan would permit retirement when the age and number of years of service totaled 85, or perhaps at sixty with 30 years or more of service or at sixty-five with 20 years of service. Sometimes a service requirement, such as 40 years, was used alone without a normal retirement age. Today these special service conditions are frequently found in plans for public employees.

[2] Commencing in November, 1956, females retiring as early as age sixty-two could elect a permanently reduced old-age benefit under the Social Security Act.

Requirements of the Internal Revenue Code sometimes make it difficult to use solely a service condition for receipt of pensions, without regard to age. A restricted form of service requirement sometimes used in current plans provides that employees becoming eligible for participation in the plan must have 10 or 15 years' service under the plan before retirement. The normal retirement age is thus automatically raised for those employees who enter the plan after some predetermined age. The alternative would be to exclude those who cannot attain the required service by age sixty-five.

Optional Retirement Ages. Although it is generally desirable to base a pension plan on a specified normal retirement age, conditions sometimes arise where it is advantageous to all parties concerned to permit retirement before that age. A disabling accident or sickness may make it necessary to retire an employee prematurely, and if there are no disability provisions in the pension plan, the adjusted retirement income may be permitted to begin at an early retirement date.[3] Various personal reasons may also make it desirable for an employee to be permitted to retire before the normal retirement age. The amount of pension payable upon early retirement is normally less than would be payable at normal retirement age, partly because a smaller amount of accumulated contributions is available at the earlier age to provide the benefit and partly because a longer period of pension payment may on the average be expected. It is customary in all types of pension plans to provide specifically that the employee may request early retirement on an actuarially reduced basis during a period (frequently 10 years) immediately preceding the normal retirement date. In many plans the granting of this request is subject to the employer's concurrence.

A provision permitting the employee to continue working beyond his normal retirement age is frequently included to take care of situations where it is to the employer's interest to continue a key employee. Usually permission for delayed retirement must be specifically given by the employer, and no further contributions are permitted to increase the benefit. Additional safeguards may be utilized, such as a

---

[3] The option of early retirement is not a complete substitute for a permanent-and-total-disability clause since such option is, in effect, a discounting—a reducing—of the accrued benefit rights due at the normal retirement age.

requirement that the board of directors act on each individual application, that permission is secured yearly for continuation of employment, and that in no event will permission be given to work more than 3 or 5 years beyond the normal retirement age. For some funding methods this provision may be troublesome administratively, since a pension plan usually contemplates payments to all employees immediately upon attainment of normal retirement age. Under an insured plan (exclusive of the deposit-administration type) the pension payments then due must be made or credited to someone. Sometimes they are applied toward reducing the employer's contributions. Sometimes they are used to increase the benefit which the employee receives ultimately upon his actual retirement. Sometimes the regular benefits commence as if actual retirement had taken place, and the employee's subsequent compensation is adjusted to this fact.

Recent union attitudes have been opposed to compulsory retirement ages for employees represented by the union. However, on the principle that the employer should have some say about when an employee ceases to meet job performance requirements because of age, most negotiated plans contain a mandatory, or automatic, retirement age set at several years later than normal retirement age. Even here, special cases may continue on the job at the employer's request.

Formula for Amount of Pension. It is the aim of many pension plans to provide an income that, when supplemented by social-security benefits, amounts to about 50 per cent of the long-service employee's normal earnings just before retirement (a somewhat higher benefit in relation to compensation, such as 60 per cent, is frequently desired in the case of the lower-paid group of long-service employees). This 50 per cent figure is used in recognition of a reduction in the employee's living costs after retirement, the elimination of certain personal expenses necessitated by working, probably reduced family expenses, and a possible reduction in standard of living. Also, the employee's own personal thrift program can be expected to augment the benefits of the plan and of social security. The percentage of previous income needed after retirement varies with income groups, normally being greatest among lower-paid workers.

There are three basic formulas (or methods) for determining the amount of pension to which an employee will be entitled upon retirement. One of these methods should be adopted and set out in clear detail in the plan so that all concerned can understand exactly the benefits to which each employee will be entitled. The three methods are (1) the *unit-benefit method,* (2) the *flat-percentage method,* and (3) the *money-purchase method.*

1. *The Unit-benefit Method.* Under the *unit-benefit formula* a definite amount of annuity is provided for each participating employee for each year of credited service. The amount of the annuity is either a stated percentage of the employee's income for the year to which the unit applies or a flat dollar amount for each year of credited service. The percentages most commonly used run from 1 to 2 per cent, although for service before the establishment of the pension plan a factor less than 1 per cent has frequently been used. Under a 1 per cent plan, for example, an employee earning $5,000 yearly will be provided a benefit of $50 yearly for each year of service. If he participates in the plan for 25 years (with salary unchanged), his yearly retirement pension will be $1,250, or 25 per cent of his annual salary. If, because of social-security benefits, the first $4,200 of income is excluded in the pension formula, his retirement pension will be 25 per cent of $800, or $200 yearly. Under the flat-amount formula the units usually will fall between $1 and $2.50 a month for each year of credited service. A common formula now is $2.25 a month for each year of service before retirement. This means $67.50 a month, or $810 a year, as the pension amount after 30 years of service. Since individuals become employed at different ages, the unit-benefit method produces differing amounts of final pension for employees, depending on the employee's total length of credited service.

2. *The Flat-percentage Method.* In order to avoid the variations in total pension that are inherent in the unit-benefit formula because of variations in length of service, a *flat-percentage method* may be used. Each employee is provided a pension that is a flat percentage of his average compensation over a specified period of time. The percentage is independent of length of service, except that some minimum period is usually specified for eligibility to receive the full pension. If the employee at retirement has not been employed for this minimum period, his pension is reduced proportionately. For bent-formula minimum-pay plans that must satisfy Internal Revenue Service re-

quirements regarding integration, the minimum period of service at retirement must be 15 years in order to secure full benefit; for shorter periods the benefits are reduced proportionately. Flat-percentage pensions vary from 15 to 70 per cent of compensation. The compensation to which the flat percentage is applied is most frequently the employee's average regular compensation over the 5- or 10-year period preceding retirement but sometimes is the average of the 5 highest of the last 10 or, possibly, the 5 highest consecutive years.

3. *The Money-purchase Method.* An entirely different approach to determining the amount of pension is provided by the *money-purchase formula.* The employer first decides what proportion of covered payroll he is willing to contribute to the pension plan; then he decides whether the employees will be asked to contribute and, if so, how much. Frequently employer and employee contribute equally. These contributions by both employer and employee are usually expressed as percentages of pay, either total regular pay or regular pay in excess of some yearly amount, such as $4,200 per employee. The amount of pension for each employee is the amount that can be provided by the predetermined contributions. This method has the advantage of definitely fixing the employer's cost at all times as a certain per cent of covered payroll. Such a cost limitation is lacking under the unit-benefit and fixed-percentage methods, where higher ages of employees, pay increases at the older ages, increases in the ratio of female pensioners, or increases in premium rates under insured plans raise the employer's costs.

One important disadvantage of the money-purchase method is that no definite amount of pension can be promised, and the employee is not sure just what his retirement income will be until he reaches retirement. A more fundamental difficulty under the straight money-purchase device is that employees who are at an advanced age when the plan is introduced will not receive significant benefits because there is only a short period during which the contributions made by them and by the employer on their behalf can be forthcoming. Even if the money-purchase arrangement is made retroactive to a degree so that the employer makes up contributions for prior years, the resulting past-service benefit is not likely to be satisfactory. For instance, under an insured money-purchase plan, if contributions had actually been made over those prior years when the employee was younger, they would have provided larger amounts of annuity than would the same amounts of contributions made currently. To overcome this difficulty, money-purchase plans sometimes apply only to the future, and an employer-financed unit-benefit or minimum-benefit method is adopted with respect to prior service for employees already advanced in years when the plan is installed. Some money-purchase plans utilize a schedule providing for contributions that are higher percentages of compensation at the older ages than at the younger ages at entry into the plan.

Past Service and Future Service. The amount of pension is directly related to the length of credited service of the employee with the employer under both the unit-benefit and the money-purchase formulas and is indirectly related to service (because of minimum-service requirements) under the flat-percentage formula.

When a pension plan is first adopted, an employer whose business has been in operation before the effective date of the plan may have many employees eligible for participation who already have put in many years of service. If provision is made in a unit-benefit or money-purchase plan for pensions for all or part of these years of prior service, they are called *past-service pensions*. Pensions based on service subsequent to the adoption of the plan are called *future-service pensions* or, sometimes, *current-service pensions*.

Past-service Pensions. Older employees who are approaching retirement age when a pension plan is adopted will not receive an adequate income upon retirement unless past-service pensions are provided. Such employees will feel that they have been discriminated against simply because the employer delayed in installing a plan. In order to avoid such discrimination, most pension plans make some provision for past-service benefits, although the cost of providing such pensions is large and must normally be borne entirely by the employer.

The amount of past-service benefit that would probably be most satisfactory to the employee is what he would have received as a future-service benefit if the pension plan had been in effect at the time he first became eligible. As a practical matter, however, most pension plans provide a lower scale of benefits for past service than for future service. For instance, pension plans providing a 1 per cent pension for each year of future service might provide only a ¾ per cent pension for past service. One reason for this is that past-service benefits are almost invariably determined as a unit percentage of the employee's salary at the time the pension plan is installed. Credit at this rate is given for each year of eligible prior service. Since wages and salaries normally increase with duration of employment, the use of a lower percentage of earnings at the effective date of the plan as a past-service benefit adjusts in a rough manner for lower earnings in the earlier years of employment. In the case of contributory plans another reason for the pension differential between past service and future service lies in the fact that no contributions have been required (nor called for retroactively) of employees over the period of such past service.

Some plans do not include a specific past-service credit but merely stipulate that a minimum annuity will be payable at retirement, such minimum annuity being in excess of the regular formula amount for entrants to the plan at the higher ages at the inception of the plan. The supplemental annuity provided for an older member (the difference between the minimum amount and the formula amount) may be funded in the same way as would a regular service benefit or may be paid for by the employer over a stipulated number of years. Retirement plans based on individual insurance contracts look to the amount of annuity to be paid at retirement and fund the cost of that pension over the employee's active years. While this type does not introduce past service directly, it usually provides full benefits to older employees with the requisite service and hence gives recognition to employees with long service before the installation of the plan.

The financial circumstances of the employer installing the plan are of paramount importance in determining the past-service credit that can be offered. In order to provide a reasonable yet financially bearable system of past-service benefits, past-service credits are frequently limited by:

1. Recognizing not more than a designated number of years of past service

2. Excluding the first 5 or 10 years of past service

3. Counting only the years of past service that are subsequent to attainment of a specified age

By using one of these methods or a combination of them, an employer may give recognition to past service and still keep the cost of these benefits within the limit of his resources.

In some instances an insurer will restrict the amount of past-service annuity that may be purchased in any year for any annuitant.

Future-service Pensions. The unit-benefit method provides a future-service pension that is a fixed-dollar unit or a definite percentage of the employee's eligible compensation for each year of participation in the plan and for whatever contributions are necessary to that end. The money-purchase method provides for contributions by the employer and generally by the employee to furnish future-service pensions; these contributions are a definite percentage of the employee's eligible compensation for each year of participation. The provisions of either type of plan regarding units, percentages, and amounts of employee contributions should be clear, concise, and simple, as should the provisions defining the pension to be provided, since those are the provisions most directly affecting the employee. In the interest of simplicity it is well to have no more than two contribution rates for employees and no more than two pension rates. Two rates permit variation for annual compensation below and above $3,000, $3,600, or $4,200, in order to recognize social-security benefits. In some instances a desirable simplification of the unit-benefit type of plan is to base benefits and employee contributions on earnings classes (proceeding by annual-pay increments, such as $240, $350, $480, or $600) rather than on exact salary and to specify amounts rather than percentages of wages provided each year for each salary class, changes in amount of employee contributions and in pension credits received being made only when employees change earnings classes. The contribution and pension is usually based on the earnings at the mid-point of the class. An example of earnings classes, benefits, and contributions under such a plan is shown in Table 4-1.

There is no hard-and-fast rule to apply in establishing the formula for the future-service pension to be paid under the unit-benefit method. The integration requirements of the Internal Revenue Service should be observed if the plan is subject to approval by the Service. It is customary to decide on the average percentage benefit which it is intended to provide at retirement, taking into account the social-

TABLE 4-1. ILLUSTRATIVE SCHEDULE OF BENEFITS AND CONTRIBUTIONS
(Based on past service at ½ per cent on first $3,000 of salary plus 1 per cent on excess; future service at 1 per cent on first $3,000 plus 1½ per cent on excess; employee contributions at 2 per cent on first $3,000 plus 3 per cent on excess)

Compen-sation class number	Base annual compensation		Mid-point compensa-tion of class	Annual benefit for each year		Employee's annual contri-bution
	Over	Not over		Of past service	Of current service	
1	$.....	$ 840	$ 720	$ 3.60	$ 7.20	$ 14.40
2	840	1,080	960	4.80	9.60	19.20
3	1,080	1,320	1,200	6.00	12.00	24.00
4	1,320	1,560	1,440	7.20	14.40	28.80
5	1,560	1,800	1,680	8.40	16.80	33.60
6	1,800	2,040	1,920	9.60	19.20	38.40
7	2,040	2,280	2,160	10.80	21.60	43.20
8	2,280	2,520	2,400	12.00	24.00	48.00
9	2,520	2,760	2,640	13.20	26.40	52.80
10	2,760	3,000	2,880	14.40	28.80	57.60
11	3,000	3,480	3,240	17.40	33.60	67.20
12	3,480	3,960	3,720	22.20	40.80	81.60
13	3,960	4,440	4,200	27.00	48.00	96.00
14	4,440	4,920	4,680	31.80	55.20	110.40
15	4,920	5,400	5,160	36.60	62.40	124.80
Etc. For each $480 increase in compensation add:				4.80	7.20	14.40

security benefit where applicable. For example, if the intent is to provide long-service employees with a pension of about 45 per cent of average earnings, the average age at which new employees will become eligible in the future may be estimated in order to obtain the typical interval from eligibility to retirement. If this interval is 30 years and a 45 per cent benefit is contemplated, a retirement benefit of 1½ per cent of salary per year of future service should be selected.

The amount of money (in terms of dollars or as a percentage of payroll) that the employer estimates he can afford to contribute to the pension plan year in and year out, with due regard to any periods when tax credits on the employer's contributions may be less favorable than at present, influences the determination of the pension formula. After a tentative formula has been decided upon, estimates of current cost based on the age, sex, length of service, and salary distribution of eligible employees should be made, together with forecasts of future costs. If these cost estimates exceed the amount the employer will probably be able to contribute, it is necessary to scale down the pension benefits, make other specifications more restrictive, adopt longer funding periods, or increase the scale of employee contributions.

A rough-and-ready estimate of the cost of future-service benefits for a retirement plan providing a yearly pension of $1\frac{1}{2}$ per cent of covered compensation is 10 per cent of covered payroll, including employee contributions, if any. Such a rule-of-thumb is, of course, subject to wide variation because of different age, sex, salary, and service compositions of employee groups. It is sometimes felt that the 10 per cent figure indicates that a money-purchase plan under which both the employee and the employer contribute 5 per cent of covered compensation would provide a satisfactory pension scale. This does not follow, because of the money-purchase structure itself. Employees at young ages when such a plan was established would secure substantial benefits by time of retirement—in fact, they might obtain pensions that were more than reasonable. On the other hand, the employees who were older at the time the plan was established would not receive reasonable amounts of benefits. Therefore, it cannot be said that because one type of plan will produce reasonable benefits at a certain over-all percentage of payroll cost a money-purchase plan using the same aggregate contribution rate would produce a comparable result.

When money-purchase plans are used for employees covered by the Social Security Act, a typical employee contribution rate is 2 or 3 per cent on that part of compensation below $4,200 a year and 5 or 6 per cent on that part in excess of $4,200 per year; the employer either matches the employee contribution or contributes better than half of the total contribution; the employer also bears the cost of whatever past-service or minimum benefits are furnished.

Benefits under the Flat-percentage Method. The flat-percentage method in its usual form does not distinguish between past service and future service. It provides a basic pension that is a flat percentage of average compensation over some base period, regardless of length of service, except for a stipulated minimum period, and regardless of whether such service occurred before or after adoption of the plan. A pro rata reduction is usually made for employees with periods of service at retirement less than the stipulated minimum for receiving full pensions. For example, a plan that calls for a $\frac{1}{25}$ reduction for each year of service below 25 at retirement would provide an employee retiring after 10 years of service with only $\frac{10}{25}$ of the normal flat-percentage pension.

The flat percentages utilized usually vary from 25 to 50 per cent of covered compensation, generally with a lower percentage for compensation below \$4,200 yearly if social-security benefits are taken into consideration. Common formulas provide pensions of 20 to 25 per cent of compensation below \$4,200 plus 40 to 50 per cent of compensation above \$4,200.

Pensions Offset by Social-security Benefits. The methods for determining a benefit formula thus far described have recognized the existence of the social-security benefit through either excluding the first \$4,200 of wages or making a differential in benefits and employee contributions between that part of pay up to \$4,200 per annum and that part in excess of that amount. In many instances the plan's benefits are more closely meshed with social-security benefits. For example, a plan's benefits may be set at 40 per cent of pay minus the actual (or approximate) amount of social-security benefit payable at sixty-five.[4]

While this type of offset arrangement appears logical, it raises many administrative difficulties and has basic drawbacks. One of these drawbacks lies in the employee contributions, if any, under the plan. The employee contributions (taxes) under the federal plan do not bear

[4] In some plans this "deduct" has been set at one-half the social-security benefit to recognize the fact that the employer's contributions under the Social Security Act are matched by those of the employee.

any consistent relationship by different pay levels with the benefits emerging under the act. Consequently, to set a benefit formula at some percentage of wages and then to deduct from such benefit a social-security amount while still keeping the same employee-contribution percentage will create differing equity relationships at different pay levels under the plan. For example, consider a plan where employee contributions are 3 per cent of salaries or wages and the retirement benefit is determined as one-half of pay less the social-security benefit. To illustrate with an extreme case, if employee A earns $1,800 annually and employee B earns $3,600 and if these two employees, both having 25 years of service, each receive a primary social-security benefit at age sixty-five based on continuous employment after 1950 under the act, then the benefits under the plan (ex-social security) and the contributions made annually by the respective employees will be as shown in Table 4-2.

TABLE 4-2.

	Employee A	Employee B
Annual earnings............................	$1,800	$3,600
Annual retirement benefit, including social security	900	1,800
Social-security benefit.....................	822	1,182
Annual benefit from plan (ex-social security)..	$ 78	$ 618
Employee annual contribution at 3 per cent...	$ 54	$ 108
Total employee contributions (25 years)......	$1,350	$2,700
Ratio of total employee contribution to annual retirement benefit from plan..............	(1,350 ÷ 78)17.3	(2,700 ÷ 618)4.4

It is apparent that employee A receives much less favorable treatment than employee B (and, in fact, A's own contributions would probably more than pay for his benefit from the plan).

Another rather difficult problem is the determination of the federal benefit. Since information concerning social-security benefits is not obtainable from the government except upon the employee's own request for such information, there is no sure way of knowing precisely what government benefits will be deductible. There is a full primary-insurance benefit due at sixty-five for the wage earner himself and an extra 50 per cent if he has a wife also over sixty-five (or less if she is sixty-two to sixty-five). Or, again, is the plan going to follow the exact incidence of payment of federal benefits? For instance, if the retired employee (below age seventy-two) earns more than a prescribed maximum in covered employment, then during the period of such employment his federal benefit is suspended. Does the benefit from the plan enlarge itself to the full amount for the period of such suspension? Another question regards early retirement. Will this benefit be level until age sixty-five is reached with the offset then occurring, or will the offset be computed in advance so that a level amount for life will result, with no offset at the time age sixty-five is attained? The fact of early retirement itself will cause the social-security benefit to be smaller when it becomes due if, from early retirement until age sixty-five, employment elsewhere in covered work is not maintained, although the 5-year dropout provision in the social-security amendments may help alleviate this problem.

Another problem lies in the small size of the benefit that is likely to come from the plan for lower-paid individuals under the offset method. The offset itself is relatively large, inasmuch as the social-security formula is disproportionately favorable to lower-paid workers. The net benefit from the plan itself can even be a negative amount, an anomalous situation, particularly for employees who had understood that they were to benefit under the plan. If these employees were required to contribute to the plan, the situation would be even more anomalous.

The above troublesome details have been multiplied by the 1956 amendments to the Social Security Act, which introduced reduced benefits for women at age sixty-two and a "disability-insurance benefit" after age fifty in cases of qualifying disability retirement.

To some employers one of the appealing features of the offset method seems to lie in the fact that increases in the social-security benefit resulting from liberalization of the act would automatically be reflected by corresponding decreases in liabilities under the plan. It is argued, however, that the same element of control is present under the terms of most other types of plans because the employer retains the right to amend the plan with respect to future-service-benefit accruals when conditions change, as long as such amendment does not permit recapture of contributions made by him. There is, of course, the problem of explaining a decrease in plan benefits to employees covered by the plan.

Compensation upon Which Pensions Are Based. When pensions are related to earnings, it is necessary to define precisely the compensation base. Conditions peculiar to the type of plan adopted largely determine whether the benefit is to be based on average compensation over the whole period of the employee's participation in the plan; over a period such as the 5 or 10 years preceding retirement; on the compensation of only 1 year, such as the final year before retirement; on the 5 consecutive years of highest pay; or on some other figure.[5]

It is desirable to state in the plan whether overtime pay, bonuses, commissions, fees, or other special pay will be included with the base pay in determining the amount of pension. Many pension plans include such additional earnings either specifically or by implication, but others definitely exclude them. The situation of the individual employer is the determining factor in making this decision, since compensation practices vary so widely. If hourly-wage employees participate, a similar determination must often be made about how many hours per week or per month are to be considered in determining credited service for pension purposes.

In recent years final-average compensation has been more widely used as the basis upon which pension benefits will be determined. Some companies with pension plans of long standing that used the career-average-salary approach (e.g., 1 per cent of each year's compensation) have found that continued inflation resulted in inadequate total benefits accrued at retirement (e.g., a 1 per cent pension plan based on career-average pay would produce an annual benefit to a participant with 40 years of credited service—his career—equal to 40 per cent of career-average pay). If, however, promotional increases and inflationary adjustments had so affected salary levels that the annual

---

[5] Some of these methods may not be acceptable to the Internal Revenue Service.

salary at retirement was twice the career-average salary, then this same benefit would be only 20 per cent of the salary to which the employee had become accustomed just before retirement.

Critics of the final-pay plan point out that under such a plan a substantial unfunded past-service liability may be created merely by granting a large across-the-board salary increase. A parallel condition is likely to arise (but not necessarily so) under the career-average pension plan because this type of salary adjustment renders the pension benefits accrued to date inadequate and makes the pension plan ineffectual unless a somewhat similar upward revision of benefits accrued to date is carried through with similar unfunded past-service liability increments. To the extent that these future increases in salary level have been taken into account through the use of salary scales in the determination of the annual contributions under the pension plan, the liability arising from the salary increases will have been funded in advance.

The advocates of the final-average-pay type of benefit determination stress that this form of plan has an advantage over the career-average type in that if there should be a period of retrenchment in business with low profits and stabilized, or perhaps reducing, pay, the funds accumulated to date may be more than adequate to finance the benefits under the plan so that funds will be released to offset current contribution requirements. Furthermore, it is often pointed out that these credits arise at the very time when the employer is most in need of them, while any increased liability developing from substantial salary increases usually arises in periods of good times with higher profits.

Minimum Pensions. Strict application of the various percentage-of-compensation formulas may produce negligible pensions for employees with short periods of service, for employees in the low-pay brackets, or for employees earning only slightly more than is required for participation in the pension plan. Such small pensions may tend to discredit the plan among the affected employees and, in any event, may be administratively undesirable. Frequently, therefore, a minimum pension is provided regardless of formula, subject to a stipulated length of service. The minimum is usually expressed in dollars, such as $10 or $20 monthly, but it may be defined as a modest percentage of average compensation for some base period. Sometimes the minimum is designed to include the social-security benefit. For plans excluding the first $4,200 of salary and thus subject to the integration requirements of the Internal Revenue Service, the permissible minimum pension may not exceed $20 monthly. The minimum itself sometimes takes account of length of service and may be subject to reduction if retirement occurs after short periods of service or in the event of early retirement.

Under a contributory plan a minimum employee contribution of $1 or $2 a month may similarly be required in order to aid in providing a minimum pension.

Maximum Pensions. Higher-paid employees are popularly supposed to be well able to provide for retirement outside a pension plan. Consequently, there has been some unfavorable publicity for pension plans that set no maximum limit for pensions, particularly when the plans have been subject to tax exemption. Actually, higher-paid executives are as reluctant as other employees to accept retirement unless their pensions are a substantial percentage of previous salary. Being subject to high individual income taxes and personal expenses, executives may find themselves unable to save sufficiently for retirement without the help of a pension geared to their rates of compensation.

In order, however, to forestall possible criticism from the public and from stockholders, some employers have set maximum-amount limits on pensions payable. These limits vary widely, from $5,000 to above $25,000. The trend has been toward increasing the maximum amounts in existing plans, and in many instances maximums hitherto established have been removed.

Subsidiary Benefits. The primary benefit in a pension plan is the periodic payment made during the retirement of the employee. Other concomitant benefits are frequently provided. For example, it may be desirable to provide life insurance along with the retirement benefit, particularly in the case of a small group of employees who would not qualify for a group-life-insurance arrangement. In such a circumstance, the death benefit is deemed a subsidiary benefit as long as the primary purpose is the provision of a pension to the employees. Another subsidiary benefit, when a definite amount of life insurance is not provided, is the payment on death of the employee before retirement, to the employee's beneficiary, of any contributions to the plan that the employee has made, with or without interest; sometimes a part of the contributions the employer has made to the plan is also paid to the beneficiary in the event of death before retirement.

A permanent-and-total-disability benefit is frequently made a part of a noninsured retirement plan.[6] The payment of a disability benefit is usually surrounded with safeguards to afford protection from adverse selection, and the benefit is not made so high as to encourage questionable claims. A fairly long period of service is generally required before an employee is eligible for a disability benefit, and a waiting period of a substantial number of months after inception of disability before benefits commence is also imposed. Following the allowance of disability payments, periodic checkups are necessary to substantiate the fact of continued disability. Arrangements for this benefit are usually entered into cautiously and are not allowed to overshadow the main purpose of the pension plan, which is retirement for age. The relationship of the plan's disability benefit to that of the disability-insurance benefit of the Social Security Act must be considered, including the concurrent definition and adjudication of "disability."

The inclusion of death, withdrawal, or disability benefits in a pension plan depends in large measure upon the employer's ability to pay the additional cost entailed by these benefits. In contributory plans it is a practical necessity to provide for return of at least the employee's contributions upon either death or withdrawal. If any subsidiary benefits are included, it is necessary to set out in detail in the plan the conditions of age and service under which the benefits will be granted. Provisions for determining the amount of each benefit and to whom it is to be paid must be clear and succinct, in order that each employee may understand exactly to what he is entitled. The amounts of these benefits are related to the basic pension benefits in the plan, but the type of pension plan also establishes the pattern of the subsidiary benefits to a considerable degree. For example, if

---

[6] Insurance companies some time ago discontinued underwriting the disability benefit in connection with group-life or regular group-annuity plans, finding great difficulty in controlling the payment of claims, particularly in the depression years. More recently, principally in connection with *deposit-administration plans* (see Chap. 8), insurers have provided for paying disability pensions out of the fund.

under stated conditions termination of employment is to carry vested rights, these will usually be patterned on the benefit formula applicable to such employee up to the time of his termination, so that his vested right is to a deferred pension proportional to his credited service. Or, again, the death benefit in a group-annuity plan may be related to the employee's contributions, while the death benefit in an individual-policy plan is frequently $1,000 for each $10 of monthly retirement income provided by the plan. Because these subsidiary benefits vary according to type of plan, more complete analysis will be presented in subsequent chapters.[7]

Funding the Pension Plan. The term *funding* relates to the methods used to pay for the benefits provided in the pension plan. Some plans are described as *funded,* while others are *unfunded.* Each year, as an active employee grows older, the present value of his prospective pension increases, and the pension liability increases correspondingly. In a funded plan this continual increase is recognized in advance and offset (amortized) by regular contributions. In an unfunded plan the benefits are paid directly as they fall due out of the current earnings or accumulated surplus of the employer. While the employee retirement plans of some concerns are still of the unfunded type, this method is rarely used for plans currently being adopted. The main reasons for the funded type lie in the reduced aggregate costs through the operation of interest on the fund; in the greater formality and specific provisions of a funded plan; in the security that the fund itself brings to the covered employee, particularly those already on the retirement rolls who could hardly turn their hand at employment for support if their pension failed; and also in the tax advantages to the employer in early deductibility of contributions toward a qualified funded plan.

The extent to which the method of funding and the employer contribution are contained in provisions of the plan runs from a very general statement, such as, "The company intends to contribute amounts which, on a sound actuarial basis, will provide the benefits of the plan," to a provision that spells out in detail how employer contributions will be determined and when they will be made. In

[7] See Chaps. 8 and 9.

the trust-fund type of plan, the funding provision for the employer is likely to be less definite than that contained in the documents establishing the insured type of plan. Frequently, even the trust-fund type of funding provision [8] stipulates clearly the employer's intended funding for future-service benefits but leaves the funding of past-service benefits flexible so that some method of amortizing past-service liability, even on an irregular basis, can be followed in the years after the effective date of the plan.

The employer's commitments in regard to funding are likely to be more clearly spelled out in the plan if it is set up on a contributory basis. This is natural since if the employees are called upon to contribute specific amounts it is felt that the employer's commitment should also be specific, particularly with respect to future service—the service periods for which the employees contribute.

Employee Contributions. When employees contribute toward the cost of a pension plan, their contributions are usually a stated percentage of the portion of their earnings on which the pension is based. When employees are covered by social security and smaller pensions are provided on the first $3,000, $3,600, or $4,200 of earnings than are provided on the excess, a correspondingly lower rate of employee contribution is required. This lower contribution rate is frequently 2, 2½, or 3 per cent of the earnings to which it is applicable. The most frequently used employee-contribution rates on the excess earnings not subject to the social-security tax are 3, 4, or 5 per cent.

The contribution rates in money-purchase plans vary considerably, but frequently employer and employee each contribute 2 to 3 per cent of the first $3,600 or $4,200 of a participant's yearly compensation and 5 to 6 per cent of compensation in excess of $3,600 or $4,200. Some plans call for contributions by the employee of two-thirds (or some other fraction) of those of the employer. Occasionally regular rates of contribution are set but are made subject to adjustment to reflect changes in the social-security tax rate.

The decision whether employees should be required to contribute toward the cost of a pension plan is of major importance. The following factors are illustrative of those normally requiring consideration:

1. The question whether the amount of money that the employer

[8] See Chap. 7.

can reasonably expect to contribute to the pension plan over a period of years, including bad as well as good times, will be sufficient without employee contributions to provide the desired scale of benefits

2. The financial ability of the employees to contribute to the pension plan after consideration is given to the general pay level and the level of take-home pay after deductions for income tax, social-security tax, group insurance, savings bonds, and other purposes

3. The amount of tax deductions that will inure to the employer as a result of his contributions to a pension plan and the fact that no such deductions are permitted the employee for his contributions

4. The fact that employer-pay-all pension plans based on minimum-compensation requirements, which are subject to the integration requirements of the Internal Revenue Code, are restricted to a maximum pension-benefit accrual rate that is a comparatively low percentage of earnings but may be increased slightly if supported by employee contributions

5. The possibility that registration with the Securities and Exchange Commission will be required if a trust-fund pension plan calling for employee contributions is set up and if membership in the plan is on a voluntary basis

6. The possibility that requirement of employee contributions will make it difficult to secure reasonably full participation without compulsion

7. The possibility that failure to require employee contributions will cause the employees to regard the pension plan as paternalistic with the result that they may not fully appreciate it

8. The possibility that employee contributions will lead the employees or their representatives to expect to have a voice in the administration of the plan

Decisions in the past regarding employee contributions toward the cost of pension plans appear to have been made too frequently on the basis of the employer's economic condition at the time the pension plan was adopted. In the decade 1930–1939, when industrial earnings were at a relatively low rate, most new pension plans provided for substantial employee contributions, while in the period of high earnings in the 1940s and 1950s to date many new plans provided that the employer would pay the entire cost. This latter trend is understandable in view of the tax situation, in which an employer paying out a very high percentage of his profits in taxes is permitted to deduct his contributions to an approved pension plan from income otherwise subject to tax and thus is enabled to meet his pension obligations by reducing his net profits after taxes by only a portion of each dollar contributed.

The employer-pay-all plan has definite advantages for the employer in that the employer has more freedom and flexibility in designing and administering the plan. It automatically assures 100 per cent participation by all eligible employees, a goal which may be difficult to attain where substantial employee contributions are required, particularly in industries with a low take-home-wage or salary level.

The argument that employees will not properly appreciate a pension plan unless they contribute toward its cost is rather specious if the plan is properly presented to them and if its benefits are kept before them by repeated employee-relations publicity. Constant reiteration of the value of a pension plan is necessary in every case, whether or not the employees contribute, if the employer is to obtain maximum benefit from its morale-building potentialities. It is an outstanding fallacy in personnel administration to assume that any welfare benefit, no matter how expensive, can be of maximum value to either employer or employee without continually keeping it before the employees.

Basically, the decision whether employees will be required to contribute must in large part rest on a determination by the employer whether he can afford, in good years and bad and in times of lesser tax incentives, to pay the entire cost of a pension plan that will provide adequate benefits to all employees whom he wishes to include in the plan.

Even if a plan is designed on an employer-pay-all basis, it is possible to include specific provisions for subsequent contributions by employees in the event the employer finds himself unable to continue paying the entire cost. If some employees do not then wish to contribute, they should be permitted to keep the pension equities already accrued for them. But it might turn out to be very difficult to persuade employees to start contributing under what had before been an employer-pay-all plan.

Voluntary Employee-pay-all Plans. Occasionally a plan is paid for entirely through employee contributions. Such a plan is usually developed to supplement an existing pension plan established along conventional lines, with costs met wholly or partly by the employer.

Unless the employer renders some indirect financial and administrative assistance to a pension plan, there is very little inducement for an employee to participate in an employee-pay-all plan, since he would feel that he could just as readily make his own pension arrangements on an individual basis through investments or the purchase of an annuity contract from an insurer. Perhaps some slight advantage costwise may accrue to an employee if he, in conjunction with a group of fellow workers, arranges to purchase a group-annuity plan or create a trust fund for pension purposes, but such savings could not be very significant.

Infrequently a situation is found where an employer has established an employer-pay-all plan and precluded any employee contributions in order better to maintain control of the plan. In such case, if the employees are adamant in their desire to contribute toward the cost of their pensions, the only course open to them is the establishment of an employee-pay-all plan with or without administrative assistance from the employer.

Employee-pay-all plans have a tendency to get into financial difficulties sooner or later. If the pension outgo is greater than the contribution input or if increase in contribution rates becomes necessary to maintain a previously set scale of pension benefits, the appeal of the plan will be concentrated more and more on those who stand to benefit soonest, with the result that it may prove difficult to bring in new members, a situation analogous to the one which developed in the past in the field of fraternal and assessment life insurance.

Compulsory Participation. All employees who meet the eligibility requirements of an employer-pay-all pension plan are automatically covered by it. In a plan providing for employee contributions, it is possible to make participation either compulsory or voluntary. Compulsory contributions may, however, result in difficulties with groups representing the employees. In practice, few contributory plans are compulsory, and these usually permit voluntary participation by employees already in service when the plan is adopted and limit the compulsory feature to employees hired after the pension plan is in effect. The predominance of the voluntary plan arises from a desire of employers to avoid any appearance of coercion in dealing with their employees, even though there is a possibility of not securing complete employee participation. Most plans provide that an employee, having once chosen to participate, must continue participation throughout his employment. Some plans, however, provide that an employee may discontinue his coverage while still remaining an employee but may not reenter the plan. Increased participation among the younger employees is sometimes obtained by requiring them to join the pension plan in order to obtain other employee benefits (e.g., hospital-and-surgical coverage).

Provisions to Protect the Employee. The 1942 amendments to the Internal Revenue Code focused attention on the need for provisions to prevent improper discrimination among different groups of employees and to assure that funds once allocated to a pension plan could not be diverted by the employer to other purposes. All pension plans qualifying under the Internal Revenue Code include provisions defining the employee's rights under the plan. These provisions are designed to minimize administrative problems by anticipating and answering troublesome questions.

Pay Changes. An increase in an employee's pay means an increase in his pension benefit in many types of plans. These increases in benefits are usually made effective annually or semiannually for all employees becoming eligible for an increase in the preceding period.

A decrease in an employee's pay under these plans theoretically means a decrease in his pension benefit. For personnel reasons, however, it is sometimes found desirable to continue providing the same benefit the employee was receiving before the pay decrease and to require the same amount of contribution from him. Most plans adjust the benefit (and employee contribution, if any) downward for decreases in pay. In minimum-pay plans, a decrease in pay below the minimum level may drop an employee from the eligible class. In this event, provision may be made to permit the employee to continue temporarily (e.g., for 2 years) as a participant in the plan, receiving the same benefits and making the same contributions as before the pay cut, or he may be excluded from further participation in the plan until an increase in earnings makes him again eligible.

Definition of Past Service. A specific definition of what constitutes past service should be included in the plan when benefits are provided for such service. Many plans specify that "continuous service" or "completed years of service" (sometimes subject to a maximum number of years or some other restriction) before the effective date of the pension plan will be counted in determining the past-service benefit. Clarification of the effect of layoffs or leaves of absence during that time is desirable.

Absences. Authorized absences caused by sickness or accident, temporary layoff, or absence on leave, vacation, or military service are normally not cause for termination of an employee's participation in a pension plan. A time limit of 1 to 2 years is, however, frequently imposed; absence of longer duration, except for military service, is cause for termination of participation.

If the employee is paid during a leave of absence, his contributions (if the plan is contributory) are deducted; employer contributions to the pension plan are normally continued. If the leave is without pay, contributions to the plan are normally suspended, but benefits already purchased remain in effect. However, provision may be made for continuance of the employer's contributions and for direct payment by the employee on leave of contributions that would otherwise have been deducted from his pay. A contributory plan may provide that the employer will pay both his own and the employee's contributions during leave of absence without pay, but usually this is limited to employees in military service.

Employer Contributions to Be Used for Benefit of Employees. Pension plans subject to the approval of the Internal Revenue Service must provide that the employer's contributions may not be diverted to purposes other than for the exclusive benefit of the employees or of their beneficiaries. Such a provision protects the employees and assures at least the older ones that part of the pension plan will be fulfilled in any event.

Assignment of Benefits. Since the benefits under a pension plan are designed for the primary purpose of supporting the employee after retirement, assignment of them is usually not permitted, nor are they subject to legal process or attachment for payment of claims against the employee or his beneficiary unless the law provides otherwise.

Loans to Employees. Borrowing by the employee against his contributions or other contingent equity is usually forbidden, since such an arrangement might nullify the purpose of the plan and would certainly complicate the investment problem by necessitating maintenance of liquid assets for loan purposes.

Beneficiaries. The employee is given the right to name a beneficiary under plans providing death benefits. He may also change the beneficiary. If the beneficiary predeceases the participant, no rights continue to the beneficiary's estate. Frequently, in lieu of paying the death benefit to the estate of the deceased participant, payment may be made under a facility-of-payment provision to one or several of the following surviving relatives of the employee: widow or widower, children, parents, brothers, or sisters—in the order of preference prescribed in the plan or determined by the insurer, pension committee, or trustee of the plan.

Provisions to Protect the Employer. Provisions to protect the employer are designed to prevent possible misunderstandings of the rights conferred upon the employee by the adoption of a pension plan. Most pension plans are fully contractual to the extent of the trust-fund or insurance contract (subject to the right of the employer to amend or discontinue), and the employee is entitled to the retirement income and other benefits specified in the plan. It is nevertheless advisable to state in the plan that certain other benefits, rights, and privileges are not conferred on the participant.

Participation in the Plan Not a Guarantee of Job or Benefits. There is usually included a provision that participation by an employee will not give him the right to be retained in the service of the employer nor give him any right to retirement or other benefits unless such rights have specifically accrued under the terms of the plan.

Reemployment Rights. Withdrawal benefits may or may not be granted, but in any event termination of employment entails termination of active participation in a pension plan. In the case of reemployment, an employee may, for the purposes of the pension plan, be considered a new employee or be allowed to rejoin on conditions different from those for a new employee.

Continuation of Participation. Under employer-pay-all plans, all employees participate as long as they remain eligible. Under contributory plans, eligible employees are usually covered on a voluntary basis, with the employee contributing in accordance with the schedule of contributions in the plan. Normally, to receive full benefits an employee must enter when first eligible; otherwise he may enter at any time after becoming eligible but may be subject to adjustments in benefits or contributions. Once an employee has become a participant, however, he is usually required to continue contributions as long as he remains an employee. Permitting employees to enter and leave the plan at will would defeat the basic purpose of accumulating pension benefits over the period of credited service. It would also create administrative difficulties. Some plans do permit employees to discontinue contributions but not to resume them, and it may be required that contributions already made under the plan must be left to provide paid-up deferred benefits.

Change or Discontinuance of the Plan. When an employer adopts a pension plan, he hopes and intends to continue it indefinitely as written. However, changes in his financial situation, amendments to the Internal Revenue Code, or modifications of social legislation may make it desirable, if not imperative, to amend or terminate the plan. All pension plans, therefore, contain provisions reserving to the employer the right to change or modify the plan at any time, including the right to reduce or discontinue his contributions. Such action should not adversely affect any rights acquired by employees before the change. In the event of discontinuance of a qualified plan, contributions made up to that time by the employer vest in the employees, subject to the limitations with respect to benefits for higher-paid employees required by the Internal Revenue Service to be effective for a period of 10 years after the plan's inception. Furthermore, the Internal Revenue Service requires that every qualified plan have provisions specifying what is to happen to employees' interests if the plan terminates. The employer cannot expect to receive back any contributions made under the plan unless an "actuarial error" (an Internal

Revenue Service euphemism for an overfunded condition) leaves a residue after the satisfaction of all liabilities under the plan. A provision in the plan that this residue may be recaptured by the employer seems to be acceptable to the Service.

The provisions of the plan must go beyond the mere statement that the employer has the right to discontinue the program. They must tell what disposition of funds is to be made under the trust or insurance contract. For example, under a trust-fund plan it is commonly provided that the fund, upon termination of the plan, will (1) provide for continuation of the pensions to the already retired group, (2) provide pensions for those already eligible for retirement or early retirement, and (3) if any balance remains, be equitably allocated—oftentimes with further categorical priorities—among the remaining employees. Such a disposition may be implemented by continuing the trust, by purchasing life annuities, or by making an outright cash distribution. Under the insured type of plan, those already retired at time of termination of the plan are in an annuity status, and no further action is necessary; those who have not yet retired either have paid-up deferred annuity rights already or the master contract provides that these shall be purchased at time of termination of the plan in some specified order of priority.

Provisions to Protect the Insurer or Trustee. Provisions to protect the plan's funding medium—insurer or trust fund—are needed to set forth the rights and the limits of responsibility of the organization acting as the funding medium for the plan.

Insurer. The principals to a group-annuity contract are the employer and the insurer (with the employee or beneficiary having third party rights). In a sense, the contract is unilateral in that, as long as the employer meets certain specified conditions, the insurer generally has no right of termination of contract. However, in order to amend the contract, the insurer and the employer must agree to the changes. In any event, the insurer reserves the right at specified intervals, generally when the rate guaranty expires, to make any modifications in the contract it feels necessary, except those which would have an adverse effect on employee benefits already purchased or on the conditions of receipt thereof previously established. While the employer is the owner of the contract, the insurer usually prohibits assignment unless mutually agreed upon.

The insurer has the right to discontinue the insured plan in event of certain specified situations such as the failure of the employer to make prompt payment of premiums or if the employee participation drops below a certain number or percentage of employees. Of course, if the employer refuses to accept any amendments to the contract made by the insurer as periodically contemplated, the contract would be placed in a discontinued status. The contract does not terminate, in the event of a discontinued status, since it must continue to govern the pensions for those already retired and the vested rights of active employees and any beneficiaries.

Under deposit-administration contracts, the insurer, while sometimes granting the employer a right to transfer the deposit account to another fiduciary, reserves the privilege to impose an administrative surrender charge, such as five per cent, on the amount transferred and to make the transfer in installments over a period of time. The deposit-administration form contains the same sort of periodic expiry of guaranties as does the group-annuity form above.

Under the individual-insurance-annuity-contract plan, the rights of revision by the insurer are limited to new contracts issued after a given date. Contracts already in the hands of a trustee or other party cannot be changed in any way as long as premium payments are met.

Trust Fund. The trustee or trustees under a trust-fund pension plan do not need to have protective clauses relative to rates and guaranties such as are necessary for an insurer, but must see to it that the trust agreement contains certain other protective provisions. If the trustee retains full responsibility for investment, he is protected from direction by others. The trustee must rely on the employer for instructions concerning benefit disbursements and is fully protected in placing such reliance on the employer and, in legal matters, upon the advices of counsel. The trustee may resign at any time on due notice. No change in the trust agreement can be made without the trustee being made a party thereto and generally no change in the pension plan itself that affects the trustee or his responsibilities is made without his approval.

If the plan is qualified under the Internal Revenue Service requirements, the trust fund thereunder is irrevocable and upon the termination of the plan the liabilities to employees and retired employees extend only to the capacity of the trust fund. If these liabilities are met in full and if the plan so stipulates, any surplus assets remaining with the trustee may be transferred back to the employer. In the administration of the trust fund, the trustee, if not compensated directly by the employer, may obtain the compensation from the fund itself.

CHAPTER 5

Governmental Regulation

It is almost universally accepted that the furnishing of reasonable incomes to retired employees through private pension plans is socially desirable. It is also widely held that the old-age-and-disability benefits payable under the Social Security Act require supplementing in order that the great bulk of employees may receive an income after retirement that is adequate to provide the necessities and at least a part of the comforts of life.

Effect of Taxation. The federal government indirectly encourages the establishment and maintenance of private pension plans by permitting reasonable contributions to such plans by the employer to be considered a cost of doing business and, therefore, exempt from business income tax. It is sometimes said that the federal government is subsidizing private retirement plans to the extent that it exempts employers' contributions from taxation. This indirect federal "subsidy" is proportional to the income tax rates. When the tax rate on net income or profits is high, the "subsidy" is correspondingly high.[1]

During 1940 to 1945 and subsequently during 1950 to 1953, excess-profits taxes were in effect, with the result that the total federal tax rates to which corporations were subject were so high that the net cost of a pension plan to many business concerns was a small percentage of the contributions, a condition which greatly stimulated the adoption of such plans. A certain danger is inherent in such a situa-

[1] "Federal subsidy" is actually a misnomer. A better view is one of "federal encouragement" of pension plans because of their social value, this encouragement taking the form of recognizing contributions to a qualified plan as being in the nature of ordinary business expenses.

tion, for with the return of more nearly normal times and a reduction in tax rates the net cost of a pension plan to many employers rises sharply. Although relatively few plans have been terminated, plans that have been carried with ease by the employer during a period of substantial profits and high tax rates may turn out to be unduly burdensome and may have to be discarded or greatly modified, with possible resultant employee dissatisfaction. For this reason, pension authorities are convinced that it is unwise to adopt a pension plan primarily for the purpose of saving taxes.

The Income Tax Law before 1942. Before 1942 the restrictions on an employer's deductions from gross income of the expense of maintaining a pension plan were rather vague and somewhat discriminatory. Not until the Revenue Act of 1938 [2] was it provided that deductible employer contributions once made could not later revert to the employer. Another important requirement of long standing has been that the employer's contributions to an employee's pension, when added to the employee's other compensation, should represent only reasonable remuneration for services rendered. Services rendered might include prior years of service as well as those of the current year. A restriction appearing in the Revenue Act of 1928, applicable only to trust-fund plans as distinguished from insured plans, was that the total cost of providing a pension for past service (service with the company before eligibility for coverage under the pension plan) had to be amortized for tax purposes over a period of not fewer than 10 consecutive years; that is, an employer could include as business expense his annual pension-plan contributions based on his employees' current year's service and a limited part of the cost of establishing past-service benefits until the total past-service liability had been liquidated.

Insured group annuities were treated somewhat more liberally. No restrictions were imposed on the method of meeting the past-service liability. An employer with a substantial number of older employees with long periods of past service was permitted to install a group-annuity plan in a year when his profits were high and deduct the entire amount of the past-service liability if paid during that year.

[2] Effective with tax years commencing after Dec. 31, 1939.

This difference between the rate of tax-deductible funding of past-service liability permitted for trust-fund and for insured plans has since been eliminated. Both are now subject to the 10 per cent per year maximum.

The Excess-profits Tax.[3] The excess-profits tax originated during World War I and was discontinued in 1922. It was reinstituted in 1940 and discontinued at the end of 1945. It again became effective during 1950 and expired in 1953. It has been instrumental in securing the return to the federal government of a substantial portion of any unusual profits of corporations during periods of heavy expenditures for war material.

Table 5-1 sets out the excess-profits-tax rates that were effective over the period 1940 to 1945 and 1950 to 1953.

The excess-profits tax was in addition to the regular corporation income tax and surtax. The regular rate of income tax plus surtax applicable to moderate and large-size net incomes [4] increased from about 32 per cent in 1940 to about 53 per cent for the years 1942 to 1945 and from about 42 per cent in 1950 to about 52 per cent in 1953, and a 52 per cent rate on amounts of taxable income in excess of $25,000 has been extended to the present time (December, 1957).

The regular income tax and surtax rates are likely to continue high for some years. While the lapse of the excess-profits tax during 1953 has removed one source of indirect federal "subsidy" of pension plans, the maintenance of sizable income tax rates and surtax rates continues the favorable treatment afforded an employer's contributions toward an employee pension program.

Wage and Salary Stabilization. The Anti-inflation Act of 1942 imposed certain restrictions on the increasing of wages and salaries after October 2 of that year but defined wages and salaries as not including "insurance and pension benefits in reasonable amounts." The restrictions imposed by this legislation and its administration lasted from

---

[3] While the excess-profits tax, the Wage and Salary Stabilization Act, and other temporary expedients may seem to be more of historical than of immediate interest, they deserve discussion because of their tremendous impact on pension-plan developments.

[4] In all cases these tax rates were applicable to taxable net incomes of $25,000 or more.

Table 5–1. Rates of Excess-profits Tax Applicable to
Adjusted Excess-profits Net Income

Adjusted excess-profits net income	Taxable years beginning in			
	1940	1941	1942, 1943 *	1944, 1945 *
World War II:				
$20,000 and under	25%	35%	90%	95%
$20,001–$50,000	30	40	90	95
$50,001–$100,000	35	45	90	95
$100,001–$250,000	40	50	90	95
$250,001–$500,000	45	55	90	95
Over $500,000	50	60	90	95
Korean War: All adjusted excess-profits net income	Taxable years ending after June 30, 1950, and beginning before January 1, 1954: 30% (subject to certain maximum amounts)			

* A corporation, for taxable years ending in 1942 to 1946, was entitled to a credit of 10 per cent of the excess-profits tax paid in each year. The rates of excess-profits tax shown above are overstated to this extent. For example, the actual excess-profits-tax rate for 1944 and 1945 was 95 per cent − 9.5 per cent = 85.5 per cent of the adjusted excess-profits net income.

October 2, 1942, until August 18, 1945; on the latter date, stabilization restrictions were drastically reduced so that the rules with respect to contributions to pension or similar plans became practically nonexistent. During the Korean War wage- and salary-stabilization controls were again put into effect and significantly affected the development of pension, profit-sharing, bonus, and insurance plans.

The fundamental purpose of the wage- and salary-stabilization restrictions was the avoidance of inflation caused by uncontrolled wage and salary increases. During a period of war or emergency, the centering of a large portion of production upon other than consumers' goods results in an unusual scarcity of a great many items. The Office of Price Administration and other agencies exercised careful control over the prices that might be charged for many of the items that are normally designated as consumers' goods, but for any system of price fixing to operate successfully it is necessary also to exercise control over the amount of consumers' funds that will be available to purchase these goods. The wage- and salary-stabilization provisions of the Antiinflation Act of 1942 and of the Defense Production Act of 1950 were devised to effect this control.

Under the administration of the latter act, reasonable contributions made by an employer toward an approved pension plan were permitted. If the contributions were made under a plan that did not satisfy the requirements for approval under Section 165(a) of the Internal Revenue Code of 1939, as amended, they were likely to be treated as compensation currently received by the employee and thus might violate the wage regulations. The penalty for such a violation could be the inclusion in taxable income of the entire payroll of the employees covered by the pension plan, with a consequent substantial increase in income taxes. If the retirement plan was in the form of an approved stock-bonus or profit-sharing plan, it was required that any employer contributions made toward the plan must be included in current compensation to the extent that they could be used to provide benefits to the employee under conditions other than death, retirement, disability, or sickness.

As a result the wage- and salary-stabilization provisions afforded an additional stimulus to approved pension plans. Many employers who were unable to increase directly the compensation of their employees could do so indirectly by contributing toward pension plans. Some deserving employees in lower wage or salary brackets might still be promoted to positions carrying greater responsibility and higher pay, but this was difficult or impossible in the case of higher-salaried employees and executives. Under wage and salary stabilization, while general salary or wage increases were restricted, an employer was afforded an opportunity to do something for his employees, in spite of the wartime controls, by contributing to an employee retirement plan.

Personal Income Taxes. As business taxes were increased during the World War II years, so were individual income taxes, and these higher rates have generally been maintained. If an employee is promoted to a higher-paying position, the consequent increase in his personal income taxes substantially reduces the effective increase in salary. If an employer contributes toward an approved retirement plan covering this employee, such contributions are not deemed income taxable to the employee in the year of contribution but rather of the nature of income postponed until his retirement.

If a particular employee's retirement takes place a number of years in the future, he may receive a more advantageous settlement than he would by receiving the amount of the contribution currently as immediate income. Through postponement of the benefits until retirement, he will defer the payment of income taxes until that time, when the general level of personal income taxes may have fallen. Also his annual income will presumably be considerably less after retirement than currently. He will probably ultimately benefit more through his employer's contribution to an employee pension plan than he would by receiving an equal amount of income currently.

Federal Legislation and Regulations to 1954. *The Internal Revenue Code.* The Internal Revenue Code (enacted in 1939) is a codification of the provisions of previous separate revenue acts. The Revenue Act of 1942 amended this code and brought it up to date. The changes with respect to pension plans (embodied in Section 162 of the 1942 act) were far-reaching. They were intended to correct the abuses previously noted by denying preferential tax treatment to discriminatory and extravagant pension plans.

Reasons for 1942 Amendments. Before the 1942 amendments some employers established pension plans that benefited only, or largely, the owners, executives, supervisors, or other high-paid employees of an organization.

The following statement outlines the situation which gave rise to the amending of the Revenue Act in 1942: [5]

The present law endeavors to encourage the setting up of retirement benefits by employers for their employees and in pursuance of this policy permits employers to take as a deduction amounts irrevocably set aside in a pension-trust or other fund to provide annuities or retirement benefits for superannuated employees. This provision has been considerably abused by the use

[5] Rep. 2333, 77th Cong., 2d Sess., July 14, 1942.

of discriminatory plans which either cover only a small percentage of the employees or else favor the higher-paid or stock-holding employees as against the lower-paid or non-stock-holding employees. Under the present law, it is contended the officers of a corporation may set up pension plans for themselves and make no provision for the other employees. Such actions are not in keeping with the purpose of this provision.

When the federal government forgoes very substantial tax income by reason of its treatment of an employer's contributions to a retirement plan as a business expense, it is clearly justified in imposing the requirement that the retirement plan must have social value. Perhaps the justification for this requirement on the part of the federal government may be more clearly understood when the magnitude of an employer's contributions to an employee retirement plan is considered.

A reasonable pension plan will frequently require an outlay of 5 to 15 per cent of the applicable payroll. If this expenditure is considered to be a valid expense of conducting a business and is, therefore, given preferential tax treatment, the tax income to the taxing authority will be correspondingly decreased. If the total amount of taxes that it is necessary to collect from all sources combined is a fixed sum, it then becomes necessary to find a corresponding amount of tax income elsewhere; i.e., other taxes must be increased to counteract the tax income lost because contributions to a retirement plan are entitled to tax relief. Therefore, the government has taken the position that all pension plans, to be entitled to a preferred tax position, must possess social value. The pensions must be reasonable and must not discriminate in favor of individuals or classes of individuals with respect to whom a transfer of tax burden to other elements of the general population would be inappropriate.

By broadening the base for eligibility of his employees, an employer will provide benefits to a larger number of employees who might otherwise require public assistance during old age. To the extent that an employee pension plan makes such public assistance unnecessary, it curtails the taxes which would otherwise be levied for that purpose. Furthermore, a retirement plan covering broad groups of employees is in itself of social value since it is an employee-welfare instrument.

The Revenue Act of 1942. The Revenue Act of 1942 clarified and unified the application of the law but, in general, was restrictive in nature; it affected employee retirement plans in four primary ways:

1. It promulgated, by amendment of Section 165(*a*) of the code, the requirements that a plan must satisfy before the contributions made by an employer toward the plan could qualify for preferred tax treatment.

2. It set forth the conditions under which the income of a trust fund established to finance a pension plan would not be taxable.

3. It established controls, by amendments of Section 23(*p*), over the extent to which contributions made by an employer to the plan would be allowable as deductions from gross income.

4. It set out the conditions, by amendment of Section 165(*b*) and 22(*b*)(2), under which the employer's contributions would be deemed to constitute income to the employee and determined the basis on which the benefits received by the employee or his beneficiaries would be subject to taxation.

Regulations of the Internal Revenue Service.[6] In addition to the law as represented by the Internal Revenue Code, regulations are promulgated by the Commissioner of Internal Revenue by authority of the Secretary of the Treasury. These regulations interpret the provisions of the Internal Revenue Code. In order to further interpret the code and in order to establish working rules for the district directors of Internal Revenue,[7] Internal Revenue agents, and others concerned, the Internal Revenue Service issued a number of Mimeographs and Bulletins (more recently designated Revenue Procedures and Revenue Rulings) containing general discussion of fundamental questions of policy in connection with approval of retirement plans.

In 1944, the Pension Trust Division of the Income Tax Unit of the Internal Revenue Service was confronted with an unprecedented flood of requests for approval of retirement plans. As a result, the responsibility for review and approval of these plans was assigned to the various decentralized field divisions. Numerous questions regarding the interpretations to be made in individual cases were submitted to the central authority, and, where these questions appeared to have application to a number of cases, digests of them (carrying the symbol *PS*) were prepared for the use of the general public. Several *PS*s dealt with

[6] Formerly the Bureau of Internal Revenue.

[7] Formerly designated collectors of Internal Revenue.

the troublesome question of discrimination in the distribution of benefits among employees; others dealt with such topics as the deductibility of contributions under Section 23(p), the approval of plans having certain unusual provisions, the appropriateness of certain beneficiaries, and, more recently, certain questions related to negotiated plans. Since 1954 the Internal Revenue Service has issued rulings from time to time, which constitute current indications covering considerations not clearly set out in the regulations. These rulings are numbered with the prefix identifying the year when issued.

The Internal Revenue Code of 1954. While the 1954 code treats some pension and profit-sharing considerations differently, for the most part it continues the general approach to what constituted a qualified plan under the prior code. An important change was made in the method of taxing annuity payments to the recipient. Significant changes have been made in the regulations pertaining to integration requirements, certain of the requirements stipulated for approval of pension and profit-sharing plans, the extent to which contributions may be deducted from an employer's taxable income, and the information which is required to be filed periodically. The section numbering of the new code is quite different from the old one. For example, Section 23(p) of the old code, dealing with the deductibility of an employer's contributions to a pension plan, becomes Section 404 of the new code, and the provisions comparable to Section 165(a) of the old code will be found in Section 401(a) (qualification of plans) and Section 501(a) (exemption from taxation of a qualified trust) of the 1954 code.

Even though the Internal Revenue Code has been interpreted in considerable detail so that it is fairly clear what retirement-plan provisions may or may not be included currently, the code itself is subject to modification. Consequently, any statements made or conclusions drawn in this chapter should be considered in the light of the most recent laws, regulations, bulletins, mimeographs, and rulings on this subject. The ramifications in the form and substance of pension plans are so extensive that no more than a broad outline of the elements involved in subparagraphs 1, 2, 3, and 4 [8] above will be attempted in

[8] See p. 88.

this chapter. Furthermore, many of the considerations are fundamentally of a legal nature, and their interpretation calls for the services of a qualified attorney.

Requirements that a Pension Plan Must Satisfy. Section 401 and the applicable regulations contain the criteria that pension, profit-sharing, and stock-bonus plans must satisfy before contributions made to them by an employer may be deemed a tax-exempt business expense.

The language of Section 401 is based on the existence of "a trust created or organized in the United States and forming part of a stock-bonus, pension, or profit-sharing plan of an employer for the exclusive benefit of his employees or their beneficiaries. . . ." The regulations define a plan as a written document communicated to the employees, intended as a permanent program. In order to qualify, a retirement program must, therefore, be formalized. An informal procedure under which the employer retires his employees and pays whatever retirement benefit he considers appropriate without having specified his pension arrangements or communicated them to his employees will not satisfy this requirement.[9]

The primary requirements of a qualified trust forming part of a plan are as follows: (1) the benefits must be reasonable; (2) the benefits must be nondiscriminatory, e.g., high-paid employees must not be favored disproportionately; (3) it must be a bona fide program for the exclusive benefit of the employees, i.e., the funds or securities making up the trust must not be diverted from the ultimate benefit of the covered employees; (4) before the meeting of all liabilities under the plan, it must not permit the employer to recover any part of his contributions once made; and (5) it must not engage in certain prohibited business transactions.

In addition, the code sets up two independent conditions or tests for coverage, one or the other of which must be satisfied before a plan (trust) may be approved. The first of these tests is based on stated percentages of defined groups of the employees. If at least 70 per cent

[9] In the case of an informal pension plan or one that does not call for payments to be made into a trust, an employer's payments to retired employees, if reasonable in amount, will be deemed a business expense, and the employer will be entitled to deduct them from taxable income when they are actually paid.

of all employees are covered by a plan, it may qualify; or if the eligibility requirements are so devised as to include 70 per cent of all employees and 80 per cent of this 70 per cent are actually covered, it may qualify.[10]

The second test is somewhat broader in scope. Under it, the employer need only include "such employees as qualify under a classification set up by the employer and found by the Secretary or his delegate not to be discriminatory in favor of employees who are officers, shareholders, persons whose principal duties consist in supervising the work of others, or highly compensated employees. . . ."

It is difficult to determine the precise point where coverage provided under a plan becomes discriminatory among employees. The fact that many of the interpretations of the law by the Internal Revenue Service deal with this problem is indicative of this difficulty. In the absence of complete formalization of the conditions prerequisite to qualification for coverage, the final determination of whether a plan is discriminatory is left to the Secretary of the Treasury or his delegate.

The regulations stipulate that discrimination must be avoided, not only with respect to the conditions of eligibility imposed upon the employee, but also with respect to contributions made by the employer, benefits made available to the various classes of employees, or any other provisions (e.g., with respect to provisions providing for the termination of the plan, the distribution of assets implementing the plan must preclude discrimination).

The requirement that no part of a trust fund may be diverted from the exclusive benefit of the covered employees is intended to remove all possibility of an employer's storing away profits or surplus for future use for his own benefit or for the benefit of his business, with avoidance of payment of current taxes. This condition, however, does not require the employer to forgo recouping any ultimate excess amount that may have been placed in the trust in good faith. To

---

[10] "All employees" as used here may exclude employees who have not worked for a specified "waiting period," which may not exceed 5 years. Employees who work fewer than 5 months in a year or fewer than 20 hours a week may also be excluded.

illustrate what is meant, rather curiously termed an *actuarial error*, consider a retirement plan for which funds have been trusteed on the necessary assumption that retired employees would die according to certain mortality rates. If the covered employees actually died on the average earlier than provided for in these assumptions, there would be a final residue left in the trust fund which could not possibly be used for the payment of the fixed benefits originally intended. The employer, if still extant, could properly receive this residue after all such benefits were paid or adequately provided for (e.g., by purchase of individual annuities).

In order to avoid the possibility of an exempt trust being used indirectly to the financial advantage of the creator of the trust (e.g., the purchasing of property or securities of the creator at unreasonable prices), Section 503 of the 1954 code designates certain transactions in which a qualified trust ordinarily should not engage. Noncompliance can result in forfeiture of the qualified status of the trust, at least until the necessary corrections are made, and serious penalties may be imposed on the employer. For this reason it is important that any transactions of the trust which possibly could be interpreted as not being conducted at arm's length between the trust and its creator should be submitted to the Internal Revenue Service for review.

In order to bring to light any prohibited transactions, extensive information about the financial operations of the trust is required to be submitted periodically to the Internal Revenue Service.

Form 990-P, required by the Internal Revenue Service for the first time in 1954, is designed to disclose any of the prohibited transactions, and Form 990-T calls for information about the receipt by the trust of any rental income on business leases, which income to a qualified trust is no longer tax-exempt.

Integration. One important item in Section 401 dealing with the problem of discrimination is the specific statement that a plan will not be deemed discriminatory merely because it is limited to salaried or clerical employees or because it excludes employees whose entire remuneration constitutes *wages* under the Social Security Act (or the Railroad Retirement Act). If the plan does exclude such employees, the benefits provided from the plan to the other employees—i.e., those eligible under the plan who earn over the social-security limit—must not be disproportionate to the relationship between the social-security benefits and the wages on which such benefits are based.

If a plan provides coverage for earnings under the social-security limit as well as for earnings over this amount, the expected benefits receivable under the Social Security Act may be recognized in determining the pension scale. Substantially, this means that a retirement plan might be designed on any one of the three following bases:

1. Provision of benefits based uniformly on the entire earnings of the employees. Here the eligibility requirements would not be related to earnings.

2. Exclusion of salaries or wages up to and including the social-security limit and provision of a restricted scale of benefits for earnings in excess of such limit.

3. Provision of a higher scale of benefits to the group earning above the social-security limit than would be permissible under 2 above by providing for a lower scale of benefits on that part of the earnings below such limit, thus taking into account indirectly their social-security benefits.

A plan that takes into consideration the benefits available under the Social Security Act in the manner prescribed in the regulations is said to be *integrated* [11] with social security as in 2 or 3 above.

The need for, or desirability of, the integration requirements as imposed has frequently been questioned.

[11] *Integration,* as the term is employed in this technical sense, should not be confused with the unifying procedure frequently used in connection with retirement plans that provide for retirement age before sixty-five, whereby an annuitant may receive an increased benefit from the time of retirement until he becomes eligible to receive the social-security benefit and a reduced amount thereafter in such manner that the aggregate pension received each year will be approximately the same both before and after the social-security benefits commence.

Internal Revenue Service Mimeograph 5539, issued in 1943, originally set out the conditions for integration. Subsequently, on May 3, 1951, Mimeograph 6641 was issued. More recently regulations issued in connection with the 1954 code have covered integration. These mimeographs and regulations dealing with the integration of pension plans where it is necessary to allow for social-security benefits are designed to take into consideration the effect of the Social Security Act as amended at the time in question. For example, the earlier mimeograph dealt with the situation where the social-security tax applied only to the first $3,000 of compensation, and the later rules applied to $3,600 and $4,200 of annual compensation, respectively.

Control of Employers' Contributions to Pension Plans. The requirements contained in Section 401 of the Internal Revenue Code and the applicable regulations were designed:

1. To prevent undue discrimination among employees in coverage or pension benefits

2. In connection with 1 above, to require recognition of the old-age benefits furnished under the Social Security Act

3. To restrict benefits to those that would be socially justifiable

4. To prevent recapture of employer contributions, once made

These conditions are imposed because the federal government in effect encourages private pension plans through (1) treatment of an employer's contributions as tax-exempt business expenses and (2) exemption of interest on the funds implementing qualified plans (insured or trusteed) from direct taxation.[12]

No less important than the requirements relating to appropriate coverage and benefits are the restrictions on the rate at which the cost of such benefits may be treated as a business expense for income-tax purposes. In the past, it has not been unusual for an employer to purchase for his employees a group-annuity contract or set up a trust fund involving a substantial amount of past-service credits and to meet the cost of these past-service credits by a single payment out of surplus or net income at the time the plan was installed. This has been done even though, for many years before the 1942 Revenue Act, there existed certain restrictions regarding the rate at which past-service payments might be deemed to be current business expenses for tax purposes. Since this practice was not unusual during periods when an employer's net income or profits were subject to only nominal rates of taxation, there would be a greatly increased tendency to make use of this treatment during periods of high tax rates, if taxation could thereby be avoided. Furthermore, many employers might tend to fund their portion of the future-service costs of group annuities (and the aggregate costs of other forms of retirement plans) at an unduly rapid rate during periods when their net income or profits were subject to high tax rates, unless adequate measures for control of these contributions were made effective.

[12] Currently the interest income under an insured plan is subject to federal taxation at a special rate, being taxed indirectly through the insurer.

Accordingly, Section 404 of the Internal Revenue Code and the related regulations prescribe upper limits to the contributions that an employer may make toward the cost of an approved pension plan and still be entitled to current tax exemption on such contributions.

The restrictions on the amount of an employer's contributions may be summarized briefly as follows:

1. An employee's total compensation plus the amount allocable to him in the form of contributions made by his employer to the retirement plan must be reasonable. This is a very indefinite restriction. It conceivably could be an item of importance in a situation where high salaries were being subjected to investigation or where there was evidence of conflict with wage- and salary-stabilization requirements, as was the case during the years when such requirements were in effect.

2. In furtherance of 1 above, the employer's contribution must not exceed that required to provide a reasonable pension to any employee.

3. More precisely, an employer may consider as a tax-exempt business expense his contributions to an approved pension plan up to 5 per cent of the annual compensation of the covered employees (but not more than is reasonably required to provide the desired pensions). If the contribution does not exceed 5 per cent, the employer will not generally be required to justify his contribution with a detailed actuarial analysis each year, but periodically, at least quinquennially, he may be required to justify the propriety of his contributions.

4. If the actuarially determined contribution to the retirement plan exceeds 5 per cent, as is more usually the case, the excess for each employee may be amortized over the period from the effective date of the retirement plan until his normal retirement date.

The purpose of this provision is to permit more generous payments than those which could be made under 3 above but, at the same time, to prevent pensions' being heavily funded over 1 or 2 years or any short period. Where a concern had a large number of older employees already near retirement age when the plan was adopted, the absence of such a rule would enable the company to establish pensions for these employees over the few remaining years of their active employment. This would in effect permit such an employer to obtain a large deduction by contributing heavily to a plan in a period of high tax rates. In order to avoid too rapid funding under this method for a few high-paid persons, it is stipulated that, for any three of the participants, in case the cost of the benefits in excess of 5 per cent of total covered compensation is greater than 50 per cent of the total cost in excess of 5 per cent of total covered compensation it will be necessary to distribute the outstanding cost for such individuals over a period of not fewer than 5 years.

5. In lieu of funding methods 3 or 4 above, an employer is permitted to deduct the *normal cost* of the plan for a particular year (by determining actuarially the cost of the plan for each covered employee on the assumption that it had been in effect from the time the employee had first been employed) and in addition to deduct up to 10 per cent of the past-service cost. In explanation of this method consider two employees, both aged forty-five, with identical earnings at the time of installation of the pension plan. If one of these employees had just been hired while the other had been hired 10 years previously, it would be necessary to calculate the *normal* annual payment required of the employer to provide the retirement benefits at age sixty-five for each of these employees separately by spreading the cost for the first employee over the actual 20-year period and for the second employee over an assumed 30-year period.[13]

Thus the normal cost for one of these employees would be the actuarial contribution figured at age thirty-five, while for the other it would be figured at his current age, forty-five. To commence contributions for the employee hired 10 years ago at the rate for his age at date of hire would not be sufficient when commenced at age forty-five to fully fund his benefits by retirement age. Consequently, some form of make-up contribution is necessary for the period of past service during which no contributions had been made, since the plan was not in existence. This extra liability for past service may be determined under the regulations by subtracting the present value at age forty-five of all the 20 annual normal-cost contributions of the future from the present value at age forty-five of the benefits anticipated. The resulting balance represents in a single sum the past-service lia-

[13] No specific procedures for performing this spreading of cost are designated; any reasonable and generally adopted actuarial determination is acceptable. See U.S. Internal Revenue Code, sec. 404(*a*)(1)(*C*).

bility (often termed the *actuarial deficiency*). Even though the employer contributed this full amount for past service at once, for purposes of tax credit he would only be permitted one-tenth of such lump-sum liability for each year in the future until the full amount had been recognized; in addition, of course, he would receive tax credit for the regular normal cost. Sometimes past service is deemed to include elements other than benefits directly related to the period of past service. This could take the form of making up for a minimum benefit or for some particular supplementary benefit called for by the plan. Hence, the regulations refer to the rule as "one-tenth of the past-service or supplementary cost as of the date the provisions resulting in such cost were put into effect. . . ."

The normal cost and past-service cost which have just been described refer mainly to that type of plan under which the funding of the normal cost (and it can also be arranged for past-service cost) will be on a level basis until retirement age—that is, level for any given employee, assuming that his salary remains the same. In the group-annuity type of plan, however, the funding is not on a level basis by the very nature of the method. Under it, a unit benefit is provided for each year of service after the effective date, and each such unit is completely purchased by contributions made during the year in which the service corresponding to that unit was rendered. As an employee's age increases, the contribution necessary to provide his service unit also increases, and it is this increasing cost per employee who stays in the plan which, in group-annuity parlance, is known as *current-service cost* or *future-service cost*. The past-service element in group annuities is obtained by adding up all benefit units for service credited for years before the effective date. This past-service benefit is then translated into a lump-sum liability on the effective date, the *past-service cost*. Here, again, the Internal Revenue Service will permit deduction of one-tenth of this past-service cost, adjusted by experience factors, in years after the effective date until the full amount of past-service benefits has been funded. However, if the employer decides to amortize past-service liability at a rate of less than 10 per cent a year, tax credit, of course, cannot be claimed on a greater amount than actually contributed toward the past-service liability.

Because of the admitted complexity of the technical clauses relating to funding of pension costs and the deductibility of contributions under a plan, the actuaries of the Internal Revenue Service made some very worthwhile attempts to indicate rules and tests which could be used by employers, actuaries, insurers, and pension consultants as a guide to what deductions the Service might find acceptable. On June 1, 1945, a Bureau of Internal Revenue bulletin was issued.[14] This bulletin goes into these funding methods in considerable detail and also covers such other matters as what information the Service needs in its consideration of claims for deduction, observations on methods of changing the provisions of plans, cost factors, and assumptions and the treatment of experience gains under a trust fund. It also provides five tests, by one or more of which an employer's contribution may be measured to determine whether all or a portion of it may be allowable as a tax-deductible item. This bulletin should be consulted by any reader who wishes to delve further into the technicalities of the governmental rules and philosophy. The bulletin is not in the nature of a firm rule; it is presented as "the best available indication of the trend of official opinion in the administration of provisions of Section $23(p)(1)(A)$ and (B) of the Internal Revenue Code," and it is stated that "it does not have the force and effect of a Treasury decision. . . ." This lack of force has been demonstrated in court.

Carry-forward of Excess Contributions, Reapplication. If an employer contributes a total amount over and above that actuarially necessary for a particular year, or, while actuarially appropriate, an amount that is in excess of one of the limitations on deductible contributions, such excess contribution will not be deductible taxwise in that year but may be carried forward and used to reduce the amount that would otherwise be contributed in the next year. When so used, the amount will be deemed to be a proper business expense in that next year and, therefore, tax-exempt, unless part of it still constitutes an excess to be carried over again.

When complete vesting in an employee of an employer's contributions has not been established under a retirement plan, any amounts that have not been vested will revert to the employer's credit when

[14] Bulletin on Section $23(p)(1)(A)$ and (B) of the Internal Revenue Code as Amended by the Revenue Act of 1942. This bulletin is still (1958) a well-recognized source of information on this subject.

an employee terminates his employment. If there is an age or service condition for participation, and in the absence of unusual rates of employee turnover, the total amount of such reversions in any year will be nominal in comparison with the employer's total contributions for that year. Customarily such reversions or refunds are immediately applied against the next year's current cost of the plan to reduce the contributions otherwise required of the employer.

Taxation of Employee on Contributions Paid. While an employer's contributions to an approved employee retirement plan are recognized as a tax-exempt business expense to the extent permitted by Section 404(a) of the Internal Revenue Code, similar treatment is not accorded employee contributions toward the plan. The employee may not enter such payments in any of the spaces captioned "Deductions" in his personal income tax return,[15] but the contributions made by the employer to a plan qualified under Sections 401 and 501 are not deemed to constitute income constructively received by the employee before the time that benefit payments are received or made available. Therefore, the employee is not required to report as income received, employer contributions made in his behalf to a qualified plan. If the plan is not qualified, however, such contributions, if the employee has non-forfeitable vested rights (even though contingent in some ways), are includable with the employee's income for the year when such contributions are paid, and tax allowance is deferred until benefits commence.[16]

Although the contributions of an employer to a qualified pension plan are not deemed compensation to the employee if they are used to pay for retirement benefits, the Treasury Department has asserted that such employer contributions do represent current compensation to the employee to the extent that they are used to provide life insurance. As such, the cost of the insurance is taxable as income to the employee in the year in which it is paid. The employer's contributions toward an approved pension plan based on individual retirement-annuity contracts are entirely tax-free to the employee, but similar contributions to an insurance-annuity contract (including the use of that form in group permanent contracts) must be separated into two por-

---

[15] See Chap. 18 for discussion of differing treatment in Canada.
[16] Special rules apply to employees of certain nonprofit organizations.

tions, the portion used each year to provide the life-insurance element and the remainder used to provide the annuity-at-retirement element. The employee is required to include the first of these two amounts as compensation on which he is taxed.[17]

The life-insurance element is taken as the net amount of insurance (usually defined as the face amount of the insurance less the cash-surrender, or reserve, value which would be released if the individual retirement-income contract were discontinued). The cost is the premium rate for this amount but not less than for 1-year term insurance according to the 1939 to 1941 population mortality rates and 2½ per cent interest.[18] If the employee contributes jointly with the employer to the retirement plan, the employee's contribution may be considered as applying first toward the cost of the insurance (but the plan should clearly so state).

Taxation of Proceeds. By the term *proceeds* is meant the payments made to the employee by reason of the retirement plan, either before or after retirement. It also includes payments made to the employee's beneficiary.

Under the 1934 Revenue Act, annuity payments were not taxed as income to the annuitant until the entire principal or consideration paid by the employee for the annuity was recouped in annuity payments. The 1936 and later amendments rendered the annuitant taxable each year on 3 per cent of the aggregate amount he contributed toward the purchase of the annuity until the aggregate of the non-taxed portion of his annuity payments received had reached his total contributions. After this time the entire amount of annuity payments was taxable. In the 1954 code, a new method was adopted whereby an individual receiving an annuity benefit is taxed on a life-expectancy basis and is presumed to receive a refund of his capital investment

[17] This requirement should not be confused with the provision in the Federal Income Tax Regulations to the effect that premiums paid by an employer on contracts of group term life insurance covering the lives of his employees, the beneficiaries of which are designated by the employees, are not income to the employees. A distinction has thus far been made between group life insurance on the term plan and "permanent" insurance provided under a pension plan.

[18] Revenue Ruling 55-747; "U.S. Life Tables and Actuarial Tables," Table 38, U.S. Government Printing Office, 1946.

ratably over his entire expected future lifetime. Only the portion of each payment in excess of this capital return is taxed as income.

Where the individual is a retired employee receiving benefits under a qualified noncontributory pension plan, all benefits are includable in his taxable income, since the payments received do not include any return of his own capital. If the plan is contributory, either of two situations is possible: (1) he does not receive within 3 years pension payments equal to the aggregate of his own contributions, in which case the life-expectancy rule is applied to his capital investment (his contributions), or (2) the pension benefits received during the 3-year period do at least equal his total contributions, in which case his benefits are not subject to income tax at all until he has received a return of his contributions, after which the total pension payment is deemed to be taxable income.

An employee earning $7,000 from age thirty-five, when he was first covered by a pension plan that recognized only salaries over $3,000, contributing 5 per cent of his eligible salary each year until he reached age sixty-five, the retirement age, would have contributed $0.05 \times 30 \times $4,000 = $6,000. Assume that he would be entitled to a pension of $175 a month, or $2,100 a year. He would then receive in the first 3 years as a pensioner $2,100 \times 3 = $6,300, which exceeds the aggregate of his contributions ($6,000). Consequently, no amounts of pension are included in his taxable income in the first 2 years, and only $300 is included in the third year, the full $2,100 being taxable thereafter.

If the amount of pension were $150 a month, or $1,800 a year, he would not receive his full amount of contribution within a 3-year period, and the life-expectancy rule would apply. His expectation of life at age sixty-five is 15 years (according to the standards adopted for this purpose by the Internal Revenue Service). Dividing his $6,000 of aggregate contributions by the life-expectancy factor produces $400. This is the amount that is tax-free each year. The balance of each year's pension payment, $1,800 − $400 = $1,400, is treated as taxable income.

The purpose of this procedure is to avoid duplication of taxation to the annuitant. His own annual contributions, whether made on a voluntary or a compulsory basis toward the retirement plan, were taxed in full as regular income in the years in which they were paid; hence, he should be entitled to receive an equivalent amount of tax-free annuity payments. In the illustration used, the annuitant receives tax exemption on the full $6,000 of his contributions either within the first 3 years of retirement or uniformly over a period of years equal to the expectation of life at retirement.

The Securities and Exchange Act. The Securities and Exchange Act of 1934 was designed to effect a measure of federal control over securities offered for sale to the general public. A concern installing a pension plan may be required to register it under the Securities and Exchange Act if the offering of benefits to employees in exchange for contributions from them may be deemed equivalent to offering them securities. Where the employees contribute toward a noninsured pension plan administered by the employer or where a trust is established into which contributions are paid, the presumption of an offering of securities to the employees is most likely to exist. If employees are compelled to contribute as a condition of employment, or if the plan is insured, this presumption is usually removed.

In a few instances the employer has set out the provisions of his pension plan, together with other information regarding the financial status of the company, the names of officers and directors, etc., in the form of a prospectus as required by the SEC. A statement has also been included to the effect that the term *securities* as used in the prospectus should be construed as referring to rights and obligations of participants under the plan and that no issuance of securities (as that term is generally understood) is contemplated.

Since the coming into effect of the Revenue Act of 1942, the promulgation of the related regulations, and the resulting control exercised over retirement plans by the Treasury Department, the Securities and Exchange Act has been of less importance for plans approved by the Internal Revenue Service, although it should not be overlooked as possibly applicable, especially if the employer should be an "investment company," as defined in the amended Investment Company Act of 1940.

State Laws. The insurance laws of each state and of the District of Columbia generally include comprehensive requirements which individual contracts of life insurance must satisfy. The laws of more than half of the states make specific reference to group-insurance contracts, but only one state (New York) has detailed requirements for their group annuities. The insurance statutes to which a pension contract must conform are largely determined by the type of pension plan. For example, if the plan is based on individual contracts, the requirements of the statutes relating to individual life-insurance and annuity contracts of the states involved must be met. An insurance contract must conform to the insurance laws of the state in which it is delivered (usually the state of domicile of the insured), and, except in the case of a few states in which an insurer may issue special contracts (because of the unusual requirements of those states' insurance laws), the contracts are designed to satisfy the most rigorous statutes of any state in which the insurer does business.

In addition to state laws pertaining directly to group and individual life-insurance contracts and to group-annuity contracts, there are a number of additional statutes that have a bearing on pension plans. These include state income tax laws, which assess taxes against the income of individuals and corporations, although taxes under such laws are generally much less onerous than are federal taxes; [19] laws levying unemployment-insurance taxes, which are a necessary business expense assessed by the individual states and borne by the employer; and rules against perpetuities, which may prohibit contracting for payment of annuities or similar benefits unless such payments will cease upon some specified contingency, such as the expiration of 21 years after the death of the last of two lives in being at the time the annuity payments commence. Some states have laws regulating the investments of trusts to a specified list of authorized securities (the "legal list") although these laws do not apply to pension-trust funds if the trust indenture is so worded as to permit investments outside the legal list.

[19] Two states, California and Minnesota, require that employee pension plans must satisfy conditions somewhat analogous to those imposed by the Internal Revenue Code. A few additional states have laws bearing directly on the exemption from state income tax of an employer's contributions to a pension plan, and a few others deal with taxation of the proceeds payable from a plan. Apparently most states will follow the Internal Revenue Service in their treatment of an employer's contributions.

While state insurance laws are still of wider application to life insurance than are federal laws (in spite of a United States Supreme Court decision that insurance is interstate commerce and therefore subject to federal legislation), pension plans must be designed primarily to satisfy the federal statutes and regulations.[20]

[20] Recent further requirements imposed by certain states (and somewhat similar regulations considered by the federal government) on some types of plans are discussed in Chap. 19.

CHAPTER 6

Advance Funding

When a pension plan is installed, it may cover some employees who are already beyond normal retirement age and others who will not retire for 40 or 50 years. Some of these employees may die shortly after retiring, while others may draw benefits for 30 or 35 years. The period during which an individual is associated with the plan can vary from a very short interval to 70 years or even longer.

If the benefit disbursements required under a pension plan covering the employees of a fairly stable company, during a period not too greatly influenced by inflationary or deflationary pressures, were to be plotted for a number of years after the plan had gone into effect, it would be observed that the curve of annual amounts disbursed would start low and increase fairly rapidly, tending to mature at a high plateau after some 30 to 40 years. A primary purpose of advance funding is to level off the annual amounts required for future pension disbursements by putting aside more than is needed for current disbursements so that these extra amounts will earn interest and serve to offset (reduce) the amounts that would otherwise be required as contributions in later years. This procedure is termed *advance funding* of pension costs.

One way of giving background to the subject of advance funding is to postulate a country with governmental monopoly, where the only securities are those of the monopoly and all workers are employed by the monopoly. A pension plan is set up which when mature will disburse B in annual benefits. The obligation to pay these B could be met in any one of three ways: (1) the monopoly as employer could pay out B each year from general revenue, (2) securities issued by the monopoly could gradually be accumulated to yield the full $B as interest, or (3) securities could be accumulated to yield part of the $B and continuing employer payments would cover the balance. But in this monopolistic society, would these methods really be different from one another? The general revenue of the first method would come from taxes or be included in the "price" of the monopoly's products. The investment return of the second method would come from the same source. The combination of the third would derive from the same source but under two names. The differences in the three methods would really be only those of semantics. The first might be labeled "pay-as-you-go" but would be no different in cause and effect from the second, labeled "benefits met by interest only," or from the third, "advance actuarial funding." The pension system would be no more costly when met by one way than by another, and the employee (active or retired) would be equally secure under all.[1]

Under a system of competitive industry, with tens of thousands of employers and billions of dollars of varied securities outstanding, the three methods take on very different characters. The methods become not at all the same thing.

Benefits paid from current revenue affect the interest of the employing corporation's stockholders at the time of payment. The increasing curve of benefits is claimed to be not only poor cost accounting but also an inequitable distribution of pension costs to stockholders. Moreover, the lack of a fund which could be liquidated for pensioners if the company were itself liquidated or merged leaves the nonmonopolistically employed person or the retired person without any security for his benefits.

The second method, that of sufficient investments for the yield alone to pay the pensions, is academic and not found among business plans. It might be considered a goal which, if attained, would satisfy employer, employees, and pensioners. This yield, however, would need to come largely from investments outside the employing company's own securities; otherwise, it would again approach the pay-as-you-go

[1] This, in part, explains why some actuaries are not too concerned about the financing methods of the social-security system, where the monopolistic taxing power of the country lies behind both the contributions called for and the debt service on the government securities held by the Social Security Trust Fund.

status costwise and the nonsecurity status benefitwise. Few employers or employees (or the Internal Revenue Service) would wish a single investment to preponderate in the fund; all the eggs should not be in one basket.

The third method, a combination of employer contribution (and employee contribution, if contributory) and a diversified investment portfolio, is the typical procedure of advance funding. The method runs a considerable gamut. Some plans are low on invested funds and high on potential contributions and vice versa. Newly formed plans may gradually pass from one status to another until (if ever) "maturity" of pension roll is reached; then the formula, benefits = contributions + interest,[2] comes into stability, with a constant for each term of the equation; benefits, contributions, and income on the fund are, each, uniform from one year to the next, again largely an academic concept or approximate goal.

Advance funding and *actuarial soundness* are not synonymous. The former is in being as soon as any contributions are made in excess of current pension requirements; a fund, however small, to carry over to the ensuing year constitutes at least a gesture of funding in advance. Actuarial soundness is achieved only by measuring the advance funding—the assets on hand and the intended contributions—by certain scientific criteria involving mortality, employee turnover, interest, and other elements depending on the provisions of the pension plan, this measurement yielding the conclusion that the scheme of advance contributions for the benefits of the plan will pay out over the long future or at earlier termination of plan. One reasonably conservative definition of actuarial soundness follows: [3]

An actuarially sound plan is one where the employer is well informed as to the future cost potential and arranges for meeting those costs through a trust or insured fund on a scientific, orderly program of funding under which, should the plan terminate at any time, the then pensioners would be secure in their pensions and the then active employees would find an equity in the fund assets reasonably commensurate with their accrued pensions for service

---

[2] *Interest* is a generic term for investment income of all sorts, such as interest on bonds and mortgages, dividends on common stock, and net capital gains.

[3] Dorrance C. Bronson, "Concepts of Actuarial Soundness in Pension Plans," Richard D. Irwin, Inc., Homewood, Ill., 1957, p. 14.

from the plan's inception up to the date of termination of plan. Note that this definition admits of a long time before all the original past service credits reach a funded condition. Note further, that I have tied this definition in with a presumption of the plan's termination. . . .

In brief, the definition means that, as a minimum for actuarial soundness, the employer should currently fund the pension credits applicable to the years elapsing after the plan's inception and should, by retirement age, have funded the past service credits for the then retiring employees.

According to this definition of actuarial soundness, a scheme of advance funding under which contributions are made only as retirements occur, each equal to the full value of each pension, would not be actuarially sound, because no protection exists or is contemplated for employees below retirement age at termination of the plan. Such a scheme is the *terminal-funding method*.[4]

A system of advance funding that meets accruing current-service costs but leaves past-service liability unfunded, paying only interest thereon to prevent its increasing, is not actuarially sound by the above definition because no method is provided for meeting that liability. This is the *interest-only method*. As decades go by and those employees for whom the liability originally existed pass over into retirement, collect their pensions, and die, the liability does not die with them but is perpetuated and shifted to new, active employees as an impairment of their accruing pension rights in case the plan one day is terminated. For governmental systems, and perhaps for monolithic enterprises whose business and corporate entity are assumed to be perpetual, complete actuarial soundness may not be essential.

Other writers may have less strict concepts of actuarial soundness, but few, it is believed, would view advance funding per se as always equivalent to actuarial funding or soundness.

Pay-as-you-go Method versus Funding. A pension plan is designed as an instrument to further good employer-employee relations. There are many reasons why it should be handled on an advance-funding basis rather than by a pay-as-you-go method.

Employees' Insecurity under a Pay-as-you-go Plan. Employees do not have the same degree of security under a pay-as-you-go system as under

[4] See Chap. 11, pp. 224–226.

a funded retirement plan. On the usual cost-accounting assumptions, the costs of an employee's retirement benefits are incurred during the period of the individual's employment rather than during his period of retirement. Under a fully funded plan the costs of the retirement benefits are met as they are incurred, so that an employee's pension is paid for by the time he retires.[5] Should the employer experience a period of unfavorable business operations after the employee retires, his pension, already funded, will not be adversely affected, nor will he be subjected to the fear (or actuality) of its discontinuance. He has a feeling of security during his later working years and his years of retirement which he cannot possibly experience under a pay-as-you-go plan.

Commitment by the Employer Involved under Formal Plan. A retirement plan that is to be presented to the employees should be a formalized plan. That is, employees should be advised of the specific retirement benefits that they may expect to receive, or they should be provided with the formula for determining them. If a formal plan is presented to the employees, the employer should regard the provision of the designated benefits as an important obligation and should make every effort to assure its being available to the employee when he retires, since many employees will rely upon these benefits for support during their old age and will adjust their savings programs accordingly. The only sound procedure for backing up the formal presentation of a plan and for making certain that the pensions will be forthcoming is the advance-funding method.

Cost-accounting Aspects. Modern cost accounting attempts to relate each cost of doing business to the period in which the cost is incurred. Employers that have met their pension-plan costs during active service as benefit credits accumulated will, when the costs to an employer with a pay-as-you-go plan are heaviest, need to contribute relatively small amounts to maintain their funded plans. They will then be in a better competitive position.

[5] Frequently the costs of a retirement plan are spread-funded beyond the date of retirement of the employees who are older at the time the plan is installed. This is a device for leveling out the heavy initial costs of the plan, but after the plan has been in effect for the period of years equal to this spread-funding period (for example, 10 years), the benefits for all employees will be completely funded upon their retirement.

Less Outlay Required for Funded Plan. The visual cost of a funded pension plan is considerably less to the employer than that of a pay-as-you-go system that provides comparable benefits. Regardless of which method (advance funding or pay as you go) is used, the same number of employees will retire, the same number of deaths among retired employees will occur, terminations of employment will be similar, and the actual pension outgo to the retired employees for a specific scale of benefits will be identical. There are, however, elements in the advance-funding structure which make for significant savings in the employer's outlay for pensions. One sort of savings results from the natural operation of compound interest; the sooner a fund is established and invested the more will the interest earnings on such fund reduce the employer outlay required in the future. Another point is that the investment income on a fund established under a plan that has qualified under the Internal Revenue Code is exempt from federal income tax. A third important feature is that the employer's contributions to such a fund are a business expense and are deductible from gross income in calculating net income for federal income tax. The payments made to employees under a pay-as-you-go system are deductible for income tax purpose only at the time they are made. If corporate income tax rates are higher now than they will be in the future, the difference in rates is saved. Even if tax rates were to remain constant or increase, it might be advantageous to the employer to receive such tax allowances early rather than to defer them. For example, if in a future year a corporation does not have taxable income, the deductions arising from a pay-as-you-go pension plan will be of little value, except in so far as these costs may be carried over into other more profitable years.

In the long run, a funded retirement plan will involve considerably less impact on net earnings than would a comparable pay-as-you-go plan.

For a given benefit a funded plan would not *cost* less than a pay-as-you-go plan. But the employer outlay, or amount of contributions, would be less because, if the contributions are placed in an invested fund, interest would later help in meeting pension payments. On the theory that money is worth interest wherever it is, it might be contended that, if the employer invests the money in his own business or elsewhere rather than in a pension fund, he will in effect be putting it to productive use to draw on later in meeting pension payments on a pay-as-you-go basis. This is perfectly true, but there are several practical objections. The argument assumes "a given benefit," but if the relatively high cost level for a proposed pension formula is not appreciated by the employer because of the absence of actuarial cost commitments, the pension level adopted for the pay-as-you-go basis may be set much higher than when it is controlled by actuarial evidence; this would result in truly higher costs for the pay-as-you-go plan. The argument assumes that the money used by the employer for other purposes, in lieu of advance pension funding, would create income, which would either be tax-deductible itself, similar to the tax-free income in a pension fund or under an insurance contract, or would be so much greater than that of the tax-free pension fund as to more than make up for the tax-free feature, an assumption hardly warranted in these days of high taxes. The argument further assumes that the pension plan will never be terminated, that the employer will be perpetual, and that the lack of a pension fund will not embarrass him costwise when the annual pension load is high, even in poor business years. Actually, a drain on his resources in bad years to meet a noncurrent production expense, such as pensions, could mean more "cost" in the effective sense than the same dollars paid earlier to a pension fund would have meant.

All in all, it is felt that, when these less tangible elements are taken into account, the pay-as-you-go method not only requires more employer outlay but is likely actually to be more *costly* as well.

Business Trends. Sound judgment would seem to dictate the desirability of putting aside during prosperous times more than the minimum amount required to keep a plan solvent in order to meet the deferred liabilities that would be incurred under any formal retirement plan. Whether it would be desirable to contribute the maximum amount permitted as tax-deductible will depend on the current financial needs of the employer. To the extent that it is possible for the employer to get ahead of the game in the funding of the plan, he will establish a cushion to fall back on later.

Employee Contributions. It was pointed out above that the outlay for a specific scale of retirement benefits, even at a constant rate of income tax, would be less under a qualified funded system than under a pay-as-you-go system by reason of the interest earned on the funds and its tax exemption. An important element influencing the cost to the employer arises from the fact that employees could not be called upon to contribute toward the benefits they would receive under a pay-as-you-go system, whereas under a funded plan they may properly be asked to contribute toward the cost during their working years. The absence of an employee contribution may add cost to the employer in a pay-as-you-go plan.

Balance-sheet-reserve Method. If an employer should provide pensions under a modified pay-as-you-go system through the establishment of a liability to be carried on its books for this specific purpose, some of the arguments against the pay-as-you-go system would be partially offset. The cost could then be met as incurred by the allocation of assets against this liability, and the employees would have greater assurance of ultimately receiving the benefits than if a wholly deferred method were used. However, the reserve assets so set up would not be beyond the control of management, and, therefore, such a plan would not qualify under the Internal Revenue Service regulations, and no amounts set aside to offset the liability would be deductible for tax purposes. According to the regulations now in effect, any amounts set aside for pensions would be deductible only when paid.

If the effect of tax allowance at the time payments were made to the retired employee were ignored (and it would be necessary for the employer to have gross taxable income in the years when such payments were actually made in order to obtain credit), it would be necessary, under a y per cent rate of tax, to divert $\$100/(1 - 0.01y)$ of gross income in order to place $\$100$ in the special reserve account. Furthermore, the interest earned on this special account would be regarded as regular income and, therefore, also taxable.

There is one possible way of avoiding being taxed on the amounts that are set aside, that is, as nonforfeitable benefits, in this special reserve fund. This is to regard them as income that is constructively received by the employees at the time they were set aside. As such they would be deductible from the employer's gross income but would be taxable to the employees. To the employees, such a method would carry no advantage over what they could arrange on their own initiative, and such a plan would have no apparent value as an instrument promoting favorable employee-employer relations.

It can be almost categorically stated that the adoption of a pay-as-you-go method (sometimes called "owe-as-you-go") even under the balance-sheet-reserve method for meeting retirement benefits will ultimately result in either financial difficulties for the employer or loss of pension payments to employees. A period of adverse business conditions frequently results in the laying off of older employees, many of whom would be eligible for retirement benefits, thus emphasizing the pension load which the company would be called upon to bear during a period of unfavorable business conditions. Changes in management, mergers, retrenchment, or discontinuance of operations all tend to interfere with the continuance of pay-as-you-go pension payments to retired employees. Moreover, it is difficult to justify pay-as-you-go methods for retirement benefits on the basis of any reasonable accounting system.

The arguments in favor of funding a retirement plan are so great, both from the standpoint of assuring each employee the retirement benefits that he has been promised and from the standpoint of the advantages in financing, with corresponding smaller variations in net income, that an employer should only under the most unusual conditions establish any retirement system other than a plan based on advance funding and qualifying under the regulations of the Internal Revenue Service.

Past-service Liability. Except for the type of advance funding that pays for the pension by level annual contributions (dollar or per cent of payroll) from the age attained at inception of plan to retirement date (e.g., the *level-premium method*), most advance-funding methods would bring out at the start a past-service liability or, in cases where this cost is not directly in a one-to-one relationship with years of past service, an *actuarial deficiency*. These terms will be used more or less interchangeably, the problem with respect to both types being to meet this liability in the same manner as any debt; i.e., payments to amortize the principal amount must also include interest. It is as if the employer owed the principal amount to the pension fund as of a given date; if it is not paid on that date, interest accrues at the assumed valuation rate. The past-service liability may also vary from time to time because of interest earnings and other gains or losses to the fund, which reflect themselves in the amount of the liability that remains unliquidated.

In a legal sense the past-service liability under a pension plan is not a liability that the employer is unequivocally committed to meet. Practically every plan provides that the employer may amend or discontinue it at any time or at some given time and limits the liability to sums already set aside, defining what is to be done with the accumulated funds in the event of discontinuance. The "liability" is thus contingent upon the indefinite continuation of the plan, and, while it may prove awkward to invoke the discontinuance provisions, it is always possible to do so.

The principal difference in the results of cost calculations by different cost methods arises from the treatment of the past-service and future-service cost elements. Some methods make no separation of the two elements in the arrangement for funding, whereas others effect a separation in varying proportions. Methods that produce the largest past-service elements provide the greatest funding flexibility (i.e., the greatest range between prudent minimum contribution and maximum deductible contribution for tax purposes).

Other Considerations. As compared with full-advance-funding methods, the meeting of pension costs on either a pay-as-you-go basis or a maturity- or terminal-funding basis (funding of pensions only as retirements take place) will generally result in lower initial costs which are subject to sharp increase for some 25 to 35 years or more until a stable pension roll has been established.[6] The ultimate annual outlay under either of these two methods will be well in excess of the ultimate outlay on an advance-funding basis, since under the latter a substantial interest-bearing fund will have been accumulated.

The chart on page 115 compares trends in pension costs between the pay-as-you-go, maturity-funding, and minimum advance-funding bases, as prepared from the statistics of a typical employing organization.

Only by virtue of advance funding does a plan come within the

[6] An exception to the lower initial cost mentioned may arise on the maturity-funding basis if there is a substantial number of retirements during the first few years of the plan.

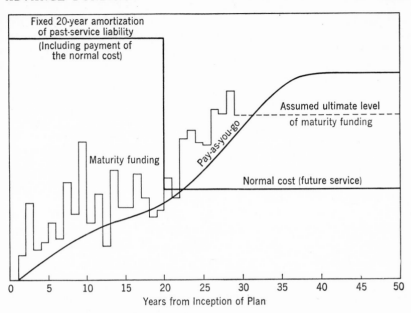

Comparison of Contribution Requirements by Illustrative Funding Methods

purview of Sections 401, 404, and 501 of the Internal Revenue Code. If a trust or annuity plan is not established on a funded basis with a third-party fiduciary or under an insurance contract, there is no basis on which to seek approval and tax exemption. Thus, for a qualified plan the Internal Revenue Service requires advance funding. But the Service does not require, or at least does not set any criteria for, actuarial soundness.[7] The Service appears to be more concerned with overfunding (high tax exemptions) than with underfunding.

[7] However, for certain special cases—one involving the right of the highest-paid employees to receive benefits during the first 10 years of the plan and the other involving a measure of the sufficiency of a cents-per-hour negotiated plan—the Service does set the criterion that "past and current contributions have been met." With respect to past service, this does not mean that the liability has been amortized or even that a start has been made; instead, it means that the past-service liability is no greater at a later date under the plan than it was at the start, a condition that could be met by paying into the fund only the required interest on the unfunded liability, by the interest-only method.

Under many collectively bargained pension plans, labor unions have insisted not only on advance funding but also on some degree of actuarial soundness. The amortization of the past-service liability over not more than 30 years is a typical commitment of the employer in labor agreements. This is not always so, as some settlements have focused only on the benefits, leaving it up to the employer to determine how they were to be met. However, unions are becoming more and more aware of the advantages of actuarially sound funding.

Certainly, the employee participants in a plan are glad to see progress in the building up of reserve assets against their accruing pension rights. They view a plan as one which is always presumptively terminable[8] (because of business conditions, bankruptcy, or merger). Provisions covering the termination of the plan usually apply the assets to provide pensions first for those already retired, next for those eligible to retire (including, frequently, early retirement), and next for the younger employees. Consequently, advance funding, and particularly actuarial funding, means security for full benefits for pensioners and older employees and benefits commensurate with service for younger employees. The more nearly adequate the funding, the greater the employee security.

When employees contribute to a plan, advance funding is almost demanded of the employer. The employee contributions are advance funds in themselves; there are no business plans (though possibly there are a few governmental plans or early "welfare" schemes) that use employee contributions, as made, to pay or help pay the pensions of those already retired. And the fact that employees contribute toward a later benefit induces their employers to do likewise. The principles of advance funding on an actuarial basis force order into a plan; the rules are formalized and observed, definite benefits are established on a basis of right, discrimination is minimized, security of the employees' interests is maximized, and industrial relations in general are improved.

Aside from the principles of orderly accounting, advance funding and the creation of an interest-earning fund offer inducement to the employer. Regardless of actuarial assumptions, the same persons are

[8] See Dorrance C. Bronson, "Pension Plans—Provisions for Termination of Plan," *Transactions of the Society of Actuaries,* vol. 8, 1955, pp. 225–269.

going to die, withdraw, and retire, and the ultimate aggregate outlay may be expressed by the formula, costs = benefits + expenses − interest. Hence, the more the interest, the less the employer's outlay; and the faster the fund is built up, the less the employer's outlay in subsequent periods.[9]

Consequently the employer has a selfish position in favoring sizable reserves and good yields—even to the extent of hedging against inflation by demanding a goodly proportion of investments in common stocks (in a trust-fund plan).

When there is no retirement plan, or where there is only a pay-as-you-go plan, employers may hesitate to terminate superannuated employees—they remain on the payroll as "hidden pensioners." With a funded plan this loss is minimized through systematic retirement of such employees on secured pensions. This security has been created by a scientific spreading of costs through the application of a combination of actuarial and accounting principles. Furthermore, these advance costs, as met, are accorded the benefit of tax deductibility, and the interest on the funds does not attract a tax under qualified trust funds.

Advance funding, of the Internal Revenue–approved type of plan, can only be accomplished through a third party—a trustee or an insurer. A balance-sheet reserve on the employer's own books does not serve, as it is not irrevocable and beyond his control.

[9] This is not to say, however, that there are not certain arguments *against* a larger and larger fund or a rapid build-up. For one thing, with tens of thousands of pension plans developing in the United States, full actuarial funding may involve investment difficulties. For extremely large pension plans, the unwieldiness of the funds creates the question whether stopping somewhere short of full funding would not be acceptable when accompanied by an understanding of the true liability under the plan. Another point is the possibility—particularly under union-negotiated plans—that a large reserve may be misunderstood as "surplus" and furnish the incentive for a drive to liberalize benefits.

CHAPTER 7

Trust-fund Plans

Development and Nomenclature. Long before insurance-company facilities for underwriting an employer's pension plan were devised, actuaries had developed pension-fund theory and practice to a point where advance contributions to a formal plan could be set aside for the purposes of leveling out costs, of protecting accrued pension rights, and of reducing aggregate outlay through the operation of compound interest.[1] These funds were established in British industries and public employment much earlier than in the United States. Following British practice the earlier funds in this country were usually set up with full employer discretion, control, and fund management and were often only a segregated account on the employer's books. A third-party intermediary was not an essential, nor even a usual, part of the pension structure. From this looseness of structure and from the employer control of the fund, the term *self-administered plan* no doubt originated.

Pension plans have become more and more definite and less and less discretionary, especially where they call for employee contributions. This development has indicated the desirability of third-party stewardship, the trend toward which was effectively accelerated by the Revenue Act of 1942 and the recent high-tax years. Hence, formal plans utilizing the services of a trustee (either a corporate body or an individual person) or of an insurer have largely replaced the discretionary and employer-controlled plans of earlier days. However, nomenclature has not kept pace with developments. The most common term for a pension plan that does not involve insurance contracts, even though it

[1] The income-tax incentives for pension plans were things of the far future.

118

must comply with today's comparatively rigid requirements, is still *self-administered plan.* A more properly descriptive label is simply *trust-fund plan,* which is used in this text. This is not to say that no truly self-administered plan is extant or can be created today. There are formalized pay-as-you-go plans with large degrees of employer control. There are funded plans in which the employer manages the fund with no insurer or trustee involved.[2] There are plans that have made no attempt, or upon attempting have failed, to qualify as approved plans with the Internal Revenue Service. In spite of attendant disadvantages, these continue to exist as truly self-administered plans.

Formal Plans. This chapter will deal with trust-fund plans under which

1. The plan is definite, its specifications being set forth in a document adopted by the employer's board of directors, shareholders, or other responsible parties.

2. There is a definite trust agreement between the employer and a corporate trustee, or between the employer and individual trustees, which has been executed as a guide for the plan's administration.

3. The plan and trust agreement are qualified under the appropriate sections of the Internal Revenue Code.

4. There is substantial advance funding, and the trustee is responsible for investing and administering a growing corpus under the trust.[3]

Basic Characteristics. Under a trust-fund plan, the contributions feeding the fund, whether paid by the employer alone or by the employer and employee jointly, are normally determined annually (although payment may be spread over the year) on an actuarial basis according to such assumptions regarding mortality, interest, and other elements as the actuary of the plan may have recommended. The annual measurement of the obligations of the plan on these assumptions is called the *actuarial valuation* of the system. The experience in any year may show a "profit" or "loss" owing to the actual experience

[2] Many public-employee plans are managed by delegated boards vested by law with wide powers.

[3] Excluded from treatment in this chapter is a plan where a trustee exists, but only to hold title to insurance-annuity or retirement-annuity contracts; for an explanation of this type of trusteed plan see Chap. 9.

differing from that assumed in the previous year's actuarial valuation. Such profit or loss will be taken into account in determining the following year's contribution requirements. The fund is built up with the trustee, its growth is guided by the actuary, and, if all contributions are paid in when due, the fund may be expected to meet its objective of furnishing all benefits due and accrued during the life of the plan.

The fund stands entirely on its own feet and is not merged with other trust funds administered by the trustee (except to the possible extent of purchasing shares in a "common fund" as part of its investment program). Its own experience determines its amount, contributions to it, interest income, markups or markdowns in year-end valuation of securities, profit or loss on sales of securities, disbursements of benefit payments, and expenses of administration, if under the plan such expenses are to be borne by the fund.

A fund of this character is not a guarantor of a *life* benefit in the same sense that an insurer offers for sale and guarantees a *life* annuity. The guaranteed life annuity of an insurer and the expected, but not guaranteed, lifetime benefit under a trust fund are fundamentally different forms of commitments. Under a trust-fund plan the fund is exhaustible before the last payment has been made to the last pensioner alive under the plan, or the fund may prove redundant for this last payment. Also, one must consider the possibility of business mortality, mergers, changes of management, discontinuance of plan for other reasons, and even failure of the fund itself. For a going concern, making contributions to maintain the plan up to par, with the actuary keeping his finger on the pulse, and with a responsible trustee, the likelihood of the fund's running dry is minimized. On the other hand, under an insurer contract, the entire assets of the insurer are behind its guarantee to make certain payments in return for appropriate premium payments, although the level of these premium rates is subject to change—i.e., not guaranteed indefinitely—and changes have frequently been made in the past.

Flexibility in Benefits. It is often said that the trust-fund plan has a considerable flexibility in benefit provision. This does not mean that, within the plan itself, benefit payment is discretionary or that alterations in amounts can be made from time to time or from employee to employee, on the criterion of need or for any other reasons. Under the Revenue Act of 1942, a specific benefit formula must apply to each employee covered by the plan. Thus, the regulations promulgated in 1956 under the Internal Revenue Code of 1954, provide that "a plan is a definite written program and arrangement" and define a pension plan as follows: [4]

A pension plan within the meaning of section 401(a) is a plan established and maintained by an employer primarily to provide systematically for the payment of definitely determinable benefits to his employees over a period of years, usually for life, after retirement. Retirement benefits generally are measured by, and based on, such factors as years of service and compensation received by the employees. The determination of the amount of retirement benefits and the contributions to provide such benefits are not dependent upon profits. Benefits are not definitely determinable if funds arising from forfeitures on termination of service or other reasons may be used to provide increased benefits for the remaining participants instead of being used to reduce the amount of contributions by the employer. A plan designed to provide benefits for employees or their beneficiaries to be paid upon retirement or over a period of years after retirement will, for the purposes of section 401(a), be considered a pension plan if the employer contributions under the plan can be determined actuarially on the basis of definitely determinable benefits, or, as in the case of money-purchase pension plans, such contributions are fixed without being geared to profits.

Flexibility, in the connotation implied in the opening sentence of the previous paragraph, means that there is more of a range of choice between admissible benefit formulas and the manners in which the benefits may be paid for under a trust-fund plan than under an insured plan. Some of these feasible choices would be difficult if not impossible to fit within the necessarily very formal, precise, and complete clauses of an insurance contract, other than one of the deposit-administration type.[5] A trust-fund plan, however, can be accommodated to just about any formula or type of retirement benefits that

---

[4] U.S. Internal Revenue Service, *Regulations Relating to Employee Pension Annuity, Profit-sharing, and Stock Bonus Plans,* Treasury Decision 6203.

[5] See pp. 149–152.

would be usable under an insured plan and may be designed to provide benefits that an insurer could not consider.

Flexibility in Contributions. The trust-fund plan is flexible with respect to costs and funding. The elements making for this flexibility are listed separately below. It will be noted that most of these elements are stated, either directly or by implication, in comparison with insured methods. This list is given from the position of the trust-fund advocate; the insurance man's viewpoint will be presented in Chapters 8 and 9.

1. There is no fixed date, or grace period, before or within which contributions must reach the fund to avoid default. If payment is delayed or omitted, the fund is that much behind in its asset position, but no contract provisions have been violated and no formal reinstatement or discontinuance proceedings are necessary. While it is dangerous practice to become casual about making contributions on time and in full, there are circumstances under which a reduced or omitted payment is desirable, perhaps is necessary—the very life of the employer's business may require this reduced outlay. Advocates of the trust-fund plan assert that it is more easily adjusted to a reduced or skipped contribution than other types of plans and is less restricted in resuming normal operations after a payment has been reduced or skipped. However, the actuary will have to reflect in his valuation the increase in the plan's liability occasioned by the reduction or omission; and since there are possible Internal Revenue Service complications as well as employee repercussions, the employer will do well not to reduce or omit contributions except for only the most valid of reasons.

2. Employer contributions may continue for an employee after his retirement; that is, his pension may become payable before the complete funding for that pension has been accomplished. This permits immediate or fairly prompt retirement at the inception of the plan of employees already near or above the retirement age fixed in the plan, without the employer's having to shoulder the entire cost of their pensions by the time they retire. The assumption, in justification of this practice, is that the employer is a going concern and will complete this *spread funding* in an orderly manner and in due time.

3. Employer contributions may be made, be the basis ever so empir-

ical, toward the advance funding of a disability benefit not usually available in other types of plans.[6]

4. Initial contribution outlay may be lowered by adopting an assumed *withdrawal rate* (termination of employment other than by death or retirement) limited by any vesting provision and by giving effect to the actuarial discount afforded by this assumption. Insured plans usually allow credit for withdrawals only as they occur; frequently this credit is withheld for withdrawals in poor health, and generally the insurance contract has imposed certain surrender charges against all withdrawal credits. Since, however, the ultimate net result costwise from terminations is substantially the same (when insurer dividends and rate credits are considered), the flexibility claimed for the trust-fund plan lies in the timing of the adjusted contributions.

5. A higher interest-rate assumption than is usually made in other types of plans may be felt to be justified by the employer or the trustee. This would further lower the initial and early contribution outlay.

6. The trust-fund plan requires, of course, an assumption of mortality rates. The 1937 Standard Annuity Table, in which the mortality rates above age sixty-five are considered to be slightly conservative (below age sixty-five this conservatism is lacking in the light of very low current death rates), is often used. A new table, the Group Annuity Table for 1951, has recently been published, and this table, or various modifications allowing for further mortality improvement, is being used more and more in both insured and trust-fund plans. There are many other mortality tables built on earlier experience and based on a higher death rate than the 1937 Standard Annuity Table. Since old-age benefits are paid to survivors while life insurance is paid at death, the mortality effect on costs of these two types of protection is opposite; that is, high mortality makes for high life-insurance premiums and low annuity premiums, and vice versa. The choice for a pension plan of a table with higher mortality than other tables results in lower initial costs. It is not unusual still to find trust-fund plans in which a lower cost table than the 1937 Standard Annuity Table is used—one such is the Combined Annuity Table (published in 1928).

[6] In some instances insurers have provided for advance funding of disability benefits under deposit-administration group-annuity contracts.

Or, again, higher mortality is in some instances assumed because of the occupational situation of the group covered by the plan. Where there is an occupational hazard, this expected higher mortality may influence the choice of a less conservative mortality table. On the other hand, where expected mortality is light—and this has been the case in certain plans for teachers and ministers—a mortality table based on a lower death rate has been adopted or has later been found to be necessary. In some cases, particularly in large public-employee plans, the pension experience has run long enough to permit the preparation of special tables based on the plan's own operations. Usually the actuary favors conservative tables, pointing out that any excess mortality above that assumed will ordinarily be reflected by a credit to the employer in future years. If the actual death rate is lower than that on which the table is based, any apparent saving in initial costs will be illusory.

The mortality element in trust-fund pension plans is claimed to be much less important than it is in insured plans, since the trust-fund method can make year-by-year adjustments for mortality experience; that is, there is no fixed, irrevocable linkage—such as exists for premiums for insured pension plans—between previous contributions and prospective pensions.

7. An assumption about the *rate of retirement* is sometimes made. For example, a trust-fund plan may set age sixty-five as the earliest age for voluntary retirement at full benefit and age seventy as the mandatory retirement age. There would then be a range of 5 years during which retirements could occur. The actuary would probably prefer to use age sixty-five as the basis for his figures, since liability fixes at that age as long as any person may elect to retire then. Sometimes, however, an assumption is made that a certain proportion will retire at sixty-five, another proportion at sixty-six, and so on up to seventy. Such an assumption can be applied under a trust-fund plan. To assume a rate at which individuals will retire is less valid than the assumption of a rate of withdrawal (item 4 above). The grounds for this statement are that the rate of withdrawal can be watched year by year in comparison with experience and gradual adjustments can be made, whereas if the rate of retirement assumed is substantially out of line, it is not discovered until employees are found to be retiring

1, 2, or 3 years before their assumed retirement date. Hence, a fund that assumed a later retirement age would be subjected overnight to a substantially higher immediate liability than that for which financial provision was made. This could be particularly true in depression times.

8. Another actuarial device used in computing costs under the trust-fund plan is that of giving some advance effect to the expected trend of pay among employees as their age increases. This is the assumption of a *salary scale*. Pay generally goes up with age. Most correlations of pay with age among business firms, in retirement-plan records, in social-security statistics, and in other figures indicate a trend that approaches a plateau at about age fifty or fifty-five and dips somewhat at ages near and above sixty. Benefits under trust-fund plans are frequently based on final pay before retirement, such as 5- or 10-year average final pay, and the salary-scale method is sometimes used in attempting to evaluate the cost effect of such final pay. Since the trend of pay is upward with age, the adoption of a salary scale increases initial costs. Some authorities feel that the use of salary scales is rather an academic exercise, especially in the abnormal periods of depression, inflation, war, and postwar uncertainty. The point is, however, that the trust-fund method can readily use this sort of assumption, and even uncertain recognition is better than none.

9. Flexibility of methods of paying the expenses of running a plan is a consideration. Under a trust-fund plan, the employer may meet expenses directly as they occur or estimate them in advance and add the result to his contribution to the fund, in which case the trustee is billed for them. The former method is the more flexible, as the timing and amount of expense charges are closely linked with the incurrence of such costs. The latter method is comparable to the loading for expenses in the insurer premium; however, any unused loading for current expenses in the trustee's hands at the end of the plan's year is required by the Internal Revenue Service to be used as a credit or offset against the next employer contribution to the fund (such an accounting is not required under insured plans where these amounts may be returned to the employer as dividends or retained as contingency funds).

Advocates of the trust-fund method hold that the administrative costs of installing and maintaining a trust-fund plan compare favorably with those of an insured plan. They point out there are no middleman commissions to pay, no state premium or federal income tax, and the overhead may be lower. However, the expense portion of the employer's contribution in either case (exclusive of state and federal taxes charged only under insured plans) is a rather low percentage of the whole. Just as with an insured plan, the trust-fund method will require of the employer the tasks of assembling records, providing information to employees, and arranging for their retirement; the trustee will have functions of making investments, keeping records, paying benefits out of the fund, and so on; there will be certain legal charges, whether the counsel is the employer's attorney, the trustee's, or an independent lawyer, and there will be fees for actuarial services if the plan is to be established and maintained on a scientific basis. Most of these expenses are incurred in any method of administering a plan. However, the trust-fund advocate points to lack of duplication of administrative effort. A minimum fee is usually set for the trustee's charges, fees rising above the minimum with the size of the fund—for example, a fraction of 1 per cent each year on the existing fund up to a certain amount, a smaller percentage on the next segment of the portfolio, and so on, plus, in some cases, a charge per employee under the plan and/or a charge per benefit disbursement made.

Flexibility in Administration. Much of the old freedom inherent in employer administration has disappeared from both insured and trusteed plans as they exist today and qualify under Internal Revenue Service regulations. First, almost all fundamental discretionary decisions by the employer have gone by the board. Second, investment policy under trust-fund plans lies mainly in the hands of the trustee, within the permitted categories of securities laid down in the trust instrument. Third, employees' rights and options have firmed considerably under modern systems, even where the employee does not contribute to the cost. Fourth, and touching on all the above points, plans are more carefully and comprehensively drawn, in an attempt to set down rather definitely what happens in each possible situation. Fifth, actuaries have been called in to a larger extent, and their natural bent for proper funding, accounting, and orderliness is added to the other influences toward the formalization of modern pension plans. Sixth, the appearance of pension clauses in labor contracts circumscribes further the employer's freedom in designing pension plans and in their administration when organized employees are to be covered.

Some administrative latitude does remain with the employer, and the trust-fund advocate will argue that there is more of it in that type of plan than under the insured method. The employer is responsible for such matters as deciding whether an employee will be retired, with or without his request or consent, under the usual early-retirement provisions of the plan; deciding whether an employee will be retained beyond the normal retirement age; and, in the case of benefits vesting at an employee's termination of service, suggesting to the trustee the best way for such equities to be paid—in a lump sum, in cash in annual installments, in benefits deferred until the age originally set for normal retirement, or otherwise, according to the possibilities offered by the plan. Also, the employer usually holds the reins on how the plan will be funded. Perhaps most important of all is the employer's right to amend the plan, in which action a trustee is usually a very cooperative partner.

Frequently, a retirement-plan committee is established by the employer to handle details of the plan and to work with the trustee. Sometimes, especially in labor-union–negotiated plans, employee representatives serve on this committee, and considerable weight is given to their opinions.

To some extent the added flexibility generally credited to the trust-fund plan arises from the lack of necessity of maintaining equity among all similarly situated employers with pension plans, which is the case with insured plans. Under insured plans, because of the pooling of funds implementing the plans, it is necessary sometimes to go to considerable length both in plan or group-annuity-contract language and in administration to avoid the possibility that one employer will receive more favorable treatment than another. The fact that this combining of funds is absent in the trust-fund approach precludes the troublesome problem of maintaining equity among plans.

Along somewhat similar lines, it is frequently pointed out that a change of a pension plan from a trust fund to an insured contract (or to another trust) may be readily carried out without penalty. A move in the other direction from insured to trust fund is not so simple. Accordingly, when some employers are faced with the necessity of installing a plan before they have had adequate opportunity to fully evaluate the relative merits of both financing mediums, they select the trust fund initially with the avowed intent of carrying out an analysis of the relative merits of the two mediums at a later date and making the final selection at that time.

Investments. What are the common practices, traditions, and characteristics pertaining to the investment of these funds? Any extended treatment of this subject is beyond the scope of this book and lies rather in the field of investments. However, certain generalizations and indicia may be mentioned. Most states have prescribed standard investment mediums as permissible for the investment of trust funds; these would normally be high-grade bonds and other securities of similar standing. Many trust-fund plans expressly stipulate in the trust agreement that the state rule does not apply but that some other basis will govern, one such basis, now used much less frequently than formerly, being investments legal for domestic life-insurance companies in the state of New York (whether or not the trust fund is located in New York). Other plans provide for specified categories of permitted investments, such as a percentage limitation on the amount of common stocks in the portfolio. Many trust agreements now leave the choice of investments to the trustee without limitation.

It is generally conceded to be inadvisable to invest a disproportionate part of the fund in securities of the employer. It would be a case of too many eggs in one basket; if the firm failed, the pension fund would fall with it, the pensioners would be suddenly cut off wholly or partially from benefits, and the active employees would be both out of a job and without pension expectations. Another objection is that this investment practice may give the employer certain powers of control and manipulation of a fund from which he is supposed to be completely divorced. Because of this possibility, the Internal Revenue Service scrutinizes closely those cases where the fund purchases, or plans to purchase, securities of the employing firm. In particular a trust is prohibited from investing in debentures of the employer (likely to be relaxed by 1958 legislation).

Many trustees of pension funds now invest a portion of the funds in common and preferred stocks. In some instances these investments have been selected with a view to obtaining higher rates of income than would be expected under high-grade bonds or other fixed-income types of investments. In other instances the trustee has emphasized growth potentialities in selecting the equities for the pension-fund portfolio. The percentages of the total funds that are so invested vary considerably with the trustee and with the size of the trust fund, but in most instances the proportion varies from 20 to 40 per cent.

As a result of these purchases made over a period of years, the rates of investment income earned by certain trusts have been much higher than the rates credited under group-annuity contracts, and in some instances a substantial excess of market value of the trust-fund assets over book value of these assets has developed. Enjoyment of these favorable results in the past is no guarantee that they will continue indefinitely into the future, but the feeling is growing that a consistent and continuing investment of a part of the assets of a pension trust fund in equities will produce more favorable results (and hence lower cost) than if the investments were to be restricted to those legal for life-insurance companies.

The contributions made to a trust-fund pension plan are invested at the current market prices of the investments selected, while in an insured plan the contributions become a part of the total assets of the insurer and, usually, will be credited with interest at the average rate for the insurer. Even for the same class of investment, the rate of investment return credited under the two financing mediums may be quite different merely by reason of the point of time at which the plan is commenced. If the insurer's assets (most of which were invested years ago at the then prevailing interest rates) earn higher (or lower) rates of return than do current investments, then the rate of return currently credited to the insured contract may be expected to be correspondingly higher (or lower) than under a trust-fund plan. For example, since at the time of writing the rates of return are relatively high on currently purchased government and corporate bonds, it appears that it would be more advantageous to enter the market directly under a trust fund for the purchase of these securities than to participate in a large portfolio of investments, a part of which was purchased when such bonds were higher priced (i.e., provided lower rates of return per dollar invested). Many employers are currently utilizing a trust fund as a supplement to a group-annuity contract established some years ago, in order to take advantage of the higher interest rates now obtainable.

The trustee is often permitted, or required, to purchase insurance contracts for some or all of the plan's participants. At one extreme, at some future time the whole fund could be turned into an insured plan. At the other extreme, annuities could be purchased only for some participants (discrimination in benefits must be avoided); for example, the trustee, not wishing to hazard the full mortality risk, might purchase life annuities for all pensioners upon their attaining age seventy or upon their retirement dates or for amounts of benefit per pensioner which exceed a predetermined amount. Annuity purchases might also be advisable when the employer is forced out of business or for other reasons has to discontinue the plan. Here, the trustee might not wish to handle a dying fund (or it might be uneconomical to do so) and would ascertain the legal and actuarial equities of participants and purchase from an insurer such benefits as the equities could provide, thus closing out the fund.

Besides the usual watchfulness over and management of the fund's portfolio, the trustee should be prepared for calls for cash over future years. To the extent that he feels the need for planning on this score, he should be guided by the actuary's estimates of the future contribution trend and the future pension load. If there are death and termination values, he will need a certain liquidity to meet these rather unpredictable disbursements.

Benefits. In Chapter 3 the more common building blocks used in the benefit structure of pension plans were described. Various types of annuities were mentioned. While the term *annuity* traditionally carries an insurer connotation, the several forms of annuities can readily be provided by the terms of a trust-fund plan, with the reservation of possible exhaustion of funds before the last death occurs. The trust-fund plan may be designed to carry benefits to be payable with no return at death or with one of the various forms of death benefits, as well as optional methods of payment to be elected by retiring employees.

The trust-fund planner should beware of certain selection pitfalls of which the insurance-company actuary is most conscious. Almost any optional choice will in the long run result in selection against the fund. Those whom option A would advantage most choose option A; those for whom option B is better choose that option. For example, statistics show that mortality is higher among those electing an option that carries a return at death than among those selecting an option of pure annuity with no return at death. Or, again, if a joint-and-survivor option [7] is offered with free election up to time of retirement, a pensioner in poor health may be expected to nominate a second life so that on the pensioner's death the system will continue a benefit to the survivor. Insurers determine their options and conditions of election with this tendency in mind. The trust fund too can be protected against this selectivity and against the danger of adverse mortality. Options should be few in number, and the actuary's suggestions for the options and for the rules applying to choosing options should be heeded. As for the mortality risk, the less the amount of the death benefit exceeds the contributions plus interest, the less the chance of mortality losses (or, for that matter, gains) to the fund. Under a plan that returns contributions with interest at death before retirement and provides a substantial *certain* period after retirement, the fund's mortality risk is little more than that of lighter mortality than expected among the reduced number of pensioners who outlive the certain period. Note the reference to the "fund's risk"; naturally, the more employees who live through to retirement age, the more the employer's contribution is needed to build up the fund.

That death benefits may be provided by trust-fund plans does not mean that group life insurance must or can be furnished by the plan. To do so might be deemed as engaging in the life-insurance business and might be prohibited or regulated by existing or future state laws. Certainly, the noninsured plan may carry death benefits not to exceed the sum of accumulated contributions with or without interest. In other words, the fund is not considered to be in the life-insurance business when the death payment is approximately the same as a refund of the contributions theretofore made by and/or for the deceased life.

[7] See Chap. 3.

Sometimes it is suggested that, since the trustee is not equipped to deal in life contingencies, his function should be limited to the process of accumulation and disbursement—that is, to building up the fund and paying it out at retirement at a certain rate of benefit until exhaustion, with the aim of paying benefits for a term certain, such as the number of years of life expectancy from retirement age. While this method may well be within the definition of a pension plan, its drawback is in the termination of income for those who outlive their expectancy. Happily, this curtate-pension idea has little place in practice, and trustees, with employer subvention, either undertake to pay benefits for life or provide for purchasing annuities at the older ages from insurers.

In disability insurance the limited period of payment has been used. Permanent and total disability has been described as premature old age and, hence, a hazard of life that a pension plan should be able to cover. Occupational disability of a prolonged nature entitles the worker to benefits under workmen's-compensation laws, sometimes for the duration of the disability, sometimes for a stated maximum period of years, or sometimes until a fixed aggregate amount has been paid— each state has its own formulas. However, severe and prolonged disabilities not incurred in employment are not widely covered, as the insurers, after heavy losses experienced in trying to provide a disability income in conjunction with life-insurance policies, largely discontinued or considerably restricted the underwriting of this coverage. Also, the previous common practice in group life insurance of maturing the face amount and paying it out in installments in case of permanent and total disability has been mostly discontinued and withdrawn from many old contracts providing for it. Again, a few insurers, in entering the group-annuity field, experimented with a disability clause but, probably because of excessive disability losses in other lines, withdrew the underwriting of this protection as well (although in recent types of deposit-administration contracts they will arrange to pay disability pensions, but without bearing the risk of disability occurrence).[8]

While some insurers and actuaries are wondering whether the pen-

[8] This point is discussed more fully in Chap. 8.

dulum has not swung too far in depriving insured plans of this benefit
—and hence it may be cautiously offered again—the trust-fund plan
does frequently include provisions for disability. Under any plan of
advance funding for pensions, a reserve is built up, and each life is
assigned a potential interest in the assets behind it. If permanent and
total disability occurs before normal retirement age, this amount (or
part of it), to the extent that it is applicable to that life, may be
considered usable for immediate payment of a pension of reduced
amount to the disabled person.[9]

In any event, even when the use of some portion of the regular
old-age assets is admitted, unless disability occurs just before normal
retirement date, the resulting disability benefit will be rather small,
and supplementation from another fund or contribution will be required for an adequate benefit. For this purpose, trust-fund plans
sometimes provide for additional funds or operate on a 1-year-term
contribution charge to meet payment of disability benefits according
to a definite formula in the plan. The benefit could be restricted, as
in some workmen's-compensation laws, to a maximum period of time;
but it is usually payable during disability and replaced with the old-
age benefit proper (based on the benefits accrued to the date of disability) when the otherwise normal retirement age is reached by the
disabled life. In any case, there is considerable latitude for covering
this hazard in trust-fund plans.

In dealing with the disability hazard, discretion is the better part
of good intentions. If the plan is to provide disability benefits, the
clause concerning them should be strictly drawn so as to cover only
bona fide essentially total long-term disability; periodic reexamination
for possible recovery should be required; the administration and claim
adjudication should be responsible and hard-boiled; a considerable
period of service should be a condition precedent to eligibility; a waiting period of several months (commonly 6 months) should elapse
after the inception of disability before benefits commence; and the
benefits should be modest enough (including recognition of their favor-

---

[9] Unless the reserve is of the sinking-fund type, its use in this way may well
disturb the actuarial assumptions of expected reserve releases from deaths, since
the disabled lives will include some of the deaths expected to occur before retirement by the tables used in the actuarial computations.

able income tax position) to be neither attractive as a substitute for full-time pay nor out of line with normal retirement benefits.

In all considerations of total-and-permanent-disability benefits due consideration must be given to the recent amendments to the Social Security Act, under which disability pensions are payable commencing in July, 1957. The administration of such disability benefits will undoubtedly affect the approval and handling of similar disability benefits under private pension plans. It is understood, however, that the administration of the feature of OASDI permitting the dropping of years of disability from recorded coverage has been strict.

In recent years, more and more interest has developed in ways and means for paying pensions with a benefit that fluctuates according to changes in the economy. This sort of arrangement is commonly known as a *variable annuity* and is described more fully in Chapter 9. While insurance companies have not yet entered this field to any appreciable degree, the trust-fund advocate feels that the variable-annuity objective is a natural function for the trust-fund plan to undertake, as being more closely allied to the investment side than to life contingencies and the guarantees thereunder of the insurers.

Provisions of Trust-fund Instruments. The retirement plan proper—that is, the legal instrument containing the governing provisions—may take several forms. In the case of insured group annuities, the master contract between employer and insurer contains the plan, except that under some deposit-administration types a separate plan document is not unusual. For insured plans using individual contracts, there is usually a plan, authorized, adopted, and set forth in writing, which provides for furnishing the benefits by the purchase of individual insurance contracts. In the trust-fund method, a plan is also formalized, with provision for the contributions to be payable to, and the benefits to be disbursed from, a fund under the control of the trustee. Here the plan is commonly a document separate from the trust agreement, although they are sometimes combined in one instrument.

The common provisions of plans are fairly uniform in their main characteristics, whether insured or trusteed. The usual provisions were explained in Chapter 4, and in view of what has already been said concerning the differences between the insured and trust-fund methods, further elaboration here would be repetitious. It is, however, important to repeat that under an insured group-annuity plan the governing instrument is the contract to which the insurer is a party. Under the trust-fund type, the plan itself may be separate from the document controlling the fund management by the trustee whose functions are governed by the trust agreement.

Summaries of the main provisions of the trust-fund instrument follow with brief comment on a few. In general, trust agreements will be made up of clauses pertaining to the following subject matter:

1. The names of the parties (employer and trustee); the purpose of, and authority for, the plan; the agreement of the parties to the clauses to follow—in other words, the "whereases" and "now therefores." Usually the plan is incorporated in the trust agreement by attachment or by reference, sometimes vice versa.

2. The trustee's responsibilities and the general duties of the employer; the former's being to manage the fund, accept payments to it, and make disbursements from it; the latter's being to keep proper books and records, suitably advise the trustee, and make contributions to the fund.

3. Definitions of the powers and duties regarding investments delegated to the trustee, including the specific types of securities or other assets that the fund may carry in its portfolio. For example, this could include investment in insurance contracts, or it could exclude such items as securities issued by the employer.

4. The administrative functions of the trustee other than those regarding investments; e.g., the right of the trustee to vote shares, register securities, arbitrate claims, or borrow money for the purposes of the trust fund, including the right and duty to make payments from the trust fund appropriate to the terms of the plan.

5. The administrative relations between the trustee and the employer. Frequently the employer appoints a committee to deal with the trustee, to direct the trustee to make benefit payments, and to furnish the trustee with any information needed for the carrying out of his duties.

6. Handling expenses and taxes of the fund. Sometimes the trust

agreement calls for all expenses to be met out of the fund; more usually the employer pays most of the expenses direct; or a combination of the two may be arranged.

7. A formal arrangement with respect to what accounts will be kept and what reports will be made, on the part of both the trustee and the employer, or on the part of the employer's committee.

8. Resignation or removal of the trustee, and the appointment of successor trustees.

9. The terms upon which the trust agreement may be amended or discontinued and, if discontinued, the manner—in conformance with the plan—in which the trust fund will then be liquidated or otherwise distributed among the pensioners or employees having an interest therein.

Internal Revenue Service Requirements. The relationship of the Internal Revenue Service to retirement plans and trusts, whether on an insured basis or on a trusteed basis, has been outlined. Most of the conditions made necessary by the Revenue Act of 1942, as amended, and the regulations and rulings promulgated since then have been set forth.[10] As most of these requirements are similar for both insured and trusteed forms of administration, there need be considered here only one or two points of difference or peculiarity with respect to trust-fund plans.

The insured plan is financed through the payment of premiums to the insurer underwriting the plan, and these premiums contain a loading for expenses and contingencies. This premium loading does not have to be accounted for either to the Service or to the employer. Consequently, if there is a margin over expenses in this loading, the margin may be used as the insurer sees fit, usually either as a long-range refund (dividend or rate credit) to the employer as experience dictates or as a contribution to meet contingencies either general or for the specific case, according to the insurer's practice. Under trust-fund plans, a specific accounting of the operations of the fund is made necessary by the Service's requirement of a balance sheet of the trust together with a statement of receipts and disbursements. Expense is one of the items of this accounting. If contributions to the trust have included an allowance for current expenses and these expenses

[10] See Chap. 5.

have actually been less than the allowance, the Service's rules require that the unused allowance must be immediately reflected in a credit offset against the ensuing employer contributions to the fund. In other words, there is no possibility of establishing a contingency or fluctuation reserve over and above the actuarial reserve proper, such as is possible under the insured plan. Since the funds under many small plans are not large, fluctuations are likely. This rule, therefore, is sometimes thought to penalize uninsured plans, especially those of smaller size.

One of the advantages of qualifying a plan and trust under the Internal Revenue Code is to secure federal tax exemption of income on the trust assets, since all investment income is exempt from tax, a favored situation not now present for the insured plan.

For both insured and trusteed plans, annual filing with the Service is necessary in order to demonstrate that the plan still qualifies and that the contributions to the plan have actuarial justification and also in order to determine what portion, if not all, of such contributions may be deductible in that year as a business expense under the appropriate section of the Internal Revenue Code. The material that must be filed is explained in the Service's regulations. Much of this material is of a technical character and requires actuarial computations and demonstrations.

General. Aside from the Internal Revenue Service and its requirements, trust-fund plans must observe such special state laws or rules as may be applicable. These may include special rules on investment, special requirements for approval of the plan and trust for state income tax deductibility (most states follow federal practice), and any rules applicable to special provisions that the trust instrument or plan might contain, such as a rule against perpetuities.

The employer's counsel should clear all proposed documents for conformity to the employer's charter, bylaws, and practice; he should also review their subject matter. Similarly, the trustee should clear all documents. The actuary of the plan should examine all documents before execution for any possible errors or omissions in the actuarial or other technical features.

In the case of contributory plans where participation of employees is voluntary, registration with the Securities and Exchange Commission may become necessary, although no requirements in this respect have thus far been promulgated. A trust-fund plan, under which the offer to join is wide-open to employees and under which a trustee, either corporate or individual, is to invest the fund (part of which is employee money), has been construed by the SEC as being in the nature of an offering of securities for sale. Consequently, the SEC considers that the Securities Act might apply and that registration thereunder is potentially required. Historically, a rather extreme argument in support of this contention is embodied in the following quotation: [11]

The standards of Section 165 of the Internal Revenue Code are not appropriate substitutes for the disclosure and liability provisions of the Securities Act. Section 165 of the Internal Revenue Code exempts from income taxes any trust forming part of an employee's stock bonus, pension or profit-sharing plan if under the plan no part of the assets may accrue to the benefit of the employer until all of the obligations of the plan have been met. There is no condition that the employer contribute anything to the plan. There is no limitation on how the funds may be invested; a plan, meeting the requirement of Section 165, might involve employees' savings in the wildest sort of speculation.

Summary. Trust-fund plans preceded the use of insurer contracts for pension purposes. The latter, however, have experienced a large growth since the 1920s. Pension plans in general have spurted ahead in the last 10 to 20 years, owing, in some measure, to the stimulus of a "security atmosphere" created by the Social Security Act and the favorable "cost atmosphere" engendered by the federal tax laws. For moderate- and large-size groups of employees the trust-fund method has grown the faster of the two during this period, and many employers who earlier established insured pension plans have more recently shifted their plans in whole or in part to the trust-fund method of financing. This increasing popularity has apparently resulted from the appeal of some of the characteristics described in this

[11] See Report of the Securities and Exchange Commission on Proposals for Amendments to the Securities Act of 1933 and the Securities Exchange Act of 1934, Aug. 7, 1941, p. 16. Consideration of these paragraphs was abandoned by Congress after the declaration of war.

chapter plus two other important developments, the aid to trust-fund plans provided by the Revenue Act of 1942 (see Chapter 5) and the emergence of pension plans at the union bargaining table, where the trust-fund method seems to have taken priority over the insured method (see Chapter 14).

CHAPTER 8

The Group-annuity Plan

Definitions. A *life annuity* is a series of periodic payments payable during the lifetime of a designated person, usually called the *annuitant* (or more generally, *pensioner*). In this chapter it will be assumed that the payments are fixed in amount, except in the case of the *variable annuity,* a relative newcomer under which payments are tied to the investment experience of the fund from which they are made. If annuity payments commence at the date of purchase of the annuity, or within 1 year after such purchase, the annuity is an *immediate annuity* (when the immediate annuity commences precisely on date of purchase, it is sometimes called an *annuity due*). If the first payment is made more than 1 year from date of purchase, the annuity is a *deferred annuity.* An immediate annuity is normally paid for by a single premium; a deferred annuity may be purchased either by a single premium or by a series of premiums payable during the period of deferment.

The term *retirement annuity* is generally used to denote an annuity which commences on the date of retirement of the individual and is a convenient term to use where retirement benefits are provided for a group of individuals under a retirement plan, such as a pension plan covering the employees of an employer.

The retirement-annuity plan covering groups of employees may be *self-insured* (discussed in Chapter 7 and frequently described as "self-administered" or "trusteed") or *insured,* that is, underwritten by an insurer. In the latter case, a *group-annuity contract* [1] is issued by the

---

[1] While the group-permanent form may conform to this description, it has other attributes that call for separate treatment. See Chap. 9.

insurer to the employer (or sometimes to a trustee), and the contract is between the employer and the insurer, although the annuity and other benefit payments are usually paid directly by the insurer to the annuitants or their beneficiaries.

Similarity to Group Insurance. The first group-life-insurance contract, which made life insurance available under a single contract to all employees of an employer, was issued in 1912, and the first group-annuity contract was issued by a life-insurance company in the early 1920s. It was natural for the early group-annuity contracts to follow soon after the inception of group life insurance, since familiarity with the handling of life insurance on a bulk basis led to consideration of the problem of furnishing retirement benefits along similar lines. Retirement benefits had previously been provided only through self-administered or trust-fund plans or had been written through individual annuity contracts.

As in the case of group life insurance, a group-annuity plan is based upon a single contract setting forth all the provisions and benefits in detail. This contract is issued to the employer, on whom rests the responsibility of transmitting the premiums (including employee contributions, if any) to the insurer. Certificates briefly describing the benefits available to the employees and the conditions entitling the employees to receive such benefits are issued by the insurer to the employer for delivery to covered employees.

The Group-annuity Contract. The *group-annuity contract* is issued by a life-insurance company. There are two broad classes of group annuities: the older form, which is sometimes simply called a *group annuity* but which, to differentiate it from the newer form, will be called a *paid-up group annuity;* and the newer form, which has come into prominence lately although originally introduced for relatively larger cases nearly 30 years ago, and which will be called a *deposit-administration group annuity.*

Under the paid-up group-annuity contract, premiums or contributions as they are received are automatically applied immediately as single premiums to purchase paid-up deferred annuities for covered employees; under the deposit-administration group-annuity contract, the premiums paid are accumulated in a fund, generally with no allocation among employee participants, and the money is applied to purchase annuities only at specified times, such as at the retirement of a participant. Many modifications are possible in the deposit-administration group-annuity contract. For example, the contract may provide that upon the employee's reaching age fifty-five all accrued units will be immediately purchased, with all future accruals to be currently purchased; from age fifty-five on this arrangement is the same as under the paid-up group-annuity contract.

The paid-up group-annuity contract may be issued either on the unit-benefit basis, under which fixed units of annuity are currently purchased as they accrue, or on the money-purchase basis, under which the money contributed for a participant is fixed in rate or amount and is used to purchase a paid-up retirement annuity.

The group-annuity contract takes its place in the insurer's group business and alongside its individual-contract business as a class of business that is intended in the long run to stand on its own feet and to develop its own cost pattern—subject, of course, to the general solvency of the insurer. In general, there is no segregation of the assets of a life-insurance company, so that the group-annuity business shares in the investment results of the insurer as do all other classes of business, but with normal adjustments to reflect the peculiarities of certain classes of investments, for example, policy loans, where the investment experience is usually credited only to those classes of business that provide for policy loans. The mortality experience, expenses, contingency reserves, and other factors of the group-annuity business are analyzed first for the entire class and then by each individual group-annuity case. The extent to which a particular case will stand on its own feet will depend on the size of the case, its own experience, the experience of the group-annuity class, the insurer's policy with respect to dividends and experience rating, and other special factors that may apply from year to year. In all of this, group annuities generally follow the pattern set by group life insurance, group hospital expense insurance, and the other group-insurance lines.

Although group annuities are issued by either mutual life-insurance companies or stock life-insurance companies, they are almost invariably participating. When issued by a mutual life-insurance company, the participation is effected through dividends; when by a nonparticipating company, through "experience rating."

One important difference between the various forms of group insurance and group annuities is that group insurance is normally issued on a 1-year-term basis (although permanent forms of group life insurance are available to some extent, as pointed out in Chapter 9), so that favorable or unfavorable experience unfolds itself each year, and the insurer can take account of these gains or losses currently. On the other hand, group annuities are long-term arrangements under which the experience emerges only gradually. For example, consider a unit benefit of $5 a month payable at age sixty-five and purchased at age thirty-five for a group of employees. Whether the premiums plus interest earnings and other income are adequate can be determined only after the last annuity payment is made, which could be as many as 60 or more years after the date of purchase.

Originally, the deposit-administration contract provided for the accumulation of money until retirement, at which time annuities were purchased. Recently a modification of this plan has been introduced, called *immediate-participation deposit administration,*[2] under which the group participates currently in the results of its own experience, and although there are some guarantees by the insurer, they are much less heavily emphasized than in the case of other forms of group annuities and consequently require much less in the way of contingency-reserve accumulation. To some degree the employer is, in effect, currently underwriting his own case.

Group annuities can be written either on a *noncontributory basis* (employer pays all) or on a *contributory basis* (employer and employees jointly contribute). When contributory, it is generally provided that the employee will always get back at some time at least his own contributions, with or without interest.

Unit-benefit Formula versus Money-purchase Formula. Under the *unit-benefit formula,* the benefit that is purchased each year is either a certain percentage of the employee's compensation for that year or a flat dollar amount. The single premium to purchase these units will increase over the years, first, because pay increases may become effective, and, second, because the cost to provide a dollar of annuity increases with age. For example, under a plan providing a $10-a-month

[2] See pp. 151, 152.

benefit per year of credited service starting at age sixty-five, the cost would be roughly $550 for a male employee now aged thirty-five, whereas the cost would be about $1,500 for this same employee when he reached age sixty-five. Under contributory plans, since the employee usually contributes the same percentage of his pay each year (so his contribution rate does not increase with age), the employer's annual contributions will be increased more steeply than indicated above to meet the residual of the higher premiums as the employee grows older.

Under the *money-purchase plan,* a stated amount of money, such as 5 per cent of pay, is used to buy retirement-annuity benefits, and the amount of retirement annuity purchased will decrease with age for a given dollar amount of premium. When the employee receives an increase in pay, the 5 per cent contribution will be increased, as also will the amount of benefit thereby provided. The money-purchase method is usually on a noncontributory basis but can also be contributory.

On the assumption that identical amounts of annuity were to be provided under the two methods, the principal difference would lie in the incidence of the funding. The unit-benefit method, which provides for equal units each year, would require an increase in premium each year. For the total annuities to be equal, the amounts of annuities purchased in the early years of an employee's coverage under the money-purchase plan would have to exceed those provided by the fixed-unit-benefit plan, while the amounts provided with the later years' contributions would be smaller than by the unit-benefit premium. Level money-purchase premiums would be greater than the unit-benefit premiums in the early years and smaller in the later years. The basic difference is that the money-purchase plan promises definite costs to the employer while the unit-benefit formula promises definite benefits.

Underwriting. The insurer will underwrite a group-annuity case more or less along the same lines followed in dealing with other group covers. Because of the long-term nature of a pension plan, because of tax considerations, because of the large sums of money involved, and because of the relationship that will exist between the insurer and the participants in the plan for many years in the future, the insurer will normally underwrite each group-annuity case very carefully. The following are a few of the factors that will be taken into account.

1. Answers to a questionnaire regarding the employer's business will show the financial history and condition of the employer, the likelihood of his being able to carry the proposed plan indefinitely, and the suitability of the plan for the employees to be covered.

2. A minimum number of participating employees is stipulated, both to meet statutory requirements and to produce a reasonable unit expense cost per employee. For many years the minimum number was usually 50, but in some states as few as 25 or even 10 can now be written under a group-annuity contract. Under a deposit-administration plan, companies originally set a minimum of 1,500 lives, later reduced to 1,000, and then to 500, and recently some companies have even accepted 200 or fewer employees.

3. Under a noncontributory plan, participation is automatic. When the plan is contributory, some states require that 75 per cent of all eligible employees must be included, and there are minimum requirements for a qualified plan under the Internal Revenue Code. Aside from legal requirements, a high participation rate under contributory plans is desirable from the insurer's viewpoint, because it reduces the possibility of selection by the employees (although this is not of as great importance as under the group-insurance covers), and, more important, a low participation rate may raise a question about the value of the plan as an employee-benefit instrument.

4. The total amount of premium to be paid in any one year may sometimes be limited by the insurer. Under a paid-up contract, this would only apply to past-service premiums because the amount of current-service premiums are fixed. Aside from tax considerations, the insurer is desirous of a more or less uniform flow of money each year from each contract because investment procedures might be adversely affected by a large influx of premium money in any one year. Under a group-annuity contract, the insurer will also insist upon a minimum contribution during the year to provide for adequate funding.

5. Sometimes insurers impose a limit on the maximum amount of annuity payment to any individual so as not to have too great a concentration of risk.

Paid-up Group-annuity Contracts. *General.* Definiteness and a guarantee, but also rigidity, are peculiar to the paid-up group-annuity contract. Each premium as it is paid buys a certain amount of benefit at predetermined premium rates, the annuity payments being guaranteed by the insurer. This benefit is allocated directly to an employee's account.

Insuring Clause. The insuring clause, usually on the face of the policy, recites that the insurer will pay the benefits to the employees as provided in the contract, establishes the effective date of the contract, and states that the contract is between the employer and the insurer.

Definitions and Plan Specifications. The contract section devoted to definitions and specifications generally contains all the pertinent provisions of the *plan,* such as persons who are eligible, the schedule of payments, the amount of past-service credit to be allowed, minimum annuities, normal retirement date, early- and late-retirement provisions, and amount of contribution.

Premiums and Purchase of Annuity Units. Premiums are applied to purchase paid-up retirement-annuity units at the time they are paid, in accordance with guaranteed rates set out in the contract (now usually based on some modification of the 1951 Group Annuity Mortality Table and $2\frac{1}{2}$ per cent interest, with a loading equal to 5 or 8 per cent of the gross premiums). The initial rates are usually guaranteed for the first 5 years of the contract, but thereafter, upon advance notice, the insurer may change them from year to year.

The contract permits the employer to pay up the past-service premiums over a number of years, sometimes subject to a minimum and a maximum contribution.

Withdrawal from Service. If no vesting of employer contributions is provided for, the withdrawal benefit is usually paid in cash and is equal to the employee's contributions, with or without interest. If there is vesting and if the employee does not cash in his benefit rights, he is permitted to take a paid-up benefit purchased by his own contributions and that part of the employer's contributions which vests. Upon the death of an employee, the employer is not entitled to any refund of his own contributions because the rates for the paid-up annuities were discounted for mortality. However, when an employee terminates employment and forfeits some retirement annuity purchased by employer contributions, the insurer is no longer liable for this part of the annuity. It is entitled to some of the assets, at least with respect to those employees who would die shortly after termination of service or who were in very poor health at termination of service, since the premium rates assume that a certain number of employees will die before retirement and that no annuity payments to them will be required. A practical solution is to provide that the entire reserve amount (arising out of employer contributions) on an employee terminating in good health will revert to the employer, but not when an employee terminates in ill health. The criterion for determining who is in good health is usually rather liberal. Reversions to the employer on account of terminating employees can be used only to reduce his contributions falling due thereafter. In the past, a surrender charge of about 4 per cent was made on these reversions, designed to permit the insurer to recoup its previous expense in connection with the terminating employee; but some insurers are reducing or even eliminating this surrender charge, and some even grant full reversions on ill-health terminations, taking the position that, unless the whole policy terminates, any such charges may be reflected in the dividend or experience-rating determinations.

Tables of Factors. The contract contains the necessary tables, such as a table of reduction factors to be applied to early retirements; a table of increase factors to be applied to late retirements; a table of OASDI adjustment factors; a table of annuity benefits purchased only by employee contributions and only by employer contributions; and various conversion factors to change from the normal form of annuity to an optional form, such as life, 10-year certain and continuous, or joint and survivor.

OASDI Adjustment Option. OASDI payments are generally designed to commence at age sixty-five. If an employee retires before age sixty-five, he usually gets a benefit under the group-annuity contract that commences at early retirement and continues for life and at age sixty-five picks up his OASDI benefit. In most cases it is desirable to provide a more or less uniform amount from date of early retirement. To this end, the group-annuity contract usually provides that the benefit otherwise payable under the contract will be increased from early retirement to age sixty-five and reduced from sixty-five so as to give this uniform benefit. Because women can now draw OASDI benefits at age sixty-two, this adjustment should be figured to age sixty-two for them.

Suspension of Premium Payments. In order that premiums may be paid when due, the contract provides that it will terminate if premiums are not paid before the end of the grace period. However, there may be situations, ranging in duration from, say, 1 month to 1 or 2 years, where this provision would cause a hardship on the employer, since he might be only temporarily unable to pay the premiums as they fall due. In order to meet such a situation, the contract also provides for a temporary suspension of benefit purchases, the contract continuing in full force without payments of additional premiums during the period of suspension. At the end of such time the employer can take up premium payments anew, with or without payment of the suspended premiums. Any prolonged suspension of premiums may involve loss of qualification under the regulations of the Internal Revenue Service.

The contract contains a provision conforming to Internal Revenue Service requirements restricting the size of benefits payable to the highest-paid employee participants if the plan should be terminated (wholly or partly) during the first 10 years.

Discontinuance of Contract. If the contract is terminated either by the employer or by the insurer (because minimum participation or other requirements of the contract are not met) all annuities purchased up to that time will usually vest in the employees, whether or not they have met the vesting requirements of the plan. This provision has, generally speaking, caused some concern to employers who wish to continue their plans but to change the funding medium to another insurer or to a trustee. In some cases insurers are willing, usually with surrender charges of up to 5 per cent, to transfer the funds pertaining to the nonretired participants under the group-annuity contract to a new insurer or to a trustee and thus enable the employer to continue the plan as before.[3]

---

[3] The insurer would continue to pay annuities to employees already retired and would retain the fund pertaining to these obligations.

Some contracts distinguish between termination of contract and discontinuance of premium payments. Termination of contract would apply when the plan itself is to be discontinued, so that the vesting of the contract assets in the participants would seem to be only equitable and may even be required by regulations of the Internal Revenue Service. Discontinuance of premium payments would apply where the plan was being continued but where future funding would be with another insurer or with a trustee; here the old group annuity would continue in full force and effect except that no further contributions by the employer would be made. In any event, the group-annuity contract remains as the governing document as long as any annuities or other benefits are an obligation of the insurer thereunder.

Reserves. State insurance laws often stipulate that the contract must state the basis (i.e., mortality tables and interest rates assumed) of the minimum reserves that are to be set up in connection with the contract; usually this is also the basis on which the premiums are computed.

Contract Changes. The contract defines the guarantees of the insurer and the extent to which it can change them. No change can be made applicable to annuities purchased before the date of the change.

Small Amounts. For administrative reasons, the contract usually provides that unless the annuity payments amount to at least $40 or some such sum a year the insurer can make an equivalent lump-sum settlement in lieu of payment of the annuity.

Miscellaneous. Various administrative provisions are usually found in the group-annuity contract, such as (1) those dealing with assignments, (2) payments to minors or those incapable of giving valid receipt, (3) adjustments to be made because of age discrepancies, (4) proof that must be submitted for entitlement to annuity payments, (5) records that must be maintained and information that must be supplied to the insurer, and (6) a statement whether the policy will participate in dividends or will be experience-rated.

Deposit-administration Group-annuity Contracts. *General.* The deposit-administration contract allows considerably more flexibility in the funding structure than does the paid-up annuity contract but to some extent loses in definiteness and in guarantees of benefits. It is aimed to cut a middle course between the rigidity of the paid-up group annuity and the freedom and flexibility of the trust fund.

The deposit-administration contract retains much of the format and many of the specifications of the paid-up type, but there are important differences.

Definitions and Plan Specifications. Rather than spelling out in detail the plan specifications, the deposit-administration contract sometimes incorporates the plan by reference.

Premiums and Purchase of Annuities. Premiums are paid into an account, and withdrawals are made from this account when annuities are purchased, generally at retirement. Subject to the requirement that the account must be adequate to meet the premiums for pensions promised to employees retiring in any given year, the insurer may leave the determination of the contribution to the employer. There is no hard and fast separation of the contribution between current-service and past-service amounts, because the employee's total benefit is purchased at retirement.

The usual guarantee in a deposit-administration contract is that the money paid in the first 5 years will earn a specified rate of interest and will be applied at a guaranteed single-premium rate in the purchase of annuities at retirement until exhausted. New guarantees will be given for contributions paid thereafter, generally on a year-to-year basis. One guarantee that has recently been announced by an insurer is of 3 per cent on the funds deposited in the first 5 contract years and 2¾ per cent on the funds deposited during the next 5 years, until such funds are exhausted by purchase of annuities. The corresponding annuity-purchase rates at retirement are based on a modification of the Group Annuity 1951 Table with interest at 2¾ per cent and a loading of 5 per cent of the gross premium. This insurer also makes an annual charge per contract (as is more or less usual in connection with deposit-administration plans) of $750 for small cases, reducing gradually to $0 for cases with annual premiums of over $100,000.

Withdrawal from Service. If an employee who is eligible to receive a cash-withdrawal payment terminates, the applicable sum of money is withdrawn from the fund and paid to him. If the benefit at termination of service is a reduced paid-up annuity starting at normal retirement date, no transfer is made until the date when his reduced annuity will be purchased.

Tables of Factors. Tables of factors are needed to show how much money is required to buy a dollar of annuity for males and females at the various retirement ages and for the various annuity options.

Suspension of Contributions. Temporary suspension of contributions need not result in the discontinuance of the contract, providing sufficient funds are on deposit to purchase annuities for employees retiring currently.

Discontinuance of Contract. The deposit-administration contract has several reasonable options available to the employer upon discontinuance of the contract. First, the funds can be transferred to another insurer or to a trustee, generally with a surrender charge, which may be up to 5 per cent of the fund. Second, the amount deposited may be left intact and used to purchase retirement benefits as retirements arise, to the extent of its capacity, no new contributions being made. Third, on the assumption that the employer decides to discontinue the plan as well as the contract, the deposit amount will be used to purchase deferred annuities according to procedures outlined in the plan or in the deposit-administration contract.

Reserves. The reserve section stipulates the minimum reserves for both the active account and the retired account.

Contract Changes. If any changes in guarantees are made, generally they will apply only to new contributions; that is, the original guarantees would hold until all previous contributions were used up in the purchase of annuities. No such change can be made applicable to annuities that have been purchased before the date of the change.

Immediate-participation Deposit-administration Group Annuity. Depending on the size of the case, some insurers offer a special type of deposit-administration plan (known by different names, e.g., *immediate-participation plan* and *pension-administration plan*) under which any gains (resulting from experience both before and after retirement) will be credited to the deposit account at the end of each year. The chief difference between this type and the regular deposit-administration type is that the employer's account is immediately credited or debited with actual expenses, any excess interest earnings (generally the only guarantee by the insurance company is with respect to a minimum rate of interest) mortality savings or losses, and other gains or losses.

As employees reach retirement age under this new form, purchases of life annuities are not effected from the deposit-administration fund, but, instead, the retiring group receives direct pensions from the fund in conformance with the plan, and each year thereafter a single-premium valuation of the pensioner group is carried out to see whether there has been a mortality gain or loss during the year. If there has been a gain, the amount is reflected as a credit to the deposit fund. If there has been a loss, the deposit fund is charged accordingly. Thus, year by year an immediate reflection of mortality among the retired lives is accomplished.

The only time purchase of a single-premium annuity for pensioners will be made is either when the deposit fund gets dangerously close to falling below the single premium for the then pension liability on retired lives or when the group contract is discontinued. If purchase is made, it will be at guaranteed rates set out in the contract; any subsequent gains will be reflected through whatever practice the insurer follows for long-term dividend provision under purchased annuities. The contract may also call for a surrender charge (up to 5 per cent) at time of discontinuance.

Death Benefits in Group-annuity Contracts. 1. *Death Benefits before Retirement.* Regardless of the form of the contributory group annuity, a benefit is payable upon the death before retirement of a covered employee. The maximum death benefit provided (without being specifically labeled "insurance") is the sum of the employee's and the employer's contributions to the date of death, together with the interest accumulated thereon. More commonly, the death benefit consists only of the return of the employee's contributions, with or without interest. The employer's contributions are almost always discounted for in the expected deaths and are just sufficient actuarially, in conjunction with the employee contributions, to provide the annuities for those employees who will live to retirement age, so that the employer's money cannot be paid at death unless the contract so provides, in which case the premiums would have to be increased for this purpose.

It is usual to include interest on the employee's contributions, but the return at death of contributions without interest calls for somewhat lower contributions from the employer, since the employer's contributions are reduced by the interest that would have been credited on employee contributions.

In the case of noncontributory plans, the employer may provide as death benefits such proportion of his accumulated contributions as he desires, and the premium he pays to the insurer will be calculated to provide the death benefit he selects. It is common practice not to provide any death benefit from the employer's contributions, this being left to the company's group-life-insurance program. Occasionally it is provided that the employee's beneficiary will be paid the current-service contributions but not the past-service contributions made by the employer, with or without interest, if the employee had completed a given period of service at the time of his death.

2. *Death Benefits after Retirement.* An amount at least equal to the employee's contributions, less the retirement-annuity payments made up to the time of death, normally will be paid to his designated beneficiary upon the death of the pensioner after retirement. Variations of this arrangement include:

a. As above, return of the employee's contributions, with or without interest, to date of retirement, less annuity payments made

b. Return of 125 per cent, 150 per cent, or 200 per cent of his contributions, with or without interest, less annuity payments

c. Guarantee of at least 60-months certain, 120-months certain, or some other specified number of monthly annuity payments

d. Payment of total contributions—employee and employer—less annuity payments made

Disability Benefits. Group-annuity plans rarely contain provisions entitling employees to pensions in the event of total and permanent disability. Life-insurance companies had such adverse experience on disability-income benefits included in both individual and group-life-insurance contracts in the late 1920s and early 1930s that most insurers discontinued offering this benefit on those forms and did not include disability coverage in their group-annuity forms, even though a disability benefit under group-annuity contracts had not been tested. The unfavorable experience was a result of antiselection on the part of insureds, many of whom feigned disability in order to obtain benefits. This situation was particularly serious during the depression, when employment was at a low level. Furthermore, liberal judicial decisions required the insurers to pay types of claims that had not been contemplated in the determination of the premium for the policy. Competition among insurers and unduly liberal provisions also contributed to unfavorable experience.

A limited form of disability benefit is available if the contract gives the employee the option of retiring earlier than the normal retirement date and receiving a proportionately reduced annuity. Since the exercise of this option is usually restricted to a period of 5 or 10 years before the normal retirement date, it affords no relief to the employee who becomes permanently disabled earlier. Also, the actuarial reduction in the benefit to fit the early retirement age tends to make it inadequate as a benefit for bona fide disability. This result has been considerably mitigated by provision of a disability-benefit feature by the 1956 amendments to the Social Security Act.

While the usual group-annuity contract no longer contains a contractual arrangement for disability, there are various ways in which it may be covered in a group-annuity contract. The employer might pay a "disability premium" to be held in a "special disability account." As disabilities occurred and where approved by the employer (not adjudicated by the insurer), sufficient single premium to purchase a life income for the permanently and totally disabled employee would be applied from this special fund. The deposit-administration method could readily accommodate a disability benefit in several ways. Benefits could be paid currently out of the deposit account as they fell due until normal retirement age, when an annuity would be purchased in the usual manner, or the annuity could be purchased at date of disability (advance retirement). Note that this paragraph deals with a real disability benefit and not just the actuarial equivalent of the accrued rights to benefits.

Level-premium Group Annuity. Practically all individual contracts of life insurance and many individual deferred-annuity contracts are sold on the level-premium basis. Premiums for a given amount of benefit (insurance or annuity) are calculated so that they will be the same each year during the premium-paying period. Under the single-premium unit-benefit type of paid-up group annuity, the cost of providing specific annuity units to a particular employee increases with age, and the total cost to retirement age is the sum of an increasing progression of single premiums. It is perfectly feasible to average out these single-unit premiums and to calculate a level yearly contribution that will produce the same prospective total annuity. This level premium applicable to any one employee will naturally be greater than the early single premiums of the unit-purchase type but less than such single premiums in the later years.

The level-premium method, unlike the money-purchase method, provides a definite benefit. The level premiums are a guarantee against rate increase throughout the life of the contract, whereas the benefit purchased by future single premiums of the money-purchase plan may be decreased by the insurer at any time, subject to the terms of the group-annuity contract. If a money-purchase plan were predicated on providing a certain amount of total annuity at retirement, an increase in the schedules of contribution would have to be made each time the insurer increased its single-premium rates.

Group annuities have been sold on the level-premium basis, but insurance companies are currently very reluctant to issue them because of the long-term-rate guarantee. An insurer writing such a contract would be justified in including greater expense and contingency margins in the premium rate than are used in single-premium rates. Usually, where a specific benefit is desired under an insured plan with a level-contribution arrangement, the group-insurance-annuity form or the individual-insurance-annuity method (see Chapter 9) is used in lieu of the group annuity.

Irregular Money-purchase Group Annuity. The regular money-purchase method contemplates year-by-year contributions at fixed percentages of payroll, the contributions to be used in the purchase of such deferred annuities as they will provide. Sometimes an even more indefinite system of benefits is established under a paid-up group-annuity contract. Contributions of an irregular nature are undertaken, to be used, if and when paid, in the purchase of deferred annuities. These contributions are to be made contingently—both in amount and in timing. The most common use of this plan calls for contributions contingent on the profit of the employer's business. This sort of arrangement is essentially a profit-sharing plan (it is so viewed by the Internal Revenue Service) which uses the paid-up group-annuity contract to provide for deferred distribution of the share of profits allocated to it. Aside from the irregular nature of the premium payments, such a contract contains most of the provisions of the usual paid-up group-annuity form.

ADVANTAGES OF INSURED FINANCING MEDIUMS

Advocates of the insured approach to the financing of pension benefits emphasize certain features of these plans. Most of these arguments also apply to the individual-annuity and group-insurance-annuity types of financing discussed in Chapter 9.[4]

Guarantees of Benefits. If a benefit once commences under an insured contract, the insurer guarantees it will be continued during the lifetime of the employee (or for such other period as is promised under the terms of the plan) despite any inadequacies in the premiums charged. In addition, where paid-up deferred benefits have been purchased, as under the traditional type of group annuity, these benefits are guaranteed to commence at retirement age and continue for the lifetime of the annuitant.

Sometimes employers interpret these guarantees as extending to the cost of purchasing future benefits. Insurers generally reserve the right to change their premium rate for each new unit of benefit purchased (at least on purchases after, say, the initial 5 years of a plan), and through the accumulation of contingency funds and control over the distribution of surplus (through dividends and experience-rating credits) they may recoup, at least to some extent, losses experienced by reason of having charged rates that prove to be too low. Costs are not guaranteed, although in the case of group or individual level-premium forms or some "permanent" forms, premium rates (which usually include substantial margins) are established for each employee

[4] The best financing medium for a particular pension plan depends on many factors. No vehicle is "best" for all plans. For a discussion of the subject, see Wendell Milliman, "The Controversy of Insured versus Trusteed Pension Plans," *The Journal of the American Society of Chartered Life Underwriters,* winter, 1956.

already covered but are subject to revision for new participants and for increases in benefits for old participants.

Investments and Interest Rates. The insurer, through its pooling of a large volume of income in various investments, obtains a desirable diversification of its investments. Life-insurance companies traditionally have invested quite heavily in mortgages, a form of investment which has, in general, provided a rather good rate of return after expenses. Because of some state laws affecting trusts and because of the expense and facilities required to administer mortgage loans, trust companies tend to utilize mortgages to only a limited degree as investments for pension trust funds.

Moreover, instances have been cited where trustees, by reason of the adoption of extremely conservative investment programs, or, on the other extreme, too speculative programs, have not obtained as high rates of investment return as have insurers, even allowing for the tax advantages of the trusts.

A fairly low rate of interest is usually guaranteed by the insurer.

Mortality. Under a group annuity the mortality of active and retired participants is pooled to some degree. If exceptionally low mortality is experienced, the amount of consideration may prove inadequate, in which circumstances other group annuities may be called upon to cover the losses which arise on a particular case, a device that is not available in trusteed plans. This, however, is an important factor only when a group annuity terminates, since otherwise, through establishing a contingency fund or raising future considerations, the insurer will usually arrange for each individual case to be self-supporting as regards costs resulting from low mortality, as well as in other respects. Of course, favorable mortality will be ultimately reflected in the dividends or experience-rating factors.

Administrative Facilities. Insurers have specific agencies for handling all phases of pension-plan management. They can provide the actuarial, legal, and financial services required, and they can handle most of the detail involved in record keeping and payment of benefits. Their nationwide facilities for these services help them keep in touch with retired employees or those who leave employment with vested deferred benefits. Partly because of their nationwide agency systems and their institutional advertising, as well as their experience in the somewhat related group-insurance field, they may be able to aid the employer in getting favorable response to an employee-welfare program. Some employees prefer to receive their retirement benefits from an insurer.

If a plan terminates, the insurer is usually in a better position than a trustee to wind it up. Mortality and other risks may be pooled with other cases, so that the last pension payment to the last surviving annuitant will practically always be met. For this reason when a plan financed by a trust fund is to be terminated, the amounts remaining in the fund are frequently applied to purchase deferred annuities from an insurer.

Expenses. Although state premium taxes, if any, and federal taxes are required to be paid, other insurer expenses compare favorably with those arising under trusteed plans, where separate fees are generally incurred for legal, actuarial, and investment-management expenses. These expenses are included in the premiums charged by the insurer, and excess expense allowances will be returned as dividends or experience credits.

An additional factor is the provision under insured plans for providing for all future expenses before the commencement of benefit payments. Thus, if a plan terminates, the employer is not subject to continuing insurer costs for the benefits already commenced or represented by deferred annuities. Such future expenses are usually charged before, or at the time, an employee retires.

Flexibility. Insured mediums, particularly some of the newer deposit-administration group-annuity forms, afford an employer a considerable amount of flexibility in designing and financing a plan.

CURRENT SITUATION

The volume of pension plans financed by group-insured methods has increased steadily since the first group-annuity contract was issued in 1921. Table 8-1 shows this growth since 1940. Regular group annuities doubled in the 5-year period from the end of 1940 to the end of 1945, when pension plans in general were greatly stimulated by the tax advantages permitted by the Revenue Act of 1942 and by the wage- and salary-stabilization controls during World War II. Through

TABLE 8-1. GROWTH OF REGULAR GROUP ANNUITIES AND
DEPOSIT-ADMINISTRATION PLANS

End of year	Regular group annuities	Deposit-administration plans	Per cent deposit administration
1940: Number of plans	770	20	2.5
Persons covered	575,000	65,000	10.2
1945: Number of plans	1,580	20	1.3
Persons covered	1,155,000	65,000	5.3
1950: Number of plans	2,460	160	6.1
Persons covered	1,950,000	275,000	12.4
1955: Number of plans	3,760	990	20.8
Persons covered	2,410,000	950,000	28.3
1956: Number of plans	4,160	1,160	21.8
Persons covered	2,495,000	1,115,000	30.9

SOURCE: "1957 Life Insurance Fact Book," Institute of Life Insurance, New York, p. 32.

1955 the business more than doubled again. Even more rapid growth shows up in the deposit-administration type of group-annuity contract. This type of contract was not much used up to 1945 but since then has spurted forward so that at the end of 1956 more than 30 per cent of the group-annuity coverage was of this form. Some of this deposit-administration business has been the result of changeovers from the paid-up type, paralleling another trend of change in whole or in part from the older form to trust-fund financing. Since it offers some of the features of the trust-fund method, the deposit-administration type has frequently been used in lieu of the trust fund where employers wished to continue certain features inherent in the insured medium without the rigidities of the paid-up group annuity.

The most recent development in the group-annuity field lies in this greater use of the more flexible deposit-administration method, with marked current activity in that type of deposit-administration (immediate-participation) plan that reflects gains and losses more promptly than through the normal processes of insurance-company dividends or rate credits.

During 1956 insurance companies reported a total of $990,000,000 in group-annuity premiums, in comparison with premium income of $927,000,000 for group life insurance and $1,382,000,000 for all other forms of group insurance (mainly accident and health). The premiums paid under group-annuity contracts amounted to between one-fourth and one-third of the premium income of the entire group business of insurance companies, although they are considerably less than the contributions made by employers currently under pension plans financed through trust funds.

Variable Annuities. Another development that may soon be adapted to the group-annuity business is that of *variable annuities*.[5] These annuities are based on a special segregated portfolio of equity investments held by the insurer, the amount of each payment under the annuity varying according to the investment value of this portfolio, although the mortality and expense experience would probably be handled in a separate account. The idea is now spreading to some of the larger insurers (although several other companies oppose the principle rather strongly).[6] The variable annuity will no doubt be available both in the individual-contract form for retail marketing and in the group-annuity form for use under insured pension plans. Combinations of fixed-dollar-annuity amounts and variable-annuity amounts will probably be permitted (or required) so that an employer's retirement plan will be balanced and so that the annuitant may have the advantages of both a fixed annuity and a variable annuity. The variable annuity is an attempt to reflect changes in the cost of living, on the theory that the variations in the market value of equity investments will bear a reasonably close relationship to them.

Split Funding. Still another development in the group-annuity field observed with increasing frequency is *split funding*,[7] or funding of an

[5] See also Chap. 9.

[6] Some states require special legislation to permit life-insurance companies to write variable annuities. Bills for this purpose have been introduced in several states but have failed to pass (as of 1958).

[7] See also Chap. 9.

annuity plan partly by a trust fund and partly by a group-annuity contract of one of the forms discussed above. Under one form of split funding, adequate funds may be withdrawn from the trust at retirement and turned over to the insurer, which, when added to the amounts already accumulated on the retiring employee's behalf in the group-annuity plan, will provide for his full annuity benefit from the insurer.

CHAPTER 9

Other Financing Mediums

INDIVIDUAL-INSURANCE-ANNUITY CONTRACTS

The Problem of the Small Concern. The small organization is somewhat restricted in establishing a formal pension plan to assist in retiring its employees. The requirement imposed by insurers or the insurance statutes of certain states that a minimum number of employees (in some states 50, in others 25, but in some only 10) must be covered under an insured group-retirement program may prevent some small concerns from using group plans. The satisfactory operation of most types of trust-fund pension plans is also more firmly grounded on the participation of a considerable number of employees.[1]

The small concern is also restricted in its opportunities to assist in providing an employee-welfare program including life insurance of a type customary for larger corporations. Group-life-insurance underwriting rules also require a minimum number of employees to be covered. While many small concerns with fewer employees than the minimum number required for group coverage may purchase life insurance on a wholesale basis, for many small concerns the only practical arrangement for providing life insurance to employees is on an individual-contract basis.

It is at least as important from the standpoint of efficient operation for the small concern as for the large corporation to replace superannuated employees with younger ones. The small concern will be at

[1] With suitable safeguards a trust-fund plan is appropriate for even a very small group, and some insurers do provide group-annuity coverage on very small groups.

a distinct disadvantage in attracting suitable employees if it cannot provide welfare benefits comparable to those offered by employers that qualify for, and maintain, regular group insurance and group-annuity or trust-fund retirement plans.

Many small concerns in recent years have met this need by the purchase for each participating employee of a life-insurance or annuity contract of the type regularly issued by the insurer to individuals. The individual contracts used are those which provide for maturity at a predetermined retirement age and for the payment of a life annuity as the main and automatic settlement at maturity. The individual contracts thus purchased in establishing an employee pension plan are usually placed in trust rather than being held by the employer or handed over to the insured employee. In this way, the employer, through the trustee, can maintain protective controls over his contributions and incorporate many of the features of a combined group-life-insurance and employee-retirement plan. The establishment of the trust has usually been a necessary prerequisite to obtaining a tax deduction for the employer's contributions.

The individual method has effectively extended pensions to employees of small businesses. The Institute of Life Insurance has reported recently (end of 1956) that about 13,600 plans utilizing individual contracts cover about 505,000 employees, an average of about 40 per plan.

It should not be concluded that pension trusts on the basis of individual contracts are necessarily inappropriate for large organizations, although it can generally be demonstrated that they involve higher costs, are less flexible, and are administratively more awkward than are bulk methods. A number of large corporations that installed pension plans some years ago adopted the individual method for their salaried employees or for such salaried employees as earned over, say, $3,000 per year. Some of these companies continue to find the individual-contract pension trust suitable for their needs, but many have introduced a bulk method of funding in order to effect economies and to overcome the failure of this type of arrangement to meet their particular pension problems.

The Individual-annuity Contract. An employer can purchase and contribute toward a separate annuity contract for each individual he employs who satisfies the conditions for eligibility which he establishes. Any of the types of individual-deferred-annuity contracts discussed in Chapter 3 would suffice for this purpose, except in the case of those individuals who have attained or are near retirement age at the time the plan is installed. For these older employees the single-premium immediate-life annuity or deferred annuity with premiums until retirement would be suitable to the extent permitted under the restrictions imposed by the government as regards tax deductions for this type of arrangement.[2]

The annual-premium form of contract is generally used where a retirement plan is based on individual contracts. This form calls for annual contributions of level amount from the time an employee is first covered until he retires. For a person aged thirty-five at the inception of the retirement plan, a level amount is deposited with the insurer each year for 30 years if retirement is scheduled for sixty-five, and at sixty-five the accumulation of these amounts will provide the prearranged annuity during retirement (this assumes that his salary remains unchanged during the interval; with each increase in salary calling for an increase in benefit, an additional level premium is normally required).

The Insurance-annuity Contract.[3] The insurance-annuity contract is an endowment-insurance contract maturing at a predetermined normal retirement age. In its customary form, as used in retirement programs, it has three principal characteristics that distinguish it from other forms of endowment contracts.

1. The unit of the contract is in terms of the amount of monthly annuity income provided during the lifetime of the insured subsequent to its maturity date (i.e., during the insured's period of retirement). The basic unit of pension is usually $10 per month (sometimes $5 or other amount), the contract providing a life annuity with payments guaranteed for a specified number of years, usually 10, regardless of whether the insured survives to receive the income for the whole of the guarantee period. One variation is the *installment-refund an-*

[2] See Chap. 5.

[3] Different insurers give this contract different names, e.g., *insurance annuity, income endowment,* and *retirement income.* The term *insurance annuity* will be used here.

nuity (sometimes called *guaranteed-minimum-return annuity*), which makes provision for monthly income to continue until at least the maturity value has been returned. For example, if the face amount of insurance just before retirement was $1,650 and $10 a month had been paid for 32 months up to the death of the employee, the $10 a month would be continued to a beneficiary for 165 − 32 = 133 additional months.

2. Before maturity the amount of life insurance per $10 of monthly income is a level amount, frequently $1,000, over a number of years following issuance of the policy, and it is equal to the cash-surrender value (as stated in the contract) for those later years preceding maturity of the contract when this value is in excess of the level amount of insurance. The number of years during which the death benefit is precisely $1,000 depends mainly on

    a. The age of the insured at the time the policy is issued

    b. The age fixed by the plan as normal retirement date

    c. The sex of the insured

    d. The underlying mortality and interest tables on which the benefits (including the cash-surrender value) are calculated

3. While insurance-annuity contracts generally make provision for optional election of any of the customary methods of payment at maturity, one form of settlement, usually the life annuity with a specified term certain, is designated as the automatic form, on the basis of which proceeds will be disbursed if no other method is elected.

The Retirement-annuity Contract. Since there is a substantial amount of pure insurance under an individual-insurance-annuity contract, particularly in the early years of coverage, the employee must meet certain standards of insurability. To be insurable the insurer must be satisfied that the employee is free from certain diseases, has no serious physical shortcomings, has had a favorable medical history, and is employed in a nonhazardous occupation. If he fails to meet these requirements, the insurer may not accept him at standard premium rates. Many insurers offer substandard insurance-annuity contracts for those employees who, while not meeting all the standard requirements, may be accepted at a somewhat higher premium rate. More and more of these contracts are being written by insurers on a nonmedical basis up to some stipulated limit of insurance.

It would be unfair to deny some of the employees the benefits of a retirement plan merely because they are not insurable. Consequently, most insurers selling individual-contract pension plans make available an individual-retirement-deferred-annuity contract for uninsurable employees or for the part of such an employee's coverage in excess of the nonmedical limit. Some insurers do not offer the retirement-annuity contract except where it is used to round out or complete a pension program based primarily on insurance-annuity contracts. Others offer the retirement annuity as the basic contract for the plan, with individual election of the inclusion of insurance (under an insurance-annuity contract) by the employee at his expense for the added cost. There is no good reason why a retirement plan should not be built entirely around such individual-retirement-deferred-annuity contracts, and while most individual-contract plans provide insurance-annuity contracts to insurable participants and restrict the uninsurable employees to the retirement-annuity form, lack of insurability is not usually a condition of eligibility for this latter contract. Allowing the form to be optional with the employee may produce a slight selection against the insurer, but the difference in cost is so little that the good lives will come in anyway and the bad will be caught by examination.

Most individual-contract pension plans have used the insurance-annuity contract as the primary annuity vehicle because the extra advantages of the insurance element could be procured for little extra cost.

Provisions of Individual Contracts. Many of the provisions which appear in individual contracts (that is, insurance-annuity and retirement-annuity forms) are required by state laws, and an insurer must satisfy not only the standard-provision laws of the state in which it is domiciled but also the laws of every state in which it does business. While there is some lack of uniformity in the requirements of the various states, the insurer usually conforms to the insurance laws of the strictest state in which it does business. Otherwise it would have to issue differing policies in different states, which would prove very troublesome administratively.[4]

---

[4] Certain states have unusual requirements that cause an insurer to issue special policies or special riders in those states.

The two principal provisions in a life-insurance contract are the *insuring clause* and the *consideration* or *premium clause*. These clauses customarily appear on the first page of the policy and are intended to give clearly the information most frequently sought in any insurance contract. This information includes:

1. The name of the insured

2. The amount of insurance and/or annuity payments

3. The contingencies upon the happening of which the insurance (or the annuity) payments will be made, how they will be made, and to whom they will be made

4. The amount of the premium, the dates upon which premiums will be paid, and the period of years over which they will be paid

The general provisions or terms of a life-insurance contract have been discussed in various texts on life insurance.[5] Retirement forms of contracts used in an employee pension plan usually include such general provisions.

General Provisions of Insurance-annuity and Retirement-annuity Contracts. Many of the general provisions of the retirement-annuity contract are similar to the corresponding provisions of the insurance-annuity contract. But there are certain areas where they differ, principally as explained in the following paragraphs.

1. *Cash-surrender Values.* The cash-surrender value of an insurance-annuity contract is usually derived by means of a formula which somewhat resembles the formula for the reserve, except that it recognizes more accurately the incidence and amount of expense. The minimum cash-surrender value—or, as is more usually specified, the maximum expense allowance that may be used in the cash-surrender-value formula—is almost always established by state law. Because commissions and other expenses are heaviest in the early contract years, it is customary to amortize the excess initial expense over a period of years rather than to try to recoup the entire amount immediately. Although it is permissible to amortize initial expenses over the entire premium-paying period, many insurers, particularly those using less than the maximum legal-expense allowance, amortize initial expenses over a shorter period, after which the cash-surrender value may be equal to

---

[5] See, for example, Joseph B. Maclean, "Life Insurance," 8th ed., McGraw-Hill Book Company, Inc., New York, 1957.

the full reserve. Under many insurance-annuity contracts the cash value reaches the full reserve very rapidly.

When applied to a retirement-annuity contract, the cash-surrender-value formula develops minimum values which during the years before annuity payments begin are somewhat less than the amount of premiums paid. As a result, some insurers provide values which are in the early years somewhat lower than the aggregate premiums paid but become greater than the aggregate premiums after a period of years during which the excess initial expenses are amortized.

2. *Death Benefits.* Under the retirement-annuity contract, the death benefit is usually a return of the premiums paid before death, or the cash value if greater.

Table 9-1 compares typical death benefits and cash-surrender values under the two types of contracts.

In Table 9-1 the retirement annuity provides for a death benefit that is never less than the total amount of premiums paid.

3. *Maturity Values.* Both the insurance-annuity contract and the retirement-annuity contract may provide the same benefits during the retirement period and, if so, would normally call for the same maturity value. The maturity values of the two contracts (at attainment of the specified retirement age) have often differed in the past mainly because of the different interest assumptions for the two forms (it requires a greater maturity value to provide $10 a month under the retirement-annuity contract if a lower interest rate is assumed for the annuity period).

4. *Extended-term Insurance.* Extended-term insurance upon cessation of payment of premiums continues the face amount of insurance for such period as the cash-surrender value will provide. It is applicable only under the insurance-annuity contract, since there is no insurance to continue under the retirement annuity.

5. *Paid-up Insurance.* Under the insurance-annuity contract the amount of paid-up-insurance annuity is determined by using the cash-surrender value as the net single premium for the attained age on the same interest and mortality assumptions as were used in calculating the annual premiums for the contract. In the case of the retirement-annuity contract no mortality cost (except possibly a small amount because of expenses paid) is incurred before maturity, and hence, upon

TABLE 9-1. ILLUSTRATIVE DEATH BENEFITS AND CASH-SURRENDER VALUES PER
$100 ANNUAL PREMIUM; INSURANCE ANNUITY AT AGE SIXTY-FIVE AND
RETIREMENT ANNUITY AT AGE SIXTY-FIVE
(Age at issue thirty-five—male)

Year	Insurance-annuity contract		Retirement-annuity contract	
	Death benefit during year	Cash-surrender value at end of year	Death benefit during year	Cash-surrender value at end of year
1	$2,027	$ 0	$ 100	$ 51
2	2,027	74	200	142
3	2,027	153	300	234
5	2,027	315	500	426
10	2,027	757	1,000	944
15	2,027	1,261	1,523	1,523
20	2,027	1,850	2,170	2,170
25	2,538	2,538	2,894	2,894
30	3,318	3,318 (maturity value)	3,702	3,702 (maturity value)
Monthly benefit at retirement (10 years and life thereafter)	$20.27		$22.62	

default in payment of premiums, the reduced paid-up amount at maturity (the specified retirement age) would be whatever the cash-surrender value at the time of default, accumulated at interest over the deferred period until maturity, would produce as a retirement benefit.

6. *Minimum Payments.* If the net proceeds of a contract would provide payments of less than $10 per quarter, settlement is usually made not under an income settlement but in one sum. This procedure would be applicable, for example, if the employee discontinued the

contract upon termination of employment before the time that its value was adequate to provide at least a $10-per-quarter annuity.

Ownership of Contract by Trustee. While both the application for the retirement form of contract (insurance annuity or retirement annuity) and the contract itself designate the individual employee as the insured, in a pension plan where the services of a trustee are utilized it is customary to vest ownership of the contract in the trustee. This may be done by either of the following procedures:

1. Using the ownership form of contract which directly designates the trustee as owner (the employee should be named as insured)

2. Amending the contract (or the application for the contract) with a rider which states that the trustee shall be the complete and absolute owner

Normally, all incidents of ownership are delegated to the trustee except the right to change or revoke any designation of beneficiaries.

Underwriting Requirements. It has been pointed out that the retirement-annuity contract has in recent years been reserved for employees who could not satisfy the underwriting criteria for the insurance-annuity contract. In many cases the retirement-annuity contract is the only one available for the older employees. Some insurers will issue insurance-annuity policies only up to and including age sixty, while issuing the retirement-annuity policy up to age sixty-four. Other insurers have required a premium-paying period of at least 10 years, but this practice is becoming less common.

The maximum amounts for which insurance-annuity contracts will be written under a retirement plan usually follow the schedule that is used by the life-insurance company for other similar forms of life insurance. These amounts are related to the age of the employee and usually increase up to about age-at-issue thirty, remain stationary for ages-at-issue thirty to forty-five, say, and thereafter decrease gradually until, at age-at-issue sixty, the maximum amounts are perhaps only one-half of those which would be granted at the median ages. The maximum amounts are generally less for females than for males.

Very large amounts of insurance may be called for by an individual-contract pension plan. Consider an executive earning $50,000 per year. If he is entitled to a pension of $1,500 a month, then under some pension plans utilizing these contracts there would have to be pur chased for him an insurance-annuity contract with a face amount of $150,000. If this amount of insurance exceeded the company's limits, reinsurance might be secured or appropriate adjustments made, such as writing the balance on the retirement-annuity form.

Life-insurance companies that offer both group-annuity contracts and pension plans based on individual contracts frequently restrict the use of the insurance-annuity and retirement-annuity contracts to plans that have few eligible employees, say, not more than 50, 100, or 200. For larger cases such insurers may offer the group-annuity form only.

While a medical examination is required (above any nonmedical limit) for the purchase of the insurance-annuity contract, no such examination is specified for the retirement-annuity contract unless the waiver-of-premium disability provision is included.

Determination of Benefit. It is rather awkward under the individual-contract method to make adjustments of retirement benefits necessitated by changes in employee earnings. If the intention is to provide a 1 per cent benefit at age sixty-five on salary in excess of $4,200, the employee aged thirty-five who is earning $7,000 at the inception of the plan would be entitled to a benefit of $0.01 \times (7,000 - 4,200) \times 30 =$ $840 per year, or $70 per month. After he has earned $7,000 a year for 5 years, suppose that he receives an increase in pay of $500 a year. This would entitle him to an increase in pension of $0.01 \times 500 \times 25 =$ $125 per year, or $10.42 per month. The trustee or employer would then purchase for this employee at the time of his raise in salary a second contract, if he is still insurable, providing the increase of $10.42 monthly annuity. Insurance of $7,000 and $1,042, respectively, will be included if the plan provides for insurance and the employee is insurable or within the nonmedical limit. More frequently the pension benefit (and insurance, if any) is determined by a schedule of salary groupings.[6] In such cases increases in earnings must be sufficient to carry employees into higher salary brackets before they are granted increases in pension benefits.

A person will have many separate contracts made on his behalf if he receives numerous salary increases. In order to avoid having to

[6] See p. 60.

issue many small policies, one for each raise in salary that an employee receives, most insurers impose a requirement regarding the minimum size of policy. Usually this has been $1,000 face amount, i.e., with $10-per-month annuity; sometimes the unit is $500 and $5. These minimums are imposed to avoid the undue expense to which the insurer would be put if it were necessary to issue a new policy each time an employee received a small raise in pay. Certain expenses, such as those for issuing the policy and setting up the records, are the same for a $100 policy (if such were issued) as for a $10,000 policy. If the unit cost were taken out of the premium for a $100 policy, there might be little premium left, but when it comes out of the premium for a $10,000 policy, the premium will be little affected. If the employee above received a $200 a year raise at age forty-one, he would be entitled to $0.01 \times 200 \times 24 = \$48$ of additional yearly retirement annuity, or $4 of monthly annuity, which would probably not satisfy the minimum contract requirements of the insurer. He would, therefore, be forced to forgo this additional benefit until he later received further increments to his salary to bring the increased retirement benefit up to the $10 or $5 mark.

These comments on effecting increases in benefits apply to other benefit formulas. Consider the percentage-of-pay formula,[7] say, 20 per cent on the first $4,200 of earnings plus 40 per cent on the excess. Here, too, a salary increase means application must be made for new contracts and medical examinations may be required. Sometimes a moving-average salary, say for the last 5 preceding years, is used to stabilize the trend, or salary classes are made wider so that substantial increases of salary are needed to bring a participant into a new class.

Under a straight percentage-of-pay formula, if the increases in salary continue up to retirement date, the pension will be related directly to the employee's final salary. This arrangement may be of questionable merit. It could favor those who receive substantial raises in the last year of their employment and might result in unfair discrimination since it would allow an employer to give a favored employee a substantial raise in salary for the year immediately preceding retirement in order to provide a correspondingly increased pension. Further-

[7] See Chap. 3.

more, it may be in conflict with the requirements of the Internal Revenue Service.

In many plans the retirement benefit is based on the average salary of the individual over the 5- or 10-year consecutive period of greatest earnings, the 5- or 10-year period immediately preceding retirement, or some other basis that will help stabilize the amount of the pension and yet reflect in the pension benefit the level of earnings near retirement. The use of some such arrangement to relate pension benefits to the average salary enjoyed during an interval near retirement, rather than the career-average salary, is increasing in popularity. Disregard of any salary increases received subsequent to a certain age, such as sixty, is an alternative method that avoids too many, or too sudden, adjustments in ultimate benefits.

Should an increase in benefit be purchased immediately following a salary increase, at the end of the fiscal year, or at some other specified time? Generally the new purchases are made all at one time each year, and frequently the date is the anniversary date of the plan. In such cases it is customary for the insurance age of the employee to be taken as his nearest age at the anniversary date, and usually he must meet the medical requirements for each increase. Delaying the purchase of additional benefit until the anniversary may appear unfair in case the employee should die before that time, since otherwise if he were insurable he could have obtained additional life insurance.

The question of how to handle a decrease in earnings is somewhat more troublesome. Many plans provide that reduction in salary must stand for 2 or 3 years before it will cause a decrease in benefit and therefore in premium. Upon such a decrease a portion of the cash-surrender value will be released, either in the form of a cash value or a paid-up benefit or as a credit toward future premiums.

Guaranteed Issue. Many insurers will agree to issue without medical examination an amount of life insurance per participant up to a stated maximum, such as $15,000 or $25,000, under an individual-insurance-annuity-contract pension trust. Sometimes this maximum is related to the average amount of insurance, such as three times the average but not in excess of $25,000. Sometimes the maximum guaranteed issue is based on the number of lives covered, e.g., $10,000 for 10 to 14 lives, $15,000 for 15 to 24 lives, and $25,000 for 25 to 50 lives.

Similar underwriting procedures are also followed when the pension trust is financed as a combination plan, utilizing, for example, ordinary-life contracts supplemented by an auxiliary fund.[8]

In view of the guarantee and the period over which it may be operating (e.g., as much as 35 years where the participant is age thirty at the time of entry into the plan) the insurer, with a view to providing for potential losses on the higher amounts of the guaranteed issue, may impose special conditions, such as reducing the regular commission scale or treating guaranteed-issue contracts as a separate dividend class.[9]

General. One of the most frequently heard criticisms of the use of the individual-insurance-annuity type of contract for medium or large groups of employees is directed at the high expense rates. The compensation of life-insurance agents for the sale of individual insurance contracts quite properly takes into account the fact that only a modest percentage of sale interviews results in the placing of contracts. To attract and hold an agency force it is necessary to pay out as commissions a substantial proportion of the first year's premiums; smaller, but sizable, commissions are normally payable thereafter for a period of 9 years or more. When an agent develops a pension case involving the placing of a large number of individual contracts under a pension trust, he may be called upon to perform considerably more work than would be required in the selling of a single contract, but the effort expended hardly justifies the aggregate commissions received on the contracts used for the pension trust. These commissions, determined on the individual-contract basis, are nevertheless usually paid on such a case.[10] The high initial expenses charged under the individual contracts are accentuated where there are included under the pension

---

[8] See p. 185.

[9] In states with antidiscrimination laws forbidding differing dividend treatment to holders of the same class of insurance contracts, a special contract form, such as a life-paid-up-at-age-eighty-six contract, is sometimes written to pension trusts financed under a combination plan.

[10] In recent years some insurers have brought out special forms of insurance-annuity contracts designed for use under a pension trust. These contracts call for lower commission and higher cash-surrender values than do the regular insurance-annuity contracts.

trust many employees who remain with the employer only a short period of time after being covered under the plan. The credits arising from the terminations of these employees may be only a small portion of the amount contributed on their behalf. Although life-insurance coverage has been enjoyed in the interim, the amount of premium expended to little real purpose, from the employer's point of view, may be impressive.

Sometimes questions have arisen between the home offices of insurers issuing the policies and the agents or brokers of record about who should perform certain of the administrative functions required under any pension plan. In a few cases the agents or brokers have seemingly lost interest once the relatively high commissions of the early years of the plan had been paid, and the employer has had to look elsewhere for the technical assistance which he expected to receive from the insurance agent.

The practice of creating a trust to act as holder of the insurance contracts also introduces an item of expense. This cost is rarely found in group-insurance-annuity plans. In a trust-fund plan the trustee's fees are charged primarily for performing the essential function of investing the funds held for pension purposes. In the strictly individual-contract pension trust, however, the trustee usually has little responsibility for investments since the contributions that he receives are normally transmitted to the insurer, and his functions are primarily administrative.

A rather awkward problem which has arisen in the case of many individual-contract pension trusts that commenced some years back is a direct result of inflation. An employer, cognizant of the OASI benefits which were originally limited to the first $3,000 of annual salary (and perhaps he was restricted in giving direct salary increases through the operation of salary stabilization during World War II), wished to furnish retirement or death benefits through an individual-contract pension trust. He therefore imposed as an eligibility condition that all employees to be covered must be salaried and earn at least $3,000. The group meeting these conditions was initially small, and consequently the outlay for the pension plan was kept within reasonable limits. As salaries increased, however (even under salary stabilization), many additional employees became eligible for the benefits of the plan by earning salaries in excess of the minimum. A very considerable increase in the number of covered employees took place (including perhaps many female clerical employees, among whom there was a high rate of turnover), with mounting costs. Furthermore, the inherent inflexibility of the individual-contract arrangement, with life insurance being granted to many of these employees who had little need for large amounts of insurance, and the rigid cost requirements of the plan resulted in its becoming a burden in many instances.

When a large number of employees is covered, the administration of an individual-contract plan raises many problems: accounting procedures are involved; medical evidence with each raise in pay is often required, and even under guaranteed-issue arrangements medical examinations are required once the maximum nonmedical amount has been passed; several contracts per employee are usually purchased; and these contracts often have different provisions and rate bases. Where, because of its small size (or for other reasons), an organization does not qualify for bulk treatment, the individual-contract pension trust may be a satisfactory means of providing retirement benefits to employees, especially if insurance protection for the covered employees is also desired. Many people feel that because of the administrative complexity and to some extent the cost of the plan it is not a suitable medium for providing pension benefits to larger groups of employees.

GROUP LIFE INSURANCE AND THE GROUP-INSURANCE ANNUITY

Group Life Insurance. Group life insurance is generally one of the elements in an employee-welfare program. Through it is made available, during an employee's working years, life insurance in an amount that is usually related to his earnings. In many cases the intent is to provide the employee's dependents with 1 to 2 years' earnings upon his death in order to afford financial assistance during the difficult period of readjustment that follows the loss of the breadwinner.

For many years group life insurance was issued almost solely on the 1-year-renewable-term plan. Under this plan, as the employee grows older, the premium rate per $1,000 increases each year. In order to remove the necessity of the employee's being called upon to bear continuously increasing costs, in most cases the employee and the employer contribute jointly to the cost of the insurance, the employee's contribution per unit of coverage remaining constant from year to year, while the employer pays the balance of the premium. For example, if the age distribution and the amounts of insurance in effect at the various ages are such that the average monthly premium rate for the group is 95 cents, the employee will pay 50 or 60 cents, and the employer will contribute 35 or 45 cents per month for each $1,000 of group life insurance in force. Although the employer will pay a gradually increasing amount of premium each year for each individual employee, this does not mean that his aggregate contribution will necessarily increase correspondingly, because older employees who die, terminate employment, or retire may be replaced by younger employees for whom lower 1-year-term premiums are charged.

One of the benefits always granted with group life insurance is the privilege of converting the insurance following termination of employment before normal retirement date (regardless of the condition of health of the employee at that time) to individual insurance on one of the permanent forms issued by the insurer in an amount not greater than that which was effective under the group plan. Since 1-year term insurance does not provide cash or other surrender values, the terminating employee who converts his group life insurance must pay the premium rate on the converted insurance that is applicable to his attained age. Many participants in group-life-insurance plans have been seriously disappointed upon learning the magnitude of the annual premium that they would be required to pay if they converted their insurance at any advanced age.

Group Permanent Life Insurance. The terminating employee may compare the premium on the converted insurance with what he would be paying had he originally been insured under the same type of contract on the level-premium basis from the age when he was first insured under the group plan. If, associated with his discontinuance of employment, there is a diminution of income, the substantially increased premium rate on the converted insurance is likely to preclude the carrying of this insurance. In practice only a very small percentage convert, and those who do are usually substandard lives, as evidenced by the high death rate among converting employees.

Accordingly, a need was felt for a group-life-insurance program where the employee could build up an equity during his working years similar to the equity he would have accumulated under one of the permanent forms of individual life insurance. *Group permanent life insurance* was developed to permit the accumulation of such equities. The cost per unit of this insurance issued at a level-premium rate is necessarily considerably greater than that charged per unit of group life insurance issued at the same age on the 1-year-renewable-term plan.

The word *permanent* here signifies a basic plan of life insurance other than term. Examples of permanent contracts are the ordinary-life, limited-payment-life, endowment, and insurance-annuity types. Under these contracts and others customarily purchased by individuals, the payment of level premiums is usual. Similarly, level premiums are contemplated under a group-permanent plan.

As in many other instances, the meaning of the terms used has become confused. The expression *group permanent* has also been used to signify another somewhat different type of group-insurance plan which presupposes the purchase of an amount of paid-up life insurance each year, this amount frequently being what can be purchased by the employee's contribution (the successive amounts purchased diminish each year as the employee grows older, if his contributions remain constant). This type of group life insurance is frequently called *group life paid-up insurance*. The cumulative total of these paid-up portions increases each year. The employer contributes for each employee each year until his retirement an amount sufficient to provide term insurance equal to the desired total coverage less the accumulated amount. Consequently the amount of term insurance provided by the employer's contributions will decrease correspondingly. When the employee discontinues employment, he will have a certain amount of fully paid-up life insurance, which will continue in effect during the remainder of his lifetime without payment of additional premiums. If he wishes to continue the full amount of the coverage which he had under the group plan, he will need to convert only the difference between the full amount and the amount of his paid-up life insurance. If he feels that he does not need the insurance, he can surrender the paid-up insurance for its cash value or he can use the equity to provide an immediate or deferred life annuity.

In order to avoid decreasing amounts of paid-up insurance per year as the employee grows older, another form of group permanent life insurance provides for the purchase of a fixed amount of paid-up insurance each year. Each paid-up unit is purchased with a single premium, which increases with age. If the employee's contribution remains fixed, the employer's portion of the contributions will increase to absorb the increasing cost. Because of the costliness (and also possible tax disadvantages) of this permanent form of group life insurance, the paid-up benefit provided each year is usually kept fairly small, and in order that a reasonable total of insurance may be provided for the employees, it is supplemented by additional group life insurance on the 1-year-term plan. Still another form provides for application of the employee's contribution as if it were a level annual premium instead of a single premium. This provides more insurance and less make-up by the employer, but it does not produce as much paid-up value for the employee who terminates or retires as does the single-premium method.

The Group-insurance-annuity Plan. Other group-permanent-life-insurance plans have been devised primarily to provide retirement benefits. A group-permanent plan providing a pension to employees when they attain age sixty-five would be based on the insurance annuity at age sixty-five. The word *permanent* seems to be superfluous in connection with this type of plan, and hence it will be called the *group-insurance-annuity plan*. Level premiums (from both employee and employer) per unit of coverage are required from the time the employee comes under the plan until normal retirement date. The benefits provided are similar to those under individual-insurance-annuity contracts.

Group-insurance-annuity policies may be issued with relationships between monthly income and life insurance other than $10 and $1,000; $10 and $500, $10 and $1,500, or other combinations are sometimes used, depending on the extent to which it is desired to emphasize the insurance element.

Fundamentally, the group-insurance-annuity plan provides a means for combining in one contract retirement benefits for employees and substantial death benefits for their dependents. As in the case of a group annuity, the insurer issues a single master contract to the employer, and each covered employee receives a group certificate which outlines in simple form the benefits and conditions of coverage which are set out in more detail in the governing master contract.

Many provisions in the group-insurance-annuity contract used most frequently for retirement plans (benefits to commence at age sixty or at age sixty-five) are similar to the corresponding provisions in individual-life-insurance contracts.

Cash-surrender values, reduced paid-up insurance, and settlement options may be available when a terminating employee withdraws from the plan, in the same way as under an individual-insurance-annuity contract. Because of lower expense per unit of benefit than is the case with the individual-insurance-annuity contract, the early cash-surrender values are usually higher under the group-insurance-annuity plan.

Where the master contract provides for dividends or experience refunds, they will be declared in a manner somewhat analogous to dividends provided for in individual contracts. The primary difference is that dividends on the group coverage are not allocated with respect to each individual covered employee but, since they represent the entire group's experience, are credited en masse to the employer's account. Also, in accordance with group principles, the larger the group, the greater the extent to which its own experience will be recognized in the dividends declared. These dividends may reflect certain administrative savings accruing from the use of group principles, including reduced acquisition expenses. On the other hand, the adoption of group underwriting without the requirement of evidence of good health before becoming insured for amounts of insurance up to the indicated nonmedical maximum (which varies with the size of the group covered, the total amount of insurance, and other underwriting characteristics of the group) means that a somewhat higher rate of mortality may be expected under a group-insurance-annuity plan than under a comparable plan utilizing individual contracts with either a lower nonmedical limit or no nonmedical privilege. Such extra mortality may tend to diminish the group-plan dividends. This extra mortality is not great, however, since under a group plan, even with a substantial amount of nonmedical life insurance, there is no great likelihood of adverse selection as there is under individual contracts.

The greater use of bulk methods of administration, automatic increases (and decreases) in coverage, nonmedical requirements (up to certain limits), lower commissions, and reductions in certain other expenses all operate toward producing somewhat lower costs than are required under plans utilizing individual-insurance-annuity contracts.

Vesting. Part or all of the employer's value (that created by the employer's portion of the premiums) in the contract may be vested in the employee. Under a contributory plan, the terminating employee is always entitled to the equity arising out of his own contributions. The employee's vested benefit may be none, some, or all of the employer's value at the time of his discontinuance of employment, depending on the provisions of the plan.

Where vesting is provided, the discontinuing employee may be given the option of continuing the existing coverage under an individual contract providing equivalent benefits. Such an individual contract carries a premium based on his attained age and is for an amount not greater than his death benefit under the group plan less any paid-up-insurance-annuity element to which he may have become entitled under the group contract.

Should the discontinuing employee desire a form of life insurance that differs from that provided by the group-insurance-annuity plan, he may purchase any of the individual forms issued by the insurer, usually with the exception of term insurance. This permits him to utilize a form with a lower premium than that of the insurance annuity and is a valuable privilege in those cases where the financial condition of the employee and his insurance needs call for maintenance of maximum insurance protection without regard to retirement benefits. This conversion privilege is of particular value to the discontinuing employee who is uninsurable, since the right to convert is conferred without regard to his insurability.

Underwriting. Group-insurance-annuity underwriting rules generally combine certain features of group-annuity and of individual-contract underwriting.

The upper limit in amount of group life insurance is determined automatically by insurer rules, which establish a maximum amount according to the size of the group covered and the distribution of coverage. In the case of group-insurance-annuity plans the nonmedical limit is determined by a similar procedure, and all amounts of insurance up to this limit will be issued without the necessity of submitting proof of insurability, while the amounts of coverage in excess of this maximum will be issued only to participants who satisfy the underwriting requirements imposed by the insurer. In this way too great concentration of risk on a few individuals is avoided. Some insurers will allow a nonmedical limit for group-insurance-annuity plans above the maximum of other group-life-insurance forms for the same employees. The reason for this is that under the group-insurance-annuity plan substantial reserves are soon accumulated with corresponding reduction in the complementary amounts at risk (the difference between the death benefit payable and the amount of the reserve).

With respect to employees otherwise eligible for this insurance in excess of the nonmedical limit who fail to satisfy the insurability requirements, there is issued the appropriate amount of deferred benefit on the group-retirement-annuity form to furnish the full pension benefit called for by the plan.

Use of group methods would suggest that all employees should be covered if they are actively at work at the time they become eligible under the plan. If the plan is noncontributory, all employees of classes to which the plan applies will be covered. If the plan is contributory, employees who would otherwise qualify for nonmedical coverage may be required to show evidence of insurability unless they join within a stated interval following the time they first become eligible. If they then fail to pass the medical examination, they will either be denied benefits under the plan or be permitted to be covered only under an annuity form that does not provide life insurance.

Under the contributory plan a minimum number of employees is usually required, and participation by at least 75 per cent of eligible employees will be necessary before most insurers will issue a group-insurance-annuity policy.

An alternative way of securing adequate participation is to require that a minimum total of insurance must be applied for (but without too great concentration of insurance on a few employees) and that a minimum amount of pensions must be provided.

Changes in Amounts of Coverage. When a participant's earnings increase, he usually becomes entitled to an increase in the amount of his coverage. As is customary in bulk-insurance procedures, the benefits are commonly related to broad salary classes in order to avoid the necessity of making frequent minor adjustments to meet slight changes in earnings. When an employee passes from one salary class to the next (frequently recognized only once a year) his retirement benefit—and his contributions, if any—increase accordingly. Where an employee's earnings decrease sufficiently to place him in a lower salary class, one of the following rules may be applied: (1) continue the previous amount of coverage without change, (2) cancel a portion of the coverage so that the revised amount will fit the reduced earnings, or (3) proceed as in (2) but continue the existing coverage for a period of, say, 2 years before effecting a reduction, in order to prevent short-term fluctuations in benefits. Cancellation of a portion of the coverage results in the release of some of the reserves accumulated previously on his account, and the cash value of the coverage after the reduction has been made will be less than the prior cash value. Therefore, it will be necessary to determine how much of the released cash value the employee will be entitled to receive—either in cash or in paid-up value—which may be done by splitting the refund in proportion to the respective contributions of employer and employee or by some other equitable procedure.

Premium-rate Guarantees. In the matter of premium rates, the group-insurance-annuity contract is rather closely allied to individual contracts. The annual-premium rate for a benefit amount provided is guaranteed for the entire contract period for each employee on the rate basis stipulated at the time he is first covered for that benefit amount. If he terminates employment before retirement and elects to pay the premiums himself, the rate that he pays on the insurance issued is identical with that charged from the time he was first covered. The premium rate for an increase in the amount of insurance annuity or for coverage on new participants is that in effect at the time such insurance is issued. Insurers customarily guarantee that there will be no advance in premium for new participants entering the plan during the first 3 years (sometimes 5 years and occasionally longer) following the issuance of a group-insurance-annuity contract. Premium rates applicable to increases in coverage for employees already in the plan may be similarly guaranteed.

Administration. The administration required under a group-insurance-annuity plan is not greatly different from that required under a pension plan based on the corresponding individual-insurance-annuity contracts. There are certain advantages in the group method, however. Increases in benefits are made automatically, although passing a medical examination will be necessary if an employee's increase takes him beyond the nonmedical limit. Bulk computing and accounting devices may be utilized. Much work is avoided, such as interviewing employees singly, completing and signing individual applications for those eligible for new benefits or increases, arranging for medical examinations (except in a few cases), and issuing individual policies, both initially and in successive series as benefit increases or decreases take effect.

It is not usual to administer the group-insurance-annuity plan through a trustee since the employer is generally the contract holder. The employee receives a certificate which sets out the principal features of the contract but is not in itself a contract. If a trustee is used, his work is much reduced from that required for the individual-insurance-annuity plan; for example, he does not need to keep records of a large number of contracts, and his storage problem is reduced to the holding of one contract in lieu of a large number.

The master contract for this group-permanent form of insured plan is a long and complicated document. Its salient benefit features are contained in the certificate distributed to each participating employee.

In summary, the group-insurance-annuity plan combines into one package the features of group life insurance and group-retirement annuity, utilizes a level-premium-funding method, and gets away from both the step-rate techniques of 1-year term insurance and of the older form of group-annuity coverage. A natural consequence of the level-premium methods used under the group-insurance-annuity form is that paid-up values develop with respect to not only the deferred-annuity element but also the permanent-insurance element. Because of the high degree of advance funding required by this plan, its original costs are likely to be somewhat higher than the comparable initial costs of a combination of separate contracts for group 1-year term insurance and group annuities providing similar amounts of benefit (later the premiums are, of course, less). In spite of the many good features of the group-insurance-annuity plan, many still feel that for many employers, especially those whose turnover is likely to be high, the less costly techniques of the traditional methods will continue to be superior. Others claim that the traditional methods should be used for employees below a given age or length of service with a transition to the group-insurance-annuity plan after the probationary period has passed. Another variation sometimes adopted is to utilize the group-insurance annuity for employees earning above a given annual salary, such as $4,200 (where employee turnover is likely to be less), and the traditional bulk methods for the lower-paid group.

A serious problem is often encountered in the application of the group-insurance-annuity plan to the older lives at the start of the plan. The level-premium concept of group permanent insurance anticipates complete funding for any given individual by the time his normal retirement age is reached. This means heavy employer costs for employees near retirement age on the effective date of the plan. It also leaves unsolved the retirement problem for employees already above the plan's normal retirement age. Consequently, it is not unusual to confine the group-insurance-annuity arrangement to employees under a certain age, such as fifty-five, with a trust-fund method utilizing a spread-funding basis [11] applicable to employees who are above that age at the commencement of the plan. Another practice is to include older employees but to set their retirement dates some 5 to 10 years into the future; but this is not very satisfactory to either party with respect to employees already over age sixty-five.

THE COMBINATION PLAN, SPLIT FUNDING

In an effort to combine certain features of the insurance-annuity arrangement and of the trust fund, some pension plans have been constructed partly on the basis of one and partly on the basis of the other medium of financing. In such a *combination plan,* once the benefit

[11] See Chap. 7.

formula has been agreed on, the scale of insurance amounts for eligible employees is established—for example, 2 years' salary. Insurance is then provided through either individual contracts or a group-permanent contract—perhaps by use of the ordinary-life form, the life-paid-up-at-age-sixty-five form, or the endowment form maturing at age sixty-five. Under each of these forms there will be available at normal retirement date, say age sixty-five, an amount of cash which will be more under the endowment-at-age-sixty-five form than under the ordinary-life form. This cash at normal retirement age may be applied under the settlement-option provisions of the contract to provide a life annuity commencing at age sixty-five and continuing through life with, where provided in the plan, a 10-year or other certain period. The balance of the pension benefit not so provided through the insurance contract is made available from the trust fund, to which the employer contributes such predetermined amounts as are estimated as necessary to provide the residue of the pension. This residual pension may be paid directly from the trust, or an appropriate amount may be transferred from the trust to an insurer as a single premium to provide the balance of the pension under an individual-life-annuity contract. By *split funding* is usually meant a combination-plan arrangement utilizing a trust fund and some form of group-annuity contract concurrently as the financing mediums. It is, therefore, an attempt to combine some of the features of each method of bulk financing.

The higher rates of return that are available under certain forms of investment suitable for a trust fund but not permitted under state laws to any extent to insurers, such as common stocks, and the opportunities for capital gains in these investments have led some insurers to endorse the use of a trust fund utilizing common stocks to a substantial degree in connection with a group annuity. Since insurers invest heavily in mortgage loans with high interest rates, while mortgages are not so frequently found in trust-fund portfolios, the split-funding approach permits substantial flexibility in the selection of investments implementing the pension plan, especially where the fund is large.

An employer utilizing split funding may work out an arrangement with the insurer and trustee whereby some predetermined portion of his annual contributions will be paid to the insurer and the balance to the trust. If the plan calls for employee contributions, these contributions may be paid to the insurer, and the employer's contributions may be paid to the trust. At retirement either the insurer will pay one part of the pension benefit and the trust fund will pay the balance, or adequate funds may be transferred from the trust to the insurer as terminal funding to provide for payment of the entire pension benefit by the insurer.

The regular form of group-annuity contract could be utilized in this split-funding method, although one of the deposit-administration forms is perhaps generally more suitable.

THE VARIABLE ANNUITY

The conventional type of pension plan, whether funded through a trust or through an insurer, is often criticized on the grounds that it provides for the payment of a fixed-dollar amount of benefit and that it makes no provision for the observed loss in purchasing power of these dollar amounts over the years.

For example, an individual who retired in 1935 after 40 years of employment on $100-a-month pension would have seen that $100 reduce in purchasing power to $98 in 1940, $76 in 1945, $57 in 1950, and $51 in 1955, or a 50 per cent drop in purchasing power in 20 years. What the future holds no one knows, but there are authorities who believe that our economic system is now "replete with inflationary bias" and that a further erosion in the purchasing power of the dollar may be expected.

The above example highlights the plight of many pensioners who retired on what was considered to be an adequate pension at the time of retirement. But if the $100 benefit had been accumulated over the 40 preretirement years based on the average (higher) value of the dollar during that period, then perhaps this $100 might still not have been adequate in terms of the value of the dollar at the time of retirement.

Since 1952, when CREF (College Retirement Equities Fund), affiliated with TIAA (Teachers' Insurance and Annuity Association), was established by a special act of the New York State Legislature, several different approaches have been developed to the problem of maintaining the purchasing power of retirement income.

One approach is to relate the pension benefit to the average salary at or near retirement age, and many pension plans have been recently amended along these lines or have been supplemented with a benefit so determined. While this type of formula or supplementation goes a long way toward correcting a serious deficiency of the type of plan that provides benefits on the basis of career-average salary, it recognizes the effects of inflation only up to retirement and does not make allowance for possible subsequent inflation.

Pension trusts have been set up which take the changes in the cost of living into account both before and after retirement. The three here briefly outlined are all noncontributory. One is a variable-annuity plan, the funds of which are invested entirely in common stocks, coupled with a conventional fixed-benefit-annuity plan. The variable part uses only annuity units with an assumed income-benefit formula used to determine the amount of the contributions. The second approach utilizes accumulation units before retirement, which are payable as a death benefit, and variable-annuity values after retirement. The funds are invested in both equity and debt obligations. Under the third approach, annuity payments are keyed to the Consumer Price Index prepared by the Bureau of Labor Statistics.

A few life-insurance companies have been organized to issue contracts providing variable annuities. One of these is CREF, mentioned above, a stock company which issues contracts on a contributory basis. Since no more than 50 per cent of the premium can be applied to buy a variable-annuity benefit from CREF, the balance is used to buy a conventional type of annuity from TIAA. CREF uses accumulation units before retirement and annuity units thereafter. Issues are almost exclusively to groups, but under individual contracts. Expenses and mortality are not guaranteed—they are reflected in the value of the units.

Two stock-life-insurance companies have been organized in Washington, D.C., to sell variable annuities exclusively, on both the individual and the group basis, contributory and noncontributory. They issue money-purchase contracts and use both accumulation and annuity units, with mortality and expenses guaranteed; both also issue a group-unit-benefit contract using annuity units only. Investments are almost exclusively in equities. Another variable-annuity insurer has been established in Arkansas.

These examples illustrate the extreme flexibility of the variable-annuity device. Other approaches are, of course, possible, such as a trust or a deposit-administration–insured contract providing funds at retirement for a final-average-pay plan, at which time the benefits may be converted to a variable annuity, also either insured or noninsured.

The concept of a variable annuity written by a life-insurance company has turned out to be a very controversial subject, both within and outside the life-insurance business. Variable annuities have created no great controversy in the pension-trust field and have had, so far, a limited effect in that field. Some life insurers vigorously oppose the idea, mainly because life-insurance companies have always dealt in dollar benefits and definite guarantees backed up generally by indebtedness investments, such as bonds and mortgages. Other life insurers just as vigorously champion variable annuities, arguing that they should give the people the kind of flexible retirement program that will reflect changing economic conditions. A committee of the National Association of Securities Administrators has taken the position that variable annuities are securities and as such should be registered with the Securities and Exchange Commission, which brought a test case against the two Washington companies. The SEC lost this case but has appealed it to a higher court.[12]

In view of the novelty of variable annuities, it is impossible to tell exactly what their future will be. But they have arrived on the scene, and it is likely that as versatile an instrument as this will be used with increasing frequency in the future. Also, it seems likely that most plans will be noncontributory or where they are contributory that they will provide, as the TIAA-CREF contracts do, that the individual participant may choose whether his benefits are to be determined solely on a fixed-dollar basis or partly on a fixed-dollar basis and partly on a variable-annuity basis.

[12] This Circuit Court appeal was denied, May, 1958.

CHAPTER 10

Actuarial Assumptions

The development of a retirement plan involves the following three major technical responsibilities:

1. The plan must be clear and definitive and satisfy all legal requirements. This is the responsibility of the employer's attorney or of specialized legal counsel engaged for this purpose.

2. The funds set aside from which the pension and other benefits will be paid must be properly safeguarded. This is the responsibility of the agency to which is delegated the stewardship of the funds— a trustee or an insurer.

3. The funds set aside, when augmented with the interest which they will earn, together with future reversions, must be adequate to meet the future pension and other payments under the plan. This is the responsibility of the actuary.

The designing of the plan as an appropriate and effective employee-welfare instrument may be undertaken by one or more of the above agencies or may be handled by specialists who have made a careful study of this problem, even though they may not be qualified in a strict sense to accept any of the responsibilities outlined. In a great many instances, particularly those involving the trust-fund form of administration, the plan is drafted by the actuary and submitted to the trustee for review. The trust agreement is drafted by the trustee and reviewed by the actuary, after which both the plan and the trust agreement are submitted for final drafting by the attorneys representing the employer.

When a pension plan is administered through an insurer, certain actuarial and fiduciary responsibilities are automatically fulfilled by the insurer, and, while competent legal advice is also rendered, the employer, union, or other organization under whose sponsorship the plan is being designed will probably still seek independent legal review of the plan and of all documents establishing the benefits. This action is undertaken in order to make more certain that the precise benefits and conditions under which the benefits will be paid are set out.

It has been said that any mistakes of legal counsel will be apparent soon after the plan is drawn, because a poorly drafted plan is not likely to satisfy the requirements of the Internal Revenue Service and, in any event, would soon run into administrative difficulties. Faulty judgment on the part of the agency to which the investing of the pension fund is entrusted will undoubtedly come to light within a reasonable period of time. But faulty assumptions on the part of the actuary may not become evident until decades after the plan is made effective unless they are periodically reviewed and adjusted in the light of experience as it develops, partly because the early years of a pension plan's existence are usually a period when substantial funds are accumulated and any underlying inadequacy to meet future pension payments may be discernible only through frequent actuarial analysis.

Enumeration of Actuarial Elements. The elements that are the particular concern of the actuary in his consideration of a retirement plan are explained in the following paragraphs. They become the continuing responsibility of the consulting actuary for each trust-fund plan he is assigned to work on and of the insurer's actuary each time the premium-rate basis is changed, future illustrative cost estimates are made, or dividend returns are computed.

Mortality Rates. Since a pension plan provides for payment of stated sums at periodic intervals during the lifetime of the participants after retirement, the determination of the proper amounts to set aside to meet these future payments is dependent on the rates of mortality among the pensioners. Where, as is the usual case, contributions are made during the working years of the participants in the plan, the mortality to which they are subject before retirement is also important, since pension payments will be made only to those who survive to receive them. Frequently a retirement plan will furnish concomitant death benefits (in addition to providing for pension payments), and the cost of these benefits is dependent on the mortality rates experienced among the group covered for such death benefits. Some plans, especially those for persons engaged in hazardous public work, such as policemen and firemen, provide a special death benefit which is paid in the event of deaths occurring in line of duty, and a smaller death benefit for nonduty deaths. This differential in benefit suggests an occupational-accident mortality rate and a nonoccupational mortality rate. This sort of refinement, however, is extremely difficult to make with any degree of reliability.

Interest Rates. The funds set aside to provide the benefits under the plan are customarily invested to earn interest.[1] The interest received on the funds so invested is used to augment reserve funds and otherwise help defray the cost of the plan. It is important to know in advance approximately what rates of interest the fund may be expected to earn over a long period of years, since this prospective interest income will be taken into consideration in arriving at the amounts to be contributed to the plan from time to time.

Expenses. The expenses of administering the plan must be provided for. These expenses may be an integral part of the amount of contributions made to the pension fund and withheld as incurred directly from the amounts contributed. Sometimes, as is common in trust-fund plans, the expenses of operating the plan will be charged to the employer as they are incurred and treated entirely separately from the benefit contributions proper. Included among pension-plan expenses are legal, investment, and actuarial costs, state or other taxes (in some cases), commissions (for insured plans), and the regular day-to-day administrative expense. These expenses are always present, as specific charges in the case of a trust-fund plan, or as implicit costs in the premiums collected in the case of an insured plan.

The three elements of mortality, interest, and expense are present in all pension plans. In many plans it will be desirable or necessary to consider certain additional elements.

Withdrawal Rates. Where no benefit is payable when a participant terminates employment before retirement or where there is vested in him only a part of the equity which could otherwise be ascribed to him, certain credits will accrue to the pension fund with respect to

---

[1] The term *interest* includes other forms of investment income.

terminating employees, and it may be feasible to discount in advance for these potential reversions. Alternatively, this situation may be viewed from the standpoint of funding benefits only for those who will fulfill the requirements for eligibility for benefits.

Retirement Rates. Frequently, especially under public-employee plans, retirement is optional on the part of the employee or may be required by the employer between a range of ages. For example, under the Federal Civil Service Retirement System any employee may retire on full benefit, with respect to service credits earned up to the date of such retirement, between the ages of sixty-two and seventy (or as early as age sixty with 30 years of service). In flexible situations such as this, the actuary is faced with the necessity of making assumptions as to when retirements will occur. Perhaps past experience under the system will offer a guide. The most conservative assumption would be to adopt the youngest possible age, but objections would be raised that this sets the costs inordinately high and that there is too long a wait for experience to deliver the offset credits arising when actual retirements are delayed beyond that minimum age. Therefore, assumed rates of retirement in some form are needed for these flexible retirement plans.

Salary Rates. At the time the rate of contribution is being determined, consideration is sometimes given to probable future rates of salary. Particularly where the benefit is scaled to the average salaries of the participants at or near retirement, it may be advisable to take cognizance of future variations of earnings scales. Generally (and particularly in the case of salaried employees whose responsibilities often increase as service lengthens), earnings tend to increase over the years of employment. If the intent is to determine a level rate of contribution (either in terms of dollars or as a per cent of compensation) per unit of ultimate pension benefit, it is important to assume rates of increase in earnings in future years and to put aside periodically into the pension fund enough to furnish the retirement benefits determined by taking such rates into account. It is, of course, impossible accurately to foresee these future rates, but attempts at estimating them and injecting these estimates into the computations are often made.

Disability Rates. The difficulties that arise in the administration of disability benefits are of considerable magnitude. As a result, a disability benefit (other than what might be provided by the early-retirement option) has been found only in relatively few pension plans until fairly recently. Currently, increased emphasis is being placed on the inclusion of a total-and-permanent-disability provision in a pension plan because of recent union pressures in this direction and because of the inclusion of such benefits in the 1956 amendments to the Social Security Act. The disability-incidence rates (the probability that a covered employee will become disabled) and the disability-duration rates (the probable length of invalidism before death or recovery) must be selected in the light of the definition of disability and the administrative procedures to be followed in determining the initial validity and subsequent continuance of the disablement. To illustrate, if a disability pension is to be paid before regular retirement in the event that two limbs are lost or eyesight is completely lost, the determination of the validity of the claim for disability benefits and its continuance is easy. On the other hand, if the definition is based on inability to engage in any substantially gainful occupation and it is presumed that the disability is permanent when it has been in existence for a stated period, such as 4 or 6 months, numerous unjustified claims may be presented, and a large proportion of recoveries must be anticipated.

The claim rates for disability are apparently influenced to a large degree by economic conditions. In a time of poor business conditions, employees, or even employers, may use the pension plan as a sort of unemployment-insurance scheme. In some situations the disability provisions of a plan have been utilized as an expedient to more easily bring about the termination of employment of unsatisfactory employees. Such retirements do not properly fall within the intended definition of *disability* and, consequently, result in an actuarial deficiency in the funds established for the retirement plan. The employer, having used the pension plan to meet objectives not contemplated at the time the plan was developed, should be called upon to make up such deficiencies as they are incurred. Some students believe that disability benefits (except in so far as the regular early-retirement provision is applicable) should not be introduced into a pension plan and, particularly, that a vested right to such benefits should never be granted. On the other hand, many believe that since disability, particularly of the total and presumably permanent variety, is a major personal catastrophe and that since its occurrence tends to increase with increasing age it should be properly recognized and coordinated with old-age-retirement benefits. The administration of disability benefits presents many difficulties, and the selection of appropriate disability rates to be representative of the disability experience over the years requires the exercising of considerable care and periodic reviews. As in the case of mortality, a refinement in disability rates is sometimes needed to distinguish between disabilities of an occupational nature and other disabilities because in some plans a different type of benefit is granted for an occupational disability from that for an ordinary disability.

Remarriage Rates. A number of plans, primarily those adopted to cover employees of municipalities, provide that certain benefits will be continued to the widow of a covered employee until she remarries. To properly value such a plan or to determine the appropriate rates of contribution, it is necessary to estimate an applicable remarriage rate for the widows.

Miscellaneous Rates. In addition to the above elements, the actuary is faced with having to utilize rates or factors for other happenings or conditions of life when special benefit systems are under consideration. For instance, sometimes an assumed rate of new entrants is needed to counterbalance the withdrawal rate assumed; at other times a rate or index of the number of dependents of persons covered by a system is needed. Especially in social-insurance studies are some of these miscellaneous factors required, such as the future birth rate, the proportion of the population likely to be engaged in covered employment, the withdrawal rate—not from any particular employer but from the country's labor force (as, for example, the fluctuations in the prewar, war, and postwar employment of women)—the in-and-out movement to and from employment covered by the system, and other demographic and economic factors.

Meaning of *Rate*. In several of these actuarial elements the term *rate* has been used. Except for the *rate of interest,* the expression *rate* commonly signifies the probability that a certain condition or event will occur within the interval of 1 year. If of 1,000 persons exposed to death 46 are to die within a year, the mortality rate for the group is $46/1,000 = 0.046$; or, restated, a mortality rate of 0.046 means that among the individuals under observation during the interval of 1 year, 4.6 per cent will die. In practice this precision of result is rarely met, and one of the functions of the actuary is to select in advance the mortality and other rates that it is expected will be representative for the group under consideration for many years into the future.

Discussion of Actuarial Elements. Mortality rates, withdrawal rates, disability rates, salary rates, and remarriage rates all display a variation by age. By following through a reasonably large group of employed persons all of the same age, it would be found that the rate of mortality would tend to increase with age, as would also the salary rate; that the rate of withdrawal would, in the absence of unusual economic circumstances, tend to decrease with increasing age; and that the remarriage rate of the widows would tend to decrease with increasing age. If a reasonably large number of persons at each of several ages were considered, some other trends would probably be noticeable. For instance, the withdrawal rates would decrease not only with age but also with duration of employment, so that of two groups of employees who are both of attained age thirty, one group having entered employment at age twenty (10 years before) and the other group having just entered at age thirty, the first group would exhibit a lower rate of turnover than would the second group.

Mortality. Except for the first few years of life, the tabular rate of mortality increases as age increases. Mortality rates also vary by sex, females generally exhibiting lower mortality rates than males of the same age. They vary by geographical location, temperate zones displaying lower mortality rates than semitropical or tropical zones. Within the United States certain geographical sections show lower mortality rates for the same age, sex, and race characteristics than do other areas. Mortality rates vary by race, the white population having lower mortality rates than do the nonwhite races. This difference is predominant at the younger ages, gradually lessening and ultimately even reversing as age increases. The death rate varies by marital status, with a distinctly lower mortality among married lives. Mortality rates vary by industry and occupation, some industries showing considerably higher mortality rates than others. In some instances this is caused by greater accident hazard; in others it is the result of a variety of causes, including working conditions and economic status. Economic status is of some significance, although probably not so much as is sometimes thought. While higher-paid employees can afford more complete and advanced medical assistance than lower-paid employees, the extra responsibilities and strains associated with their work are seemingly productive of extra mortality.

An important element requiring consideration in connection with a pension plan is the tendency toward improving mortality rates, with the passage of time, for groups with identical characteristics otherwise. For instance, consider a group of persons of certain age, sex, race, industry, and other characteristics during one interval, say the decade 1920–1929. If the experience of earlier periods established a guide, it is likely that a similar group in the decade 1950–1959 will display a significantly lower mortality rate. At the lower ages the improvement of mortality rates since the beginning of this century has been very striking. In the absence of evidence to the contrary, there is reason to believe that some improvement will continue in the future, especially in the light of many recent medical discoveries, such as the antibiotics. Increased attention is being given to the improvement of mortality at the higher ages, although the major lowering of mortality rates has taken place at the lower ages.

The experience of insurers shows that the rates of mortality for insured persons are lower than the mortality rates for the general population (some of whom are insured and some not). This difference is partly a result of the rejection by medical examination of many persons who are regarded as uninsurable. The experience also demonstrates that the mortality rates experienced among persons covered by life-annuity contracts are lower than those among persons who are not so covered. Here the weeding out arises from the automatic selection exercised by the purchasers of individual annuities, since they do not generally purchase life-annuity contracts unless they expect to collect annuity payments for many years to come. To some extent the favorable mortality is probably caused by merely being annuitants, as it is generally believed that the assurance of regular annuity payments acts to prolong life. Retired persons covered under group-annuity plans or other bulk pension plans also appear to exhibit lower mortality than groups of comparable age who do not enjoy benefits from pension plans, although there is much less likelihood of any personal selection among such groups than among individual purchasers of life annuities. There is, however, a group selection through having been in good enough physical condition to fulfill the duties of their employment until retirement.

Comparisons of rates from representative mortality tables will serve to demonstrate the above observations. Table 10-1 shows for repre-

TABLE 10-1. EXPECTED DEATHS AND ACTUAL DEATHS PER 1,000

Age	Expected deaths per 1,000 according to tables used for life-insurance premium rates				Deaths per 1,000 according to Census Bureau
	American Experience *	American Men (5) †	1941 CSO ‡	Table X-17 §	U.S. Life (population), white males, 1949–1951
10	7.49	2.37	1.97	0.60	0.60
20	7.80	3.92	2.43	1.46	1.62
30	8.43	4.46	3.56	1.82	1.82
40	9.79	5.84	6.18	3.30	3.91
50	13.78	11.58	12.32	7.84	10.12
60	26.69	26.68	26.59	20.20	23.81
70	61.99	61.47	59.30	49.79	50.27
80	144.47	135.74	131.85	109.98	109.93
90	454.55	280.35	280.99	228.14	228.90

* Based on insurance experience before 1868.
† Based on insurance experience 1900 to 1915.
‡ Based on insurance experience shortly before 1940.
§ Based on insurance experience 1950 to 1954. This table has been proposed but is not actually used for calculations of premium rates.

sentative ages certain of the mortality rates used in calculating life-insurance premiums over the last century. These rates were based primarily on life-insurance experience (but include certain loadings), and for comparison purposes there is included a table of rates derived from statistics compiled by the Bureau of the Census.

Table 10-2 sets out mortality rates in certain tables that have been used for determining the premiums or rates of contribution for annuities.

TABLE 10-2. EXPECTED DEATHS PER 1,000
(Males)

Age	McClintock's Annuitants *	American Annuitants †	Combined Annuity ‡	1937 Standard Annuity §	1937 Standard Annuity (set back 1 year in age)	Ga-1951 ¶
10	7.55	......	1.53	1.26	1.26	0.48
20	7.85	......	2.05	1.33	1.31	0.62
30	8.63	4.99	2.36	2.07	1.94	0.99
40	10.56	7.51	4.64	4.36	4.04	2.00
50	15.42	13.15	10.35	9.29	8.61	6.48
60	27.50	25.66	23.02	19.75	18.32	15.56
70	57.22	53.05	50.81	41.76	38.76	39.30
80	127.90	111.65	110.18	87.16	81.05	99.68
90	282.96	230.04	229.99	177.14	165.32	200.59
100	561.48	456.79	442.94	362.12	331.84	365.46

* Insurance company annuity experience to 1892.
† Insurance company annuity experience to 1918.
‡ Published in 1928.
§ Group insurance experience (clerical occupations) 1932 to 1936 for ages under sixty-five (American Annuitants set back 2 years in age thereafter).
¶ Annuity experience 1946 to 1950 for ages over sixty-five (adjusted and projected to 1951).

Table 10-3 compares mortality rates for white male lives with those for white females during various periods.

Table 10-4 compares mortality rates for nonwhites with those for whites in the general population.

Table 10-5 compares rates representative of mortality among annuitants in recent years with certain "forecast" (projected) and adjusted rates believed by some actuaries to be representative of the rates that will emerge in the future. The methods of projecting and adjusting mortality rates are discussed later in this chapter.

TABLE 10-3. U.S. LIFE TABLES (POPULATION)
DEATHS PER 1,000

Age	1900–1902		1939–1941		1949–1951	
	White males	White females	White males	White females	White males	White females
10	2.74	2.46	1.00	0.70	0.60	0.40
20	5.94	5.54	2.12	1.45	1.62	0.73
30	7.99	7.72	2.79	2.20	1.82	1.15
40	10.60	9.31	5.13	3.68	3.91	2.42
50	15.37	13.37	11.55	7.62	10.12	5.61
60	28.59	25.06	25.48	17.14	23.81	13.40
70	58.94	53.69	54.54	42.33	50.27	34.09
80	133.53	121.15	124.71	108.19	109.93	90.60
90	262.78	245.32	248.94	231.41	228.90	206.57

TABLE 10-4. U.S. LIFE TABLES (POPULATION)—1949 TO 1951
DEATHS PER 1,000

Age	White males	Nonwhite males	White females	Nonwhite females
10	0.60	0.84	0.40	0.55
20	1.62	3.14	0.73	2.27
30	1.82	4.92	1.15	3.90
40	3.91	8.79	2.42	7.70
50	10.12	19.09	5.61	15.99
60	23.81	36.76	13.40	29.54
70	50.27	56.20	34.09	45.53
80	109.93	90.86	90.60	73.27
90	228.90	182.55	206.57	155.35
100	391.12	385.52	388.39	382.08

TABLE 10-5. EXPECTED DEATHS PER 1,000
(Males)

Age	Basic * Ga-1951	Projected and/or adjusted rates		
		Basic Ga-1951 (projected 14 years to 1965)	Ga-1951	Ga-1951 (projected 3 years to 1954, set back 1 year in age)
20	0.68	0.57	0.62	0.57
30	1.10	0.92	0.99	0.90
40	2.22	1.86	2.00	1.78
50	7.19	6.03	6.48	5.59
60	17.28	14.49	15.56	13.85
70	43.67	36.62	39.30	34.61
80	110.75	100.85	99.68	88.96
90	222.88	222.88	200.59	188.54

* The Basic Ga-1951 Table (author's designation) is the Ga-1951 Table with certain ɔadings deleted.

Of 1,000 persons alive at age thirty the numbers remaining alive 35, 15, 55, and 65 years later are set out in Table 10-6.

These various tables reflect the following facts: (1) that mortality ɪas shown great improvement over recent years, particularly in the lower and early middle ages but also to some extent at the higher ages; (2) that white persons show generally lower rates than nonwhites although the difference is diminishing; (3) that, in general, females show lower rates than males; and (4) that insured lives are subject to lower mortality than is the general population.[2]

Two of the columns in Table 10-6 are captioned "1-year set-back in ɑge." For the "1-year set-back" the mortality rates at age twenty-nine ɑre used as applicable to age thirty and so on for each age in the table. This device provides, in effect, a more conservative table (with lower rates of mortality) without necessitating the derivation of a completely

[2] The effect of these various characteristics on the cost of retirement-plan benefits will be discussed in Chap. 12.

TABLE 10-6. NUMBER OF PERSONS ALIVE AT CERTAIN AGES
(From 1,000 alive at age thirty)

Age	American Experience	American Men (5)	1941 CSO	Table X-17	Combined Annuity *	1937 Standard Annuity		a-1949	Basic Ga-1951 (projected 14 years to 1965)	Ga-1951 (projected 3 years to 1954)	
						No set-back in age †	1-year set-back in age †			No set-back in age †	1-year set-back in age †
Males											
30	1,000	1,000	1,000	1,000	1,000	1,000	1,000	1,000	1,000	1,000	1,000
65	577	629	625	725	676	709	727	782	796	789	806
75	307	336	342	440	404	466	492	549	547	538	569
85	64	80	85	140	128	190	214	226	193	197	228
95	0	3	3	10	10	28	36	22	17	22	29
Females											
30					1,000	1,000	1,000	1,000	1,000	1,000	1,000
65					751	790	804	884	865	861	872
75					518	593	616	716	687	679	702
85					225	320	348	381	369	365	400
95					35	86	103	55	71	79	97

* For females the male table is set back 4 years (i.e., female mortality rate at age thirty is the male mortality rate at age twenty-six).
† For females the male table is set back 5 years.

new mortality table. At the lower ages the mortality rates in the 1937 Standard Annuity Table are much higher than are those found in actual experience. On the other hand, from about age sixty the rates in this table are conservative and probably still contain some margin for future improvement in mortality, although it is to be expected that any such margin will tend to vanish as mortality at the higher ages continues to improve. Through the use of the set-back some allowance may be made for future improvement in mortality. When the 1937 Standard Annuity Table was derived, it was concluded that a reasonable approximation to the mortality rates to be expected among females could be obtained by using the male table of mortality rates with a 5-year set-back. Consequently, it was decided to construct a single table representative of the mortality among male lives rather than separate tables for males and females. In the use of the male table for females, the probability that a female aged thirty-five would live to age sixty-five was found by determining the equivalent function from the male table, i.e., the probability that a male aged thirty would live to age sixty.

The question of mortality rates suitable for determining contributions and accumulating reserve funds under pension plans has recently received considerable attention. Under an insured pension plan making certain guarantees, where the maintenance of equity among various employers is important, it is essential that a conservative mortality basis is used. Under a trust-fund plan, the selection of mortality bases is of somewhat less importance.

Table 10-7 sets out the expectation of life (average after-lifetime) according to several tables used in the past by insurers as mortality bases for group annuities.

1937 Standard Annuity Mortality Table. Over the years the insurance companies have experienced considerable improvement in mortality at the higher ages. The most striking improvement, that at the lower ages, has not been recognized to anywhere near an adequate degree by the 1937 Standard Annuity Table. In fact, while the 1937 Standard Annuity Table has been regarded as a reasonably conservative representation of the mortality to be expected at the higher ages (although there are certain peculiar twists in the table at these ages), it has greatly overstated the mortality at the lower ages. At the lower

TABLE 10-7. LIFE EXPECTANCY ACCORDING TO REPRESENTATIVE MORTALITY
TABLES USED FOR GROUP-ANNUITY VALUATIONS

Used extensively in period	Mortality table	Life expectancy for male lives at age 65 (years)
Before 1921	McClintock's Annuitants Table	11.8
1922–1928	American Annuitants Table	12.5
1929–1932	American Annuitants Table (set back 1 year)	13.1
1933–1937	Combined Annuity Table	12.7
1938–1940	1937 Standard Annuity Table	14.4
1941–1951	1937 Standard Annuity Table (set back 1 year)	15.0
After 1951	a-1949 Table, or	15.0
	Various modifications of the Ga-1951 Table	14.8 *

* 14.8 years is the life expectancy (as of 1952) under the Ga-1951 Table (projection *C*) without special modification. For further explanation of the use of various projection scales in connection with the Ga-1951 Table, see *Transactions of the Society of Actuaries* vol. 4, pp. 246–307.

ages mortality rates about half as great as those found in this table are more nearly representative of the mortality to be expected among participants in a pension plan.[3] Although the mortality rates at the lower ages are usually deemed to have a considerably smaller effect on pension-plan-contribution requirements than do turnover rates, the authors believe that it is desirable to utilize as realistic a basis of mortality at all ages as is possible, and to bear in mind that allowances must be made for possible mortality improvement in the future.

Ga-1951 Table and Modifications. Certain modifications of the Group Annuity 1951 Mortality Table have been made and adopted recently in one form or another by a number of insurers for the calculation of premiums and reserves for group-annuity plans. While the Ga-1951

[3] Although the mortality rates in the 1937 Standard Annuity Mortality Table are considerably overstated at the early ages, when used for group annuity premiums this overstatement is partially compensated for by the insurer by controlling the refunds to the employer for ill-health terminations.

rates are based on recent experience under insured group-annuity retirement plans (actually they constitute 90 per cent of the "basic" Ga-1951 rates, which are representative of experience during the years 1946 to 1950 projected forward to 1951 by applying certain reduction factors), they do not by themselves take into consideration the continuing improvement in mortality that is to be expected in years after 1951. Accordingly, the Ga-1951 rates are usually modified (i.e., reduced) in one way or another before being used for pension-plan calculations. One modification that has obtained rather wide acceptance in group-annuity work is that of projecting the Ga-1951 Table ahead 3 years (i.e., to 1954) and then setting the age back 1 year. In determining contributions for a trust-fund plan some consulting actuaries feel it unnecessary and perhaps undesirable to attempt to introduce a great degree of conservatism. Rather than attempting to introduce factors designed to produce contingency-fund accumulations and credits, it is better to select a mortality basis which, in the opinion of the actuary, will be representative of the mortality which will actually be experienced. If it is believed that mortality will continue to improve in the future, some reasonable recognition of this belief should be introduced into the mortality bases adopted, but reducing mortality by a flat 10 per cent (12½ per cent for females), as was done in the table discussed above, before effecting the adjustment designed to reflect continuing mortality improvement in the future is of questionable merit when used for a trust-fund pension plan.

It is generally conceded that the most suitable way of representing mortality among employed persons covered by a pension plan and among pensioners is through a generation or forecast type of table. Under such a table the rates of mortality depend not solely on the attained ages of the participants and pensioners but also on the particular year in which they enter on retirement under the plan (e.g., under a forecast table the mortality rate for pensioners who attain age eighty in 1957 will be higher than that for pensioners who attain age eighty in 1967). In practice the use of such a system of mortality rates for valuing a pension fund and calculating contribution requirements could give rise to unwieldy computations. For this reason some form of static table (with mortality rates varying by attained age only and not by duration—e.g., for group annuities the Ga-1951 Table

projected 3 years with ages set back 1 or 1½ years) is often selected
with the margins there included intended to allow for anticipated
improvement in mortality in the future.

Mortality Trends. In a recent report to the Society of Actuaries, the
mortality experienced among pensioners under five noninsured pension systems was presented. The experience among these five group
of employees is set out in Table 10-8.

TABLE 10-8. NONINSURED PENSION PLANS
RATIO OF ACTUAL DEATHS TO EXPECTED DEATHS
EXPECTED DEATHS ACCORDING TO 1937 STANDARD ANNUITY TABLE
(Males)

Group	Per cent		
	Late 1930s *	Early 1940s *	Late 1940s *
A (government employees)	123	121	117
B (public utilities)	146	137	126
C (electric utility)	136	124	111
D (manufacturing)	118	128	122
E (electrical manufacturing)	...	...	105
Weighted total †	127	123	117

* Approximately.

† This averaging (weighted by number of actual deaths) can produce only the very
roughest index for comparison purposes since there are differences in these plans, in
the treatment of disability pensioners, in the proportion of early retirements, and in
the administrative procedures followed.

While these results are indicative of a steady decrease in the mortality rates experienced among retired persons under noninsured
pension plans, it must be borne in mind that the bulk of this experience has been at ages close to sixty-five. There is little experience
as yet at the higher ages of retirement.

Interest Rates. Except for periods of war and rare epidemics, the
long-term trend of mortality has been downward, particularly at the

ower ages. From the standpoint of practical application, the aberrations in this trend, caused by wars and epidemics, may be leveled out over a period of years.

This is not the case with interest rates on bonds, debentures, and other evidences of indebtedness. When relatively free of governmental control, they appear to follow a cyclical trend, rising for a number of years, then falling for a period, eventually rising again. In general, this cyclical trend conforms to changing business conditions and to the demand for capital. During the last two or three decades, the control exercised by the government over interest rates apparently disrupted this cyclical trend temporarily, and until very recently interest rates have been uniformly low.

The forecasting of interest rates is a problem for the specialist in investments rather than for the actuary, although the determination of the effect on the pension fund and the rate of annual contribution or premium that would result from variations in the interest rate is an actuarial problem. Some pension plans established in the past either have become underfunded or have required extra contributions because of the assumption of overly optimistic rates of interest.

Insurers have had to follow this trend in interest rates in determining the scale of premiums required to fund the costs of insured pension plans. Two or three decades ago the assumption of a 4 per cent interest rate was not uncommon. The insurers that used such an interest assumption have decreased the interest rate used in their calculations by successive steps until the most commonly used rate has become 2 per cent. Currently, many insurers writing group annuities are using $2\frac{1}{2}$ or $2\frac{3}{4}$ per cent.

An insurer adopts the interest rate that it believes to be appropriate for all the retirement plans that it administers, generally with provision for later adjustment through crediting of dividends or increasing premiums so as to take into consideration the individual experience of each retirement plan as it develops. An insurer does not segregate and invest separately the contributions of each retirement plan; consequently, the crediting of individual experience here means that each plan would receive an interest credit or debit in its dividend determination that is related to the size of the reserve at the time consideration is given to dividends.

Under a trust-fund plan it is possible to select investments to yield a variety of interest rates. Here the general rule that "the higher the interest rate, the greater the risk" needs to be borne in mind. A retirement plan provides that pension payments will be forthcoming many years in the future. It should not lightly be entered into, and it is of paramount importance that the trustees responsible for the administration of the trust fund select for the bond portion of the portfolio securities that will provide reasonably regular income.

While some part of the assets of trust-fund retirement plans are invested in preferred and common stocks and perhaps mortgages, it is customary to restrict a substantial proportion of the investments to top-grade corporate bonds and government obligations. In selecting a rate of interest for the purpose of valuing liabilities and determining contribution levels for a trust-fund plan, it is customary to adopt a rate somewhat below what it is expected the trust will earn, on the average, on its investments. This is because (1) there is no assurance that current rates will continue throughout the life of the trust fund, (2) it is not possible to have all the contributions invested continuously from the time they are made, (3) the payment of benefits may require a certain amount of liquidity in future years which would make it necessary for some cash to be readily available, and (4) it is thus possible to set up what is in effect a contingency fund under the trust.

Where a trustee believes that the earnings of the trust will run between $3\frac{1}{2}$ and 4 per cent per year, the actuary would probably adopt $2\frac{3}{4}$, 3, or $3\frac{1}{4}$ per cent as the valuation rate. Any interest earned in excess of this assumed rate is automatically included in the assets of the trust and applied toward decreasing current or future contributions under the plan. If, however, the financial climate should so change that over the long pull it appeared that a rate below the assumed rate would be earned on the trust investments, the reserves established would be inadequate, and some form of supplementation would be required, which would usually take the form of increased contributions.

In practice, in certain recent years, the problem faced by pension trusts has been one not only of increasing interest earnings but also of high capital gains (both realized and unrealized but predominately unrealized). In some plans the amount of realized capital gains in a articular year indicated almost fantastic earned investment rates, and the unrealized capital gains constituted, at least at the time, significant contingency funds.[4]

Since the assets of most pension trusts are valued on a book-value (cost) basis, one of the most difficult considerations that is encountered is whether to take into account, in determining future contributions, some part of unrealized capital gains. Many economists feel that over the long range the trend will continue to be inflationary, as it has been in the past. If this is the case, then there would seem to be merit in treating a portion of any seemingly permanent unrealized gains as available to reduce future contributions, with the balance of unrealized gains treated essentially as a contingency fund or cushion to soften possible future reversals in market conditions.

Expenses. The expenses incurred in the establishment and maintenance of a pension plan may be classified broadly as follows:

1. Development. The cost of developing a pension plan includes the selling and other acquisition expense incurred by an insurer in connection with compensation of its agents and field representatives, salaries and other expenses paid by insurers and trust companies for promotional activities, and fees paid to independent consultants specializing in this field. It is not possible to set down the amount of each of these expenses because they vary considerably from case to case. They usually bear some relation to the amount of service rendered.[5]

2. Legal. When a trusteed plan is selected, legal fees are incurred in the final writing of the plan and trust agreement. Legal fees are also incurred whenever a plan is amended or revised. When an insured plan is installed, the insurer's comparable legal expenses are met from

---

[4] Some pension trusts, benefiting from the inflationary tendencies of recent years, earned rates as high as 5 to 8 per cent. Cases can probably be found where unrealized capital gains constituted 50 per cent of the recognized assets of the trusts.

[5] One notable exception occurs in the case of individual-insurance-contract pension-trust plans where the soliciting agent frequently receives the regular commissions paid on individual contracts individually distributed. Since these commissions were originally designed to provide an agent with a reasonable remuneration for work required in the sale of individual policies, it follows that in a large pension-trust case he may receive commissions entirely unrelated to the value of the services rendered.

the premiums paid. Law firms generally maintain a record of th
time spent on a plan, and the fees are usually determined with thi
in mind.

3. Actuarial. The comments made on legal fees are also applicabl
to actuarial fees, but there is one difference. In the absence of majo
revisions or amendatory treatment, the legal expense will normall
be only incidental in renewal years. Actuarial expenses for a plar
administered with proper regard for long-term financial implication
will be a recurring element, since an annual valuation and actuaria
review will be desirable, if not essential. This is true regardless o
whether or not the plan is insured. In the case of an insured plan
the actuarial expense is provided from the loading. In trust-fund plans
it is usually handled as a separate item. In some cases, outside actuaria
talent is engaged to audit the financial transactions under an insured
group-annuity plan.

4. Financial. The investment of the fund implementing the plar
calls for the service of financial experts in the form of either insure:
personnel or corporate or individual trustees. The expense of these
services is usually related to the size of the funds handled. In New
York State, for the purpose of determining their investment-expense
allowance under Section 213 of the Insurance Law, insurance com
panies are permitted a maximum of $\frac{1}{4}$ per cent of the amount o
their invested assets.[6] The maximum investment-expense deduction ir
the federal tax return is also $\frac{1}{4}$ per cent.

There is some variation among corporate trustees in the amoun
of fees for investing pension-plan funds and disbursing benefit pay
ments. While most trustees charge a fee which is related to the amoun
of the pension fund (with the charge per unit of fund grading down
ward as the size of the fund grows) and with additional charges pe
check issued, other trustees relate their fees to the amount of invest
ment income earned by the trust.

5. General Administration. Any administrative operations involve
expense, whether in the form of salaries paid to employees, properly
allocated overhead expense of the company maintaining the pension
plan, fees paid to outside actuaries or other consultants, or costs

[6] Insurer investment expenses, exclusive of federal taxes, usually stay well within
this limit.

ncurred for services rendered by an insurer. These expenses are generally related to the amount of administrative work and to the compensation of the people performing the work. In the interest of economy, it is desirable to avoid unnecessary duplication of administrative operations in so far as possible.

In the case of group annuities, it is generally contemplated that the expenses borne by the insurer will fall well within the premium loading. Expenses, in terms of percentages of premiums, generally decrease as the size of the group-annuity plan increases, since some of the expenses are constant and are, therefore, not related to size.

One element of expense that is difficult to justify is the great amount of free work performed by insurers, and more recently to an increasing extent by trustees also, on what might be termed a speculative basis. If an employer wishes, he may receive without charge proposals for a pension plan with cost estimates (and even sometimes rough drafts of the plan itself) from 20 or more agencies interested in selling it. While generally these proposals conform to a standardized pattern, their preparation does involve considerable expense, which, in the long run, must be borne either by the existing clients of the agency or by the small proportion of cases that actually install a plan with a particular agency.

In comparing the administrative expenses (and to some extent other expenses) incurred under insurer-administered pension plans and trust-fund plans, it should be borne in mind that the insurer's expense is held back out of the premiums, contributions received, or investment income earned. Consequently, when an employee retires, the expenses of administering his particular benefit can properly come only from a reserve fund built up for this purpose during the years that premiums were collected in his behalf. In practice, with a continuing group annuity, such precise equity may not be maintained, administrative and other expenses for the retired employee being provided from the general income under his and other group-annuity plans. In the case of a trust-fund plan, expense may be handled entirely aside from contributions and other income of the fund, and even if the trust fund had no income an expense charge might be incurred. Consequently, the expense incidence may be quite different under these two forms of administration.

6. Taxes. An element of cost (usually treated as an expense) which is difficult to justify is the premium tax assessed by the individual state on premiums collected on life-insurance contracts.[7] This tax varies from state to state but, on the average, is about 2 per cent of the premiums collected. In a number of states, group-annuity contributions are regarded as insurance premiums and are subject to the same tax as life-insurance premiums. In other states, a different tax rate (usually lower) is applied to group-annuity considerations; and in still other states, group-annuity premiums are exempted from the state tax. Trust-fund plans enjoy an advantage in this respect, since the contributions collected for such plans are not subject to state tax.

In the years immediately preceding 1956, the federal government taxed life insurers at the rate of $3\frac{3}{4}$ per cent of the first $200,000 of annual net investment income plus $6\frac{1}{2}$ per cent of net investment income over $200,000. In 1956 these rates were generally increased so that for a large company the federal income taxes are roughly 20 per cent higher than they would have been on the previous rates. Since a pension plan involves the accumulation of large sums of money, it follows that a diversion of investment income for taxes has a significant effect on the cost of the plan. It has been estimated that if a tax rate of $6\frac{1}{2}$ per cent of net investment income were to be continued indefinitely, it would ultimately increase the annual cost of the plan by 5 per cent over the cost of a similar plan where no tax rate was applicable. The current increase in the federal tax rate still further emphasizes this differential.

Withdrawal Rates. While it is conceded that every concern will experience terminations of employment before retirement, it is sometimes difficult to forecast appropriate rates of turnover for any long period of time. In the case of mortality and interest, the experience that accrues over a period of time is usually only in small part related to the particular concern under consideration, and the fluctuations from the norm are usually not great. Withdrawal rates are, on the other hand, very likely to vary from industry to industry, among organizations within any one industry, and between the salaried and

[7] For a thorough discussion of the discrimination aspects of the taxation of insurance companies, see Joseph B. Maclean, "Life Insurance," 8th ed., McGraw-Hill Book Company, Inc., New York, 1957, pp. 463–464.

hourly employees of one firm. The economic health of a company is sometimes reflected in its withdrawal rates. Older established concerns showing moderate growth have more stabilized employment than do newer concerns which are frequently developed to satisfy a current temporary demand. A decision whether to use withdrawal rates among employees requires considerable study, as does determination of the rates to be used.

In the absence of an expense or other charge for the settlement of the equities of terminating employees and with uniform corporate tax rates over the years, there will be no difference in the cost to employee or employer, whether or not withdrawal rates are introduced into the calculations. Under these circumstances, if withdrawals are not discounted for in advance when an employee withdraws from a plan (without vesting), he receives the accumulation of his own contributions, and the employer receives as a credit against his future contributions the accumulated amounts which he had contributed for this particular employee. In the long run this must produce the same net result as if the withdrawals had been discounted for in advance so that the employer did not set aside any funds for employees who would not remain in his service long enough to become eligible for a vested benefit provided by part or all of the employer's contributions.

The introduction of a withdrawal rate into actuarial computations may have a considerable effect on the incidence of the employer's contributions. If no withdrawal rate is introduced, at least under the level-premium method of funding, the employer may expect a decreasing rate of contribution over the years, which might be deemed to favor the stockholders at a later date, as compared with the present stockholders. If the withdrawal rates introduced are truly representative of the future rates of termination of employment, the employer's contribution will be level over the period to which the withdrawal rates are applicable.[8]

In view of the difficulty of predicting with any degree of accuracy the future termination-of-employment experience of a specific em-

[8] This contemplates a static situation where no unusual changes in payroll take place and where mortality, interest, retirement rates, and other factors also follow the actuarial assumptions.

ployer, it is customary to use conservative (low) withdrawal rates. If withdrawal rates in excess of those experienced are used, the funds set aside into the pension fund will be inadequate and will require later supplementation. If the rates are too low, gains or credits will develop to reduce future contributions. Frequently it is desirable to show the effect on the initial rate of contributions required under two sets of actuarial assumptions, the first of which introduces a conservative rate of withdrawal and the second, a higher rate of withdrawal. The withdrawal rates used may then be selected with due regard to the future situation as seen by the employer.

Since withdrawal rates are greatest in the early years of employment, the adoption of an eligibility period of several years, only after which an employee may come under the pension plan, automatically eliminates a great deal of the effect of turnover. But withdrawals taking place among employees who have been under the plan for a period of years will have a much greater effect costwise than withdrawals taking place in the early years because the aggregate amounts contributed by the employer for any particular employee increase as the years of coverage increase.

Since rates of withdrawal tend to decrease with increasing periods of service, it may seem desirable in some cases to use a select table of rates. Under this type of table a separate rate is shown for each age at entry into the plan and for each year of service thereafter until ultimately the withdrawal rates will show little variation as the period of service increases. An example of a portion of such a select table is shown in Table 10-9.

According to this table, employees entering the plan at age twenty-five are expected to experience a withdrawal rate of 9 per cent during their third year of employment. Of all employees now aged thirty-three who have been with the company for 4 or more years, 5 per cent are expected to terminate employment within a year.

Usually, for convenience and in order to make a conservative approach to the question of withdrawal rates, only the ultimate portion of the table of withdrawal rates is used. Through this procedure, turnover rates varying by attained age (and not by duration) are used, thus reducing considerably the mathematical work required in valuation of a plan.

TABLE 10-9. EXPECTED NUMBER OF EMPLOYEES WHO WILL TERMINATE
EMPLOYMENT WITHIN 1 YEAR * PER 1,000 ACTIVE EMPLOYEES

| Age at entry into plan | Years of employment | | | | Attained age |
| | Select rates | | | Ultimate rates | |
	First	Second	Third	Fourth and on	
20	330	195	105	70	23
25	250	150	90	60	28
30	200	110	70	50	33
35	150	85	55	40	38
40	110	60	40	30	43
45	75	40	30	20	48
50	50	25	20	10	53
55	40	15	10	5	58

* For causes other than death or retirement.

Perhaps the most satisfactory way of arriving at a set of withdrawal
rates varying by attained age only is to weight the basic rates at each
attained age and duration by the average reserves that would be
accumulated at the attained age. This procedure reflects the relatively
small financial effect of an employee terminating with a short period
of coverage and the much greater effect of an employee terminating
after a long period.

A device sometimes used to produce contribution rates that will
be unaffected by turnover at the lower ages is a reasonable set of
eligibility conditions for the plan, such as attainment of age thirty
with 5 years of service, but to defer making contributions for an
employee until he reaches, say, age forty. His benefit would then be
funded over the period from age forty until attainment of retirement
age. If the plan is contributory, the employee's contributions commence when he satisfies the eligibility conditions of the plan. On the
other hand, the adoption of a lengthy eligibility period very frequently

obscures the true long-range cost of a pension plan because, if the firm is growing, substantial increases in the covered payroll, and consequently pension costs, will develop when the ineligibles attain eligibility. In true bulk funding, especially where the plan is noncontributory, there is much to be said for a plan for which all employees are eligible.

Withdrawal rates are closely related to the particular concern under discussion, and there is considerable variation from firm to firm. The mere fact of the institution of a pension plan may exert considerable holding power on the employees and affect subsequent withdrawal rates. But in many instances, where employees are covered by a pension plan from the time they enter employment, it will be found that the reduction in cost resulting from a discounting for future withdrawals will be greater than the effect of discounting for future mortality. The introduction of an eligibility period (such as 3 or 5 years) makes the withdrawal discount have less effect (because withdrawal rates decrease with length of service) and makes the mortality discount have relatively more effect on the initial cost (because mortality rates increase with age).

Salary Scale. The result of inflation has been that pension benefits comprised of separate units based on each year's compensation are rather inadequately related to the earnings of employees at the time they retire, and therefore it is becoming increasingly common to relate pension benefits to the compensation earned at or near retirement.

A prospective salary scale is frequently adopted in order to take into consideration the current effect on costs of basing pension benefits on, say, the average annual earnings of employees over the 5-year period preceding retirement.

One such salary scale is the ratio of the projected final salary on which the pension benefit is based to current salary (at each attained age of the employees). The scale may presuppose that salaries will increase in arithmetical progression (i.e., by constant amounts each year), or in accordance with more complicated algebraic formulas. Sometimes the salary scale is obtained very simply by first taking the average salary at each age and dividing that salary into the average salary earned by employees who are in the age brackets where the pension benefit is determined. For example, if the benefits are based on a 5-year final average plan (preceding age sixty-five), if the average annual salary earned by employees aged sixty to sixty-four is $6,000, and if the average salary earned by the employees aged twenty to twenty-four is $3,000, then the salary-scale factor for ages twenty to twenty-four is 2. This factor decreases as ages increase, and a representative set of salary-scale factors of this type might be as shown in Table 10-10.

TABLE 10-10. ILLUSTRATIVE SALARY-SCALE FACTORS

Attained age	Average annual salary	Salary-scale factor
20–24	$3,000	2.00
25–29	3,530	1.70
30–34	3,870	1.55
35–39	4,290	1.40
40–44	4,800	1.25
45–49	5,220	1.15
50–54	5,450	1.10
55–59	5,710	1.05
60–64	6,000	1.00

Customarily, separate salary scales are adopted for male and for female employees. Also, there may be certain groups of employees for whom promotions are at a quite different rate from that for the bulk of the employees, and sometimes special salary scales are adopted for them (e.g., the executive group).

A salary scale of the type discussed above is designed to reflect only the type of salary progression which results from increases related to length of service and from increased responsibility for some employees as they grow older. It is not designed to reflect any increases caused either by future inflation or by improvement in the efficiency of the employees. These increases tend to be of the across-the-board type, in which all employees share more or less uniformly, and in the opinion of some actuaries they may properly be reflected in pension costs only as they arise. In fact, when annual pension costs are considered in relation to total salaries (i.e., as percentages of covered compensation rather than as dollar amounts), the effect of inflationary increases in compensation do not usually throw these costs out of line in comparison with comparable costs of the prior years.

General. It is not possible in this discussion to cover more than a few of the major points to be considered in the selection of the actuarial bases appropriate for a pension-plan survey. No one set of assumptions is applicable to all circumstances. Actuarial hypotheses may not be fulfilled in later experience; consequently, it is necessary to have periodic and frequent review and evaluation of the factors used.

All too frequently someone inadequately trained in this field will state that these actuarial factors possess a much greater degree of definiteness and stability than is generally the case. While the special skills of the actuary lie in estimating trends of mortality, disability, withdrawal, and the other factors discussed in this chapter, it must always be remembered that these are inherently only estimates and, as such, are subject to some extent to the vagaries of the actuary. The actuary meets his professional responsibilities only if he periodically analyzes and interprets his prior assumptions in the light of the continuously changing conditions affecting these factors.

CHAPTER 11

Funding Principles

That higher or more extensive benefits bring increased costs is an obvious truth that even the novice in the pension field immediately recognizes. That funding method A, involving lower contribution requirements per year than funding method B, means lower costs usually seems to the novice (and sometimes to others, for that matter) to be an obvious truth, whereas actually it does not follow at all. For a given benefit formula and other equal provisions, the same employees will enter the plan, earn their pay, terminate service, retire, and die. The outgo will be identical, and the present value of the outgo is the same at any given rate of interest. The assumptions on which to compute contributions will be adjusted up or down as experience emerges. If contributions are high in the early years of a plan, they will be lower later, and vice versa.

The details of determining such factors as exact contributions, premiums, reserves, and projected disbursements and the derivation and application of the tools for such determinations (such as decrement tables, interest tables, symbols, and functions) require the trained actuary. As in any specialized business, know-how is not acquired by merely walking through the office door. However, an understanding of the broader aspects of pension financing, its objectives, and the variety of methods does not require much in the way of mathematical gymnastics. The purpose of this chapter is to set forth some of these aspects, objectives, and methods in a broad and nontechnical manner.

Pension funding, like all monetary transactions, is merely a "put-and-take" proposition, with the different methods patterned by the incidence, in time and amount, of the "put." For present purposes, it may be assumed that the "take" on the part of those who have been or will be retired is the same for a given plan, regardless of the manner of funding the plan.[1]

Under any plan the employee characteristics of the employing organization must be analyzed, including the distributions by sex, age, wage, length of service, and sometimes other factors, such as occupational or departmental classification. These elements, together with the particular type of plan and benefit formula, will determine costs and their incidence. The trained actuary, whether associated with the insurer under an insured plan or retained under a trusteed plan, will perforce give full consideration to these factors. In what follows it is assumed that the above statements are fully understood by the reader.

To examine the relative timing and magnitude of costs (the "put") required to produce the benefits, the following items will be postulated. They are kept to a minimum to avoid complexity.[2]

1. The John Doe Company has all male employees, between the ages of thirty and sixty-four at the time the period of observation commences; the age distribution of these employees and their death rates by age follow those of a current life table; [3] new employees enter the pension plan each year at age thirty (a common qualifying age), and all employees not dying sooner retire at age sixty-five; there are no terminations under the plan except by death. These assumptions mean that ultimately—in 35 years if age one hundred is taken as the limiting age—the number of new employees entering at age thirty in a year will equal the number of employees, active and retired,

---

[1] In practice there are influences that would vary the "take" and its incidence; for example: benefits large enough to encourage prompt retirement, as contrasted with benefits which are small; employer practices in effecting mandatory retirement; or the right to a cash termination value at retirement age, which competes with the acceptance of the monthly pension.

[2] When one of the authors was associated with the Office of the Actuary of the Social Security Board, he assisted in the preparation of a report (W. Rulon Williamson, Robert J. Myers and Eugene A. Rasor, Various Methods of Financing Old-age Pension Plans, Actuarial Study 10, Social Security Board, Office of the Actuary) on the financing variations in the theory of social-security old-age benefits. The approach used in that report is drawn on herein to some extent.

[3] Group Annuity Table for 1951—Male (except that age one hundred will be deemed the limiting age, or that, in other words, none survive beyond age ninety-nine).

who die in that year and that in the thirty-sixth and each subsequent year the same equality will continue. The number who attain age sixty-five and retire is the same for each year. This is a "stationary-population" situation.

2. The John Doe Company pays uniform annual salaries of $3,000 to its employees and plans to provide $1,000 per year for life as a uniform pension to commence at age sixty-five (augmented by old-age pensions under the social-security law, this would mean roughly two-thirds of pay). All absolute figures shown are simplified and hypothetical; the relationships between the figures are more instructive than the figures themselves.

3. Money earns 2½ per cent interest compounded annually, and no profits, losses, or expenses connected with the plan are considered.

4. Costs are borne entirely by the John Doe Company, and no benefits are provided beyond the $1,000 pension terminating at death.

Under the stated postulates, the period of observation will be taken as 35 years, that is, until the last survivors of the company's first group of pensioners, who reach retirement age sixty-five during the plan's first year, die at the end of year of age ninety-nine, after the receipt of their last (thirty-fifth) annual pension checks. By that time the pension roll is completely filled out and will be constant thereafter. Table 11-1 depicts these distributions at the beginning and end of the period.

With the hypotheses set and the employee age pattern of Table 11-1 available, including work sheets on the corresponding distributions for the second through the thirty-fifth years, several different methods of funding by the John Doe Company will be examined. Each, as fundamental to the entire analysis, supports the same benefit outgo. For brevity, Table 11-1 shows 5-year age groupings, and subsequent tables will be shown for the first, second, and fifth years, and by 5-year time intervals thereafter for the 35-year period of observation.

I. Funding by Current Disbursements. Funding by *current disbursements* merely calls for the John Doe Company to meet each year's pension needs out of current company funds; it is an extended, or quasi, payroll charge. It is sometimes called the *pay-as-you-go plan, pension payroll costs, paying out of the till, assessment plan* (when a group is meeting the costs), and perhaps other names. Of all methods,

TABLE 11-1. AGE, PAYROLL, AND PENSION DISTRIBUTION FOR
THE JOHN DOE COMPANY *

Age group (1)	Beginning of first year		End of thirty-fifth year	
	Active employees (2)	Payroll (3)	Active employees (4)	Payroll (5)
30–34	491	$1,473,000	491	$1,473,000
35–39	488	1,464,000	488	1,464,000
40–44	484	1,452,000	484	1,452,000
45–49	476	1,428,000	476	1,428,000
50–54	462	1,386,000	462	1,386,000
55–59	440	1,320,000	440	1,320,000
60–64	409	1,227,000	409	1,227,000
30–64	3,250	$9,750,000	3,250	$9,750,000
	Retired employees	Pension roll	Retired employees	Pension roll
65–69	None	None	365	$ 365,000
70–74	None	None	303	303,000
75–79	None	None	225	225,000
80–84	None	None	141	141,000
85–89	None	None	68	68,000
90–94	None	None	24	24,000
95 and over	None	None	6	6,000
65 and over	None	None	1,132	$1,132,000

* These distributions should not be considered typical of employed populations.

it is probably the least worthy of either the term *actuarial basis* or the term *actuarially sound*. Later discussion herein will attempt to draw a distinction between these two terms. About the only application of actuarial techniques to this method would be some effort to measure ahead of time the magnitude of pension disbursements in some future year or years.

Under the assumptions, for the John Doe Company the pension outgo can be traced year by year and in the aggregate. Table 11-2

TABLE 11-2. FUNDING BY CURRENT DISBURSEMENTS

Year of plan	John Doe Company contribution		Pension payments	Reserve	Interest on reserve fund	Balance in reserve fund
	Amount	Per cent active covered payroll				
(1)	(2)	(3)	(4)	(5)	(6)	(7)
1	$ 77,000	0.8	$ 77,000	None	None	None
2	152,000	1.6	152,000	None	None	None
5	365,000	3.7	365,000	None	None	None
10	668,000	6.9	668,000	None	None	None
15	893,000	9.2	893,000	None	None	None
20	1,034,000	10.6	1,034,000	None	None	None
25	1,102,000	11.3	1,102,000	None	None	None
30	1,126,000	11.5	1,126,000	None	None	None
35	1,132,000	11.6	1,132,000	None	None	None
35-year total	$29,491,000	8.6	$29,491,000	None	None	None

shows the rise in company contributions over the years, contributions which under this method are one to one with pension disbursements. They start out at less than 1 per cent of active payroll and reach an ultimate level at slightly over 11½ per cent. There are no reserve funds or interest income at any time.

The method just outlined is the type followed to a considerable extent in years past, or sometimes still in the early period of an employer's coming face to face with an immediate pension problem. It is a method by which many pension promises have been destroyed, a likely vicious trend of increasing costs with no protective reserve. For an institution in perpetuity with ample revenue or taxing power, a case can be made for its use. For the John Doe Company and its like, subject to business hazards, few would recommend the current-disbursements method.

II. Reserve Set up at Retirement (Terminal Funding). Under a plan whose benefits are confined to a lifetime income commencing at a given age of retirement (here, age sixty-five), the retired lives at any time would be better protected if a fund were on hand from which these pensions could be paid in the future. They would not have to depend upon the continued existence of the employing unit, competence of later management, or willingness of the employer to pay the pensions counted upon.

A straightforward way to create this security reserve fund would be to set it up at the time each employee retires at age sixty-five. This would be analogous to taking enough funds from surplus or current revenue to purchase or otherwise provide for an immediate lifetime pension for each retiring employee. Under the stationary population which is assumed in this outline, there are 77 employees retiring at age sixty-five each year in the future. With an annual pension of $1,000 to be provided to each of these 77 lives each year, the single premium required to provide pensions is $11,950 per new pensioner, or a total for each year's new group of 77 such persons of $920,000. In Table 11-3 column (2) indicates this amount as being set aside at the end of each year over the period of observation.

In column (4) of Table 11-3 the pension outgo is the same as in Table 11-2, and for more than 15 years this outgo is less than the level contribution of column (2). This creates an interest-bearing reserve fund, illustrated by column (6) which gradually increases over the whole period to reach a stabilized maximum of $8,470,000 at the end of the period. The interest of column (5) helps out, of course. After 35 years the $212,000 annual interest on the reserve fund when added to the $920,000 contribution is just sufficient to meet the pension

TABLE 11-3. FUNDING BY SETTING UP RESERVE AT TIME OF RETIREMENT
(TERMINAL FUNDING)

Year of plan	John Doe Company contribution		Pension payments	Interest on reserve fund	Balance in reserve fund *
	Amount	Per cent active covered payroll			
(1)	(2)	(3)	(4)	(5)	(6)
1	$ 920,000	9.4	$ 77,000	$.........	$ 843,000
2	920,000	9.4	152,000	21,000	1,632,000
5	920,000	9.4	365,000	76,000	3,682,000
10	920,000	9.4	668,000	143,000	6,115,000
15	920,000	9.4	893,000	183,000	7,510,000
20	920,000	9.4	1,034,000	202,000	8,165,000
25	920,000	9.4	1,102,000	209,000	8,403,000
30	920,000	9.4	1,126,000	211,000	8,463,000
35	920,000	9.4	1,132,000	212,000	8,470,000
35-year total	$32,200,000	9.4	$29,491,000	$5,761,000	$8,470,000 †

* Reserve fund at the close of the year after interest income and pension outgo.

† Reserve fund stabilizes at this figure; the oldest original entrant has reached age ninety-nine; the total receipts, column (2) plus column (5), are equal to the total pensions paid, column (4), plus the amount on hand after 35 years, column (6).

payments amounting to $1,132,000 annually, leaving the reserve fund intact.

This method may be compared with that of current disbursements in Table 11-2. Table 11-3 requires an immediate employer cost of 9.4 per cent of payroll, whereas in Table 11-2 only 0.8 per cent is needed the first year. It is not until more than 15 years have elapsed that Table 11-2 costs reach the 9.4 per cent level of Table 11-3. Thereafter Table 11-2 costs are greater. Not only are such costs greater, but no reserve fund is on hand, so that the pensioners under Table 11-2 have nothing to fall back on should the contribution source dry up.

In contrast, the pensioners of Table 11-3 are always assured that the proper fund stands behind their pensions.

In practice, there are probably few pension plans that are funded in exactly this manner. However, the method is approximated when large sums are initially contributed to fund the past-service benefits for employees close to or above the retirement age when a plan commences. Also the method is sometimes used in accumulating a general fund and at retirement transferring therefrom the appropriate sum into a specific fund representative of the required single premium or reserve to pay the benefits for each newly retired life.[4]

III. Level Contributions from Entry Age.[5] The establishment of a reserve fund at the time of retirement, as illustrated by the method shown in Table 11-3, gives those already retired a comfortable feeling, it is true, but goes no distance in underwriting the benefits for employees before retirement. In Table 11-3, if the John Doe Company ceases its $920,000 contribution at any time, the reserve fund of column (6) is only sufficient to pay off the current pensioners with no money applicable to any active lives. Thus, those employees aged sixty-four, who have looked forward to benefits a year hence, will be out of luck and had better have some personal anchor to windward or count on remaining on the job. This latter solution may not be too easy, since disability or loss of incentive may cause the loss of the job or a reduction in salary, and, indeed, if the John Doe Company cannot pay the pension cost as previously, the business itself may be disintegrating.

If active employees are to have an earnest of their future pension expectations, a reserve fund larger than that of Table 11-3 must be accumulated. One way of doing this in an orderly, equitable, and actuarial manner is shown in Table 11-4. Here the age of each employee at the time the plan is installed serves as the determinant of a level contribution or premium paid at the beginning of the year by the John Doe Company to the pension fund or on an annuity contract. For those aged sixty-four at the start, a 1-year amount is needed; for those sixty-three, a level 2-year amount; and so on until

[4] However, a number of negotiated plans include a minimum-funding provision based on this terminal-funding method.

[5] For those presently employed, the contribution is based on their attained ages.

TABLE 11-4. LEVEL ANNUAL CONTRIBUTION FROM AGE OF ENTRY
UNTIL RETIREMENT AGE

| Year of plan | John Doe Company contribution | | Pension payments | Interest on reserve fund | Balance in reserve fund * |
| | Amount | Per cent active covered payroll | | | |
(1)	(2)	(3)	(4)	(5)	(6)
1	$ 3,483,000	35.7	$ 77,000	$ 87,000	$ 3,493,000
2	2,593,000	26.6	152,000	152,000	6,086,000
5	1,645,000	16.9	365,000	292,000	11,596,000
10	1,077,000	11.0	668,000	432,000	17,059,000
15	820,000	8.4	893,000	509,000	19,964,000
20	683,000	7.0	1,034,000	546,000	21,365,000
25	610,000	6.3	1,102,000	562,000	21,930,000
30	575,000	5.9	1,126,000	566,000	22,095,000
35	565,000	5.8	1,132,000	567,000	22,115,000
35-year total	$35,181,000	10.3	$29,491,000	$16,425,000	$22,115,000 †

* Reserve fund at the close of the year after interest income and pension outgo.

† Reserve fund stabilizes at this figure; the oldest original entrant has reached age ninety-nine; the total receipts, column (2) plus column (5), are equal to the total pensions paid, column (4), plus the amount on hand after 35 years, column (6).

for the youngest employees, aged thirty, a 35-year annual contribution must be figured.

At the start of the plan, the highest cost develops, with each year showing a lesser figure until, after 35 years, all active employees will have entered the plan at age thirty and the annual contribution will be stabilized at $565,000. The reserve fund will grow over these years until it too levels off, at a figure of $22,115,000.

Under this structure, if the John Doe Company at any time discontinues its contributions, there is a fund for paying pensions on retirement of active employees commensurate with their age and length of time under the plan. For example, if the company supports the plan for 9 years, employees just reaching age sixty-four at the time of cessation of contributions will have had 9 out of 10 payments made toward their pension, and over 90 per cent of it will be represented in the reserve on hand (it is *over* 90 per cent owing to the action of interest and accretions from "reserves released" by similar lives who died during the 9 years). Likewise, those aged fifty-four will have over 45 per cent of their benefit provided for, and so on.

Method III shown in Table 11-4 removes the sharp boundary line between the ins and the outs that exists in the method shown in Table 11-3. True, it requires the John Doe Company to contribute much more in the early years than later on, but in a sense this is making up for not having started a plan earlier; it is a reflection of the heretofore unfunded past-service or accrued liability.

Method III of Table 11-4 illustrates a funding device commonly found in practice, either under an insured arrangement or through trust-fund facilities. In practice, the steady and substantial drop in column (2) of Table 11-4 is more indicative of trend than of magnitude. This is because the John Doe Company might be an expanding plant with more and more younger lives requiring contribution recognition; or the levels of salaries and wages over a period of time might rise, as they have done in the past, so that pension benefits would also be forced higher, requiring a natural increase in the annual contributions supporting the system. Sometimes a different type of downward cost curve is obtained by spreading the high costs of the early years over a longer period than to retirement age. On the other hand, sometimes the past-service costs are brought even more prominently to the fore as an initial lump-sum accrued liability.[6]

IV. Full Reserve Fund for Past Service with Annual Contributions for Future Service. The method shown in Table 11-5 is based on the concept that each person's pension is the sum total of "pieces" of pension, one for each year served. If an employee is aged fifty at the plan's installation, he has 20 units of past service and 15 units prospectively of future service; which, using the $1,000 pension, means $20/35$,

---

[6] For this latter method, see Table 11-5.

TABLE 11-5. RESERVE FOR PAST SERVICE AND LEVEL PREMIUM
FOR FUTURE SERVICE

Year of plan	John Doe Company contribution		Pension payments	Interest on reserve fund	Balance in reserve fund *
	Amount	Per cent active covered payroll			
(1)	(2)	(3)	(4)	(5)	(6)
1	$12,605,000	129.3	$ 77,000	$ 315,000	$12,843,000
2	750,000	7.7	152,000	340,000	13,781,000
5	712,000	7.3	365,000	405,000	16,220,000
10	661,000	6.8	668,000	483,000	19,134,000
15	624,000	6.4	893,000	530,000	20,842,000
20	596,000	6.1	1,034,000	554,000	21,681,000
25	578,000	5.9	1,102,000	564,000	22,012,000
30	568,000	5.8	1,126,000	567,000	22,105,000
35	565,000	5.8	1,132,000	567,000	22,115,000
35-year total	$33,761,000	9.9	$29,491,000	$17,845,000	$22,115,000 †

* Reserve fund at the close of the year after interest income and pension outgo.
† Reserve fund stabilizes at this figure; the oldest original entrant has reached age ninety-nine; the total receipts, column (2) plus column (5), are equal to the total pensions paid, column (4), plus the amount on hand after 35 years, column (6).

or about $570, of past service and $15/35$, or about $430, to be credited in future years.

Suppose the John Doe Company wants first to meet completely the liability for past service; to do so it will take, including the first year's future-service contribution, $12,605,000, or over 100 per cent of payroll. Then suppose that the company wishes to proceed with the funding of future-service cost as in method III, by level contributions until retirement age. This is accomplished through contributions of the amounts in column (2) in Table 11-5. Finally, the thirty-fifth-year values are identical in Tables 11-4 and 11-5.

An important variant of method IV is to treat past service as just described but to change the incidence of funding the future-service credits so that each year's unit benefit is funded on an as-earned basis, that is, without the anticipated benefit credits of any later year being taken into account costwise. This is the *unit-benefit* or *unit-purchase method*. It is commonly used under a group-annuity plan and can also be handled through a trust fund. Because of similarity in fundamentals between method IV (level purchase) and this unit-purchase variant, a separate table is not shown for this method.

Under the unit-purchase method, it is not infrequent that future-service costs increase somewhat rather than remaining uniform as in the illustration. Wherever an employer's "age center of gravity," taking into account salaries and sex, is tending upward, the yearly unit costs will increase. Hence a declining business might incur a steadily increasing pension cost, even though the number of employees were becoming fewer.

Under either of these two variants of method IV, the company could meet the large past-service liability through an annual budget, amortizing this value over a period of 10, 15, 20, or more years.

V. Full Reserve at Entry Age. An even stricter means of advance funding than the past-service purchase of method IV would be to establish a reserve fund for the whole anticipated pension at the time of an employee's initial entrance into the system. The John Doe Company would contribute once and for all for each employee between the ages of thirty and sixty-four upon the start of the plan and yearly thereafter would pay in a sum sufficient to provide the future pensions for the year's group of new employees entering the system at age thirty.

A very sizable outlay would be needed at the start, $21,286,000 as shown in Table 11-6, followed by only $388,000 annually thereafter. For the thirty-fifth year and after, with a pension load of $1,132,000 to meet, there must be a stabilized reserve fund large enough so that when it is increased by the current year's contribution of $388,000 it will yield $744,000 of annual interest, which with the annual contribution of $388,000 will just meet the pension outgo. This reserve fund, as shown in Table 11-6, is $29,372,000.

VI. Fully Funded Perpetuity. Suppose, with the stationary employee population of the John Doe Company, it is asked what sum might

TABLE 11-6. RESERVE AT ENTRY AGE

Year of plan	John Doe Company contribution		Pension payments	Interest on reserve fund	Balance in reserve fund *
	Amount	Per cent active covered payroll			
(1)	(2)	(3)	(4)	(5)	(6)
1	$21,286,000	218.3	$ 77,000	$ 532,000	$21,741,000
2	388,000	4.0	152,000	553,000	22,530,000
5	388,000	4.0	365,000	608,000	24,580,000
10	388,000	4.0	668,000	675,000	27,013,000
15	388,000	4.0	893,000	715,000	28,409,000
20	388,000	4.0	1,034,000	734,000	29,064,000
25	388,000	4.0	1,102,000	742,000	29,304,000
30	388,000	4.0	1,126,000	744,000	29,365,000
35	388,000	4.0	1,132,000	744,000	29,372,000
35-year total	$34,478,000	10.1	$29,491,000	$24,385,000	$29,372,000 †

* Reserve fund at the close of the year after interest income and pension outgo.

† Reserve fund stabilizes at this figure; the oldest original entrant has reached age ninety-nine; the total receipts, column (2) plus column (5), are equal to the total pensions paid, column (4), plus the amount on hand after 35 years, column (6).

be set aside at the start so that ever after the pension outgo would be met without any further payment by the company. This figure, under the assumptions, can readily be computed and is given in Table 11-7 as $36,806,000. The accumulation of this amount at interest, minus pensions as they become due, results in a growing reserve for 35 years until a stabilized investment is reached, the interest return on which just meets the thereafter constant pension outgo of $1,132,000 a year.

For the business as such this method would be least likely to produce a feasible pension solution. If, however, some philanthropist, windfall reversion, or other extra situation produced the money, its use in this way to provide income for superannuated employees might be deemed

Table 11-7. Fully Funded Perpetuity

Year of plan	John Doe Company contribution		Pension payments	Interest on reserve fund	Balance in reserve fund *
	Amount	Per cent active covered payroll			
(1)	(2)	(3)	(4)	(5)	(6)
1	$36,806,000	377.5	$ 77,000	$ 920,000	$37,649,000
2	None	None	152,000	941,000	38,438,000
5	None	None	365,000	996,000	40,488,000
10	None	None	668,000	1,063,000	42,921,000
15	None	None	893,000	1,103,000	44,317,000
20	None	None	1,034,000	1,122,000	44,972,000
25	None	None	1,102,000	1,130,000	45,212,000
30	None	None	1,126,000	1,132,000	45,273,000
35	None	None	1,132,000	1,132,000	45,280,000
35-year total	$36,806,000	10.8	$29,491,000	$37,965,000	$45,280,000 †

* Reserve fund at the close of the year after interest income and pension outgo.

† Reserve fund stabilizes at this figure; the oldest original entrant has reached age ninety-nine; the total receipts, column (2) plus column (5), are equal to the total pensions paid, column (4), plus the amount on hand after 35 years, column (6).

a legitimate social benefaction. Something of this nature was actually the purpose and theory behind the Carnegie Foundation for the Advancement of Teaching, which set up a fund whose income was supposed to furnish pensions for retired teachers. It did not work too well, for the teachers increased in numbers, lived longer than was expected, and secured higher salaries, and the investment opportunities did not furnish the yields necessary to support the system. The perpetuity capital sum can only be figured accurately if the actual number and amount of future pensions are known in advance, an impossibility except for the fictional John Doe Company.

The Completed Circle. The highest level of advance funding is illustrated by Table 11-7, where all pensions are paid from interest on the fund. Assume that the fund is owned and was set up out of the business resources of the John Doe Company. Table 11-2 shows the ultimate pensions of $1,132,000 as paid entirely from the current business operations of the John Doe Company. Thus the circle is complete; the only difference between Table 11-2 and Table 11-7 (if we disregard legal rights and measure solely in terms of the business enterprise that must produce the funds, one way or another, for current pension payments) is the investment source of the perpetual pension payments. If the funds of Table 11-7 were all invested in securities of the John Doe Company itself, Table 11-2 might be called identical in end results with Table 11-7. Perhaps this demonstration is a novel Q.E.D. for the principle that the pension reserve fund should not be invested in the obligations of the company itself. The full reserve in such case becomes a current disbursements method, and again all the eggs, but with a different name, are in the same basket.

The graduation between the six funding methods may be seen, in the ultimate status, by the chart that is shown below, which summarizes

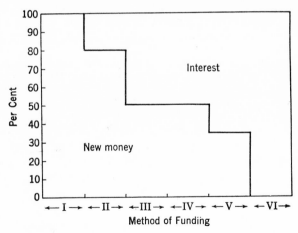

Comparison of Funding Methods for the Long Run (Source of Funds for Thirty-fifth Year and Later)

the components of the stabilized pension load between new money from the company (100 to 0 per cent) and investment returns on the fund (0 to 100 per cent). This chart distinguishes the methods graphically in end product, but prime differences between methods also lie in initial costs and early incidence, as given in the preceding tables. Most plans in use today may be typed as being based on one of the methods described in this chapter, although there are in-betweens, including *partial-reserve plans,* whose implications may be understood from this discussion.

Actuarial Methods and Standards. Any one of the methods just reviewed may be said to follow actuarial principles and procedures. While each is funded on an *actuarial basis,* they are not all of the same degree of *actuarial soundness,* or perhaps a better term, *actuarial conservatism.* There is a considerable looseness and misunderstanding surrounding the use of these terms. To claim that a plan is actuarial gives no real clue to its funding, other than that a structure of some sort has been adopted for meeting costs. Even that can be vague, however, as witness the 1935 Social Security Act, where "annual premiums" were called for on "accepted actuarial principles," but no one ever really knew what Congress intended by this wording, least of all the actuary.

Therefore, a plan may be described as on an "actuarial basis" and yet be far from conservative in its funding. In method, it could range from something just a little better than method I, shown in Table 11-2, to something as ultraconservative as method VI, shown in Table 11-7. It is well to ask for the form of funding structure itself in looking behind the term *actuarial basis.* Having learned the structure, one may then ask whether the mortality tables are "safe," whether the interest assumption is likely to be realized over the years ahead, what withdrawal rates are used, what future salary assumptions are, and what incidence of actual retirement may safely be expected. In other words, even with the adoption of a conservative funding *method,* the basis of computing contributions and reserves thereunder might be quite nonconservative.

The Revenue Act of 1954 and the regulations, bulletins, and other interpretations promulgated by the Internal Revenue Service practically force plans to measure themselves by some actuarial standards, conservative or otherwise. Upon analysis an existing plan may be found to be weak in its actuarial assumptions and reserve position, or the commencement of a new plan may be, in blueprint, on a low plane as regards funding. Many authorities believe that neither of these situations needs to discourage the project. There is hope for success as long as some definite actuarial structure is adopted with the intent of living up to it and with the objective of gradually moving to greater conservatism when possible. Even though, technically, such a plan could fit the label "an actuarial plan," it should not be held out to employees as being safe and sure and soundly financed by such a loose and too reassuring designation.[7]

[7] For further discussion of this subject see Dorrance C. Bronson, "Concepts of Actuarial Soundness in Pension Plans," Richard D. Irwin, Inc., Homewood, Ill., 1957.

CHAPTER **12**

Cost of Benefits

For a pay-as-you-go pension plan, the *cost* is the same as the amount of benefit outgo (plus the employer's administrative expense of keeping records, mailing checks, and tracing the payees), and the incidence of cost coincides with the due dates of the benefits. The cost usually increases each year for decades into the future, as was explained in the preceding chapter. In this chapter, when reference is made to *cost of benefits,* an advance-funded plan is assumed, supported either by single-premium or by annual-premium contributions. The terms *single premium* and *annual premium* are used in a generic sense, as applicable to either an insured plan or a trust-fund plan. There is no actuarial terminology to distinguish the contributions under the two types of plans, for, in effect, the same processes are gone through in arriving at the actuarially appropriate contributions in either type, and *premium* is the traditional actuarial designation for contributions to systems of protection against life contingencies (death, disability, and old age).

Single Premiums. The single-premium principle is used in the unit-benefit-per-year-of-service type of pension plan for meeting the cost of both past-service credits and units of current-service credit as they arise in the future. It is also used in the money-purchase type of plan to provide such amounts of deferred benefit as the contribution of the year will produce, according to the age and sex of the employee and the premium basis (mortality table, interest rate, and expense loading) adopted. The single-premium principle is also applied where purchase of specific insured benefits is deferred until retirement occurs, at which time monies are drawn either from an existing trust, conventional

TABLE 12-1. SINGLE-PREMIUM COST OF PENSION BENEFITS—UNIT-BENEFIT PLAN

Employee's age	Amount of annual earnings	Annual benefit purchased		Single premium per $1 annual benefit (no death benefit)	Cost of indicated benefits	
		Past service	Current service		Past service	Current service
60	$4,000	$600	$ 40	$ 9.62	$5,772	$ 385
61	4,200	....	42	10.01	*	420
62	4,500	....	45	10.44	*	470
63	4,200	....	42	10.90	*	458
64	4,200	....	42	11.40	*	479
65 (retires)	.....	....	..	.....	*	
Totals............		$600	$211		$5,772	$2,212

* Nothing, unless past-service cost of $5,772 is amortized instead of being paid in an initial lump sum.

deposit-administration fund, or from current revenue to furnish the premiums for the specified retirement benefits.

Purchase of a 1 per cent per year of service benefit for a particular employee will illustrate the application of the single-premium principle. This employee was aged sixty at the effective date of the retirement plan, at which time he was credited with 15 years of past service. Table 12-1 shows what the cost of this employee's benefits would be.[1]

[1] Unless otherwise noted, the Group Annuity Table for 1951—Male with 2½ per cent interest (expense loading omitted) is used as the basis for premiums and yields shown in this chapter. Many insurers are supplanting the 1937 Standard Annuity Mortality Table, which has been used widely in the past, with various modifications of the Ga-1951 Table. While the 1937 Table greatly overstates the mortality to be expected at the early ages, it is still regarded by many actuaries as a suitable mortality basis for pensioners, particularly for pension plans financed through trust funds. It is believed that the 1937 Table (and 2 per cent interest) is still used by the Internal Revenue Service as the most conservative actuarial basis in testing deductibility of contributions from taxable income, and this same

TABLE 12-2. SINGLE-PREMIUM COST OF PENSION BENEFITS—
MONEY-PURCHASE PLAN

Employee's age	Amount of annual earnings	Contributions made		Single premium per $1 annual benefit (no death benefit)	Amount of annual benefit purchased	
		Past service	Current service		Past service	Current service
60	$4,000	$6,000	$ 400	$ 9.62	$624	$ 42
61	4,200	*	420	10.01	....	42
62	4,500	*	450	10.44	....	43
63	4,200	*	420	10.90	....	39
64	4,200	*	420	11.40	....	37
65 (retires)	.....	*				
Totals............		$6,000	$2,110		$624	$203

* Nothing, unless past-service allocation of $6,000 is amortized instead of being paid in an initial lump sum.

Table 12-2 gives an illustration of the purchase of benefits under a money-purchase plan. It shows the amount of pension which would be provided on a no-death-benefit basis with employer contributions of 10 per cent of the employee's salary for each credited year of past service (15 years) and 10 per cent (e.g., 5 per cent from employee, 5 per cent from employer) of salary for each year of current service.

The introductory remarks in Chapter 11 stressed the fact that real costs are determined by the experience of each plan. However, the addition of supplementary benefits to the basic pension benefit means added cost. With respect to the first point, a plan can start out on any given premium basis, high or low, until experience indicates over- or under-funding. Examples given below will show the effect on premium rates caused by varying the assumed interest rate, varying the mortality assumptions, or introducing a withdrawal postulate. Death bene-

table (with a 1-year set-back in age) is used currently in determining the portion of a life annuity that is subject to federal income tax.

fits before retirement are frequently included in a plan as supplements to the basic pension benefit. The effect on costs of introducing such supplementary benefits into a plan will also be indicated.

In the several tables that follow, the straight life annuity,[2] with the first payment falling due at age sixty-five (or immediately, if indicated age exceeds sixty-five), is used as a base with which to make comparisons. The annuities are in the amount of $100 a year, payable at the beginning of each year, with the final payment falling due at the beginning of the year in which death occurs.[3] The first set of comparative tables (Tables 12-3 to 12-9) deal with the single-premium type of annuity; the annual-premium type is discussed later with a corresponding set of comparative tables.

Effect of Changing the Interest Rate. The first comparison to examine is that of the relative decrease in costs resulting from an increase in the assumed rate of interest. Since single premiums are, in effect, present values of future-benefit payments, the higher the rate of interest earned on a fund organized to meet such payments, the lower the initial fund (single premium) need be. This comparison is shown in Table 12-3.

Table 12-3 illustrates how single-premium costs decrease as the assumed interest rate increases. The decrease is not uniform relatively between ages but differs very little percentagewise for any given age for successive changes in interest rate of a uniform amount. The 79.1 per cent of column (4) for age twenty-five means that the cost is 20.9 per cent less (as ½ per cent is added in the interest assumption) than the cost given in column (1), the 62.7 per cent of column (6) (as another ½ per cent is added) represents a decrease of 37.3 per cent from the cost in column (1), and the decrease between column (8) and column (1) is 50.2 per cent.[4]

The higher the age is, the smaller are the differentials between costs resulting from using different interest rates, the reason being that the older the annuitant or prospective annuitant is, the shorter is his

[2] The term *straight life annuity* means that the income is payable for life from its date of commencement, with no surrender values or death benefits.

[3] In practice, pension benefits are usually paid monthly, and slight adjustments would be thereby required.

[4] 100 per cent minus the 49.8 per cent shown in column (9).

TABLE 12-3. SINGLE-PREMIUM COMPARISONS—EFFECT OF VARYING INTEREST RATES
COST OF $100-A-YEAR STRAIGHT LIFE ANNUITY *—GROUP ANNUITY TABLE FOR 1951—MALE

| Age | At 2 per cent interest | | At 2½ per cent interest | | At 3 per cent interest | | | At 3½ per cent interest | | |
	Single premium (1)	Per cent of column (3) (2)	Single premium (3)	Per cent of column (1) (4)	Single premium (5)	Per cent of column (1) (6)	Per cent of column (3) (7)	Single premium (8)	Per cent of column (1) (9)	Per cent of column (5) (10)
25	$ 438.38	126.4	$ 346.71	79.1	$ 274.79	62.7	79.3	$ 218.24	49.8	79.4
35	539.68	120.4	448.22	83.1	372.96	69.1	83.2	310.90	57.6	83.4
45	671.54	114.7	585.68	87.2	511.64	76.2	87.4	447.68	66.7	87.5
55	872.14	109.2	798.75	91.6	732.57	84.0	91.7	672.79	77.1	91.8
65	1,242.55	104.0	1,195.03	96.2	1,150.67	92.6	96.3	1,109.20	89.3	96.4
75	804.85	102.6	784.22	97.4	764.60	95.0	97.5	745.94	92.7	97.6

* Commencing at age sixty-five, except that for age seventy-five the annuity commences at seventy-five.

probable remaining lifetime and the less opportunity there is for interest to be compounded.

Effect of Changing Mortality Basis. The effect of changes in the assumptions of mortality rates is indicated in Table 12-4. Here again, logic can supply the general answer in advance, since the lower the death rate is, the more employees will live to retirement age and the longer the benefits will be payable beyond that age—a double effect.

The differentials in Table 12-4 under differing mortality assumptions are fairly constant by age, unlike those produced by changes in interest rate in Table 12-3. Columns (13) and (14) in Table 12-4 deal with the common technique, for purposes of premium computation, of assuming a person to be 1 year younger than he actually is; this adds conservatism when the table itself is thought to be insufficiently conservative.

The table used for columns (5) and (6) is derived from Census Bureau studies made from the data of the 1940 census, and for columns (7) and (8), of the 1950 census. It is based on the general-population experience for white male lives and includes all sorts of health conditions, the hale and moribund alike. It consequently shows heavier mortality than among individual purchasers of annuities or among employees actively at work when first observed, but the mortality improvement from one census to the next is of considerable significance.

A more recent mortality table based on the mortality experience among lives covered under group-annuity contracts is the 1951 Group Annuity Mortality Table, on which the entries in the second column in Table 12-4 and the third column in Table 12-5 have been based. This mortality table was developed by Ray M. Peterson after a study of the intercompany group-annuity mortality experience for the years 1946 to 1950. In preparing this table, Mr. Peterson analyzed the long-range improvement to be expected in mortality rates, and projection scale C was developed for the purpose of giving effect to this expected improvement. Under projection scale C, the annual rate of decrease in mortality per year assumed in projecting the mortality table is 1.25 per cent for ages twenty to seventy, 1 per cent at age seventy-five, 0.67 per cent at age eighty, 0.33 per cent at age eighty-five, and 0 per cent at age ninety. Appropriate percentages apply at intervening ages (see Table 12-5).

TABLE 12-4. SINGLE-PREMIUM COMPARISONS
COST OF $100-A-YEAR STRAIGHT LIFE AN

Age	Ga-1951— Male, 2½ per cent, single premium	1937 Standard Annuity, 2½ per cent males		Census Actuarial Tables, 2½ per cent, white males			
				1939–1941		1949–1951	
		Single premium	Per cent of column (2)	Single premium	Per cent of column (2)	Single premium	Per cent of column (2)
(1)	(2)	(3)	(4)	(5)	(6)	(7)	(8)
25	$ 346.71	$ 314.54	90.7	$ 248.97	71.8	$ 274.14	79.1
35	448.22	411.05	91.7	327.79	73.1	357.56	79.8
45	585.68	549.31	93.8	441.66	75.4	475.92	81.3
55	798.75	770.92	96.5	634.03	79.4	673.57	84.3
65	1,195.03	1,201.34	100.5	1,046.13	87.5	1,092.37	91.4
75	784.22	834.36	106.4	681.21	86.9	728.23	92.9

* Commencing at age sixty-five, except that for age seventy-five the annuity commences at seventy-five.

† For a discussion of the Ga-1951 Table, see Ray M. Peterson, "Group Annuity Mortality," *Transactions of the Society of Actuaries*, vol. 4, p. 246. The 1937 Standard Annuity Mortality Table appears in the *Transactions of the Actuarial Society of America*, vol. 39, pp. 8–23. For the Census Actuarial Tables, see T. N. E. Greville, United

There is also included in the 1951 Group Annuity Mortality Table a basic safety margin to allow for groups that have a lower mortality experience than the average. This basic safety margin was injected by reducing the rates in the basic table (derived from the experience of the years 1946 to 1950) for males by 10 per cent and for females by 12½ per cent. The 1951 Table is coming into widespread use, but numerous adjustments are frequently made when it is used by insurers for calculating group-annuity rates; for example, an insurer may utilize the projection factors for a short period, such as 3 years, and then set the age back by 1, 1½, or 2 years in order to introduce mar-

—Effect of Varying Mortality Rates
nuity * on Mortality Bases † Indicated

Basic ‡ Ga-1951—Male (projected 14 years to 1965), 2½ per cent		Ga-1951—Male (projected 3 years to 1954), 2½ per cent			
				1-year set-back in age	
Single premium	Per cent of column (2)	Single premium	Per cent of column (2)	Single premium	Per cent of column (2)
(9)	(10)	(11)	(12)	(13)	(14)
$ 356.38	102.8	$ 354.07	102.1	$ 375.10	108.2
460.40	102.7	457.57	102.1	484.48	108.1
600.76	102.6	597.45	102.0	631.44	107.8
815.77	102.1	812.88	101.8	853.81	106.9
1,207.46	101.0	1,209.10	101.2	1,254.55	105.0
775.88	98.9	792.39	101.0	830.32	105.9

States Life Tables and Actuarial Tables, 1939–41, U.S. Bureau of the Census, Vital
Statistics Division; and Actuarial Tables Based on United States Life Tables, 1949–51,
National Office of Vital Statistics.
    ‡ This is the Ga-1951 Table with certain loadings (10 per cent and 12½ per cent in
the case of males and females, respectively) deleted.

gins for their annuity business. In trust-fund determinations, these
margins are not so widely used. Some actuaries feel that for this purpose a more logical procedure would be to use the basic (unloaded)
1951 Table and, except where unusually heavy mortality is expected,
project it into the future for, say, 10, 15, or 20 years.[5]

    The substantial reduction from the mortality rates in the 1937
Standard Annuity Table at the lower ages has a significant effect on the
contribution required to provide a pension benefit. The effect is illustrated by Table 12-6.

[5] See Chap. 10.

TABLE 12-5. EXPECTED DEATHS PER 1,000 LIVES PER YEAR BY
VARIOUS MORTALITY TABLES
(Male lives)

Attained age	1937 Standard Annuity Table	1951 Group Annuity Mortality Table projected by scale C to				
		1951	1952	1962	1972	1982
25	1.561	0.758	0.749	0.660	0.582	0.513
35	2.981	1.374	1.357	1.196	1.055	0.930
45	6.362	3.580	3.535	3.117	2.749	2.424
55	13.554	10.436	10.306	9.087	8.013	7.066
65	28.751	24.418	24.113	21.263	18.750	16.533
75	60.464	62.427	61.803	55.893	50.549	45.716
85	124.837	146.852	146.363	141.561	136.917	132.426

TABLE 12-6. COMPARISON OF NET PREMIUMS TO PROVIDE A
$100-A-YEAR STRAIGHT LIFE ANNUITY FROM AGE SIXTY-FIVE
(Males—2½ per cent interest)

Age	Single premiums			Annual premiums payable through age 64		
	1937 Standard Annuity Mortality Table	Ga-1951 Table	Basic Ga-1951 (projected 14 years to 1965)	1937 Standard Annuity Mortality Table	Ga-1951 Table	Basic Ga-1951 (projected 14 years to 1965)
25	$ 314.54	$ 346.71	$ 356.38	$13.09	$14.03	$14.39
35	411.05	448.22	460.40	20.78	21.99	22.51
45	549.31	585.68	600.76	37.55	39.05	39.88
55	770.92	798.75	815.77	92.26	94.14	95.79
65	1,201.34	1,195.03	1,207.46			

Effect of Introducing a Withdrawal Rate. Employees terminating service other than by death or retirement would reduce the number living through to receive retirement benefits under the plan. In some plans the terminating employees are granted a full, or partial, right to retirement benefits accrued on account of service rendered up to their termination date; in these cases a benefit liability (*vested deferred right*) continues to exist beyond the date of termination. Under the single-premium forms, where such liability continues, no savings have occurred by reason of the fact of termination. Where, however, no such vested right exists, the reserve assets representing the liability canceled may be credited to the employer's account and thereby reduce the cash requirement for subsequent single-premium purchases. The figures below illustrate the cost effect for two assumed sets of withdrawal rates, one with moderate rates of termination of service and the other with fairly high rates.

Column (2) of Table 12-7 again shows the basic measuring rod used in this chapter, which does not include a withdrawal discount (or,

TABLE 12-7. SINGLE-PREMIUM COMPARISONS INTRODUCING A WITHDRAWAL RATE Cost of $100-A-YEAR STRAIGHT LIFE ANNUITY*—GROUP ANNUITY TABLE FOR 1951 —MALE—2½ PER CENT—AND INDICATED WITHDRAWAL BASES

Age (1)	No withdrawal, single premium (2)	Moderate withdrawal		High withdrawal	
		Single premium (3)	Per cent of column (2) (4)	Single premium (5)	Per cent of column (2) (6)
25	$ 346.71	$ 72.90	21.0	$ 17.90	5.2
35	448.22	237.41	53.0	159.38	35.6
45	585.68	443.45	75.7	420.40	71.8
55	798.75	671.18	84.0	671.18	84.0
65	1,195.03	1,195.03	100.0	1,195.03	100.0
75	784.22	784.22	100.0	784.22	100.0

* Commencing at age sixty-five, except that for age seventy-five the annuity commences at seventy-five.

indeed, any form of attrition except deaths). Columns (3) to (6) show illustrative reductions in cost by reason of the introduction of such a discount. The rates of termination (which exclude deaths) are principally those for quits and discharges, which are assumed to decrease as age increases and become zero after age fifty, but they also include rates for total and permanent disablement, a form of termination which may occur up to age sixty-four. The greatest volume of withdrawals is found at the lower ages, where costs are lighter. Hence, the relative effect in *dollars* of a withdrawal discount is typically much smaller than the corresponding effect in *number of persons* withdrawing. For this reason, cost reductions taken in advance for assumed withdrawals do not make as much difference as at first might be supposed; the numerically higher turnover at the younger ages is considerably offset by the greater weight of the fewer withdrawals at the higher ages.

Male versus Female Mortality. In Table 12-8 appears the effect on single-premium costs of population experience by sex. Mortality of white lives and nonwhite lives is recorded separately in the mortality studies made by the Census Bureau in conjunction with the 1950 census.[6] The single premiums have been computed from these census tables for white lives and are shown in comparison with the Group Annuity Table for 1951 used in preparing the earlier tables in this chapter.

The purpose of Table 12-8 is to give some indication of the effect on costs of (1) substituting female for male experience and (2) introducing the concept of *selective lives* (according to a table intended to be representative of mortality among those purchasing annuities) instead of the general population experience. Column (7) shows how much greater is the single premium for an age-sixty-five benefit for a woman than for a man. A comparison of column (10) with column (4) gives an indication of the mortality differential by sex in the general white population. The single premiums shown for the census table are not available on the market; that is, no insurer would offer these prices since they cannot expect purchasers to represent a cross section

[6] Actuarial Tables Based on United States Life Tables 1949–51, U.S. Department of Health, Education, and Welfare, Office of Vital Statistics, Special Reports, vol. 41, nos. 1 and 2.

TABLE 12-8. SINGLE-PREMIUM COMPARISONS BY SEX

Cost of $100-a-year Straight Life Annuity *
(2½ per cent interest)

Males

| Age | Ga-1951 Table, single premium | Census Actuarial Tables, 1949–1951, white | |
| | | Single premium | Per cent of column (2) |
(1)	(2)	(3)	(4)
25	$ 346.71	$ 274.14	79.1
35	448.22	357.56	79.8
45	585.68	475.92	81.3
55	798.75	673.57	84.3
65	1,195.03	1,092.37	91.4
75	784.22	728.23	92.9

Females

| Age | Ga-1951 Table | | Census Actuarial Tables, 1949–1951, white | | |
| | Single premium | Per cent of column (2) | Single premium | Per cent of column (6) | Per cent of column (2) |
(5)	(6)	(7)	(8)	(9)	(10)
25	$ 455.00	131.2	$ 372.21	81.8	107.4
35	586.30	130.8	481.95	82.2	107.5
45	760.55	129.9	631.92	83.1	107.9
55	1,003.32	125.6	855.27	85.2	107.1
65	1,389.54	116.3	1,250.60	90.0	104.7
75	912.05	116.3	815.07	89.4	103.9

* Commencing at age sixty-five, except that for age seventy-five the annuity commences at seventy-five.

of the general population; rather, they expect selective purchasers whose lighter mortality will necessitate the higher premiums of columns (2) and (6).

In the past, many mortality tables were constructed from data for male lives only or from data containing only a small proportion of female lives. Premium rates for females were based on an arbitrary set-back of (usually) 3 to 5 years (i.e., female lives were assumed to be subject to the same mortality as male lives at a somewhat younger age). The Group Annuity Table for 1951, in keeping with more modern practice, was derived from data for males and females separately, two distinct tables being published.

The single premiums for females at ages twenty-five and thirty-five are practically the same as for males aged thirty-five and forty-five, a difference of about 10 years in age. This difference tends to decrease to about 5 years of age in the range at which joint-and-survivorship functions are normally calculated, and for purposes of simplicity a level difference in age between male and female mortality is sometimes assumed in connection with the Group Annuity Table for 1951—Male.

Effect of Introducing Death Benefits. A significant increase in costs is caused by the introduction of collateral benefits in addition to the basic life-income benefit at retirement age. Collateral benefits frequently used are some form of death benefit payable either at death before retirement or at death after retirement, or both. In Table 12-9 the effect of this influence is shown under a plan that undertakes to refund the single premium (without interest) [7] that has been paid at death before retirement but to make no payment if death occurs after retirement. A second set of figures is given where the reverse is assumed, i.e., no payment at death before retirement but a guaranteed duration of income after retirement. The third comparison is of the effects of both, a refund of premium at death before retirement and a guaranteed period of payment after retirement.

When the single premium paid at the age indicated is to be refunded in event of death before retirement, it adds about 15 per cent to the cost, as shown in column (4); similarly, if a period of 10 years

---

[7] In most plans interest is allowed at the valuation rate or a slightly lower rate.

TABLE 12-9. SINGLE-PREMIUM COMPARISONS INTRODUCING DEATH BENEFITS COST OF $100-A-YEAR STRAIGHT LIFE ANNUITY * WITH DEATH BENEFITS INDICATED (GA-1951—MALE—2½ PER CENT)

Age	No death benefits, single premium	No death benefit after age 65; premium refunded at death before age 65		No death benefit before age 65; death within 10 years after retirement, remainder of 10 payments continued		With both the death benefit before age 65 of column (3) and after retirement of column (5)	
		Single premium	Per cent of column (2)	Single premium	Per cent of column (2)	Single premium	Per cent of column (2)
(1)	(2)	(3)	(4)	(5)	(6)	(7)	(8)
25	$ 346.71	$ 388.38	112.0	$ 379.63	109.5	$ 425.26	122.7
35	448.22	513.86	114.6	490.78	109.5	562.65	125.5
45	585.68	684.24	116.8	641.30	109.5	749.22	127.9
55	798.75	912.51	114.2	874.60	109.5	999.16	125.1
65	1,195.03	1,195.03	100.0	1,308.50	109.5	1,308.50	109.5
75	784.22	784.22	100.0	1,034.77	131.9	1,034.77	131.9

* Commencing at age sixty-five, except that for age seventy-five the annuity commences at seventy-five.

certain is guaranteed for payment of benefits after retirement, the single premium is increased about 9½ per cent, as shown in column (6). To grant this latter benefit to a person already well along in age, such as age seventy-five, where the annuity would begin immediately, the increase from the no-refund-at-death type would be much larger— 31.9 per cent in the example above. Column (8) gives the percentage increase when both benefits, refund of single premiums in the event of death before retirement and 10 years of benefits in any event after retirement, are combined. In this case, the single premiums are increased about 25 per cent except for the expected irregularities at the higher ages.

The several tables thus far presented in this chapter are illustrative of changes in size of single premiums when age, interest rate, mortality rate, withdrawal rate, sex, and death benefit are considered separately. The successive changes cannot be combined from these tables to produce a correct composite result; that is, any two percentage changes, each of which is shown in these tables, when taken together are neither sums nor products of the individual changes. For example, Table 12-3 shows that at age forty-five changing from an interest rate of $2\frac{1}{2}$ per cent to one of 3 per cent causes a 12.6 per cent reduction in premium; in Table 12-4 changing from the Ga-1951—Male Table to the 1937 Standard Annuity Table causes a 6.2 per cent reduction in premium. However, changing from the Ga-1951—Male Table at $2\frac{1}{2}$ per cent interest to the 1937 Standard Annuity Table at 3 per cent interest causes neither a reduction of 18.8 per cent (12.6 per cent plus 6.2 per cent) nor a reduction of 18.0 per cent (100 per cent minus the product of 87.4 per cent times 93.8 per cent). The accurate reduction may be obtained only by direct computations from the 1937 Standard Annuity 3 per Cent Table itself; for age forty-five the result would be a single premium of $479.27, a reduction from the single premium shown by the Ga-1951—Male—$2\frac{1}{2}$ per Cent Table of 18.2 per cent. The product of the individual changes more closely approximates the correct total change than does the sum of the individual changes.

Annual Premiums. Annual-premium funding calls for a level yearly contribution of a fixed amount per unit of benefit, payable for a predetermined number of years, usually until retirement, but ceasing at an employee's death. The annual-premium principle is used (1) for benefits of either the flat-amount or the level-percentage-of-pay type, (2) for the group-permanent type, and (3) for the insurance-annuity or retirement-annuity type based on individual contracts. If employees at or above retirement age are included in the plan when funding commences, only one annual premium, identical with the single premiums previously shown, is payable on the account of each (unless some spread-funding device is adopted, such as making contributions over a 10-year period for these older lives).

The annual-premium tables that follow proceed by the same variations and in the same order as the single-premium tables above. As before, they are related to a basic straight-life-annuity rate for male employees retiring at age sixty-five (or over) and are the net premiums (without expense loading) for a $100-a-year retirement benefit.

TABLE 12-10. ANNUAL-PREMIUM COMPARISONS—EFFECT OF VARYING
INTEREST RATES
COST OF $100-A-YEAR STRAIGHT LIFE ANNUITY *—GROUP ANNUITY TABLE
FOR 1951—MALE

Age	At 2 per cent interest		Annual premium at 2½ per cent interest	At 3 per cent interest		At 3½ per cent interest	
	Annual premium	Per cent of column (4)		Annual premium	Per cent of column (4)	Annual premium	Per cent of column (4)
(1)	(2)	(3)	(4)	(5)	(6)	(7)	(8)
25	$ 16.41	117.0	$ 14.03	$ 11.99	85.5	$ 10.23	72.9
35	24.92	113.3	21.99	19.40	88.2	17.12	77.9
45	42.96	110.0	39.05	35.51	90.9	32.32	82.8
55	100.70	107.0	94.14	88.11	93.6	82.55	87.7
65	1,242.55	104.0	1,195.03	1,150.67	96.3	1,109.20	92.8
75	804.85	102.6	784.22	764.60	97.5	745.94	95.1

* Commencing at age sixty-five, except that for age seventy-five the annuity commences at seventy-five. Single premiums are shown for ages sixty-five and seventy-five.

Effect of Changing Interest Rate. Table 12-10 shows the effect of varying rates of interest while holding the other basic assumptions constant.

The same general effects on annual premiums follow from varying the rate of interest as for single premiums.[8] However, the effect of change from one interest rate to the next is not so marked as on single premiums. The reason is that under the single-premium form the full contribution for the benefit is made in one sum at the entry age, so that the difference in interest rate (with its compounding) affects the whole period before benefit commencement. Under the annual-

8 See pp. 239–240.

TABLE 12-11. ANNUAL-PREMIUM COMPARISONS
COST OF $100-A-YEAR STRAIGHT LIFE AN

Age	Ga-1951—Male, 2½ per cent, annual premium	1937 Standard Annuity, 2½ per cent		Census Actuarial Tables, 1949–1951, white males, 2½ per cent	
		Annual premium	Per cent of column (2)	Annual premium	Per cent of column (2)
(1)	(2)	(3)	(4)	(5)	(6)
25	$ 14.03	$ 13.09	93.3	$ 11.41	81.3
35	21.99	20.78	94.5	18.12	82.4
45	39.05	37.55	96.2	32.86	84.1
55	94.14	92.26	98.0	81.72	86.8
65	1,195.03	1,201.34	100.5	1,092.37	91.4
75	784.22	834.36	106.4	728.23	92.9

* Commencing at age sixty-five, except that for age seventy-five the annuity commences at seventy-five. Single premiums are shown for ages sixty-five and seventy-five.

premium form the contribution is paid in installments, so that the difference in interest rate operates over the whole period only on the first installment, a shorter time on the second installment, and so on.

Effect of Changing Mortality Basis. Table 12-11 is based on varying the mortality rates while the other basic assumptions are constant.

Much of the discussion of Table 12-4 is also pertinent to Table 12-11. The respective changes in annual premium caused by varying the mortality rates are approximately equal, irrespective of whether single premiums or annual premiums are being compared. Since the single premium is the present value of the annual premiums, changes in mortality tables will have roughly the same effect on one as on the other.

Effect of Introducing Withdrawal Rates. The next annual-premium-cost element for examination is that of employees terminating service without taking with them any vested rights to benefits under the pen-

—Effect of Varying Mortality Rates
nuity * on Mortality Bases Indicated

| Basic Ga-1951—Male (projected to 1965), 2½ per cent | | Ga-1951—Male (projected to 1954), 2½ per cent | | | |
| | | Annual premium | Per cent of column (2) | 1-year set-back in age | |
Annual premium (7)	Per cent of column (2) (8)	(9)	(10)	Annual premium (11)	Per cent of column (2) (12)
$ 14.39	102.6	$ 14.31	102.0	$ 15.11	107.7
22.51	102.4	22.41	101.9	23.62	107.4
39.88	102.1	39.74	101.8	41.76	106.9
95.79	101.8	95.61	101.6	100.01	106.2
1,207.46	101.0	1,209.10	101.2	1,254.55	105.0
775.88	98.9	792.39	101.0	830.32	105.9

sion plan. In such instances, there is a twofold influence on costs. One (which was absent in the single-premium form of Table 12-7) is the cessation of annual premiums or contributions for such terminated employee. The other is the release, to the employer's credit, of reserve assets theretofore held against the growing pension liability for such employee. Where the plan provides that the employee takes with him full vested rights to accrued benefits, only the first of these cost influences applies. The figures in Table 12-12 are based on the assumption that no vesting is granted, so that the combined effect of both influences is reflected in the indicated comparison.

The effect of a withdrawal assumption on the single premiums of Table 12-7 is considerably reduced in the similar comparisons of Table 12-12. Here, again, it is because of the installment character of the annual premium. If a person pays $72.90 at age twenty-five to receive

Table 12-12. Annual-premium Comparisons Introducing a Withdrawal Rate Cost of $100-a-year Straight Life Annuity *—Group Annuity Table for 1951—Male—2½ per Cent and Indicated Withdrawal Bases

Age (1)	No withdrawal, annual premium (2)	Moderate withdrawal		High withdrawal	
		Annual premium (3)	Per cent of column (2) (4)	Annual premium (5)	Per cent of column (2) (6)
25	$ 14.03	$ 7.03	50.1	$ 3.42	24.4
35	21.99	16.07	73.1	14.10	64.1
45	39.05	32.53	83.3	32.21	82.5
55	94.14	83.25	88.4	83.25	88.4
65	1,195.03	1,195.03	100.0	1,195.03	100.0
75	784.22	784.22	100.0	784.22	100.0

* Commencing at age sixty-five, except that for age seventy-five the annuity commences at seventy-five. Single premiums are shown for ages sixty-five and seventy-five.

an annual retirement benefit of $100 at age sixty-five on the condition that he is then both alive and a member (employee) of the system (plan), the annual probabilities of his withdrawal from the system over the whole period have been taken into account in discounting the cost down to the $72.90 level. But if only annual installments of, say, $7.03 of the cost are to be paid, the person's withdrawal during the early portion of the period does not release as much to apply toward those who stay as would have been the case had he initially paid the single premium of $72.90. Thus the single premium discounted for withdrawal is 21.0 per cent of the single premium without such discount, while the annual premium discounted for withdrawal is 50.1 per cent of the undiscounted rate.

Variations Owing to Sex of Employees. Similar to Table 12-8 for the single-premium form, Table 12-13 gives the effect on annual premiums when sex of the general population is given consideration. These comparative results are derived from the Census Bureau mortality tables previously cited.

Males

| Age | Ga-1951 Table, annual premium | Census Actuarial Tables, 1949–1951, white | |
| | | Annual premium | Per cent of column (2) |
(1)	(2)	(3)	(4)
25	$ 14.03	$ 11.41	81.3
35	21.99	18.12	82.4
45	39.05	32.86	84.1
55	94.14	81.72	86.8
65	1,195.03	1,092.37	91.4
75	784.22	728.23	92.9

Females

| Age | Ga-1951 Table | | Census Actuarial Tables, 1949–1951, white | | |
| | Annual premium | Per cent of column (2) | Annual premium | Per cent of column (6) | Per cent of column (2) |
(5)	(6)	(7)	(8)	(9)	(10)
25	$ 18.09	128.9	$ 15.07	83.3	107.4
35	28.09	127.7	23.60	84.0	107.3
45	49.08	125.7	41.80	85.2	107.0
55	114.87	122.0	99.92	87.0	106.1
65	1,389.54	116.3	1,250.60	90.0	104.7
75	912.05	116.3	815.07	89.4	103.9

* Commencing at age sixty-five, except that for age seventy-five the annuity commences at seventy-five. Single premiums are shown for ages sixty-five and seventy-five.

Table 12-13 shows that the annual-premium rates for white male lives of the composite character found in population statistics are considerably lower than under more selective experience (that is, of purchasers of annuities).

A similar set of comparisons applies with respect to female lives, as shown in the lower portion of Table 12-13. The annual premiums for white female lives based on population statistics are moderately higher than those determined on the selective Ga-1951 Table for Males as given in column (2) above. In other words, white females of the general population involve pension-plan costs somewhat higher than those for selective male lives.[9]

Effect of Introducing Death Benefits. Table 12-14 is similar in its illustrative purposes to Table 12-9. Where Table 12-9 showed the effect of refunding the single premium if death occurred before retirement, Table 12-14 shows the effect of refunding the sum of the annual premiums paid up to time of death. Similarly, Table 12-14 shows the effect on annual premiums of providing for a guarantee after retirement of benefits payable for 10 years certain. In general, the effect of adding a death benefit before retirement is slightly more pronounced for the single premiums of Table 12-9 than it is for the annual premiums of Table 12-14. The reason for this is that up to retirement age there is more death benefit at risk under the single-premium form than under the annual-premium form; in the former case, the whole cost is refunded, while in the latter, only that portion of the cost paid up to the time of death is refunded. The addition of a death benefit after retirement increases both the single premium and the annual premium in the same proportion.

Salary Scales. Past experience indicates two forms of pay increase during a person's working years. One is a proficiency increase, pay going up with maturity and experience and as managerial, supervisory, or executive abilities reveal themselves. This form of increase is largely a function of age and length of service, although there is a tendency for it to flatten out, or even dip a little, above age fifty-five. The other type of increase is due to underlying economic causes; it follows the secular trend of both money wages and real wages and follows an irregular but seemingly persistent upward movement.

[9] This is an oversimplification from the actuarial standpoint.

TABLE 12-14. ANNUAL-PREMIUM COMPARISONS—INTRODUCING DEATH BENEFITS
COST OF $100-A-YEAR STRAIGHT LIFE ANNUITY * WITH DEATH BENEFITS
INDICATED (GA-1951—MALE—2½ PER CENT)

Age	No death benefit, annual premium	No death benefit after age 65; premiums refunded at death before age 65		No death benefit before age 65; death within 10 years after retirement, remainder of 10 payments continued		With both the death benefit before age 65 of column (3) and after retirement of column (5)	
		Annual premium	Per cent of column (2)	Annual premium	Per cent of column (2)	Annual premium	Per cent of column (2)
(1)	(2)	(3)	(4)	(5)	(6)	(7)	(8)
25	$ 14.03	$ 15.99	114.0	$ 15.36	109.5	$ 17.51	124.8
35	21.99	25.15	114.4	24.08	109.5	27.54	125.2
45	39.05	44.27	113.4	42.75	109.5	48.48	124.1
55	94.14	103.00	109.4	103.08	109.5	112.78	119.8
65	1,195.03	1,195.03	100.0	1,308.50	109.5	1,308.50	109.5
75	784.22	784.22	100.0	1,034.77	131.9	1,034.77	131.9

* Commencing at age sixty-five, except that for age seventy-five the annuity commences at seventy-five. Single premiums are shown for ages sixty-five and seventy-five.

Early actuarial writers on the theory and practice of pension funds took cognizance of the proficiency type of increase by using in their computations a rising rate of pay by age, usually following a simple mathematical function, such as an arithmetical or geometrical progression.[10]

[10] In the determination of annuity premium rates, not the initial rates of pay assumed but rather the ratios between amounts of pay at different times are important. For example, if the salary scale is based on an assumption of a 50 per cent increase in pay over a 20-year period, the effect on the unit-premium rate is the same regardless of whether the initial amount of pay is $1,000 or $5,000.

The use of salary scales is almost always combined with the assumption of a withdrawal rate, another rather unpredictable function. Withdrawal rates and salary scales, at least in nonvested plans, work in opposite directions in their effect on initial costs. The higher the assumed rate of withdrawal, the lower the initial costs; while the higher the assumed rate of increase in salary, the greater such costs. However, actual experience under the plan will determine the true costs in any event, and the assumptions made about withdrawal rates and salary scales will only influence the incidence of such costs.

Because of this compensating effect and because the experience under a plan will fashion its ultimate cost in any event, some actuaries do not attempt to attain the high degree of exactitude implied by taking account of withdrawal rates combined with salary scales. In practice, a plan that does not vest the accumulated funds in an employee who terminates service will be credited with reserve funds released from such terminations, and the plan, which usually bases benefits on pay levels, will be debited with higher contributions when pay increases take place. The introduction of a salary scale is of considerable importance, however, in a pension plan that provides benefits related to the final average annual rates of compensation at or near retirement. In this type of plan the current rates of compensation do not determine the pension benefit, and it is customary, in essence, to attempt to forecast the future compensation levels through the application of salary scales. For this type of plan particularly, annual pension-plan costs should be thought of as percentages of covered compensation rather than as dollar amounts. Where the thinking is directed in this way, it is of less importance to attempt to forecast compensation changes attributable to inflation than to forecast the regular promotional or career changes.

The following comparative table (Table 12-15) gives a quantitative indication of the effect of a salary-scale assumption. For the purposes of this example a salary is assumed that will increase according to an arithmetical progression scale such that the salary at age twenty-five will be 61 per cent of the salary at age sixty-four, increasing by 1 per cent per year of age (or service) for 39 years as shown in column (2). The benefit is assumed to be known and to be a straight life annuity of $50 a year per $100 of final salary starting at age sixty-five.

TABLE 12-15. ANNUAL PREMIUMS TO PROVIDE AN ANNUITY OF 50 PER CENT OF FINAL SALARY FOR A MALE AGED TWENTY-FIVE (BASED ON THE GROUP ANNUITY TABLE FOR 1951 AT 2½ PER CENT—MALE—AND ASSUMPTIONS SHOWN)

Attained age (1)	Salary index (2)	Without assumptions of withdrawal or increasing salaries		With assumptions of high withdrawals but not of increasing salaries		With assumptions of both high withdrawal and increasing salaries	
		Amount of premium * (3)	Per cent of column (2) (4)	Amount of premium * (5)	Per cent of column (2) (6)	Amount of premium * (7)	Per cent of column (2) (8)
25	61	$7.02	11.5	$1.71	2.8	$1.53	2.5
35	71	7.02	9.9	1.71	2.4	1.78	2.5
45	81	7.02	8.7	1.71	2.1	2.03	2.5
55	91	7.02	7.7	1.71	1.9	2.28	2.5
64	100	7.02	7.0	1.71	1.7	2.50	2.5

* Per $100 of final salary.

Column (3) shows the level dollar amount of premium which would be required for one employee entering the plan at age twenty-five, assuming no withdrawals and no salary increase. Column (4) shows this amount expressed as a percentage of the salary at attained ages twenty-five, thirty-five, etc., until the last contribution is due 40 years hence. In practice, these rather large premiums would in the aggregate be considerably offset by large credits accruing to the employer year by year as withdrawals occurred. Moreover, in practice, the amount of premium initially set aside might well have been chosen so as to purchase an annuity of only $30.50 a year (50 per cent of $61), and as the salary showed a tendency to climb toward the (unknown) final salary the contributions would have had to be increased to purchase the additional annuity over the decreasing remaining period of expected employment.

On the other hand, columns (5) and (6) show what would happen if a high rate of withdrawal were originally assumed. The initial costs are considerably reduced. Again, if the contributions were set so as to purchase an annuity of 50 per cent of the current salary, with additional premiums applied each year as the salary increased, the percentages shown in column (6) might start at a figure of about 1.7 per cent (0.61 per cent of 2.8 per cent) but would increase rapidly thereafter.

In columns (7) and (8) are shown the effects on costs of providing the same $50-a-year benefit if an increasing salary scale is assumed, in addition to the same withdrawal rate, and if, as shown in column (8) the premiums are computed as a level percentage of the salary at each duration. These premiums will need no adjustment (if the experience follows the assumptions) and will enable the employer to estimate his pension costs as a level percentage of payroll in all future years.

Rate of Retirement. The age of retirement or of benefit commencement affects pension costs. If benefits commence at age seventy,[11] there will be fewer payments than if they commence at age sixty-five. Unless extra benefit credits are granted in one way or another for the additional 5 years, the costs for retirement at age seventy will be substantially lower. Even if higher benefits are granted, the incidence of cost will be lighter because the costs are spread over a 5-year longer period.

To give a quantitative illustration of the cost differences between the different retirement ages, Table 12-16 is based on a benefit of $100 a year provided in one instance by single-premium methods and in the other by annual premiums payable to age of retirement. The figures are for male lives and are based on the Group Annuity Table for 1951—Male—2½ per cent net rates with no return on death.

Most pension plans provide for retirement at age sixty-five for both sexes, as does the Social Security Act.[12] Occasionally, however, the normal retirement date for females is age sixty, and a few business plans use age sixty for both sexes. In nonbusiness plans, age sixty is more common, especially in public employment.

---

[11] In some plans benefits commence at a fixed age whether or not the employee continues on the job.

[12] The recent amendment to the Social Security Act permitting women to obtain benefits at age sixty-two imposes an actuarial-reduction factor (except for widows), where the age at which benefits commence is below sixty-five.

TABLE 12-16. COST RELATIONSHIPS FOR DIFFERENT AGES OF RETIREMENT
(BASED ON THE GROUP ANNUITY TABLE FOR 1951—MALE—2½ PER CENT)

Single-premium costs

Age (1)	Age of retirement, 55 (2)	Age of retirement, 60 (3)	Age of retirement, 65 (4)	Age of retirement, 70 (5)
25	$ 714.99 (206.2) *	$ 512.82 (147.9) *	$ 346.71 (100.0) *	$215.68 (62.2) *
35	924.32 (206.2)	662.96 (147.9)	448.22 (100.0)	278.83 (62.2)
45	1,207.81 (206.2)	866.29 (147.9)	585.68 (100.0)	364.34 (62.2)
55	1,647.21 (206.2)	1,181.44 (147.9)	798.75 (100.0)	496.89 (62.2)
60	. . . .	1,422.40 (147.9)	961.66 (100.0)	598.23 (62.2)
65	. . . .	. . . .	1,195.03 (100.0)	743.40 (62.2)
70	. . . .	. . . .	. . . .	980.16

Annual-premium costs

Age (6)	Age of retirement, 55 (7)	Age of retirement, 60 (8)	Age of retirement, 65 (9)	Age of retirement, 70 (10)
25	$ 34.01 (242.4) *	$ 22.25 (158.6) *	$ 14.03 (100.0) *	$ 8.29 (59.1) *
35	59.16 (269.0)	36.35 (165.3)	21.99 (100.0)	12.63 (57.4)
45	137.58 (352.3)	71.04 (181.9)	39.05 (100.0)	21.17 (54.2)
55	. . . .	253.65 (269.4)	94.14 (100.0)	43.20 (45.9)
60	. . . .	. . . .	208.72 (100.0)	72.59 (34.8)
65	. . . .	. . . .	. . . .	164.61

* Figures in parentheses give percentage ratios to age–sixty-five costs.

Some employers feel that, while it costs more for pensions, clearing the decks as soon as possible by providing for a low retirement age will, by reducing the number on the payroll or by substituting lower-paid and more efficient employees for higher-paid retiring employees, be compensated for by the wage savings. Hence, some plans provide for compulsory retirement at a given age. Under plans where retirement is voluntary, economic conditions may give rise to irregular experience in the effective rates of retirement. For example, during the war, with excellent employment opportunity and high wages, few employees retired on their own volition; in fact, many existing pensioners returned to gainful employment. Another factor to reckon with is that the rate of termination of employment by age experienced before the adoption of a plan is not necessarily an index to rates of termination or retirement after a plan is installed. The plan itself may keep employees from terminating employment before retirement age when benefits commence, while employees who, in the absence of the plan, would have continued as long as possible beyond retirement age, may now, with benefits available, leave the employer much sooner.

Consequently, the cost of two plans providing similar benefits may be quite different if one stipulates compulsory retirement upon attaining a specified age while the other permits the participants voluntarily to determine whether to retire at that age or to continue in employment. Sometimes a plan will provide that retirement benefits will commence in any event upon reaching the specified age.[13] Unless a plan permitting voluntary retirement so provides, this possibility of deferment of retirement date is another cost influence. Since it is difficult to forecast either the extent to which superannuated employees will continue in employment or the extent to which management will encourage retirement, the effect of this factor on costs is not accurately measurable in advance. Table 12-16 does, however, give an indication of the effect when assumed retirement ages are compared.

Expense Rates. Premiums for insured group-annuity retirement plans usually include a 5 to 8 per cent loading for commissions, taxes, actuarial costs, and other general expenses. If the margin permits,

---

[13] Often the employee's earnings are reduced thereafter so that it is not necessarily to his financial advantage to continue beyond normal retirement date.

contingency reserves may be set up from this loading, and it may also make some provision for future dividends or rate credits. It is desirable to recognize to some extent in advance the expenses that an insurer may incur (e.g., the cost of disbursing pension checks) after premiums cease owing to termination of the plan.

A different loading formula is generally used for the premiums of group-permanent retirement plans, which combine life insurance and old-age protection, and less uniformity prevails among insurers than in the case of group-annuity plans. The results of a typical loading formula for group-permanent-insurance-annuity premiums is shown in Table 12-17. These results are expressed here in terms of a single

TABLE 12-17. ILLUSTRATIVE LOADING * IN GROUP-PERMANENT PREMIUMS
ANNUAL PREMIUM FORMS—RETIREMENT AT AGE SIXTY-FIVE

Male age (1)	Percentage of annual premium which is loading (2)	Female age (3)	Percentage of annual premium which is loading (4)
35	15	35	14
45	12	45	12
55	9	55	9

* For expenses, contract-holder dividends, and contingencies.

percentage, although the underlying loading formula is usually more complex.

Premiums for individual-contract plans, the type where a trustee holds the contracts until time for distribution of proceeds, probably involve as many different loading formulas and factors as there are insurers in the business.[14] Loading is only one of several factors in competitive rate making under individual forms; mortality, interest, and other elements also enter into the premium equation. Because of

[14] This type of plan also entails trustee's expenses for holding, changing, and releasing contracts and for general administration.

the diversity in the loading factor and because of the many forms of individual contracts used in this type of pension trust, it is impracticable to discuss it in detail here.

There is equal diversity of practice among trust companies in determining their charges for administering trust-fund plans. Sometimes a loading is added to the benefit contributions paid over to the trustee. The trust instrument may direct the trustee to meet part or all of the plan's expenses from this loading. In some cases, the trustee is to meet only the trustee fees or other specified costs from the loading; in others, the trustee meets none of the expenses, the employer bearing them all as incurred. In any event, expenses paid from the trust fund must be reported annually by the trustee, and any excess loading over and above such expenses must be applied to reduce subsequent contributions in accordance with the regulations of the Internal Revenue Service.

Disability Costs. Long-term invalidity among employees (permanent and total disability) is a hazard causing work stoppage and loss of earned income. It is one of life's catastrophes. The difficulties encountered in underwriting and administering these benefits were discussed in earlier chapters. In discussing disability costs it is also necessary to emphasize the unreliability of any figures given. Employers or unions often ask how much disability benefits will cost, but it is extremely difficult, or impossible, to answer such a question satisfactorily. This is particularly the case when the query is presented in advance of any planning or setting up of specifications for the benefit. Even with the exact terms of a long-term disability program known, including a specific definition of compensable disability, and even after some administrative experience has been gained thereunder, forecasts of future cost are still unreliable. In the absence of these advantages of specific definition and experience, cost figures are even more uncertain. In addition to the benefit formula and the specifications of the plan, disability experience and related disability costs are also influenced by definition, administration, and economic conditions. The clause defining disability for the compensable purposes of the plan is important; an original intent of restricting compensable cases to the more serious and permanent types of disability may be defeated over the years by such loose wording that a constant whittling away of the intended restrictions could gradually take place and result in significant cost increase. The firmness of the administration and the administrators over the years would have much to do with maintaining conformity to the original intent and to the disability clause contained in the plan; general liberalization, lack of adequate follow-up for recoveries, or favoritism could adversely influence the cost trend. Economic conditions have an effect on costs; in bad times, an employee will hold his job as long as possible, but if he sees its loss coming in any event and he has some symptoms of poor health, he is more inclined to think of himself as a disability case. On the other hand, if the disability clause is susceptible to use for short-term sicknesses, a period of high prosperity and short labor markets also encourages disability claims, and the employee can have a rest from his job without worrying about reemployment. Indications are pretty clear that economic conditions do have an effect on disability claims and malingering. Disability costs are therefore indeterminate and are most suitably presented as perhaps falling within a range between high-cost and low-cost assumptions.

Advance funding for disability benefits may take one of three forms: single premium, annual premium, or 1-year-term premium. Under the first two methods a reserve is built up for both active employees and employees who become disabled. Under the term form, each year's premiums or contributions for the whole group of active employees are assumed to be sufficient to offset the full reserve necessary to pay out the benefits for the number of lives among the group who become disabled in the year for which such premiums or contributions are paid. Each of these funding methods is complicated by the fact that reserve assets already exist at time of disability under the pension plan proper. How should this fund be treated? Should it be released? Should it be used to offset disability costs? Or should it be maintained to be used to pay the ultimate old-age benefits if the disabled life recovers and returns to his job or lives through as a disabled life to the normal age of retirement? The analysis of these complexities lies in the specialized field of the actuary.

For a quantitative illustration of disability costs it will suffice to use the 1-year-term-premium method under a set of *low* assumptions and also under a set of *high* assumptions.[15] Both sets assume certain restrictions, for instance, that disabilities of an obviously partial or short-term nature are not covered; that benefits will not be available to employees before a specified length of service has elapsed; that medical attention will be required at onset of, and during, disability; that only disability benefits well below 100 per cent of pay will be granted; and that benefits will cease if substantially gainful employment is resumed.

Table 12-18 gives the 1-year-term cost for male lives, the incidence

TABLE 12-18. COST ILLUSTRATIONS FOR LONG-TERM-DISABILITY BENEFITS
1-YEAR-TERM COST OF BENEFIT OF $100 A YEAR FOR PERIOD OF DISABILITY

Male age (1)	Low incidence and short duration		High incidence and long duration	
	Cost (2)	Per cent of column (4) (3)	Cost (4)	Per cent of column (2) (5)
25	$0.37	18	$ 2.11	571
35	0.45	18	2.57	571
45	0.81	18	4.60	571
55	1.93	18	11.01	571

rate being based on the assumptions indicated in the table. The duration of disability is assumed to have an average present value per dollar of yearly benefit of $7 for disabilities of "short duration," and $10 for those of "long duration." It is not unusual to double the disability-incidence rates among males to secure the corresponding rates for females, so that for the latter the cost figures in Table 12-18 may be multiplied by 2. The benefit is a life annuity, unless discontinued

15 These "low" and "high" designations are in no way intended as limits; careful, conservative systems could incur less than the low costs and liberal, or mismanaged, systems, more than the high costs.

because of recovery, and no recognition is given in these calculations to any existing pension reserve fund at onset of disability. The figures, as in previous tables, use $100 a year as the illustrative benefit unit.

Provision in a pension plan for a moderate disability benefit with neither extreme restriction nor laxity in its definition, coverage, or administration might entail a cost of 1 to 2 per cent of covered payroll. A study by the Social Security Administration of the cost of adding to the old-age-and-survivors protection a benefit payable for serious or total disabilities of permanent or protracted duration indicated the possibility of an even wider range in payroll costs, from about 1 to 2½ per cent.[16] The Civil Service Retirement System of the federal government has had a large experience with a rather loosely worded disability clause. Out of about 250,000 retired employees on the pension roll in 1956, some 65,000 had been granted disability pensions; over one-third of the female pensions were the result of retirement for alleged disability. These Civil Service figures are the proportions of disability cases at the time indicated and do not, of themselves, permit translation into costs expressed as percentages of payroll. Since the level actuarial cost of the system has been computed to run to some 15 per cent of covered payroll, it seems clear, from the large proportion of disability cases already among those in receipt of benefits, that if the level-cost figures for disability were available they would be responsible for a significant part of the 15 per cent. This will be even more the case after amendments of 1956 liberalizing the disability benefits become fully effective.[17]

Employee Contributions. If it were estimated that a noncontributory plan would call for an employer contribution of, say, 12 per cent of covered payroll, it would seem that the introduction of employee contributions at, say, a 4 per cent rate would leave 8 per cent as the employer's share. It is not so simple as this, and usually the employer

[16] These costs were made for a more extended eligibility for disability benefits than was added by the 1956 amendments, under which no benefit commences before age fifty and the definition of disability and conditions for receipt of benefits are quite strict; the 1956 amendments call for an extra ½ per cent tax.

[17] By reason of the 1956 amendments to the Civil Service plan, cost estimates have raised the 15 per cent to some 19 per cent of payroll, of which employees contribute 6½ per cent rather than the former 6 per cent.

does not secure this much reduction. In some instances, he may secure more.

Usually the plan will provide for the return of employee contributions, frequently with interest, in event of death or termination of employment. With these collateral features, the 4 per cent rate must anticipate a refund of itself when the participant dies or withdraws. Consequently it cannot all be counted as providing pension payments. This prevents the full reduction's being reflected as savings to the employer. Another factor often restricting employer savings from employee contributions is setting the benefits in contributory plans at a higher level, e.g., at a total cost level of 15 per cent of payroll instead of 12 per cent, against which the 4 per cent would apply. Consider a plan which has been noncontributory and which is being changed to the contributory form. Unless benefits are raised at the same time, the appeal to employees of paying toward the same benefits that they were previously getting free will not be very strong.

Employers might benefit by more than would be indicated from the percentage rate of employee contributions. This would occur where the plan provided that employees who died or terminated employment before retirement would receive no return of their contributions, which would be left to augment the fund and thus operate as a further offset against the residual cost borne by the employer. Although such plans would seem to have little appeal, especially among younger employees, they are occasionally found. Such a forfeiture arrangement is possible only where compulsory provisions can be enforced, as in some public-employee plans; in some labor-union plans where dues include forfeitable pension contributions; and even, in a sense, in the social-security plan, where if a person drops out of covered employment before 10 years' (more precisely 40 quarters') credits are accumulated he may forfeit his right to benefits. If the employee contributions are returnable without interest, any interest otherwise creditable thereon is applied to reduce employer costs; or if the employee contributions are returnable with interest at a lower rate than has been earned, some modest credits are applicable to the employer costs.

Summary. By referring to the earlier tables of premium comparisons, Table 12-19 has been drawn up to give rough indications of the effect on initial contributions of the several actuarial assumptions outlined.[18] For this purpose the annual-premium tables are used. Ages twenty-five and forty-five are chosen for purposes of illustration. Costs based on the Group Annuity Table for 1951—Male, with 2½ per cent interest and without expense loading are taken as the bench mark (line 1) for comparative purposes.

Other rates and elements could be used to extend such a table indefinitely; even different combinations of the elements of the above table would produce over 2,000 more indexes in columns (9) and (11). Those given, however, are representative combinations and are a rough guide to the interrelation of costs on different assumptions. Any combining of these indexes is probably more nearly correct if it is done by multiplication rather than by addition; that is, instead of adding the deviations (plus or minus) from 100 per cent with respect to any two indexes in order to accomplish a transition, multiply the two indexes, and the product will be the approximate index. For example, suppose it were desired to find the index for age forty-five for a set of assumptions the same as those for line 15 in Table 12-19, except that the interest rate would be 3½ per cent instead of 2½ per cent. In line 9, an index for an interest rate of 3½ per cent is given, which is 17 points below the standard index of 100. Line 15 has an index which is 24 points above the standard index. If 17 points were deducted from 124, an index of 107 would result. If, however, the index of 83 in line 9 were viewed as a percentage and multiplied by the 124 of line 15, the result would be an index of 103. While neither of these results by the combination method is exact, 103 is a closer approximation than 107.

Table 12-19 sets out cost indexes at ages twenty-five and forty-five. It may be helpful to close this chapter with a table based on an assumed frequency distribution of employees, giving the resultant costs under a few of the sets of assumptions of Table 12-19. Assume an employer with all male employees who are covered by a retirement plan that provides for a pension of $1,200 a year commencing at age sixty-five. This plan is to be funded by the level-annual-premium

---

[18] It cannot be too frequently recalled that these assumptions merely pattern (1) the initial costs and (2) the funding structure. The actual costs and incidence will come only from experience.

TABLE 12-19. INDEXES OF EFFECT ON COSTS OF VARIOUS ACTUARIAL

Line no.	Normal retirement age (1)	Interest rate, per cent (2)	Mortality table (3)	Withdrawal rate (4)	Sex (5)
1	65	2½	Ga-1951—Male	None	Male
2	65	2½	1937 Standard Annuity	"	"
3	65	2½	Census (1949–1951) White	"	"
4	65	2½	Basic Ga-1951 (projected to 1965)	"	"
5	65	2½	Ga-1951 Table (projected to 1954)	"	"
6	65	2½	Ga-1951 Table (projected to 1954), 1-year set-back in age	"	"
7	65	2	Ga-1951—Male	"	"
8	65	3	Ga-1951—Male	"	"
9	65	3½	Ga-1951—Male	"	"
10	65	2½	Ga-1951—Male	Moderate	"
11	65	2½	Ga-1951—Male	High	"
12	65	2½	Ga-1951—Female	None	Female
13	65	2½	Ga-1951—Male	"	Male
14	65	2½	Ga-1951—Male	"	"
15	65	2½	Ga-1951—Male	"	"
16	55	2½	Ga-1951—Male	"	"
17	60	2½	Ga-1951—Male	"	"
18	70	2½	Ga-1951—Male	"	"

* Level annual premium to age sixty-five for straight life annuity of $100 per year.

method so that benefits are fully paid for by age sixty-five, except that any employee above age fifty-five at the start will have his premium spread over 10 years, even though such an employee commences to receive his benefit at age sixty-five. For simplicity, assume that the

AND BENEFIT ASSUMPTIONS AT AGES TWENTY-FIVE AND FORTY-FIVE

Refund at death		Age 25		Age 45	
Before retirement (6)	After retirement (7)	Annual premium * (8)	Index of initial cost (9)	Annual premium * (10)	Index of initial cost (11)
None	None	$14.03	100	$39.05	100
"	"	13.09	93	37.55	96
"	"	11.41	81	32.86	84
"	"	14.39	103	39.88	102
"	"	14.31	102	39.74	102
"	"	15.11	108	41.76	107
"	"	16.41	117	42.96	110
"	"	11.99	85	35.51	91
"	"	10.23	73	32.32	83
"	"	7.03	50	32.53	83
"	"	3.42	24	32.21	82
"	"	18.09	129	49.08	126
All contributions	"	15.99	114	44.27	113
None	Balance of 10 years' payments	15.36	109	42.75	109
All contributions	Balance of 10 years' payments	17.51	125	48.48	124
None	None	34.01	242	137.58	352
"	"	22.25	159	71.04	182
"	"	8.29	59	21.17	54

average pay for any age group is $3,000 a year. The initial data are then as shown in Table 12-20.

The age distribution is, of course, artificial but will nevertheless permit an initial cost measurement under any of the sets of assump-

TABLE 12-20. COMPOSITION OF EMPLOYEES AND PAYROLL

Male age (1)	Number of employees (2)	Average salary (3)	Covered payroll (4)	Anticipated average pension (5)	Total benefits per annum at age 65 if none dies or resigns (6)
25	100	$3,000	$300,000	$1,200	$120,000
35	85	3,000	255,000	1,200	102,000
45	70	3,000	210,000	1,200	84,000
55	30	3,000	90,000	1,200	36,000
65	15	3,000	45,000	1,200	18,000
Total.....	300	$3,000	$900,000	$1,200	$360,000

tions already examined. If lines 1, 2, 9, 10, and 15 are chosen from Table 12-19, the resultant costs for the above distribution are those shown in Table 12-21. Note that under the specifications outlined above there are 15 employees living at age sixty-five who will commence to receive benefits immediately, although contributions for such benefits will be spread over the first 10 years of the plan or until prior death.

By these figures, the results of changes in the assumptions discussed in this chapter are illustrated, showing a range in cost as a percentage of payroll from 12.2 to 17.8 per cent. Table 12-21 has been prepared on the assumption of a noncontributory plan. It should be borne in mind that these percentages represent a fairly liberal benefit formula, 40 per cent of pay, exclusive of the OASDI benefit.

General. In this chapter have been discussed the several common cost elements about which actuarial assumptions must be made in establishing the contribution and valuation structure for a pension plan. Certain numerical comparisons of premium, or contributions, based on several different assumptions have been shown, both by the single-premium and by the annual-premium methods and both at individual ages and compositely for hypothetical age distributions. It is important to reiterate that these are merely the pegs on which

TABLE 12-21. ILLUSTRATIVE COSTS FOR DISTRIBUTION OF TABLE 12-20

Number in Table 12-19 (1)	Basis of actuarial assumptions (2)				Employer's initial annual cost *	
					Amount (3)	Per cent of payroll (4)
1	Ga-1951	2½%	No withdrawal	No death benefit	$133,400	14.8
2	1937 Standard Annuity	2½%	No withdrawal	No death benefit	129,600	14.4
9	Ga-1951	3½%	No withdrawal	No death benefit	113,100	12.6
10	Ga-1951	2½%	Moderate withdrawal	No death benefit	109,600	12.2
15	Ga-1951	2½%	No withdrawal	Death benefit before and after retirement	160,500	17.8

* Level premium to retirement age except that in the case of employees within 10 years of retirement age at the time the plan becomes effective the costs are funded over a 10-year period.

the monetary funding of a plan is established and operated and that the ultimate aggregate cost of a plan is not determined by these pegs but rather from the actual evolving experience under the plan. The actuarial pegs for a plan are put into place according to what appears to be conservatively reasonable for the future, but this view is only a snapshot taken currently. A snapshot taken at a different point in time would probably bring out a different picture of reasonable assumptions. This point may be amply demonstrated by a brief review in columns (2) to (6) of Table 12-22 of the premium history over nearly 15 years of an actual insured group-annuity plan. Column (7) gives typical 1956 insurance rates on one of the variations of the

TABLE 12-22. ILLUSTRATIVE CHANGES IN COSTS CHRONOLOGICALLY
SINGLE PREMIUM AT AGE INDICATED, REQUIRED TO PROVIDE $100 A YEAR FOR
MALES RETIRING AT AGE SIXTY-FIVE
(Pensions payable in equal monthly installments)

Age	1934 premium rates	1939 premium rates	1942 premium rates	1947 premium rates	Per cent 1947 rates of 1934 rates	1956 premium rates	Per cent 1956 rates of 1934 rates
(1)	(2)	(3)	(4)	(5)	(6)	(7)	(8)
30	$194	$304	$ 398	$ 493	254	$ 423	218
40	289	421	524	618	214	549	190
50	447	602	710	798	179	725	162
60	753	926	1,030	1,102	146	1,020	135

Ga-1951 Table. This indicates that rates can go down as well as up;
the reduction is due largely to a return to 2½ per cent interest.

If comparable rates were included in Table 12-22 on premium bases
in effect before 1934 (insured group annuities commencing in the late
1920s), it would be seen that rates still lower than those of 1934
prevailed in those years. The 1934 rates in Table 12-22 are based on
the Combined Annuity Table with 3¾ per cent interest; for 1939,
on the Standard Annuity Table with 3 per cent interest; for 1942, on
the Standard Annuity Table set back 1 year in age with 2½ per cent
interest; for 1947, on the Standard Annuity Table set back 1 year in
age with 2 per cent interest; and for 1956, the Ga-1951 Table set back
1 year in age with 2½ per cent interest. In all the cases, the premium
rates include the usual loading for expenses, taxes, and contingencies,
generally 8 per cent of gross premiums, except for 1956, where the
loading is 5 per cent of gross premium.

The experience illustrated by Table 12-22 shows that the underlying
cost bases of a plan—whether insured or trusteed—are subject to periodic review and change as conditions require. Under insured plans,

conditions are taken into account by a revision in future premium rates and by dividends or rate credits; in trust-fund plans, they may be taken into account by a revamping of the actuarial assumptions or by periodic adjustments in the employer's contributions to the trust fund.

CHAPTER 13

Valuation

The term *valuation* in its broadest sense connotes the setting of a price or value. It may require nothing more than looking up the worth of a security in a financial publication, or it may mean a highly complex operation, such as the valuation of the liabilities of a life-insurance company. When one is speaking from the standpoint of a life-insurance company, the term generally means the periodic determination (at least annual) of the reserve liability under its outstanding insurance and annuity contracts. The expression *reserve* as used in connection with life insurance and pension plans has a meaning quite different from that of the same word when used in connection with general business operations. The reserve of a business concern is usually the amount which has been withheld from profits made in prior years and set aside to meet such future contingencies as taxes, replacement of depreciated property, or operating losses. It is usually built up from small portions of the company's normal annual income.

In the case of an insurer, the *principal reserve* is the total amount needed in addition to future premiums or contributions and interest income to meet such obligations as future death benefits, annuity payments, or surrender values. It is a definite liability of the company and is more in the nature of the deposits held by a bank than of a contingency or administrative reserve, though reserves of the latter types are often carried by insurers. The reserve liability of an insurer, at the end of a particular year, develops from adding to the previous year's reserve the income items of new premiums received during the year and interest on the amount of the previous reserve and deducting

276

the outgo items of claims paid and previous reserve liability canceled through lapse or surrender of policies.

In annuity or pension plans, *valuation* means (1) the initial estimate of costs before a plan is put into effect, (2) the final precise determination of the amount of contributions for the first year of a plan, or (3) a measurement of the financial condition or outlook of a plan after it has already operated for a period, whether financed through an insurer, trust-fund, bookkeeping-reserve, or pay-as-you-go system. *Valuation,* as discussed in this chapter, has to do with the actuarial principles and processes used in, and the results of, measuring [1] the financial status of a going system, mainly old-age benefits.

Elementary Valuation. An illustration of a simple valuation is the following: Series E savings bonds are sold to return $1,000 after 8 years and 11 months for each $750 of their purchase price; compound interest at the rate of 3¼ per cent over the period is responsible for the $250 increase in value at maturity. At any point, a valuation could be made to show that the Treasury liability in anticipation of the maturity of the bond was the original payment of $750 plus compound interest at 3¼ per cent up to the date as of which the valuation was made.[2]

Or, again, assume that a life annuity of $100 a year for a male aged sixty-five can be purchased for $1,195. Consider an individual aged forty-five today, who could bank a payment of $45.64 at the beginning of each year; at 2½ per cent interest, this would amount to $1,195 in 20 years, when the individual would be sixty-five. The valuation of that arrangement at any point during the 20 years would show a "reserve liability" on the books of the bank equal to the payments thus far made plus 2½ per cent interest accumulations.

While this illustration uses the expression *life annuity,* it will be observed that, before attainment of age sixty-five, the procedure followed is merely that of making periodic payments into a bank. If the individual fails to live to age sixty-five, his estate would receive only the accumulations of his bank account.

---

[1] The assumptions and methods involved in this measurement have been dealt with in Chaps. 10–12.

[2] Actually, the Treasury does not value these bonds in this way because the redemption value before maturity is taken into account. Bonds cashed in before maturity yield less than 3¼ per cent.

These valuations are called "simple" because they introduce only one element, compound interest, which is applied to the original purchase price or annual deposits. Valuation becomes more complex when, in addition to compound interest, the element of mortality (survivorship) or any other factor is introduced. Discounting for mortality is necessary to a valuation of life-insurance contracts, life-annuity contracts, and pension plans.

Valuation Introducing Mortality. Suppose a man enters a benefit plan with 999 other males all aged forty-five. Under the plan each one is to receive $100 a year for life commencing at age sixty-five *if he lives* to that age; if he dies before that age, the scheme is to owe him nothing. There is now more than an interest rate to deal with, since whenever a death occurs the fund is relieved of all obligations to the deceased. In fact, his accumulation is released upon his death and applied to augment the amounts of those who survive. On this basis, again by using 2½ per cent interest and assuming the deaths among the group occurring between ages forty-five and sixty-five will be in accordance with the Group Annuity Mortality Table for 1951—Male, the annual contribution for each of the 1,000 entrants is reduced from the previous $45.64 to $39.05. The valuation of this system at any point during the interval between ages forty-five and sixty-five results again in the aggregate payments theretofore made by the members plus the interest accumulations, but only if the deaths up to that point have occurred in accordance with the mortality table assumed when the $39.05 contribution was computed. If 10 years should pass without a death, the system would show a deficit,[3] which the valuation would bring to light; conversely, a heavier death experience than assumed would produce a surplus which would be brought out by the valuation.

The extreme deficit would be incurred if all 1,000 members were still alive at age sixty-five; each would need $1,195 as indicated previously, but only $1,022 for each would have been accumulated in the

[3] Because of the fact that no deaths have occurred while several have been anticipated in the calculation of the annual contribution of $39.05 per member, more members than have been counted on will probably survive to age sixty-five, and more annuity payments will be required than have been allowed for in the calculations.

fund, a 14 per cent deficit. The extreme surplus would be accumulated if all 1,000 members died before age sixty-five, leaving a 100 per cent surplus since no annuity payments would ever be made.[4]

Retrospective Valuation. Examples of a straightforward type of valuation may be found by referring to Table 11-4. There a group of 3,250 persons are alive initially at various ages from thirty to sixty-four. At the end of the first year a valuation would show the system's liability to be $3,493,000. This amount derives from the contributions at the beginning of the year of $3,483,000, plus a year's interest at 2½ per cent on the contributions, amounting to $87,000, minus the $77,000 of pension payments at the end of the year to those attaining age sixty-five and retiring at that time. The second-year valuation would follow a similar determination, but there would be added to the interest element 2½ per cent on the $3,493,000 amount of reserve liability outstanding at the end of the first year. Thus the second year's terminal liability would be $6,086,000. And so the process would develop year after year. This is an illustration of a *retrospective valuation,* that is, a determination from past operations of the income and outgo of the requisite reserve liability. In order to be called fully funded to date, the system must show equivalent assets in the form of bonds, mortgages, or other securities or cash. Such retrospective valuation is sound only if the annual contribution requirements have been properly computed in advance and timely met; if an arbitrary contribution is chosen and accumulated in this manner, the resulting amount would be an entirely unreliable measure of the reserve liability.

Prospective Valuation. Another type of valuation method producing values identical with those produced by the retrospective method—but only if the same assumptions are used—is *prospective valuation.* In this case the future is looked to instead of the past. Future benefit payments for those employees expected by the mortality table to reach retirement age are discounted at an assumed rate of interest and expressed as a present-value lump sum as of the valuation date. On

---

[4] This example illustrates one theoretical factor: the pendulum cannot swing as far in one direction, when all members live to become annuitants, producing a 14 per cent deficit, as it can in the other direction, when they all die before reaching age sixty-five, producing a 100 per cent surplus.

the other side of the balance sheet are placed the contributions that are expected to be made to the system in the future under the mortality table used, which contributions are also discounted at interest and expressed as a present-value lump sum. The extent by which the lump-sum measure of future benefit payments exceeds the present value of future contribution income is the reserve liability. The existing assets of the system (purchased with the excess of prior years' contributions over pension payments) must be tested for sufficiency by being compared with this prospectively determined reserve liability.

It is not unusual to find an uninsured plan which has been in operation for years without an actuarial valuation. The contribution rate may have been originally determined in an unscientific manner (or even on what then seemed to be an appropriate actuarial basis of mortality and interest) and that rate followed willy-nilly ever since. It may appear adequate to the managers of the fund because sizable assets have accumulated, which have been growing each year. Perhaps they first become concerned when the rate of increase in assets begins to taper off as pension payments increase. To look at either the aggregate contribution rate or the total assets of such a system tells nothing about its inherent long-run condition, but a prospective valuation will bring out the deficiency of the system's assets (or, as is more rarely the case, their redundancy) in comparison with the benefits promised if the previous contribution rate should be maintained in the future as in the past.

More Complex Valuations. One chapter cannot constitute a treatise on valuation, but for perspective some of the complicating elements and assumptions may be mentioned. Previous sections outlined the simple cases of an E-bond valuation, a valuation of deposits made periodically to a savings account, a valuation of a group of annual-premium-deferred-life annuities, and the difference between retrospective and prospective methods of valuation. The principles involved in these examples are applicable to all valuations, although collateral benefit features or actuarial assumptions (such as a withdrawal rate) in addition to mortality and interest may necessitate elaboration of the processes thus far explained.

In the illustration above from Table 11-4, the only disbursements assumed were for straight-life-pension payments. The specifications of many plans, as explained in previous chapters, provide for death benefits before or after retirement or both, for benefits at termination of service, for disability benefits, and for optional settlements of one kind or another.

When death benefits are included, the valuation must recognize them; this can be done either retrospectively or prospectively, by figuring into the accumulation of the past or the discounting of the future expected deaths and the consequent benefits, according to the mortality table adopted. With this added form of disbursement, both the premium (or contribution) per unit of annuity benefit and the reserve liability must be always greater than under the simpler type of no-death-benefit plan.[5]

The valuation of a system that pays benefits when a participant withdraws from service also has its special problems. These depend on whether the premium or contribution rate has already been adjusted for anticipated terminations; if so, the use of methods paralleling those used when a death benefit is involved will automatically take care of expected terminations according to the table used. When no advance adjustment has been made in the contribution rate because of anticipated withdrawals from the system, at withdrawal an amount will be released equal to the average reserve liability pertaining to the age, sex, duration in plan, and benefits of the terminating participant. This reserve (or, if there is a withdrawal benefit payable, the amount by which the reserve exceeds such benefit) may be considered a *gain* to the plan and be used for strengthening existing reserve assets or for reducing subsequent contributions. Here the valuation method will not make direct use of withdrawal factors, but the results will show the effect of the withdrawal benefits as they are paid and of any gains from the excess of amounts released over amounts paid out to the withdrawing members.

In systems providing disability benefits, additional valuation problems arise. Usually disability-reserve liabilities are set up apart from the retirement, death, and termination-benefit valuation. If the con-

---

[5] The actuarial processes for valuations of this nature are beyond the scope of this book but may be found in textbooks on actuarial science. See, for example, Chester Wallace Jordan, Jr., "Society of Actuaries' Textbook on Life Contingencies," Society of Actuaries, Chicago, 1952.

tribution for the disability feature is of a 1-year-term type—that is, estimated as just about sufficient to fully fund the disability cases whose inception is expected to fall in the year of the contribution— there will be only one kind of reserve-liability account, i.e., for persons already disabled. If, on the other hand, a level premium (or contribution) has been computed for use over a period of years, there will be two such accounts: (1) an account for active employees against the increasing likelihood of disability with increase in age and (2) an independent account for those already disabled to which an amount is added at the time each disability benefit commences. Valuation problems are, of course, simpler under the 1-year-term-funding method than under the level-contribution method, but the latter basis leads to more nearly level costs.

Optional modes of settlement of death or retirement benefits are readily handled by the actuary in his valuation processes. As a rule, the actuarial value of the elective form of benefit is equal to the value of the normal form of benefit, although some insured or trust-fund plans impose either time limits or medical requirements for electing certain options [6] or provide for a safety factor in the rates upon which the optional benefit is determined. An illustration of the imposition of a safety factor is one where the retiring life is assumed to be 3 or 5 years older than is actually the case. The actuarial-reduction factor for the higher age is then applied against the normal benefit to determine the optional benefit, and the amount of this optional benefit is less than would have been the case if the factor at the employee's true age had been used. In the subsequent valuations of this optional benefit the true age of the individual would be used, because to use his artificially adjusted (increased) age in such valuations would be tantamount to releasing reserves which should be maintained. In fact, it could be argued that if a high degree of conservatism is being sought

[6] For example, in group-annuity contracts it is customary for an insurer to require that a participant must make his election at least 5 years before his normal retirement date if he wishes to have his annuity reduced at retirement so that his wife may receive after his death part or all of the reduced periodical amount which he would receive. If, however, he submits to a medical examination to demonstrate that he is not merely substituting a second life in contemplation of death, the 5-year requirement may be waived.

the actuarial-reduction factor used in determining the amount of the optional benefit should be that for an age higher than the true age of the participant, while the age used for valuation purposes should be lower than the true age.

The usual settlement options (though not all of them are always available in any given plan) are (1) to retire early (before normal retirement date) at an actuarially reduced benefit, (2) to choose delayed retirement benefits starting later than normal retirement date, (3) to choose a larger benefit with no death return (used when the normal benefit carries a death return), (4) to choose a smaller monthly benefit with 10, 15, or other certain period of years' payments guaranteed (used when the normal benefit carries no death return), and (5) to choose a reduced benefit with continuation of part or all to a second person if the retired employee dies first.

A great many plans are jointly contributory, with employees sharing in the cost. In these plans it is general for the employee's contributions (with or without interest) to be returned at death or termination of employment, but in many the employer's contribution is not so vested in the discontinuing employee.[7] Consequently, the death, termination, and optional-benefits assumptions introduced in determining the amount of the reserve liability on account of employee contributions are of a different nature and/or application from the corresponding assumptions related to employer contributions only. For valuation purposes these are treated as split cases, one set of valuation factors being needed for the employee part of the liabilities and another for the employer part. For example, consider a plan which provides that, in event of death before retirement, the employee's beneficiary will receive the aggregate employee contributions plus interest but none of the employer contributions. The valuation of the employee's part in this case would involve an interest-only accumulation if handled retrospectively, or an interest-only discount if handled prospectively. On the other hand, the valuation of the employer's part would include interest, a mortality factor, and perhaps a withdrawal factor if em-

---

[7] Other plans provide that in the event of termination of employment the employee (with vested rights) will be entitled to a deferred benefit starting at normal retirement date; usually a condition of this deferred benefit is that the employees' contributions must also be left in the plan.

ployer contributions were computed to take account of withdrawals. Only if employee and employer premiums or contributions are applied identically for establishing benefit values can they be treated as an undivided unit for valuation purposes.

Valuation Processes. Actuaries use a variety of techniques in their valuation work. These techniques are mathematically complex, but a brief nontechnical explanation of their general features will be presented.

Seriatim Method. The most direct and simplest valuation process is the *seriatim method.* Here each covered employee is treated individually, and the reserve liability on his account is determined.[8] The summation of all these individual items establishes the amount that should be balanced by the system's assets if the system is to be fully funded. The seriatim method is not particularly onerous for small systems and may even be found in use for large groups if the plan is such that death or termination benefits are a function of the individual reserve liability, for in that case at one point or another this reserve must be computed individually. A manual record card, or a punch card, for each covered employee is the usual informational and computing medium for the seriatim method.

Group Method. When there is a substantial number of persons in a system under which benefits are dependent on sex, age, length of service, salary, and other such factors, it is possible to group the persons with the same valuation characteristics, or *likes,* and to treat each set of likes as a unit in any computation process. In valuation work a segregation by sex, age, and duration of membership is common and may be the basis for application of the *group method.* If, for instance, one male group, or set of likes, has been in the plan for n years and the past yearly contributions for the group are known (assuming that the contributions were actuarially correct under the valuation assumptions in use), the accumulation of these contributions (the *retrospective method*) may readily be made for the whole group as a unit. Or, as prospective benefits for the group would be ascertain-

---

[8] Such individual reserve liability assumes all persons to be creatures of the mortality table, i.e., all alike with respect to probability of death. While this is not so in fact, the assumption is the essence of the annuity concept, and all equities and values under the scheme are based on this principle.

able and the future rate of contributions toward those benefits known, the discounting of both elements could readily be handled, with the difference between the results producing the reserve liability for the whole group as a unit (the *prospective method*). Thus the group procedure requires fewer computations than the seriatim procedure; instead of making a calculation for each individual, there is only one calculation for each class of likes.

Attained-age Method. Another form of group treatment that can be adapted to pension-plan valuation (although probably feasible only for insured plans where the insurer uses the method for its other business) is the *attained-age method*. This method is most effective where punch-card equipment is available. The principle behind it is that almost all annuity forms can be cast into actuarial expressions containing constant factors depending on the *attained* age at date of valuation. All the data are punched on cards, which are then sorted by attained age. Tabulations are prepared showing the appropriate totals for each year of birth (which determines the attained age). These totals are then multiplied by the proper factors, and the appropriate totals are taken. The details of this method vary considerably by type of deferred annuity, and the technicalities involved are extensive.[9]

Aggregate Method. The *aggregate method* [10] is a fourth process sometimes used in valuing plans financed through a trust fund or a deposit-administration group-annuity plan, where the benefit provisions permit it. It is not so much a valuation method for determining reserve liability as a means for periodically adjusting the employer contribution rate. In effect, this method determines by the prospective valuation procedure the extent of total benefit liability not met by funds then on hand and future expected employee contributions, if any. This balance of liability is converted into an annual employer contribution payable until a subsequent similar valuation calls for another adjustment. This valuation and conversion are often linked to covered payroll, the resultant employer-contribution rate being expressed as a percentage of payroll. Whether the payroll goes up or

---

[9] See Richard A. Getman, "Attained Age Valuation of Life Annuities," *Transactions of the Actuarial Society of America,* vol. 38, p. 463.

[10] Sometimes called the "percentage-of-payroll" method.

down before the next valuation, this percentage is used to determine each year's dollar amount of contribution from the employer.

Insured Plans and Trust-fund Plans. The principles and many of the procedures of valuation are the same under both insured plans and trust-fund plans. Retrospective or prospective devices may be applied to either type of plan, and seriatim or group methods may be followed under either. In view of the general similarity of valuation procedures between insured and trust-fund plans, it may strike one as paradoxical to say that the results of a valuation have two quite different connotations or applications in the two types of plans. The insured contract is funded by premium payments which are merged with premium income from all other contract holders; benefits are not included in full under the valuation if premiums therefor are in default; that is, no assumption is made that the premiums will be made up in the future or resumed; the insurance reserve liability adheres strictly to a past-performance basis. The amount of actuarial reserve brought out by the valuation enters the liability accounts, and its effect mingles with that of all other reserve liabilities in influencing the size of the insurer's surplus account.

Quite differently, under the trust-fund medium, contributions do not merge with those of other plans, nor do the actuarial obligations of a given plan mingle with liabilities of other plans handled by the same trustee or with the trustee's own corporate accounts. In fact, the actuarial reserve liabilities do not as a rule appear, as such, in the trust fund's accounts at all. The only essential accounting for the trustee is to show that only to the extent of the funds it has received do liabilities of the trust (as apart from the plan) exist. Perhaps the plan has been underfunded by too small contributions, or perhaps some contributions have been omitted; in either case the actuary's report will show the amount needed to bring the funding up to par, but the trustee's report to the employer will not include this statement. While defaults in contributions may occur in trust-fund plans, the provisions with respect to benefits do not automatically reduce the amount of expected benefit, as would usually be true in the insured plan. The trust-fund plan can hope that contributions will be made up; insurance methods are less optimistic and consider only the experience to date (except for the deposit-administration contract mentioned on page 290).

The insurer's actuary makes the valuation, and it is not necessary to compare this answer with another answer, as the past performance of premium payment definitely determines the one answer.[11] The trust-fund actuary, on the other hand, will compare his valuation results with the assets of the trust fund as evaluated and reported by the trustee. If the actuary's calculated reserve liability is greater than the trustee's statement of the fund's assets (as is usually the case in the early years of a pension plan) the actuary reports to the employer the extent to which the plan is unfunded. If the trustee's statement shows assets in excess of the reserve liabilities determined by the valuation, the plan is correspondingly overfunded.

There are also differences when the valuation shows that a gain from interest, mortality, withdrawal, or expense charge has resulted from past experience. Under individual-contract insured plans, these gains under any given retirement plan are not segregated from the general gains for similar types of contracts in the insurer's general insurance business; that is, the dividend returns on contracts implementing the retirement plan are the same [12] as those paid to individuals holding the same type of contract but not subject to the plan.

For insured group-annuity plans, or group-permanent plans, this merging of experience is modified by the use of *case-experience* (or *credibility*) factors which are applied to the plan's own gains (or losses) and ultimately influence the allowance and size of the dividend credit to the employer's account. The larger the plan the greater the credibility factor and the more the plan stands on its own experience. The gains emerging from the valuations, however, may be applied by the insurer in other ways than as future dividend credits; existing reserves may be strengthened, either directly or through allocation of the gains to general contingency reserves or to specific-case contingency reserves. The insurer has complete control and discretion about where and how any such gains will be used. Some years ago insurers found it necessary to lower the rate of interest assumed in their calculations

---

[11] This does not mean that there can be no unfunded liability with respect to an insured plan; it is of course common to amortize the cost for already established past-service benefits over a period of years.

[12] There are recent instances of attempts to establish a separate "dividend class" for these contracts when used for pension plans (e.g., the guaranteed-issue type), but not for separate pension plans.

of contribution rates and in the determination of the reserve liabilities for their group-annuity plans (recently this trend has been reversed). This reduction in interest rate made it evident that the reserve liabilities previously posted for the group-annuity plans then in effect were inadequate, and consequently they were strengthened by being augmented by additional allocations. In this strengthening the insurers drew upon their contingency reserves and general surplus to increase group-annuity reserves. The funds so drawn upon were then replaced gradually by withholding dividends which otherwise might have been paid to employers and by increasing the rates of future contributions.

Different principles and practices obtain in arriving at the valuation results under trust-fund plans. As explained above, the consulting actuary compares the reserve liability resulting from his valuation with the trustee's assets. If an underfunded condition exists, it may be due to not having completed the amortization schedule, but, if not, he recommends added contributions to increase the assets and correct the condition. If an overfunded condition exists, he could, like the insurer, recommend holding the extra amount as a contingency reserve. This course would be his natural inclination until such time as a reasonably good cushion was built up; the desirable cushion would be in inverse order of proportion by size of case, since random fluctuations among small groups of employees could disturb the fund's liabilities considerably more than among large groups. The obstacle to a trustee's following the actuary's advice of building up a contingency fund from experience gains lies in the insistence of the Internal Revenue Service that for a trust-fund plan such gains must be used to offset the employer contributions next due and must not be used for contingency-reserve purposes unless an equal amount is made subject to inclusion with taxable income of the employer for that year. With insured plans free of this restraint, it appears to be not only discriminatory but, considering the nonpooling of trust-fund protection, anomalous as well.[13]

An illustrative actuary's valuation report for a typical trust-fund

[13] For further discussion on this point and a suggestion which would prevent misuse of contingency reserves for trust-fund plans, see discussion of Dorrance C. Bronson, "Pension Fund Valuation," by Robert J. Myers, *Transactions of the Actuarial Society of America,* vol. 46, p. 397.

plan (of the type negotiated with certain unions in the steel industry) is summarized as follows:

ILLUSTRATIVE VALUATION RESULTS FOR TRUST-FUND PLAN

(Valuation as of December 31, 1956—Effective Date of Plan, January 1, 1955)

This particular plan provides 1 per cent of final 10-year average earnings multiplied by years of credited service, reduced by $85 per month (in lieu of the exact OASDI benefit). It provides for a minimum pension credit of $25 a month for 15 years of service plus $2 a month for each year of service over 15 with a $55 minimum for 30 or more years of service; also for a permanent-total-disability pension. The entry-age normal-cost method of valuation has been followed.[14]

1.	Number of covered employees (not retired)...................	909
2.	Average annual pension payable from plan................... $	796
3.	Number of retired employees...............................	82
4.	Average annual pension being paid......................... $	322
5.	Gross actuarial reserve liability as of December 31, 1956	
	a. Retired employees....................................... $	231,300
	b. Nonretired employees beyond normal retirement age.........	471,800
	c. Nonretired employees under normal retirement age..........	2,981,000
	d. Total gross liability.....................................	$3,684,100
6.	Assets in trust fund as of December 31, 1956 (per statement of trustee)...	627,000
7.	Unfunded liability on December 31, 1956 (item 5 minus item 6)...	$3,057,100
8.	Annual normal cost...................................... $	110,000
9.	Annual normal cost and annual budget for item 7 over 20-year period from the effective date of plan.........................	317,800
10.	Annual normal cost and interest on item 7...................	184,600
11.	Maximum contribution for year on tax-deductible basis (based on 10 per cent of adjusted original past-service liability, plus normal cost)...	429,200

[14] The entry-age normal-cost method makes the assumption that if the plan had always been in effect in the past the employees would have entered the plan years ago when they were first hired and a level annual contribution based on their respective entry ages would have commenced and would by now be represented by a large pension fund with a continuation until their retirement age of the same contribution based on their original entry ages. Consequently, this hypothetical entry-age contribution is viewed in the aggregate as continuing in the future as the "normal cost" and the pension fund which would have accumu-

Comparison of the prospective average pension of item 2 with the much smaller average now being paid per item 4 indicates that the early retired cases apparently had lower pay and/or shorter service than is expected over the years ahead. Item 5a brings out the lump-sum liability on the fund for already retired employees; item 5b shows that about twice as large an amount is attributable to active employees already eligible to retire. The total of these two, about $700,000, means that the trust fund of item 6 will meet the obligation for the retired group but, until another year's contribution is made, falls a little short of meeting the obligation for the nonretired eligibles of 5b.[15]

Items 10 and 11 give the employer a fairly wide range within which to decide upon his contribution for the year. Item 9 is one possible intermediate basis, i.e., using a 20-year period for the amortization of the original liability (past service). It would be possible for this company to contribute more than item 11, but the excess would be "carried over" for tax deduction in a subsequent fiscal year. Because of the unfunded condition of items 5b and 5c, it would be well for this employer to decide on a larger payment than the "minimum" of item 10.

The above discussion of trust-fund valuation also applies in many respects to the deposit-administration contract used by insurers as a funding medium for pension plans. In this form of group-annuity contract, the valuation standards described earlier for insured plans are not followed. An actuarial valuation similar to that for a trust fund is made. The same actuarial-funding methods would be available for use in the valuation as for a trust-fund plan. A table of results such as that above would allow the employer to decide on his next contribution (premium deposit) to the fund. There would be one important difference. Line 5a, giving the liability for retired lives, would not

---

lated, if such "normal cost" had been paid in past years, becomes, instead of a fund in hand at the inception of the plan, an "actuarial deficiency" or a "past-service" value to be met in one way or another over future years. At each valuation after the plan becomes effective, the unfunded liability becomes the total liability for all benefits under the plan less the present value of future normal-cost contributions and less the assets accumulated to date of valuation.

[15] No funding has yet been made for active employees, when the fund is viewed in this light. This fund has been operating only a short time.

show on the deposit-administration valuation table since as retirements occurred definite purchase of annuities would have been effected (thereby reducing line 6), and from then on these annuities would revert to the usual rigid form of insurer valuation. Even this practice, however, has given way in some "modern" deposit-administration contracts so as to parallel the more flexible trust-fund method of immediate reflection of mortality gains and losses among the retired group.

Importance of Reserves. The appropriate measurement of a system's reserve liabilities and their balancing by the system's assets are essentials of sound procedure for business and other nongovernmental pension plans. This need is automatically fulfilled for insured plans (deposit administration excepted) by the insurer's reserve methods as prescribed and generally supervised under statute by state insurance departments. In trust-fund plans, the consulting actuary, trustee, and employer are responsible for the soundness of the plan's financing and must not only adhere to correct procedures but also take responsibility for the underlying technical assumptions on which these procedures develop. The actuary is particularly charged with responsibility for such assumptions.

In the trust-fund plan, the fund's own assets represent the extent of the guarantee of benefits. The more the assets of the fund lag behind the reserve liability as brought out by valuations, the closer the fund gets to the no-guarantee character of pay-as-you-go methods, without, perhaps, the employees' or retired pensioners' being aware of the inadequacy of the fund. If the actuary's valuations indicate a steadily increasing gap between the fund's assets and the computed liabilities, it is time either to find ways of augmenting contributions (such as having employees contribute) or frankly to reduce the plan's benefits to a point within the scope of the assets and anticipated future contributions. In extreme circumstances, perhaps all accruals of benefit beyond what the assets will then support should be canceled. These comments apply to some extent to the insured deposit-administration medium as well.

The Treasury, too, is concerned with valuation results. If assets lag behind reserve liabilities to a serious extent, the Internal Revenue Service may insist that higher-paid employees, including those who have already retired, must have their benefits (even though already accrued) adjusted to lower amounts.[16] Also, a discontinuance, or partial discontinuance (by reduction of benefits), of a plan through neglect to contribute adequately may subject the employer to scrutiny for the cause of his neglect. If no justifiable cause is presented, he may be subjected to a retroactive disallowance by the Internal Revenue Service of previously granted tax credits for contributions to the plan.

Comparison of the assets with valuation results is the actuarial diagnosis of the "health" of a plan.

Modified Reserve Plans. The various stages or degrees in reserve financing have been set forth,[17] from pay as you go, around the circle, to a fully funded perpetuity. The importance of an adequate reserve structure for private pension plans has just been explained, with particular attention to trust-fund plans, since, except for deposit-administration plans and plans in which there is a yet-to-be-funded past-service liability, insured plans are automatically on full-reserve standards.

One of the prime reasons for concern with reserve liabilities is the continual risk of business mortality. When the business dies, the employee payroll vanishes, and without reserve assets pension promises die, too. But there are organizations that are not subject to "business mortality" and that may, for practical purposes, be regarded as *perpetual*. Such organizations are the state and federal governments, perhaps municipalities, highly endowed funds or foundations, governmentally subsidized institutions, and other quasi-public enterprises. The reserve basis of plans organized or sponsored by this type of institution may well be different from that of plans found in business. It is an entirely pertinent question whether a high degree of reserve financing is always necessary, or even desirable, for the plans of these institutions. It is true periodic actuarial valuations of these systems should be conducted, but it is by no means unanimously conceded that sufficient assets need to be on hand to balance the reserve liabilities.

Consider, for example, the federal civil service retirement system

---

[16] U.S. Internal Revenue Service Mimeograph 5717 states that during the first 10 years of a plan certain restrictions will be imposed on the amounts of benefits to be provided to the 25 highest-paid employees if current costs are not met.

[17] See Chap. 11.

covering most of the employees of the federal government. In spite of periodic valuations and annual actuarial reports, Congress has not deemed it necessary either to follow a rigorous funding program or to become disturbed about the low proportion of the reserve liability for which assets are in hand; these assets are probably not adequate to meet the sum of pensioner liability and the employee equity in the system represented by employee contributions alone. It is true that a desultory sort of program for funding past service by 1998 has been announced occasionally as the "intention," but Congress has not implemented this intention. Similar observations, although leading into the realm of general governmental fiscal policy, may be made concerning the social-security system, and also, with its own particular qualifications, the railroad retirement system.

As the consideration of reserve funding moves its focus from the federal government to states, municipalities, and other political subdivisions or to endowed funds, foundations, and other quasi-governmental institutions, the appropriateness of some degree of reserve funding becomes evident. Not only is "mortality" possible for some of these subdivisions or institutions, but also their taxing power is limited or nonexistent. If the pension costs without reserve financing go beyond a certain point, reductions in, or cessation of, benefits may occur. Also in these lower echelons of public institutions a considerably greater psychological stimulus pervades the employee membership if they know that their employer is contributing advance funds to protect the pension promise. In general, the lower the degree of permanence or the smaller the size of this type of employing unit, the more advisable full reserve funding becomes.

CHAPTER 14

Negotiated Pension Plans

The earliest pensions were paid by the employer on an informal discretionary basis, and when pension plans came to be formalized, they were still subject to employer decision and control. As pension plans were more and more often placed on an actuarial basis of advance funding by the employer, it seemed even further to strengthen the innateness of these unilateral characteristics. Even when plans calling for employee contributions began to arise, these characteristics were not altered; sometimes representation of contributing employees was called for, or permitted, on an administrative committee or board, but the employer seldom gave up any prerogatives of ultimate direction or control of the plan or of its fund. There were numerous early attempts of unions or other employee groups to provide pensions from their own dues or contributions; most of these were failures because of unsound funding and lack of appreciation of the costs.

For some time after collective bargaining on wages and other conditions of employment had become common, the question of pensions (and other benefit schemes, such as group insurance and hospitalization) was not generally thought of as a bargainable issue, at least by management. Furthermore, unions were uninterested in, distrustful of, or antagonistic toward employer-financed pension plans because of their use by employers as a paternalistic device to forestall unionism; because of their tendency to restrict the mobility of workers by tying them to one employer; and because of their general unattractiveness as an alternative to cash in hand. Plans were occasionally installed on the "request" of organized employee groups, but their establishment was viewed as being a gratuitous action of the employer and as having the same unilateral character as if the employer had taken the initiative in the first place. Perhaps not over 350 formal and funded private pension plans were in effect by 1930, and only some 1,500 by 1940. Most of these plans covered salaried employees only, though some included all employees. A plan for the hourly-rate group alone was almost unknown, and a plan only for employees of a given union was unheard of. By 1958, about 40,000 private pension and profit-sharing plans were in operation (substantially over half of which were pension plans), including coverage of several millions of hourly and union employees.

If widespread existence of pension plans had obtained in the 1930s, no doubt the formulation of the Social Security Act would have been along somewhat different lines. Actually, the act was the precursor of widespread private pension plans in business. Indeed, the so-called inadequacy of the governmental pensions (although in the beginning, at least, they were intended to be no more than a subsistence benefit) spurred on the supplementary-pension movement by creating something on which to build.

Pensions as a Negotiable Issue. Before 1949, the negotiated pension plan was uncommon in most industries, although the 1947 Labor-Management Relations Act permitted employers to make contributions to jointly managed pension funds. It was not until 1948 that the issue came into the open to be tested by the courts. The Inland Steel case, involving pensions, and the W. W. Cross case, involving health and accident insurance, were the deciding vehicles in this important landmark in bargaining history. The following excerpt from a report of a congressional committee is a succinct statement on the issue and its background: [1]

Although a number of employers voluntarily bargain with labor organizations representing their employees on health, welfare, and retirement plans and agree to the incorporation of various phases of the subject in labor-management contracts, there remains for final adjudication the question of

[1] Report of the Joint Committee on Labor-Management Relations, 80th Cong., 2d Sess., 1948, pp. 94–95.

whether the subject is within the area of mandatory collective bargaining. In April of 1948 the NLRB ruled on this issue. In a 4-to-1 decision the Board adopted the recommendation of its trial examiner in the *Matter of Inland Steel Company* and *Local Union, Nos. 1010 and 64, United Steelworkers of America (CIO)*, (77 N.L.R.B. No. 12), ruling that pension and retirement plans are within the area of compulsory bargaining. In this case, the Board found that the company had refused to discuss with the union the amendment and application of the terms of an old-age retirement and pension plan originally established by the company. This refusal to bargain, the Board found, amounted to an unfair labor practice under section 8(5) of the National Labor Relations Act, in that the company's unilateral action on amendments to the plan changed the employees' "wages" and "conditions of employment" as the terms were used in section 9(a) of the National Labor Relations Act. The Board construed the term "wages" to include "emoluments of value, like pension and insurance benefits, which may accrue to employees out of their employment relationship." The company's contribution to the plan, the Board said, "constitutes an economic enhancement of the employee's wages." With reference to the effect of the company's unilateral action upon "conditions of employment," the Board held that "matters affecting tenure of employment, like the respondent's retirement rule, lie within the statutory scope of collective bargaining."

The Board found in the legislative history of the amended act what to it was compelling evidence that Congress intended to encompass pension and retirement plans within the meaning of "wages or other conditions of employment" as those terms were used in the original act. It also found that in reenacting these provisions, there was evidence of congressional willingness "to allow that conclusion to stand."

The case of W. W. Cross and Company and *United Steelworkers of America, CIO* (77 N.L.R.B. No. 1162), carries the doctrine of the Inland Steel case into additional areas. It involves the union's right to have included in contract negotiations the terms of a company-sponsored group health and accident insurance plan under which benefits are afforded the company's employees. For the reasons given in *Matter of Inland Steel Co.,* the Board found that the company had a statutory duty to bargain collectively concerning the terms of its group health and accident insurance program.

On appeal of the Board's Inland Steel decision, the United States Circuit Court of Appeals for the Seventh Circuit on September 23, 1948, unanimously held—that the order of the Board insofar as it requires the company to bargain with respect to retirement and pension matters, is valid.

The courts refused to review the earlier decision in either case, so that pension and other employee-benefit bargaining has become the general practice.

Another important issue involving pensions arose soon after the Inland Steel case. This was in the matter of the United Steelworkers of America (CIO) demand in 1949 that certain major steel companies must bargain immediately on pensions, even though the labor contracts did not expire until some time later and contained no language with respect to pensions. A strike was threatened, and against the employers' objections President Truman appointed the Steel Industry Board (referred to as the Fact-finding Board) to examine the issues in dispute. The board was of the opinion that pensions were properly bargainable immediately but felt that a preliminary study would be advisable. The board went further, however, and enunciated two far-reaching indicia for steel-industry pension plans. One was a definite statement that the plans should be noncontributory, and the second was a suggestion that a flat minimum pension of approximately $100 a month, including benefits under OASDI, would be a reasonable benefit formula (they roughly estimated that an employer contribution of 6 cents an hour would finance such a benefit).

The Noncontributory Principle. It was the noncontributory principle of the board's report that the union grasped in immediately pressing their pension demands without waiting for the suggested study. The employers contested this basis, no doubt feeling that it would leave out of control the costs for future liberalization in benefits, since no part of any increased cost would be felt by those covered. A large-scale strike in the steel industry ensued in the fall of 1949. Owing in part perhaps to the psychological influence of a noncontributory settlement by the Ford Motor Company while the strike was in progress, the steel union essentially won the noncontributory-pension issue, Bethlehem Steel being the first to sign the agreement, followed soon after by others.

Because of the importance of the question,[2] the following quotation from the report of the board is pertinent (this excerpt was directed to

---

[2] Employee contributions are also discussed in Chap. 4. See p. 70.

the subject of health benefits and insurance, but the board referred to these points in the pension discussion): [3]

We are recommending, however, that in general the system of insurance established by the parties should be noncontributory. We have come to this conclusion for the following reasons:

1. The general trend is in that direction. The Bureau of Labor Statistics Bulletin No. 946, reporting a study of collective bargaining plans in effect by mid-1948 and covering over 3,000,000 workers, states that most of these plans are financed entirely by the employer. That this is a recent development can be seen from the fact that only 600,000 workers were covered by collective bargaining plans in 1945, and 1,250,000 by early 1947. Union exhibit 19 shows that almost 80 per cent of the workers under this union's collective bargaining plans whose financial provisions are known are on a noncontributory basis. . . .

2. Such noncontributory plans will cover all the workers in a plant instead of making the individual employees elect, subject to individual temptation, to remain out of the plan in order not to forego any part of his current spendable income.

3. There will be no reduction in the present take-home pay of workers.

4. Stability will be promoted because costs can be better integrated into the labor cost structure.

5. Taxwise, more insurance can be bought for a given number of dollars than if the employee contributed from his own earnings after he had paid a tax on them himself.

The companies urged that making pensions noncontributory would tend to discourage the hiring of other than younger men. The union did not concede this; but it is apparently convinced that, in any event, other advantages outweigh this consideration. Moreover, the existence of a pension plan would be of benefit to the employers in that workers would be less apt to quit their jobs, having a stake in the pension plan, and the resulting drop in labor turn-over would to a degree result in reducing the expense of training replacements.

We have carefully considered and discussed the arguments on the other side. The claim was made that the contributory system is more calculated to preserve the dignity and self-reliance and incentive of the worker. There is no evidence, however, that workers in industries where the employer pays

[3] The Bureau of National Affairs, Inc., Special Report on the Steel Case—Report to the President on the Labor Dispute in the Basic Steel Industry by the Steel Industry Board, submitted September 10, 1949, Washington, 1949, pp. 49–51.

all are any less dignified or self-reliant than other workers, or that their employers are more paternalistic. So long as the cost of the plan is integrated into the labor cost structure and has a bearing on the rates set in wage negotiations the worker will know that he is in fact paying for his own insurance. Therefore, he will be just as careful about abuses and malingering as if he were contributing to the insurance fund directly. It is true that Government insurance is predominantly contributory, except with respect to unemployment insurance. But in private industry the general trend in collective bargaining is the other way.

Private Pensions and OASDI. The Fact-finding Board's report spoke of a pension-level objective "including the Social-security benefit." The Bureau of Internal Revenue had already made rules on the meshing, or integration, of the OASDI benefit amount with the pension of the private plan. Furthermore, a number of plans of a unilateral type were already functioning with a pension formula "inclusive of OASDI." It came about naturally that the steel companies, who had lost on the issues (1) of not bargaining at all on pensions and (2) of employee contributions, proceeded—as they were able to do with the unions—on the principle of a "deduct" equal to the OASDI benefit. The symbolic $100 a month seemed to be the immediate union goal, regardless of its component parts. At that time, about $46 a month was the highest OASDI old-age benefit being paid, which would leave $54 for the plan to meet; later, in 1950, the top OASDI benefit became $80 a month, in 1952, $85—this last amount leaving only $15 for such a plan to meet—and in 1954, $108.50, an amount in excess of the $100 criterion. No doubt the companies viewed this deduct as protection against the advance, partly at their expense, in OASDI benefits, and, up to 1954 at least, it did protect them. Considerable dissatisfaction arose, however, on the point of OASDI increases' becoming private-plan reductions, the gross pension remaining the same; this seemed particularly unfair to already retired employees. Whether the deduct principle (the maximum amount of such deduct has been set at $85 per month) can or will be maintained in the future by the steel industry is questionable; other benefit formulas that started on that basis have been replaced by formulas that do not involve any such deduct.

The $100 amount was only part of the pension formula for most of the steel companies. Some of them already had a plan that expressed benefits per year of service as a percentage factor applied to compensation. Most negotiated plans in the steel industry provided for computing the pension at 1 per cent of average pay over the 120 months (10 years) before retirement, for each year of service, again deducting OASDI benefits, if this basis would produce amounts in excess of the formula of $100 a month minus OASDI. Subsequently the steel-industry type of plan was generally revised, through negotiation, to set the minimum pension at $140 per month reduced by $85 (in lieu of the exact OASDI benefit). The resulting $55-per-month minimum was further reduced by $2 for each year short of 30 years of service at retirement; since at least 15 years of such service was required, the absolute minimum pension under the plan was $25 per month. The negotiated revision in 1956 again increased the minimum pensions, establishing a formula of $2.40 per month for each year of service before November 1, 1957, and $2.50 for each year thereafter, subject to a total credited service period of 30 years.

The steel-pension settlement did not emphasize the funding of the pension plan other than to provide that the cost would be met by the employer. Some of the agreements were silent on the matter, while others stipulated that the employer would assure full funding with a third-party trustee or insurer of any pensions entered into upon retirement during the period of the agreement. This is *terminal funding* and requires no advance funding before retirement. However, the agreements put no strings on the employer who wished to effect advance funding, nor did they attempt to control the investments of any fund. Many employers in the steel industry that initially adopted a terminal-funding approach have since swung over to an advance-funding method.

During September, 1949, the Ford Motor Company settled with the UAW-CIO Union for a noncontributory $100-a-month pension formula inclusive of the OASDI Primary Insurance Benefit (now Primary Insurance Amount, or PIA), the basic benefit under Title II (OASDI) of the act, upon retirement at age sixty-five or later, exclusive of any extra for wife or children.

Another provision in the original Ford settlement that later became an issue both in Ford and in other automotive pension negotiations was that Ford would contribute only a fixed cents-per-hour cost. Here was an actuarial anomaly of a fixed-benefit formula and a fixed unit cost geared to a "work" index and not a "pension" index. Several other agreements were made on this basis. The unscientific character of this arrangement was explained by one labor representative as follows: [4]

Much to the chagrin of the actuary, contracts in large numbers specify both fixed benefits and contributions. While their relationship may be loose in the formal sense in which the actuary would like to see them tied down, such a procedure is not confounding to the collective bargaining parties. They have immediate objectives such as retiring specific groups of persons, or laying a foundation for future developments. They are aware of the working relationships within the collective bargaining process which allow for periodic reviews and frequent changes in the light of later developments. The flexibility of the collective bargaining process is as applicable to pension programs as to any other phase of the bargaining relationship. The actuary operating on conservative principles of loading his cost figures against all eventualities, and assuming the ultimate termination of plans, and insisting on accelerated funding, must learn to relax them "where the parties so desire" in view of the underlying assumption of the continued existence of the business, one on which the accountant constructs his accounts, and the opportunities for recurrent adjustments in the rate of contribution. Long periods for amortizing past service costs are preferred by unions since they permit more liberal immediate benefits and lower annual costs.

Proceeding in accordance with the bargaining latitude suggested in this quotation, many plans negotiated originally on this unscientific cents-per-hour basis later changed over to the "actuarial basis," whereby costs bear a relation to the accruing benefits instead of to the number of hours worked during a year.

Benefit Formulas. The agreement in the original Ford settlement, recognizing the OASDI offset, has also given ground. On the original basis, each increase in the Primary Insurance Amount of OASDI reduced by that much the benefit of the private plan. Further, the inclusive $100 a month was reduced proportionately for service at retirement of less than 30 years (25 years in some similar plans). This meant that with a PIA of $46 before 1950, an employee with fewer than 15

[4] Solomon Barkin, Labor's View on Actuarial Requirements for Pension Plans, Proceedings of Panel Meeting Sponsored Jointly by the American Statistical Association and Others, Chicago, Dec. 29, 1952.

years of service at retirement would get no benefit from the plan; after 1950, with the top PIA increased to $80 (and later to $85), employees with service of 25 years or fewer would get nothing.

In the General Motors Corporation settlement on pensions in May, 1950, both of these problems were avoided. The cents-per-hour basis was not used, but the employer agreed to contribute for the duration of the labor contract (1) the actuarial normal cost for the year and (2) the cost for the actuarial deficiency (the cost of past-service benefits) so as to amortize that deficiency over a 30-year period. General Motors agreed to a benefit formula that was independent of OASDI by granting a pension of $1.50 a month for each year of credited service not to exceed 30 years (i.e., $45 a month maximum). Hence no "zero benefits" could emerge for short service (10 years of service by retirement was generally required for coverage under the plan, which established a $15-a-month minimum pension).

A considerable number of settlements after that with General Motors followed similar lines; in fact, most employers who had used the Ford offset formula soon changed to the General Motors type, including Ford itself. General Motors did include the symbolic $100-a-month-inclusive-of-OASDI formula as a catchall minimum, but it could apply only in very unusual patterns of combined General Motors and OASDI coverage or lack thereof.

There were many other varieties of benefit formulas worked out in the negotiated plans of 1949 to 1952. One type retained the inclusive $100 formula but avoided zero benefits by prorating for short service on the net amount instead of on the gross. For example, if the PIA was $80 a month, the net benefit for full service was $20 from the plan alone; if the retiring employee had only one-half the requisite service for full benefit, he would get one-half of $20, or $10 a month as his pension, as compared with a zero pension according to the original Ford method of first taking one-half of $100 and then deducting the $80 PIA.

Another variation was to use the $100 formula up to some given length of service, such as 25 years, and then to add a unit of pension, such as $2 a month, for each year of further service.

Because of amendments to the Social Security Act increasing the

PIA, it was not long before some plans gave way by upping the symbolic $100 to a higher figure, e.g., $112.50, $125, or $140.

The next change in the UAW-CIO bargaining area was to adopt, with the General Motors type of formula, a unit of $1.75 for each year of service up to 30 years instead of a $1.50 unit. Effective June 1, 1953, Ford agreed to this formula, thus abandoning both cents-per-hour costs and the offset formula. Many other automotive companies followed, and General Motors also increased its benefit unit from $1.50 to $1.75 in 1953. The negotiations taking place at the end of the 5-year-contract period (1955 for many companies in the automotive industry) produced several important further changes in the pension formula. For example, the $1.75 rate of benefit accrual was upped to $2.25. The 30-year limitation on credited service went by the board so that all covered service up to retirement would be credited. Employees who terminated employment after age forty and who then had 10 or more years of credited service were entitled to a vested benefit (deferred to age sixty-five) based on their years of credited service after age thirty.

In the CIO area in the steel, automotive, rubber, and other such industries,[5] bargaining for noncontributory pension plans has resulted in a variety of benefit formulas and other provisions. This variety has now narrowed, and the dollar-unit formula has become the usual pattern with frequently an alternative of a per cent of pay if a higher pension results.

It has been found that it is not practicable to present a comprehensive listing of other provisions of these negotiated plans nor to discuss them at length. In general, the same sorts of provisions as have been described in Chapter 4 are necessary, depending on the benefit formula and conditions of eligibility and receipt of pension.

Form of Labor Contract. Sometimes the contract with the union contains all the provisions of the plan; sometimes the plan stands alone, and the contract includes the plan only by reference, with cer-

---

[5] Excluding textiles where relatively few pension plans are found; in some cases a severance-pay benefit has been granted in recent years in lieu of pensions, and in other cases the plight of the industry has not permitted the pension issue to make much headway.

tain auxiliary clauses, which in some instances modify those in the plan for the duration of the contract. Under this latter arrangement, for instance, the labor agreement may call for more specific funding of pensions during the period of the contract than is provided for in the plan. The contract may provide for a more detailed and joint method—union and employer—of administration than that contained in the plan. The labor contract may modify a mandatory retirement age contained in the plan and may spell out the exact basis of credited service, such as how many hours worked, or compensated, represent 1 year of credited service. The question of what constitutes a break in credited service or in seniority must be covered in one or the other of the two documents. When reduction in pension is to be made to allow for OASDI benefits, workmen's compensation, legislated disability benefits, or unemployment compensation, the reductions must be defined and explained in one of the documents.

Disability Pensions. Provision of disability pensions has been greatly stimulated by the union-negotiated approach to pensions. The insurance-company difficulties of the 1920s and 1930s with disability-income provisions in life-insurance contracts cast a pall on the whole field of long-term-disability benefits. Insured pension plans have almost wholly omitted the disability-pension feature, and even today insurers generally will not underwrite the risk but will only arrange for payment on the direction of the employer or plan administrator, for example, by charging the payments against the fund or the employer on a pay-as-you-go basis. The unions have seen permanent and total disability as a premature forced retirement and have demanded that the pension formula must apply to it. Hence, most negotiated plans include some provision for disability pensions, and the clauses seem to be carefully drawn to apply only to bona fide cases of serious disability. On this basis, costs can be controlled, but if administrative decisions gradually whittle down the original restrictions in these clauses, they may again get out of hand. The appearance of the disability pension in union plans has initiated a similar movement in the field of non-union-employee plans. There can be no doubt about the need for protection in bona fide cases. The disability-insurance benefit under the OASDI program (equal to the full PIA with certain possible deducts) will raise many problems with respect to like benefits under private plans and could exercise both good and bad influences on these plans.

CIO Plans. Before the AFL and the CIO merged in late 1955, there were important differences in pension-plan approach and philosophy between the two groups. While the merging of the two bodies may influence a change in these attitudes toward greater uniformity, it seems advisable to record some of these differences. The typical plans that the CIO negotiated with employers had three features in common: (1) they were noncontributory, the employer meeting the full cost, but with no set pattern for funding; (2) they placed more emphasis on flat-amount benefits than on benefits related to pay level; (3) length of service increased the pension, but, until certain revisions of 1955, a maximum credit of 25 or 30 years usually obtained. Early in this recent pension movement, there was some talk of industry-wide identical plans, even possibly handled in one or more large, pooled trust funds, with the unions largely controlling these funds or forming a union-sponsored insurance company for the purpose. Except to a limited degree, the identical plans have not emerged,[6] and the funds are mostly held under trust agreements or insurance-annuity contracts between the individual employer and the trust company or insurer; nor has the union-sponsored insurance company for pension purposes as yet been formed. Also a certain amount of pressure was exerted for a vesting feature in these noncontributory plans, and recently this objective was obtained through providing for vesting after a given age and/or length of service.

AFL Attitude. The approach to pensions of the American Federation of Labor was somewhat different and of a longer duration than that of the CIO. The AFL seemed to have placed considerable emphasis on the need for actuarially sound financing: [7]

In negotiating the pension agreement, the union should make sure that the plan will be adequately funded. A provision binding the employer to the payment of certain pension benefits is not sufficient. In definite-benefit plans, no less than in fixed-contribution plans, there should be an additional

[6] Several area plans have been negotiated between employers in a particular industry domiciled in a limited area, such as one city, and their unions.

[7] "Pension Plans under Collective Bargaining, a Reference Guide for Trade Unions," American Federation of Labor, p. 66.

provision setting forth clearly the manner in which those benefits are to be financed through current contributions to a trust fund or insurance company.

The most desirable provision is one which obligates the employer to maintain the plan on a full advance funded basis; that is, through current contributions sufficient to finance the full amount of all future service credits as they are earned, plus an installment on the past service liability, large enough to assure that the past service will eventually be paid off in full. Anything less than this should be strongly resisted.

The AFL early stressed the importance of vesting: [8]

Where the scope of these plans is limited to individual establishments, and where workers have no vested rights in the funds contributed by the employer, broken service with different employers will deprive them of pension rights—even though they may have a long record of active membership in their union, and may spend their working lives in the trade or industry. While plans of this type may help to meet some of the immediate needs of a few of the older members of a union group, they offer little in the way of benefits to the majority of the members, and so little to help solve the broad national problem of economic insecurity and dependence among the aged.

Plans of this sort may fairly be said to serve more of a management purpose than a trade union purpose. They follow the pattern of the typical precollective bargaining unilateral "company" plan; set up as an instrument of, by, and for management—out of "efficiency" and "personnel relations" considerations.

They offer the employer a cheap means of getting rid of superannuated workers, with a specious show of generosity. They give the employer a sort of invisible chain with which to tie workers to their jobs with a particular company, and to prevent them from bettering themselves elsewhere, through the promise of a pension plan if they stay and the threat of its loss if they leave.

The AFL took a far less dogmatic position than did the CIO about employee contributions: [9]

Although a great deal of attention has been devoted to this issue in some quarters, actually the question, as to whether a plan should be contributory or noncontributory, cannot be regarded as a basic one. It is entirely possible to set up a plan which will prove reasonably satisfactory on either basis, provided the plan is sound in other more fundamental respects.

[8] *Ibid.*, pp. 69–70.   [9] *Ibid.*, pp. 75–76.

As far as any question of principle is concerned, there is no sound argument in favor of employee contributions to private negotiated plans. However, some employers are emotional on the subject, and, in such a situation, it might be possible to use it as a lever to get concessions that could not otherwise be obtained—on other more vital issues—by agreeing, in exchange, to go along with a contributory approach.

General Labor Attitude. Union groups seem to believe strongly in joint administration—by employer and union—of the plan's operations and in availability to the union of employee data and actuarial findings. They seem emphatically opposed to a hard and fast mandatory retirement age. Apparently, they feel that the federal government, through the Social Security Act, should do more and more in the way of higher and more comprehensive benefits. In fact, from remarks made in certain labor areas, employer plans may almost be viewed as only a temporary expedient or stopgap until the federal law can be employed to do the whole pension- and survivorship-benefit job.

Multiemployer Plans. This chapter has touched on only the highlights of pensions negotiated between the unions and the single employer. There are many large plans of a union-negotiated nature that are not the single-employer type but are of an area- or union-wide character. Because of its skilled-trade categories (and the diffused employment among large numbers of small employers or on spot jobs), these plans are principally found in the craft-union group. Examples of this multiemployer type of pension fund (as well as funds or insurance contracts for other types of benefits) are those of the International Ladies Garment Workers Union, the International Longshoremen's Association, and the International Brotherhood of Electrical Workers. Of these, the plan of the last-named is probably the widest in scope geographically, encompassing union members throughout the United States and Canada. Under these multiemployer funds, each employer contributes on some unit basis—cents per hour or percentage of payroll—and the pension is set at the amount deemed, or hoped, to be supportable by such contributions. It is generally realized that fixed costs and fixed benefits are not inherently linked indefinitely; either contributions or benefits may have to be adjusted according to the experience over a long period. In some of these plans the union members contribute to the cost. The great advantage of these plans is the possibility of migration from employer to employer within the industry without loss of pension rights, a form of vesting.

Perhaps the most publicized multiemployer union pension plan is that of the United Mine Workers, which—with other benefits—is supported by royalty payments per ton of coal, the present rate being 40 cents per ton. The fund from which benefits are paid—and which has had several experiences in the courts and before federal bureaus— does not purport to be established on an actuarial-reserve basis. The underlying principle apparently is that monies will be produced as needed by increasing the tonnage royalties through collective bargaining. In support of this characteristic of the plan are the following statements in the 1951 report: [10]

All benefits authorized are subject to termination or revision in the discretion of the Trustees. No vested interest in the Fund extends to the beneficiaries; all benefits are on a "pay-as-you-go" basis. . . .

Pension payments are made from a separate account established by the Trustees solely for paying pensions. From time-to-time the Trustees transfer irrevocably to this account from royalty payments received by the Fund such amounts of money as are required to satisfy current pension obligations. Payment of pensions is therefore assured insofar as possible under a Fund whose continued existence depends upon industry-wide collective bargaining.

Area Plans. A few area plans have developed covering the union employees of employers in certain localities. The best-known plan is the Toledo Plan, established at the behest of the (then) UAW-CIO to provide pensions to employees of several—generally smaller—employers in the Toledo area. Among the participating employers are representatives of a variety of industries. The Automotive Tool and Die Association Plan in Detroit is an example of an area plan restricted to employers in a specific industry. Other illustrations are the plans covering the brewery workers of certain cities, the longshoremen of several cities, and the milk drivers of the dairies in several cities.

The Taft-Hartley Act. A phase of union pension plans, structure, and funding that remains vague lies in the application and intent of

[10] United Mine Workers of America, "Welfare and Retirement Fund, Four Year Summary and Review for the Year Ending June 30, 1951," Washington, September, 1951, pp. 10–11. According to the 1957 report, this characteristic of the plan has not changed.

the Labor-Management Relations Act (the Taft-Hartley Act), Section 302(*c*) of which deals with welfare and pension funds. The act lays down certain conditions to be met when a labor representative establishes a trust fund from employer contributions to provide benefits for the employees of one or more employers participating in the arrangement. One condition is that the fund must be exclusively confined to the payment of such benefits, which may include life insurance, sickness benefits, unemployment benefits, or pensions. Another requirement is that a written agreement must be made with the employer detailing the benefit program and calling for equal employee and employer representation in its administration, with provision for one or more neutral representatives. An annual audit of the fund is called for, to be publicly available. If any contributions are to be used for pensions or annuities, the trust must have a separate fund earmarked solely for that purpose.

This law does not apply to trust funds established before January 1, 1946. Its application to later funds is not clear; it appears that the usual pension plan, under which the employer rather than the union representative sets up the trust, would not be subject to it. Furthermore, a fund that is subject to, and conforms to, these provisions does not thereby escape the requirements of approval under Sections 401(*a*) and 501(*a*) of the Internal Revenue Code. It is required under a ruling of the National Labor Relations Board that where an employer contributes an amount based on total payroll to a negotiated pension plan (or other employee benefit plan) all employees, union or nonunion, must benefit from the plan, even though it is established under an agreement with the union.

Other Legislation. Welfare-plan laws have recently been enacted in the states of Washington, New York, Connecticut, California, Wisconsin, and Massachusetts. The law of the state of Washington is loosely worded and unclear but would seem to carry disclosure requirements and admit of quinquennial examinations. The New York welfare law calls for registration and reporting of such welfare plans (including pensions) as fall within its purview, and, more importantly, it includes the portent of insurance-department approval and supervision. However, under a ruling of the attorney general of New York State, the scope of this act encompasses only plans jointly established or maintained, so that the more numerous unilateral pension programs—whether insured or noninsured—fall outside the legislation.[11]

At the federal level, the Douglas committee, during the 1956 session of Congress, studied welfare plans and was shocked by a few flagrant irregularities among union-management funds, mainly not of a pension character. Supported only by these few notorious examples, legislation was introduced in Congress during 1956 which would require stipulated procedures for welfare plans—a welfare plan being widely defined to encompass all types, insured and noninsured, unilateral and multilateral, even seeming to include group life insurance. One bill would have all such plans register if 25 or more employees were covered, and with 100 or more employees covered, full disclosure would be required. However, it is believed that no federal bill introduced would set up machinery for *examination* and *supervision* of plans. In the Douglas committee's bill, the registration and reporting would be made to the SEC. An advisory council would be established reporting to the SEC, and proposals have been made in certain bills introduced in 1957 for even greater regulation at the federal level.

Tax Deductions. In the Internal Revenue Service's earlier administration of Sections 165(*a*) and 23(*p*)—now 401(*a*), 501(*a*), and 404—dealing with approval of, and tax deduction for, pension plans, the union-negotiated plan, whether or not a Taft-Hartley type, brought up special problems. For example, did a contract calling for terminal funding only mean that the funding was entirely for past service and hence subject to the 10 per cent maximum rule for annual deductions? Or, again, did a specified cents-per-hour contribution constitute funding adequate to justify the Service's acceptance of the plan as of a "permanent" character and not one that would be gradually "terminating" through actuarial inadequacy of the underlying contributions? Another problem lay in the multiemployer field, where a union had arranged a pooled plan and trust supported by identical rates of contribution from all employers—sometimes hundreds—such as a rate of

---

[11] The laws of some of the above-mentioned states contain detailed requirements for registering and annual reporting of welfare plans, while others leave more of these requirements to the discretion of the administrative department head. In any event, the actual results of the operation of these laws will not be known until they have been in effect for some years.

cents per hour or per cent of payroll. Should the Service ignore the fact that some employers in the pool were high-pension-cost cases (with older long-service employees) while others were of the low-cost type? By paying the same unit cost, some would be paying less and some more than the correct amount for their own coverage. Was a blanket tax deduction under Section 23(*p*)—now 404(*a*)—suitable in these circumstances?

It is not feasible to go into a full discussion of these and other points, since the situation is still in flux and statements might soon be obsolete. Numerous rulings have been made which, on an up-to-date basis, are available for study when such questions arise. Suffice it to say that so far the Service seems to have taken a practical attitude and has resolved such questions in a manner that minimizes roadblocks to the establishment of bona fide union-negotiated pension plans.

Conclusion. In summary, it appears that the present movement among unions in putting pensions on the bargaining agenda has thus far not resulted in many wild schemes. The influences of employer caution in a competitive milieu, the supervision of pension plans and costs by the Internal Revenue Service, and the general acceptance by both union and employer of the usually conservative advice of consultants, actuaries, trustees, and insurers have contributed to this healthy result. During the war and postwar periods of highly competitive bidding for employees, the federal wage-stabilization agencies, while in the end not promulgating really confining rules, did introduce a psychological slowdown on ultraliberal plans on the part of both labor and management.

CHAPTER 15

Widows' Benefits and Allied Protection

Once a system of employee benefits is established, pressure is always exerted for expanding or liberalizing it. This is true not only of government programs but also of union-negotiated programs and even of unilateral employer plans, particularly when business is profitable and tax rates are high.

The purest concept of the term *pension plan* is that of a program providing lifetime benefits at or after a given age upon retirement from the active service of the employer after a long period of employment. However, this pure form of pension has come to be enlarged in numerous cases to include one or more of the following: pensions at disability before the normal retirement date of the plan, options for nondisability earlier retirement at reduced amounts of pension, vesting of a deferred pension for employees terminating service even a long time before their normal retirement age, inclusion of a lump-sum payment at death before or after retirement, provision of a term-certain period with payments for life thereafter, and choice of a variety of options at retirement so that a reduced pension will carry on for a temporary period or for the life of a spouse or other dependent after the death of the retired employee. From time to time, and particularly in the last few years, discussion of pension plans has appeared, suggesting that what has been done—even the full roster of the benefits described above—is not enough and that, after an employee's death, the widow (and sometimes the children) should also be granted a pension under the employer's plan. For instance, to quote from *The New York Times* of Sunday, July 26, 1953:

How to protect widows of employes who have died before retirement, or shortly thereafter, from serious loss of income is being recognized more widely as a major problem in employe welfare planning. There is a growing demand for greater effort to increase such protection.

Since few private pension programs provide adequate incomes for widows of employes who die before realizing their full pension benefits, and since high taxes and living costs add to the difficulties of employes in providing for the necessary protection of their families, the need for increased incomes for many widows has become urgent.

The purpose of this chapter is to discuss briefly some aspects of proposals that an employer provide pensions for widows under his pension plan.

Widows' pensions provided as a part of a pension plan are not new, although in this country this type of family benefit is rare. In England such pensions, as well as orphans' pensions, have not infrequently been provided. But pension plans have had a considerably longer history in Great Britain than in this country, and long before the days of group life insurance the British provided employee death benefits. Modest widows' pensions were made an integral part of some pension plans; in other cases a completely separate but adjunctive fund for widows was established. As a result, even today, group-life-insurance protection in England is much less widespread than in this country.

Optional Equivalent Benefits. Among the optional-benefit provisions of pension plans is the *joint-and-survivor* or *contingent-annuitant option*. This option provides for the continuation of a reduced pension, after an employee's retirement and his subsequent death, to his widow, if she survives him, or to another named dependent. It does not increase the cost of a pension plan, because the cost of the payments for the survivor or contingent annuitant is met by a reduction in the employee's own pension. Another option—indeed the automatic provision of many insured pension plans—is to pay a reduced pension for a term certain and for life thereafter (the reduced pension has the same actuarial value as the regular no-term-certain life annuity); this would furnish protection of considerable value to a widow. These options, which are, by reason of providing reduced pensions to the employee, the actuarial equivalent of the employee's lifetime benefit, do not increase costs. They are considerably different from the *full widows' pension* discussed below.

Numerous pension plans that provide no death benefit before normal retirement date (other than a refund of any employee contributions) carry a provision whereby, on proper election, the pension payable upon retirement at or after the regular retirement age is decreased and becomes payable as long as either the pensioner or his designated contingent annuitant (often confined to the spouse) survives. In this way, the pensioner can, in effect, buy a life-insurance value for his widow by taking a reduction in his own pension, the amount of the reduction being the cost of the insurance. The respective values at retirement age of the two possibilities—of taking the pension in full or of taking a reduced pension under the option—are the same; this option, as well as other joint-and-survivor options, is based on the principle of *actuarial equivalents*.

The amount of reduction in pension for the option depends on the respective ages of the employee and his contingent annuitant at the time he retires. The applicable factors are illustrated in Table 15-1.

TABLE 15-1. ILLUSTRATIVE FACTORS FOR JOINT-AND-SURVIVOR (WIDOW'S) OPTION

Age of employee at retirement (1)	Age of wife when employee is the age in column (1) (2)	Per cent of employee's full pension, payable as long as either lives * (3)
65	60	65.7
	65	72.0
70	60	55.1
	65	61.8
	70	69.3

* Basis: 1951 Group Annuity Table, $2\frac{1}{2}$ per cent interest. Percentages shown are approximate.

The factors in Table 15-1 provide for the reduced pension to be paid as a *level* amount. It is common to provide for a somewhat smaller reduction in the pension to be applicable while both live, a further reduction if the retired employee dies first, or another example, a moderately reduced pension at retirement age with payments equal to one-half or two-thirds of the initial amount to be continued after the first death. Other combinations, including a term certain instead of a contingent annuity, are possible, but all would meet the actuarial-equivalent criterion.

Because this option is a form of life insurance, its election, if permitted to be made or canceled at will, could become very costly. It is confined to the nonretired employees when first introduced, and it is usually required that, except for a short period of grace following the announcement of the provision, the employee must either elect it several years before regular retirement age or satisfactorily pass a medical examination. Once elected, it may not be canceled, although if the spouse dies before the regular retirement date, the option is automatically void and the employee becomes entitled to the full pension. On the other hand, if the employee dies before the retirement date, the option is also void and no pension is payable to the survivor.

The option is effective only *upon retirement at* or *after* the normal retirement age. It entails many complexities and cost problems if permitted on any other basis. Consider first the period before regular retirement date. If the option were to apply upon retirement for disability (if the plan had a disability-retirement provision) or at other early retirement, considerable antiselection against the fund would appear, since a person in poor health could, in effect, substitute a healthy life to be the recipient of the pension that would otherwise cease at his death. Even the election of the option a number of years before the time the employee would retire would not eliminate this selection, since the actuarial costs would have been based on the assumption that a certain number of deaths would occur before the normal retirement age and that those pensioned for disability would receive payments only as long as they lived. For these reasons, unless the employer is willing to face a substantial increase in cost, this option should not apply to disability or other retirements before the regular retirement age.

Even after the normal retirement age, there are certain difficulties. For instance, if an employee has previously elected the option but at normal retirement age continues to work—perhaps at the behest of the employer—under the usual operation of the option, his death before his actual retirement will cause the option to be void and his widow will receive no pension. This situation has been a subject of some concern, particularly among employers who have had occasion to persuade employees to continue to work beyond the normal retirement age. As a consequence, some plans have provided that the option, if elected, will be effective at the normal retirement age whether or not the employee lives to a later actual retirement date. This would mean that, if he were still employed at his death, his widow would receive the same pension (or approximately the same) that she would have received if the employee had retired at the normal age. But, suppose the wife dies before his actual retirement. Must he accept the lower pension when he does retire because the option was effective at his regular retirement age? In some cases this is the rule, but in others the employer meets the additional cost of giving the employee the full pension on actual retirement.

An illustrative provision for the joint-and-survivor option in a pension plan is given below. Its terms go about as far as would be prudent, unless one is willing to add substantially to costs. This provision protects the employee who continues to work beyond his normal retirement date.

A participant may nominate his spouse as beneficiary and may elect, by written application filed with the employer, a joint-life-and-survivor benefit of equivalent actuarial value, as determined by the actuary, to the retirement benefit to which he would otherwise be entitled. If the application is filed less than three (3) years prior to his actual retirement date (except that this option is not applicable to disability retirement before normal retirement date), the participant must submit evidence of good health to the employer unless he files such application within three months after the effective date of the plan. The annual retirement benefit, payable monthly, shall be determined on the basis of equivalent actuarial values according to the ages of the participant and of the beneficiary nominated under this option at the time the participant retires. The reduced amount so determined shall be payable so long as either lives. If the beneficiary dies before the participant has actually retired, the election will be void, and the participant will be treated as though he had made no election. The election shall remain in effect if the beneficiary dies subsequent to the participant's actual retirement date. The election shall remain in effect if the participant dies subsequent to his normal retirement date even though prior to his actual retirement date. Once an election has been made and accepted by the employer, it cannot be changed or rescinded without consent of the employer in accordance with rules of uniform application to all participants similarly situated.

While a joint-and-survivor option has been included in a large number of plans—particularly of the insured variety—the use of the option among employees who have retired has been surprisingly small. The option seems attractive, and yet few choose it. This may be due to the employee's feeling that he needs the full pension, without reduction; or he may have sufficient regular life insurance, savings, or survivor protection in the form of OASDI or railroad-retirement benefits. Or, perhaps, there are older children who he expects will look after their mother after his death. Of course, if the option were thrown wide open, it would probably find much greater usage; it would be to the advantage of everyone to elect it and to decide whether to continue it or cancel it as retirement age approached.

In order to keep the joint-and-survivor option on an actuarially equivalent basis, the limitations and conditions explained above must be observed. At times employers may wish to relax these conditions, permitting more flexibility in the use of the option. However, the greater such relaxation, the higher the cost of the plan. For example, under a plan that has an early retirement privilege on a reduced benefit, consider an employee who has satisfied all the requirements for advance election of the regular joint-and-survivor option—i.e., to take effect on an actuarially equivalent basis at normal retirement date—who dies while actively employed before attaining normal retirement age but at an age above that stipulated in the plan as the lowest age at which he could have applied for early retirement. Under the usual form of option the death of the employee would not provide a widow's pension. It would be possible, however, to provide a reduced pension for her under such conditions, but this would not be an option without cost. It would be akin to a full widows' pension as discussed below, but for a limited group, only those who had elected the normal-retirement-age joint-and-survivor option. Why should this limited—and rather accidentally limited—group share in the widows' pension in event of death while still employed after early retirement date; that is, why not have it apply to all? Choice of benefits not based on actuarial equivalents can cause misunderstanding and difficulties.

Full Widows' Pension. The full widows' pension is a pension benefit applicable to all widows that is *not* related by the criterion of actuarial equivalents to the employee's own pension. This type of pension is rarely found in private pension plans in the United States (or, except for bank plans and branches of British companies, in Canada) but is not uncommon in Great Britain. Public-employee plans, where competitive costs are not an element and where political persuasion can overcome actuarial argument, frequently carry either a full widows' pension (sometimes children's too) or provide a joint-and-survivor option far more liberal than the principle of actuarial equivalents would permit.

Full widows' pensions would be payable to widows of all employees who pre-deceased their wives—in the broadest form of such provision either before or after retirement—with no change in the amount of the employees' own pensions. The provision could, of course, be more restrictive and apply after retirement only, or after the normal retirement age only, or in the event of death before retirement age but subject to qualifying conditions based on the employee's age or length of service. A provision might be included for cessation of the pension at, or shortly after, the widow's remarriage. In any event, the provision could be costly. It has the characteristics of life insurance rather than of pensions in the usual pension-plan sense. Where a plan is contributory, the use of a widows' pension unrelated to actuarial equivalents might be deemed to discriminate in favor of employees who happen to be married at the time of their death or, among those married, who happen to have very young wives. It would be wholly unfeasible to have only the married employees bear the cost by special employee contributions. If, on the other hand, the cost of the widows' pension were to fall on the employer, it might be objected to by the stockholders because they were being called on to foot the bill for the individual insurance needs of certain employees. Most employers, after reviewing the problem, either look to liberalization of their group-life-insurance program or to the Social Security Act (or

Railroad Retirement Act) survivors' provisions or to both and decide not to go beyond the actuarially equivalent option.

Cost of Providing Full Widows' Pension. What would be the added cost of a pension plan if a full widows' pension were payable (1) in the event of the retired employee's death after retirement and (2) in the event of the employee's death before retirement? To establish cost indicia for these provisions, it is necessary to assume a formula for determining the widows' pension and to make certain other broad assumptions.

Tables 15-2 and 15-3 will be used in estimating the cost of the above-mentioned benefits. They were derived from the latest available data published by the Bureau of the Census in connection with its monthly population sample survey. Table 15-2 shows how the age of

TABLE 15-2. MARITAL RELATIONSHIP IN THE UNITED STATES *

Age of wife	Per cent at each age if husband is age 65 to 69
Under 35	0.3
35–44	2.6
45–54	9.2
55–64	54.7
65–69	27.6
70–74	5.0
75 and over	0.6
Total......................	100.0

* Data as of April, 1953.

SOURCE: Based on data obtained in connection with the monthly population sample survey of the U.S. Bureau of the Census. See U.S. Bureau of the Census, "Current Population Reports, Population Characteristics," ser. P-20, no. 53, Apr. 11, 1954.

wives ranges in relation to husbands aged sixty-five to sixty-nine. Table 15-3 shows for various age groups the percentage of the male population that is married.

Suppose that a pension plan is set up to provide $100 a month for an employee upon his retirement and that the effective average age of retirement of the employees covered by the plan will be sixty-

TABLE 15-3. PERCENTAGE OF MALE POPULATION IN THE UNITED STATES THAT
IS MARRIED *

Ages	Per cent married
14–19	2.4
20–24	50.4
25–29	75.0
30–34	83.6
35–44	87.9
45–54	85.8
55–64	83.6
65–74	76.2
75 and over	55.6
Total 20–64............	80.8

* Data as of March, 1956.
SOURCE: U.S. Bureau of the Census, "Current Population Reports, Population Characteristics," ser. P-20, no. 72, Dec. 21, 1956.

seven. Suppose further that the full widows' pension—which will not cause an actuarial decrease in the employee's own $100 a month—is payable on the same basis as the OASDI relationship, namely, 75 per cent of the employee's own pension—in this example, $75 a month.

The value of the $100-a-month pension for the employee retiring at age sixty-seven is about $12,700, so that, regardless of the method of funding used under the pension plan, this $12,700 may be considered as the final cost of the plan with respect to that employee. From Table 15-3 it is seen that about 80 per cent of the employees age sixty-five to sixty-nine would be married, and if from Table 15-2 it is assumed that the average age of the wife of an employee retiring at age sixty-seven is 5 years younger than her husband, it is necessary to determine the value of the $75 a month payable, if and when she becomes a widow, to the wife now age sixty-two for the period that she will live beyond the death of her husband (the effect of the re-marriage rate at this age would be small). The value of this $75 survivorship pension is some $5,400. However, since only 80 per cent of those retiring are married, the average for all employees, married and unmarried, is $4,300. By comparing this $4,300 with the value of the employee's pension alone, $12,700, it is found that the increased cost for the full widows' pension after retirement might be in the area of 30 to 35 per cent. If the widows' pension were only 50 per cent of the employee's full pension, the increased cost would be 20 to 25 per cent.

Next, what would be the added cost for a full widows' pension at death before retirement? By referring again to Table 15-3 it is seen that about 81 per cent of the males at ages twenty to sixty-four are married. The percentages increase somewhat with advancing age, so that for the range of ages at which eligibility under the plan would be heaviest and mortality rates would be increasing, assume that 85 per cent of the employees will, on the average, be married. It may be further assumed that the pension plan will cover mostly male lives.

From a typical age distribution of an employer's male personnel over age thirty with 5 years of service (assuming these are the conditions for becoming eligible for coverage under the pension plan)—excluding terminations of service—20 employees will die for every 80 living through to retirement. Under a simple type of pension plan with no death benefits or other optional features, the actuarial costs will have been determined on the assumption that these 20 employees will die, thereby lowering costs, since the pensions otherwise due at retirement will not eventuate for them. If, however, it is estimated that 85 per cent of the 20, or 17, will be married at time of death, and if a widows' pension is substituted for what would otherwise be an anticipated reversion credit to the fund because of the death of these 17, the cost of the plan will be increased by the value of the pension payable to the 17 widows. In fact, depending on the amount of annual pension for a widow, because of her lower age on the average and lower mortality, this substituted value could exceed the value that had accumulated for the employee on the basis of the probability of his living to receive his pension.

What this substituted value might be would depend on the exact provisions of the pension plan containing the widows'-benefit provision. For purposes of illustrating costs of the provision, it is perhaps suitable to assume that the amount of annual pension payments to the widow would be chosen so as to have a present value at the time of the employee's death that would be equal to the present value at the time of the employee's retirement (if he lived through to that date) of the pension to which he would then become entitled.[1] By adopting this simplified assumption and ignoring the technical adjustment for interest, the cost of the program would be increased some 20 per cent [2] by reason of the provision of a full widows' pension for death before retirement. If we assume the average widows' pension would have a present value of only one-half the value of the employee's pension at normal retirement date, the cost increase would be over 10 per cent.

If the costs were combined for death after retirement (20 to 35 per cent) and death before retirement (10 to 20 per cent), a widows' pension might well increase pension costs by some 30 to 55 per cent, depending on the pensions granted.

These extremely rough cost illustrations indicate that the death-before provision would not generally be as expensive as would the death-after provision. However, it is difficult to visualize a program that would provide widows' pensions only for death before retirement and would not make similar provision for death after retirement, especially since there is usually a group-life-insurance program for death before retirement which is frequently not continued—at least in full—after retirement. Consequently, when the costs of widows' pensions for death before retirement are considered, the likely greater costs for death after retirement should be borne in mind.

There is no feasible or equitable method whereby employee contributions to the pension plan can finance a full widows' pension. A main reason is that some employees are not married and never will be; others are not married but will be; still others are or will be married, but the wife will die first; and some wives are considerably younger than the husbands and vice versa. Furthermore, some widows will remarry soon, some later, and some never. In a complex situation

[1] Assume that an employee now aged fifty would become entitled to a pension benefit of $100 a month upon reaching age sixty-five and that the present value of the pension at that time would be $15,000. If he dies now (while aged fifty) and leaves a widow aged forty-five, the present value of her monthly benefit commencing immediately would be about $15,000 also (this particular value of a widow's benefit is being used here solely for illustrative purposes).

[2] In addition to providing pensions to the 80 employee survivors who retire, pensions will be provided to the 17 widows of the employees who die before retirement. This constitutes a 21 per cent increase in the pension roll.

such as this, how can appropriate employee contributions be established? Therefore, the cost of the widows' pension would fall upon the employer even under a contributory pension plan.

To what extent does the employer's obligation—or, indeed, the right to apply the stockholders' funds—extend to supporting the employee's family after his death? It is natural for management to feel a responsibility, shared by the stockholders, to the employees, but does this extend to monthly incomes to their families? Group life insurance is uniform; it is payable whether a named beneficiary survives or not, but for an employer to meet the costs of widows' pensions is a selective process under which only certain employees may benefit. An employee with an age, salary, and service record identical with that of another would be given very different values under the plan depending on whether he was married and, if so, whether his wife happened to be younger or older than the wife of his counterpart. Yet is one of these employees more valuable, or more loyal, to the employer to an extent that would warrant the differential costs?

When a full widows' pension is made a part of a pension plan, a pertinent question arises about the position of the widows' benefit relative to the employees' pensions. Which would have priority on the fund if the plan terminated? Suppose that the full-widows'-pension feature provided for death before retirement and that a catastrophic series of deaths among active employees occurred. Would the widows of those deceased active employees stand on a par with the then pensioners? Could the money from the fund be used to pay this unexpected claim load, even though it ate into the funds for the remaining active employees? Should, then, the employer contributions for the widows' pension be established under a separate fund?

Widows' and Children's Benefits under OASDI. The present OASDI of the Social Security Act provides (and the Railroad Retirement Act similarly provides) that at the death of an employee or a retired employee certain survivors' benefits are payable if he has met the applicable service conditions. In such instances, the widow is eligible to receive a benefit immediately following the death of the employee if she is then aged sixty-two or over, or regardless of her age if she has a child in her care (the child will also receive a benefit). The amount of this widows' benefit (as of the time of writing) can reach over $80 a month and will be payable to her until death or remarriage if she is already sixty-two or over, or until death, remarriage, or until she has no child in her care (including a child's reaching age eighteen), whichever occurs first. If her benefit ceases because her youngest child has reached age eighteen, she will again become eligible for it when she reaches age sixty-two.[3] This amount of $80 a month assumes the top wage of $350 a month. For a widow age sixty-two, a lifetime benefit of $80 a month represents roughly about $14,000 worth of life-insurance value (decreasing, of course, at higher ages).

Under OASDI all benefits are free of federal income tax to the recipients. The tax situation of the widow under a private plan, providing either the joint-and-survivor option or the full widows' pension, is not so clear. There have been several changes in the attitude of the Internal Revenue Service with respect to these pensions.

Group Life Insurance. It is not within the scope of this book to cover the subject of group life insurance; however, a short discussion of that form of protection in relation to pension plans is pertinent.

Group life insurance for employees is principally written on the 1-year-renewable-term form, under which no permanent values build up and the premium for a given employee increases with age. While most of the group life insurance in force is written on this basis, other forms are often used in an endeavor both to stabilize costs and to provide some employee equities and paid-up values in case of termination of employment (including retirement) or in case of discontinuance of the contract by the employer.

One of these other types is group permanent life insurance.[4] Here, as the name implies, a level-premium form of insurance is established which builds up policy values that are absent under the 1-year-term method. This may be particularly valuable with respect to the status of *pensioners* under group-life-insurance protection.

Still another type of group-life-insurance structure is the group-life paid-up method. In its rather infrequent use, this method is customarily contributory, the employee's contribution being used to purchase a small unit of paid-up insurance each year and the employer paying

---

[3] See Chap. 2.

[4] Explained in Chap. 9 in its function as a vehicle for providing pensions.

for the cost of the residual insurance of the death-benefit formula on a 1-year-term basis.[5] With a fixed amount of employee contribution, the unit of paid-up insurance purchasable decreases each year with increasing age, but over a period of time a significant amount of this paid-up insurance can be accumulated and be permanent protection (or provide cash values) for the employee even though he terminates service, retires, or finds the contract discontinued.

If the employee contribution is not applied wholly against immediate death-benefit costs—as it is in the case of 1-year term group life insurance—but instead is largely set aside for future mortality, the residual part of the death benefit for the employer to meet is substantially increased. For example, consider an employee aged forty-five who is called upon to contribute 60 cents a month ($7.20 a year) toward a group-life-insurance amount of $1,000.[6] Depending upon the type of group contract, the amount of life insurance for the first year provided by his contribution and the balance left for the employer's premium to meet would be as shown in Table 15-4, under the 1-year-term type of contract, the unit-paid-up type, and the level-premium type.

The 1-year-term type is considerably less expensive to the employer as long as the age of the employee and duration of his participation in the plan are below certain points. The exact determination of these points is beyond the scope of this chapter, but the figures shown for an 11-year duration indicate the basic trend of the three methods. It may be generally stated, moreover, that the continuation of group life insurance beyond retirement age will be more costly to the employer under the 1-year-term type of contract than under the other types. For example, the 1-year-term premiums for $1,000 insurance at higher ages are as shown in Table 15-5.

[5] A variation of this is sometimes found in the application of the employee contribution as if it were a level annual premium used to purchase as much level premium insurance as possible, which would be a greater amount than under the unit-paid-up basis, thereby leaving a smaller residual amount for the employer to meet on the 1-year-term basis, but with correspondingly less in the way of termination equities to the employee.

[6] Under types of contracts other than the 1-year-term type the employee is frequently called upon to contribute $1 monthly per $1,000 of insurance.

TABLE 15-4

Type of contract (1)	Amount bought by employee contribution of $7.20 for the year * (2)	Balance of the $1,000 insurance for employer to buy (3)	Annual cost of column (3) to the employer on 1-year-term basis * (4)

Age 45—first year of participation

1-year term.............	$857	$143	$ 1.20
Unit paid-up............	13	987	8.29
Level premium to age 65..	186	814	6.84

Age 45—eleventh year of participation (attained age 55)

1-year term.............	$410	$590	$10.35
Unit paid-up............	132 †	868	15.22
Level premium to age 65..	186	814	14.28

* Illustration only—net premiums based on CSO Mortality Table, 2½ per cent interest, no loading.

† Accumulated amount purchased over 11-year period.

TABLE 15-5

Attained age	Annual cost of 1-year term insurance of $1,000 *
65	$ 42.96
70	64.27
75	96.07
80	142.91
85	210.41

* U rate exclusive of flat loading. The U rates are widely used by life insurers as group-insurance premiums.

This increasing cost of 1-year term insurance on pensioners is avoided when the employer has been willing and able (and without stockholder objection) to meet the considerably higher costs at the earlier ages under one of the other types of contracts. In such cases, either the full insurance may be continued beyond retirement age at a relatively low cost to the employer or premiums may cease with a paid-up-insurance value of a substantial portion of the face amount.

Since group life insurance is usually of the 1-year-term type, serious cost problems arise with respect to insurance after retirement age. Various policies have been followed, ranging from the employer's meeting the mounting cost and keeping the insurance intact to an automatic termination of the insurance when retirement age, or actual retirement, is reached. Intermediate practices are decreasing the insurance by some percentage of the face amount, such as 50 or 75 per cent, or dropping it to a burial-benefit amount, such as $500. Other practices gradually reduce the amount by age after retirement date. To illustrate this graduated method, the following excerpt gives the after-age-sixty-five-group-life-insurance program for employees with 10 or more years of service of a large industrial concern as provided for in the current contract with its union employees. Note that this program starts at age sixty-five whether employees are retired or not, and employees do not contribute after age sixty-five.

On the first day of the calendar month following the month in which the 65th birthday of the employee occurs, his life insurance in force immediately prior thereto shall be reduced by 2% thereof, and shall be further reduced by an equal amount on the first day of each succeeding month as follows . . . such reductions shall be made until the life insurance is reduced to 1½% of the amount in force on the employee's 65th birthday, times the number of full years of participation, not in excess of 20, at age 65, but in no event to less than $500, and such remaining life insurance, called "Continued Life Insurance," will be continued thereafter until death of the employee, subject to the rights reserved to the Corporation to modify or discontinue this plan.

The earlier discussion of the full widows' pension indicated several possible objections thereto, including that of applying the employer's money unevenly among the employees according to marital status and age of wife; the unfeasibility of constructing a system of employee contributions to pay for this provision on an equitable basis; and the substantial cost increase entailed. Some employers, who have approached this matter with an initial interest in the full widows' pension, have, after analysis, abandoned the idea and, instead, have adopted a group-life-insurance program or have raised the benefits in an existing group-life-insurance program. Many employers have, irrespective of the widows' pension, taken steps to modify group-life-insurance programs as they apply to retired employees.

In the United States at the end of 1956, over 117 billion dollars of group-life-insurance protection was in force, practically all of which covered employees in the labor force or retired employees.[7] In addition to this, the population of the United States carried more than 238 billion dollars of ordinary life insurance and over 40 billion dollars of industrial life insurance. To this may be added about 44 billion dollars of federal life insurance for veterans; 12 billion dollars of insurance in force with fraternal and assessment associations, burial societies, etc.; and nearly 1 billion dollars of savings-bank life insurance. The death-benefit-insurance value of the old-age-and-survivors program under the Social Security Act of some 300 to 400 billion dollars gives a total of about 800 billion dollars of death-benefit protection without regard to other avenues of savings and thrift. Potential widows are designated as the beneficiaries of a major proportion of all this death value. Even though it is realized that this huge volume of protection is spread unevenly among the population, its very magnitude is impressive and raises a basic question about the need for the additional full widows' benefit, as well as about the pertinence of this benefit as a supplement to a pension plan. If still more death benefit is needed, should it be handled directly through a death-benefit vehicle rather than through what has been primarily a retirement vehicle for employees?

[7] Exclusive of group life insurance covering borrowers ("credit insurance") in the amount of some 17 billion dollars.

CHAPTER 16

Public and Nonprofit Employee Plans

As noted in Chapter 2, the Old Age, Survivors, and Disability Insurance (OASDI) [1] Title of the Social Security Act for some years excluded certain large categories of employees. Through gradual amendment most of these categories became partly or wholly covered or were given the opportunity to obtain coverage on an elective basis. Thus, more and more employee groups obtained the basic protection of OASDI, with supplementary benefits through localized private plans being a problem of each group. Many large categories of workers, because of their loose and heterogeneous composition, are not susceptible to inclusion in staff pension plans in the usual manner, which requires an employer-employee relationship of a size and character not often present in these groups. The groups in question are agricultural laborers, domestic servants, and the self-employed; for them, OASDI is the only group program for old-age protection.

OASDI continues to exclude most of the civilian employees of the federal government, although efforts are periodically made to bring them within the purview of the act; on the other hand, oddly enough, military personnel are covered by OASDI. Another group, railroad employees, while covered by their own retirement program, are also covered by OASDI because of an interlocking arrangement between the two programs under which for the first 10 years of railroad service the benefit coverage of OASDI is operative.

Other groups of public employees (state, municipal, etc.), while not

[1] Before the 1956 amendments which brought in disability benefits, the designation was OASI. Even though at times in this chapter reference is made to dates before 1956, the designation OASDI is used for uniformity and convenience.

automatically covered by OASDI, can, through compacts between the state and federal governments, elect to become covered by OASDI, the state being the party making the election for its own employees or those of a political subdivision. This is predicated in some instances on a referendum among the particular employee group if the group is already covered by a local pension plan.

As for employees of various nonprofit organizations, here too there is in general no mandatory coverage by OASDI, and a process of election of coverage through waiver of exemption from taxes can be used if two-thirds of the employees are in favor of coverage. This chapter will deal briefly with pension plans for these public and nonprofit employees.

PUBLIC EMPLOYEES

Under the heading of *public employees* fall not only those of federal, state, county, and municipal governments and their subdivisions by departmental or occupational classification but also those of certain quasi-governmental establishments, such as publicly owned corporations, municipal transit companies, the Tennessee Valley Authority, and the Federal Reserve System. Moreover, the employees of international bodies, such as the United Nations Relief and Rehabilitation Administration (UNRRA, now defunct), the United Nations, the International Bank for Reconstruction and Development, and the International Labour Office, may reasonably be included as public employees (excluded from OASDI).

The earliest attempt at placing public employees within the purview of a formal pension system was made in England, where a plan for civil servants of the central government was established in 1810. This plan has continued through various phases to the present time, although the legislation in the 1940s implementing much of the Beveridge report superseded the basic stratum of benefits of this staff pension system and made it an arrangement supplementary to the national social-security system.

Public-employee plans in the United States were inaugurated well over 50 years ago. The retired-pay measures of the armed services have long been in effect, but they are not pension systems in the usual sense; they continue a certain proportion of *pay;* the recipients are subject to recall to duty, and there is no advance funding or thought of employee contributions. Agitation for a general staff pension plan for federal civilian employees commenced around 1900, but it was not until 1920 that enabling legislation finally brought its realization.[2] Several special plans for certain segments of federal employees have been enacted since 1920 (as listed later), among them the one covering members of Congress.

The earliest state plans for public employees were those to care for superannuated teachers, starting in New Jersey in 1896, when a noncontributory plan was adopted. The first contributory state teachers retirement plan was adopted in 1913 in Massachusetts. General state-employee plans began with that of Massachusetts in 1911; their growth was slow at first, then rapid; there were 38 such plans in 1955 as against 12 in 1940. There were at least 10 plans for policemen and firemen by 1900, but large municipal-employee systems came later, in 1916 for Philadelphia, in 1920 for New York City, and in 1922 for Chicago. Smaller cities followed, but many of them and many towns, counties, and other jurisdictions among the tens of thousands of political subdivisions of the country have no local pension plans worthy of the name.[3] In some states progress has been made on the problem by opening up the state-employee plan to participation by local governmental units and their employees.

The approximate magnitudes of covered and noncovered civilian public employees in the United States, by broad category, are shown in Table 16-1.

In the federal service by far the largest group of employees is subject to the Civil Service Retirement and Disability Act as amended, which provides for the largest staff retirement plan in the world,[4] having about 2,000,000 active and (by 1956) about 250,000 retired members and nearly 100,000 survivor annuitants.

[2] Pub. Act 215, 66th Cong., May 22, 1920.

[3] Counting all types and sizes of school districts, sanitary districts, and other similar subdivisions, there are perhaps 100,000 subdivisions.

[4] Some authorities view the Railroad Retirement System, which exceeds the Civil Service plan in number of participants (active or vested), as tantamount to a staff retirement plan.

TABLE 16-1. PUBLIC EMPLOYEES COVERED BY RETIREMENT PLANS (1958)

	Covered active employees * (1)	Per cent of total active employees * (2)	Not covered active employees * (3)	Covered retired employees receiving benefits (4)
Federal civilian employees †.	2,100,000	93	150,000	250,000
Public-education employees ‡..............	1,800,000	90	200,000	220,000
State, municipal, county, and other local employees §..............	1,900,000	74	660,000	200,000
Total public employees.....	5,800,000	85	1,010,000	670,000

* Regular full-time employment.

† Excluding the Armed Forces and quasi-federal employees.

‡ Nonfederal except for the District of Columbia.

§ Excluding public-education employees.

SOURCE: Unpublished study prepared by Mrs. Weltha Van Eenam, Social Security Administration, Office of the Actuary, Washington.

There are many smaller plans among federal employees. Table 16-2 is an almost complete itemization of the federal plans, including the retired-pay types of the armed services.

There is considerable variation in the specifications and administration of public-employee systems. While some are noncontributory, most require employee contributions; joining the plan is mandatory in most cases; retirement age is usually quite flexible, optional, say, from age sixty or sixty-two on and perhaps mandatory at seventy or optional after a specified period of service, such as 20 or 30 years; benefit formulas in relation to pay vary substantially; some vesting of benefits at termination of service is common; widows' benefits are provided by some plans but frequently are an elective retirement option reducing the benefit otherwise payable to the retired employee;

TABLE 16-2. RETIREMENT SYSTEMS FOR FEDERAL EMPLOYEES AND
YEAR OF FORMATION

1. Civil Service employees, 1920
2. Alaska railroad employees, 1935 (now merged into item 1)
3. Canal Zone employees, 1931 (now merged into item 1)
4. Foreign Service officers, Department of State, 1924
5. Judges of United States courts and justices of the United States Supreme Court (early date)
6. Judiciary of territories and possessions, 1938
7. District of Columbia police, 1895; United States park police and White House police, 1942; also certain Secret Service employees
8. District of Columbia firemen, 1895
9. Public school teachers of the District of Columbia, 1920
10. Federal Reserve System employees, 1934 *
11. Tennessee Valley Authority employees, 1939 *
12. Office of the Comptroller of the Currency, Examining Division employees, 1936 *
13. Civilian teachers of the United States Naval Academy, 1936
14. Coast Guard and Lighthouse Service, 1915
15. Coast and Geodetic Survey commissioned officers (early date)
16. Public Health Service commissioned officers, 1930
17. Army Nurse Corps and Navy Nurse Corps (separate plans), 1926
18. Army commissioned officers (early date)
19. Army enlisted men (early date)
20. Navy commissioned officers (early date)
21. Navy enlisted men (early date)
22. Marine Corps commissioned officers (early date); came under Navy, 1934
23. Marine Corps enlisted men (early date); came under Navy, 1934
24. Panama Canal construction employees (practically a closed group), 1944
25. Land-grant-college employees, 1940

* Quasi-federal.

administration and funding vary from life-insurance contracts to trust funds and from pay-as-you-go benefit payments (made from the general revenue of the political subdivision, based on its taxing power or on revenues from specific sources) to full advance funding.

To illustrate the benefits, contributions, and other main specifications of retirement plans for public employees, Table 16-3 presents plans for three levels of governmental employment—federal, state, and municipal (however, to call these plans typical would be misleading as there are as many variations in pension plans in the field of public employment as there are among private plans).

TABLE 16-3. ILLUSTRATIVE MAIN FEATURES

Item description	Federal Civil Service plan
Date of plan..........................	1920
Retirement ages......................	Optional, 62; compulsory, 70. Certain early retirement possible
Retirement-benefit formula (annual basis).	Best 5-year average salary times 1½ per cent for service up to 5 years; times 1¾ per cent between 5 and 10 years; times 2 per cent above 10 years; or, for each period, times 1 per cent plus $25, if greater
Options at retirement................	Form of survivorship option
Employee contributions................	6½ per cent of salary
Death benefit	½ of accrued-service benefit to widow; children also have significant benefits
Disability benefit....................	After 5 years of service, the lesser of 40 per cent of average salary, or benefit counting prospective years to age 60
Termination benefit and vesting........	Employee contributions refunded without interest (except before 1957 or during first 5 years' service). In lieu of refund, vested deferred benefit at age 62

* In this tabulation, where an item would carry more than one method, condition, or alternative in a fuller description of the plan, the most widely used, or applicable, method is shown.

OF THREE GOVERNMENTAL PLANS *

New York State Civil Service Employees' plan †	Chicago Police Department plan
1920	1922 (replaced plan of 1915)
Optional, 60; compulsory, 70	Optional, 50, after 10 years; compulsory, 63
$\frac{1}{70}$ of "best" 5-year-average pay times years of service	Annuity benefit that $15\frac{7}{8}$ per cent of pay will provide (minimum—after 25 years' service and age 55—50 per cent of average salary for 5 highest consecutive years)
1. Form of cash-refund annuity 2. Reduced survivor's benefit 3. Others possible	No options—automatic widows' benefits
Vary by age and sex—to provide $\frac{1}{140}$ final pay times years of membership service	6 per cent plus 1 per cent for widows' benefits
Employee contributions with interest, plus $\frac{1}{12}$ of annual pay per year of service (maximum, 50 per cent of pay) ‡	Widows' and children's benefits provided by 3 per cent of pay in addition to the $15\frac{7}{8}$ per cent of pay. Special provisions for death from "duty"
90 per cent of accumulated service benefit after 15 years' service but generally not less than 25 per cent of pay	"Duty disability," 75 per cent of pay plus children's benefit, to 100 per cent maximum. "Ordinary disability," 50 per cent of pay for not over 5 years of benefit
Employee contributions with interest; if involuntary after 20 years' service, vested annuity also granted	Employee contributions with interest; proportional vesting after 10 years with full vesting after 20 years

† Several municipal plans have specifications similar to this plan.

‡ If death or disability occurs in performance of duty, more comprehensive benefits are payable from the retirement plan but reduced by any "workmen's compensation."

The departmental plan of the Chicago police shows considerable deviation from the other plans in specifications in the direction of liberality. This is generally true for specialized occupations of a hazardous nature, where youth and physical stamina are important and where means are sought to remove employees from the payroll when they fail to meet these criteria. But the early retirement age, the disability feature, the widows' benefits, and the high-benefit formula mean considerable extra cost. Undoubtedly some of these liberalizations are misdirected. Why, for instance, should a person in sound health and effectiveness be allowed to elect a pension at age fifty, say, and immediately take another job at full pay plus pension? [5] A deferred benefit at early retirement would seem wiser.

Turning to supragovernmental plans, tendencies in the direction of larger contributions and higher degrees of vesting are found. The plan in effect for the employees of the old League of Nations probably set the pattern for the later retirement plans, or "provident funds," of UNRRA, the International Labour Office, the United Nations, and many allied groups. Table 16-4 gives highlights of the pension plan for the principal such international organization, the United Nations Joint Staff Pension Fund. The comprehensiveness and liberality of benefits and conditions are evident. The cost is some 21 per cent of payroll, as indicated by the table, and may well exceed that figure.

NONPROFIT EMPLOYEES

Although many nonprofit organizations are not compulsorily subject to the OASDI provisions of the Social Security Act, many others are so subject. The line of demarcation is not distinct and has been the subject of much argument and uncertainty. The nonprofit-exclusion provisions of the act, in addition to listing such smaller groups as certain agricultural organizations and employee-benefit associations, define the largest excluded nonprofit category as follows:

Corporations, and any community chest, fund, or foundation, organized and operated exclusively for religious, charitable, scientific, testing for public

[5] Some municipal plans specify that if a pensioner earns in excess of a stated amount, such as $1,200 (or $2,400) in a year, from municipal employment, his pension will be reduced or discontinued.

TABLE 16-4. UNITED NATIONS JOINT STAFF PENSION FUND (1956 EDITION)

Effective date:	January 23, 1949
Eligibility:	Regular full-time staff members under age 60 with 1 year of service
Normal retirement age:	60
Benefits—age retirement:	$\frac{1}{60}$ of final 5-year-average pensionable remuneration times number of years of contributory service up to 30 years (at retirement employee may take up to $\frac{1}{3}$ capital value of benefit as a lump sum)

Total and permanent disability:

1. Fewer than 20 years' contributory service at disability
   a. Entered fund before age 40—30 per cent of final 5-year-average base salary
   b. Entered fund after age 40—90 per cent of pension benefit otherwise payable at age 60 if continued in plan at present salary to 60
2. 20 or more years' contributory service—90 per cent of $\frac{1}{60}$ of final 5-year base salary times years of contributory service (maximum 30 years)

Death—before retirement:

1. Married male employee—widow receives 50 per cent of employee's total-and-permanent-disability pension (if employee is over age 60 but not retired, widow receives 50 per cent of regular pension)
2. Married female employee—if husband is disabled at her death, he will receive pension equal to widows' pension in (1) above
3. Other employees—lump-sum payment of accumulated employee contributions (at $2\frac{1}{2}$ per cent interest)

Death—after retirement: If employee is married when death occurs, widow receives 50 per cent of employee's pension

Children's benefits: Payable in certain amounts at retirement or death

Withdrawal:

1. Fewer than 5 years' contributory service—employee contributions accumulated at $2\frac{1}{2}$ per cent
2. 5 or more years' contributory service—present value of deferred benefit accrued to withdrawal; payable as lump sum or as an immediate (in some situations) or deferred annuity

Eligibility for total-and-permanent-disability benefits: Medically substandard employee not eligible for first 5 years or until he passes medical examination if earlier (such employees similarly restricted regarding widows' benefits)

Employee contributions: 7 per cent of salary (plus voluntary additions)

Employer contributions: 14 per cent of salary (plus special contributions if required to make up actuarial deficiencies in fund)

safety, literary, or educational purposes, or for the prevention of cruelty to children or animals, no part of the net earnings of which inures to the benefit of any private shareholder or individual, no substantial part of the activities of which is carrying on propaganda, or otherwise attempting, to influence legislation, and which does not participate in, or intervene in (including the publishing or distributing of statements), any political campaign on behalf of any candidate for public office.

It should be borne in mind that nonprofit groups excluded from compulsory social security are narrower than nonprofit groups excluded from federal income taxation. Exemptions from income tax set up additional nonprofit entities; in this field, there are numerous subcategories, of which the following list summarized from Section 501(c) of the Internal Revenue Code (1954) contains certain important groups that are exempt from income tax although in the main compulsorily subject to social-security taxes in regard to their employees. The employees themselves are subject to both kinds of tax.

Community Chests and other charitable organizations
Credit unions
Fraternal orders
Cemetery companies
Certain benevolent insurance associations
Boards of trade, chambers of commerce, business leagues, civic leagues, etc.
Labor organizations
Clubs for pleasure, recreation, and other nonprofit purposes
Small mutual insurance companies (other than life or marine)

Nonprofit groups not electing coverage under the Social Security Act have the whole pension problem to cope with, whereas nonprofit groups covered by the act face only the question of pensions supplemental to the government plan in the same way as do industrial employers. Under the law as now amended, nonprofit groups do not have to be excluded, since practically all categories may now waive exemption subject to a two-thirds vote of the employees in favor of coverage; thus they can arrange to get at least the basic protection of OASDI, after which supplemental pensions can be considered.

Nonprofit groups exempt from income tax avoid the necessity for justifying their pension-plan contributions as tax-deductible items, but it is usually desirable to obtain Treasury approval of their plans as "qualified" [6] in order that the investment income of the trust fund (if used) may be tax-free and that all possible tax advantages may be secured for the employees covered by the plans.

Certain nonprofit nuclei have affiliations that own or control active businesses. Employees of these businesses are usually ruled to fall compulsorily under the Social Security Act, and any previous income tax exemption of these affiliations or ownerships has largely been canceled. Undoubtedly, pension plans do exist, or can be established, among these allied operations, even where the nonprofit controlling entity has no plan for its direct employees or has a quite different type of plan.

Many nonprofit groups, whether or not compulsorily or electively covered by the Social Security Act, have pension plans in existence, often of long duration. In fact, this was one reason for early opposition to inclusion in the social-security plan—that the latter would supersede the organization's own plan. The fallacy of this reasoning has been amply demonstrated by the experience of industry, where the application of the social-security plan seems to have acted more as a stimulant than as a deterrent to maintaining old plans and to starting new ones. Nonprofit groups, especially the religious groups, were wary of inclusion under the Social Security Act because it levied an excise tax on employers; it was feared that this would be the entering wedge for further taxation or regulation and a lessening of the separation of church and state. More recently, many of these doubters have been reconciled, and the nonprofit groups as a whole see the basic disadvantages for their employees (and, to a degree, for themselves as employers) of social-security exclusion; they seem more willing to entertain proposals for coming within the purview of the act.

Religious Bodies. Ministers, priests, and members of secular orders and groups, dedicated as they are to spiritual matters and to helping other human beings, are doubly in the nonprofit class, since their employers are assumed to be in the nonprofit class and they themselves presumably are not seeking enrichment in worldly goods. Their financial support, in cash or kind, is relatively small, lower on the average

6 See p. 88.

than for college or intermediate school faculties. What is their status when age forces them from their charge? Dignity and respect are clearly due and require some arrangement for benefits to sustain them in their declining years. There are probably around 300,000 persons, both clergymen and laymen, employed in work and services of a religious nature.

The Roman Catholic Church takes care of the dependent years of its bishops, priests, members of orders, and others of the full hierarchy. This is a matter of course and is implicit in the arrangements made and expected on all sides. The Protestant groups, however, with numerous denominations and autonomous parishes and with clergy permitted to marry, raise families, and have bank accounts, have had to face the pension question more as separate, special problems than has the Catholic Church.

Even the denominational genus may contain many species, as witness certain large Protestant denominations shown in Table 16-5.

TABLE 16-5

Denomination	Approximate number of subgroups
Methodist............	15
Baptist..............	15
Lutheran............	20
Presbyterian.........	10

In large urban centers, a church may have many compensated employees in addition to the clergy. Pension provision, if any, for the former is likely to be set apart from that for the latter. Pension funds for clergymen are numerous and in many instances run to millions of dollars—some to tens of millions—in reserve assets. Pensions now being paid from these funds amount to 25 or 30 million dollars per year. However, the average pension is small, diluted, no doubt, by the large number of rural parishes where cash is only a part of the pension.

Some of the funds are formal, contractual, and founded on actuarial principles; many others are loose and inadequately funded. Some of the funds are contributory, but most of them are supported entirely by the church as employer.

The funds may be representative of the denomination as a whole or applicable only to particular subdenominations. When the denomination as a whole measures the coverage of the fund, clergymen may move freely within that denomination and retain past credits and accumulate additions.

Many funds are on questionable funding bases; many small churches or church groups do not have the number needed to commence a fund and secure the advantages of averages. Suggestions have been made that an insurance company similar to the Teachers Insurance and Annuity Association [7] might be established under state supervision to assist in old-age provision for the religious groups by a general pooling on a sound actuarial basis.

As with other nonprofit categories, the Social Security Act has been amended so that clergymen and members of religious orders not subject to a vow of poverty can obtain OASDI coverage through the employing organization by electing coverage by an affirmative vote of two-thirds of the eligibles. This means that sole reliance on localized pension plans for religious groups is no longer necessary.

Educational Groups. Among nongovernmental educational institutions—universities, colleges, and private schools of various types—there may be in the neighborhood of 300,000 employees who are not compelled to be covered by OASDI and additional employees automatically subject to OASDI coverage but whose employers are not subject to income taxes. They comprise academic employees, nonacademic employees, and employees of business enterprises, usually of an investment nature, owned or controlled by the institutions. In most cases, the employees of these business enterprises are automatically subject to the Social Security Act.

This question of OASDI coverage is important in a discussion of pension plans because the presence or absence of the basic benefits of the federal program influence most of a plan's specifications and funding treatment; indeed, the influence may reach the point of determining whether there is to be any staff retirement plan at all.

Educational groups have at their disposal all the benefit devices and funding mediums available to industrial employers. Trust-fund

[7] See below, p. 342.

plans, insured plans (individual-contract, group-annuity, and group-permanent plans), employer-reserve systems, and formal or informal pay-as-you-go methods are all possibilities for meeting the retirement problem. While examples of each of these types could probably be found in the large field of educational employment, an additional facility established especially for this category (including many publicly administered or tax-supported educational institutions) has been largely utilized.

The organization called the Teachers Insurance and Annuity Association of America (TIAA) was incorporated in 1918 in New York State as a nonprofit legal-reserve life-insurance company. This company was founded to avoid perpetuating the adverse experience of the Carnegie Foundation for the Advancement of Teaching. The foundation had a fixed endowment to provide free pensions for college staffs, an endowment which proved inadequate, particularly because of upward trends in payrolls and salaries and rapidly expanding staffs shortly before and during World War I. To obtain a self-supporting actuarial basis and to offer life insurance as well as pensions, the Carnegie Corporation financed the formation of TIAA and met its expenses for many years. A further gift of over 6 million dollars in 1938 permitted complete separation.

The institutions whose employees are eligible for TIAA protection comprise colleges and universities in the United States and Canada, certain junior colleges, some private secondary schools, research institutions, and certain other educational institutions. While both the academic and the nonacademic staffs of these institutions are eligible, there is some question whether the pension methods used by TIAA are as suitable for the nonacademic groups as other more flexible means of meeting the problem.

The TIAA method of handling pensions is a mixture of individual-contract methods and group methods. A separate contract is entered into between TIAA and each covered employee, there being no master contract with the employing institution as there is in standard group coverage. However, the employing institution sets up the plan and its main specifications by a resolution of its governing body and agrees to deduct the employee's contribution from his pay and to forward, along with the institution's contribution, the aggregate premiums to

TIAA. The plans are set up as money-purchase arrangements, the contributions of the employee usually being matched or exceeded by the employer; in addition, provisions for past-service credits may be arranged for. Since each employee has his individual contract and all premiums become vested on payment, he may transfer from one covered institution to another without interrupting coverage and may make contributions (pay premiums) independently of any plan.

TIAA contracts are subject to dividends if experience warrants. Because mortality rates in the teaching profession are lower than in industrial-employee groups, TIAA premium rates for annuities must be set high enough to anticipate this lighter mortality. On the other hand, TIAA operates with certain expense economies which permit less premium loading than is used for industry groups. In general, their current premium-rate basis is very little, if any, higher than that for the group-annuity contracts of insurers that write mainly industry groups. Since the ultimate cost of most forms of insured pensions is derived from experience—mortality, interest, and expense—over a long period of time, gross-premium comparisons between insurers are not particularly meaningful. TIAA also issues life-insurance contracts on a similar basis to the same classes of employees, and the lighter mortality has, of course, an opposite effect on premium rates.

This discussion of one particular organization has been included because, when the pension status of employees of educational institutions is considered, it must be recognized that this organization, its history, and its methods are unique and of great importance. Currently TIAA has pension arrangements with over 500 institutions and old-age-protection contracts with perhaps 50,000 employees or former employees of such institutions.

More recently, TIAA has established a separate organization, the College Retirement Equities Fund, from which eligible employees may elect to purchase pension benefits based on the variable-annuity principle.[8]

Most institutions of higher learning have established pension plans for their academic employees, largely through TIAA, but pension gaps exist for the nonacademic groups. Among the larger institutions, some

[8] See Chap. 9, pp. 187–189.

utilize trusts, the funds implementing the pension plan being invested in the same manner as the college endowment. In this way they have been able to obtain somewhat higher rates of investment return than are possible through TIAA. Among intermediate schools of a non-profit character, whether publicly or privately controlled, there is an even greater lack of pension provision, or there is inadequate provision. These smaller groups do not have sufficient funds, political influence, or opportunity to set up adequate pension plans. Like small groups everywhere, they are faced with these difficulties in getting action; for them, particularly, the elective extension of social security is proving a boon in providing at least a basic measure of old-age protection.

Social Service Agencies and Allied Groups. Large numbers of employees in federal, state, and local government are engaged in what is rather vaguely designated as "social work." Whatever governmental employees this category may emcompass are classified as "public employees." But there are numerous nonprofit groups of a nongovernmental or quasi-governmental nature for whom the pension problem must be faced as it becomes more and more serious with the aging of the groups in these categories.

While rather homogeneous in the nature of their enterprises, these nonprofit, social-agency types of employers vary significantly in size, in geographical distribution, in the extent to which they have elected OASDI coverage, in the source of their funds, in their degree of likely permanence, and in their employee composition by sex, age, length of service, and salary levels. Taken together they comprise a large group, having perhaps upward of 400,000 employees. They include such organizations as hospitals, community chests, philanthropic funds and foundations, a multiplicity of charitable offices found in any city, YMCAs, home-economics groups, local housing authorities (even though subsidized federally), and others too numerous to mention.

These groups have their own paid staffs of employees, who seem to be in a sort of no man's land pensionwise, except for elective social security. Public-employee systems are not available to them as a rule, and they are usually individually too small to form an adequate base either for insured-group coverage or for trust-fund treatment. In addition, it is often difficult to convince their governing bodies of the need or feasibility of establishing a plan for each small group. Some of these groups have plans of their own; for instance, certain local housing authorities are enabled by state legislation to come within the purview of social security or of the public-employee plan, or both; also it is understood that the YMCA has a satisfactory system covering their employees on a national basis.

In order to make a start in solving this problem of the small non-profit employer, the National Health and Welfare Retirement Association, Inc., was organized to act as a vehicle for centralizing the pension planning and funding of such of these numerous nonprofit groups as wish to subscribe as members. The association was formed in January, 1945, and incorporated under Section 200 of the insurance law of New York State, which provides for the supervision of the plan by the state superintendent of insurance. The benefit payments and guarantees are further protected through the association's having effected reinsurance under a group-annuity contract with an established life-insurance company.

The association's plan is built on the fixed-cost concept of the money-purchase principle (as in the case of TIAA). The plan calls for contributions by both employing unit and employee. Benefits on withdrawal usually take the form of deferred annuities, fully vested in the employee, which have been purchased by the total of the combined contributions made before termination. The usual options at retirement are available under the plan.

The availability of this centralized pension organization for non-profit groups of the social-agency type offers not only a solution to the small-size problem but also continuity of protection if an employee shifts from one employer member of the association to another. For this continuity to be effective, a large measure of success on the part of the association will be required in bringing within its membership substantial numbers of similar employers of the type eligible, especially in the same locality, since many employees probably shift over to like employers in the same vicinity.

The field of possible eligibility for the association's plan is very large, but as it comprises a multiplicity of small employers requiring individual action throughout, rapid growth is not to be expected, although a steady increase to sizable proportions is not unlikely. Up to the middle of 1956 about 2,400 subscribing employer members had signed up, and about 30,000 employees are now enjoying the protection offered by the system.

This description of a special organization, the National Health and Welfare Retirement Association, as with TIAA for educational groups, has been emphasized because, aside from social security (if the group can qualify), it is the only nationwide, activated movement for solving the no-man's-land pension status of these groups. It is not the only possible solution. Where groups are large enough, separate trust-fund plans or insured group plans could be used, or an individual-contract plan might be found to be suitable as the pension medium for some of the smaller employers.

Labor Unions. Labor organizations per se are exempt from income tax, but they and their employees are subject to the contributions and benefits of OASDI. Likewise most railway-labor groups and their employees are subject to the Railroad Retirement Act; for example, the employees of the railway brotherhoods are in the service of a subject "employer" as defined in that act. Consequently, when the pension status of regular employees of labor unions and affiliated organizations is being considered, it may be assumed that, as a rule, they have basic mandatory protection under a statutory program. To this extent, they are on a par with business employers and employees.

Most international unions have established pension plans of one sort or another for their officers and staff, and many either include their clerical employees or have established entirely separate plans for them. More recently, consideration has been given to establishing pension systems for the officers and employees of local unions, and in 1956 one large union established such a plan, financed jointly through contributions of the participants and, as are all administrative expenses of a union, by the dues of its membership, which were raised by 10 cents a month coincident with the inception of the plan.

Before the merger of the AFL and CIO, the plan for the AFL headquarters employees was of a standard type with the usual provisions and safeguards of a properly devised and well-funded contributory system. It was similar to hundreds of plans established by employers for their employees. The benefit formula was not particularly liberal as such formulas go; the future-service annuity was modest indeed, the ratio of the employee contribution to the annual retirement benefit being $3\frac{2}{3}$ to 1; that is, for every $3.67 the participating employee contributed during his working years he was entitled to receive an annual benefit of $1 upon retiring at normal retirement age. The withdrawal benefit carried with it no vesting of employer contributions to the plan, although such vesting is not uncommon in business plans, and a union's proposal to an employer would, of course, seek as high a degree of vesting as possible. All in all, the American Federation of Labor, in designing a retirement plan for its own employees (the plan was established before the surge of labor-management–negotiated plans), followed time-tested provisions found in the plans adopted by business.

Following the merger of the AFL and CIO, this contributory AFL plan was superseded by a new plan patterned on the former non-contributory CIO staff plan (AFL employee contributions were re-funded to the participants). The new plan, effective December 5, 1955, is of the money-purchase type with the union contributing 6 per cent of salary to a trust fund, of which contribution, seven-eighths is allo-cated to individual employee accounts and one-eighth to a contingency account. There are also certain past-service credits for which 6 per cent allocations are made from funds built up under the prior plans. The interest accumulation on the individual accounts is governed by the rate on United States Savings Bonds (Series E) even though such bonds are not, in current practice, purchased for the fund (previously, under the CIO plan, they were the main investment).

When a covered employee terminates employment as a staff member prior to retirement, the amount of his individual account is available, and probably will normally be taken in a lump sum because of tax advantages. Whether or not this is preserved for retirement purposes is up to the ex-employee. An active employee is eligible for retirement at or after age 60 with at least 10 years of continuous service. The benefit then available is either the aforesaid lump sum or the monthly amount determined by dividing his applicable pension equity (some-what more than the aforesaid lump sum) by his life expectancy ac-cording to the most recent U.S. Life Table (population, white lives) subject to certain minimum benefits (based on OASDI). If the individ-ual account is not used up prior to the pensioner's death, the balance is payable to the beneficiary; if the individual account is exhausted, the contingency fund is relied upon to continue the payments for the pensioner's life.

Thus, the amount of monthly pension depends upon the accumulation of fixed employer contributions over the employee's period of service. For an employee hired at a young age, if his salary did not increase greatly with service, the relative benefit would be quite generous; for short-service employees, the pension can seem quite small. For the normal employee having a reasonable length of service and making good progress in his work, the monthly pension generated is apt to be inadequate in relation to his salary just prior to retirement. These effects are generally found in pension plans when the money purchase principle (rarely found now) is followed.

The extension—partially mandatory and partially elective—of the nationwide coverage of the governmental system of social security and increased employer responsibility in setting up supplementary plans have given the workers in these two fields of endeavor—public employment and nonprofit organizations—greater uniformity of protection both within the two categories themselves and in relation to the employees of other employment categories.

CHAPTER 17

Profit-sharing Plans

In a broad sense, profit sharing may be regarded as including any form of gift, reward, or remuneration deriving from the success of the business that employees are given in excess of compensation and other benefits furnished as a condition of employment.

The regulations (Treasury Decision 6203) of the Internal Revenue Service include the following definition: [1]

A profit-sharing plan is a plan established and maintained by an employer to provide for the participation in his profits by his employees or their beneficiaries. The plan must provide a definite predetermined formula for allocating the contributions made to the plan among the participants and for distributing the funds accumulated under the plan after a fixed number of years, the attainment of a stated age, or upon the prior occurrence of some event such as layoff, illness, disability, retirement, death or severance of employment.

The term *profits* is subject to variations in interpretation, but for present purposes, unless otherwise defined, it will mean the net balance of the income of an employer for a given period remaining after all specified expenses of the employer have been met. In addition to regular operating expenses, including wages and salaries, these current expenses might include such items as interest on outstanding debt, dividends on preferred stock (possibly also a predetermined rate of

[1] The previous regulations provided that the plan must be "based on a definite predetermined formula for determining the profits to be shared." This requirement does not appear in the current regulations.

dividend on common stock), taxes, capital gains or losses, and contributions to a pension plan.

A profit-sharing plan is, then, a device for the orderly distribution among some or all of the employees of a portion of the employer's residual funds arising out of current operations after expenses and other specified current obligations have been met.

Retirement Plans. Profit-sharing plans are of two main types: those that provide for the immediate or periodical distribution of all funds allocated to the plan and those that provide for *deferred distribution*.[2] This latter type generally makes available some or all of the funds accumulated to a participant's credit only on the occurrence of one or more of such specified contingencies as termination of employment, disability, death, or retirement. Since many deferred-distribution plans are designed primarily to provide retirement benefits, a brief discussion of profit-sharing methods is included in this text.

Profit-sharing retirement plans have considerable appeal to employers who hesitate to assume the long-term obligations that are incurred in adopting a formal pension plan providing fixed retirement benefits or requiring stated contributions. Just as a pension plan providing a meager benefit is usually better than none at all, a profit-sharing retirement plan is generally preferred to no plan at all. But the current requirements of the Internal Revenue Service for allocation of distributable funds make it impossible for a profit-sharing plan by itself to meet employee-retirement needs in full in the early years of the plan.[3]

Past experience indicates that a profit-sharing plan rarely takes the place of a pension plan of conventional type. There are some businesses whose margins of profit are likely to be erratic from year to year or whose periods of existence are likely to be brief. In these instances, a deferred-distribution profit-sharing plan may be more appro-

[2] Some profit-sharing plans provide for the distribution in cash of certain employees' (say the younger and lower paid) equities after a stated period, such as 2 years, while for other employees the plan provides retirement benefits. Other employers offer two profit-sharing plans on an elective basis. If the employee elects one plan, he receives a current distribution; if the other, a deferred distribution. Usually if he elects the deferred plan, he must continue in that plan.

[3] Particularly the requirements that, in effect, prohibit allocation on any basis involving the respective ages of the participants.

priate than a formal pension plan involving more definite commitments. It may sometimes also be used advantageously to supplement benefits provided under a conventional retirement plan, but even in this limited capacity it leaves much to be desired as a pension vehicle, largely because of statutory and regulatory restrictions.

Contribution Formulas. Infinitely varied contribution formulas are used to determine the portion of a company's annual profits to be set aside in the profit-sharing fund. While most formulas may seem rather arbitrary (and, indeed, under the 1954 Internal Revenue Code there need be no formula, the contribution being left entirely to management), the aim is frequently to give those who have provided the capital—the stockholders—and those who have produced the materials or services that were sold—the employees—their respective shares of the total profits of the enterprise on a basis deemed by management to be equitable and conducive to furthering employee incentives. Where a contribution formula is used, the definition of apportionable profits varies considerably. Some plans allot to the profit-sharing plan a fixed percentage of gross profits, while others apply a larger percentage to net profits or to the excess of net profits over an amount based on invested capital. Among the types of contribution formulas, in which the figures are illustrative but not necessarily typical, are the following:

1. *Percentage-of-gross-profits type*—e.g., 5 per cent of gross profits before allowance is made for taxes, depreciation, etc.

2. *Percentage-of-net-profits type*—e.g., 10 per cent of net profits

3. *Contribution-after-dividends type*—e.g., after sufficient sums are set aside to pay $3 a share on common stock, the balance of distributable profits to be split, 50 per cent to the profit-sharing plan and 50 per cent to common stockholders

4. *Flat-deduction type*—e.g., after the first $50,000 of net profits, 25 per cent of remaining profits [4]

5. *Graded-percentage-of-net-profits type*—e.g., 4 per cent of the first $20,000 of net profits, 6 per cent of the next $20,000, 8 per cent of the next $20,000, and 10 per cent of the balance over $60,000

---

[4] A similar type excludes a percentage of invested capital—e.g., after 10 per cent of invested capital has been deducted, 50 per cent of profits are apportioned to the profit-sharing plan.

Regulations of the Internal Revenue Service. The net profits of an industrial concern are taxable, but, subject to certain conditions, the portion of the profits set aside in a qualified profit-sharing plan are tax-deductible at the time they are so set aside. And, as under qualified pension plans, they are taxable to the participants only when they are deemed to be received by them.

In order to prevent an unduly large amount of profits from receiving tax exemption by reason of being set aside in a profit-sharing plan, the 1954 Internal Revenue Code, like the preceding code, and the related regulations of the Internal Revenue Service specify the employer will not be permitted to deduct in any one year an amount greater than 15 per cent of the total compensation of all participating employees.[5]

Since profits fluctuate widely and the amount available for the profit-sharing plan may be less than the 15 per cent limitation in a particular year, the difference between 15 per cent and any greater amount set aside in another year may be carried forward to be treated as a deduction in a subsequent year or years. Tax exemption in any one year is granted only to the extent that the accumulation of the unused deductions, plus the deduction (limited to 15 per cent) for the year in question, does not exceed 30 per cent of the aggregate compensation of the participating employees in that year. An employer may contribute more than this amount to his profit-sharing fund, but the amount in excess of the limits is subject to taxation for the year in which it is contributed, although any such excess amount may again be carried over for tax exemption in later years. There is no limit to the amount that may be carried over.

To qualify for approval by the Internal Revenue Service, a profit-sharing plan may not provide to a participant specific retirement benefits, such as 1 per cent of wages for each year of credited service or 30 per cent of average earnings over a period of years. The evidence of intent to furnish specific benefits, the cost of which is actuarially determinable in advance, would render the plan a pension plan, and

[5] Depending on the allocation formula in the plan, the amount credited to an individual employee may be more or less than 15 per cent of his compensation if the total amount set aside is not more than 15 per cent of the aggregate compensation.

as such it would be subject to many other regulations.[6] The retirement benefits furnished under a profit-sharing plan may be only those, necessarily indefinite in amount in advance of actual retirement, which can be provided by the funds accumulated in the plan for the particular employee at his retirement.

One other serious handicap to the use of a profit-sharing plan to provide retirement benefits lies in the stipulation that a profit-sharing plan may not be used as a "feeder" for a pension plan. That is, while the funds accumulated in the profit-sharing plan may be used to provide retirement and other benefits, they may not be deposited to the credit of a separate pension plan.

In order to qualify for approval by the Internal Revenue Service, the eligibility requirements (for participation) adopted must satisfy the same conditions as are stipulated for a pension plan.[7] It is permissible to exclude workers who have not been employed at least 5 years or whose customary employment is for not more than 20 hours in 1 week or more than 5 months in any calendar year. It is also permissible to limit the plan to hourly workers or to salaried employees or to exclude those employees who earn $4,200 a year or less and whose full salary is subject to the OASDI title of the Social Security Act.[8] The Internal Revenue Code provides further that the plan need only include "such employees as qualify under a classification set up by the employer and found by the Secretary of the Treasury or his delegate not to be discriminatory in favor of employees who are officers, shareholders, persons whose principal duties consist in supervising the work of other employees, or highly compensated employees."

Eligibility Conditions. In accordance with the permissive regulations of the Internal Revenue Service, many profit-sharing plans impose eligibility conditions, and many are restricted in scope. While it may be argued that only the principal executives should be covered, on the theory that they are primarily responsible for the success of a business and that therefore a profit-sharing plan does most for the business if it serves to stimulate these executives to greater endeavor,

[6] See Chap. 5.

[7] See Chap. 5, p. 90.

[8] This last exclusion is not common, and if it is used the plan must satisfy certain integration requirements similar to those for pension plans (see Chap. 5).

it may be difficult to demonstrate that such a restriction would not constitute improper discrimination. Some plans include all managerial and executive employees; others are extended to salaried employees; and still others include both wage and salaried employees. Occasionally a plan excludes executive employees.

A service condition is widely found. This condition eliminates the necessity of establishing records for temporary employees. It also awards a greater share of profits to employees of longer service who were probably more responsible for the creation of the profits. Exclusion of a period of up to 5 years of service may be imposed under a qualified plan, and periods of 1, 2, or 3 years are frequently found. On the other hand, the plan may provide that all employees are covered, but the vesting provisions are so set that employees who terminate after short periods of service receive little or nothing.

Some pension plans, particularly those requiring employee contributions, exclude from participation all employees until they have attained a specified age, such as twenty-five or thirty. The imposition of this condition not only serves to exclude the temporary employee but also to postpone making contributions for very young employees for whom retirement is far distant. An age restriction is much less frequently, though occasionally, found in profit-sharing plans, since such plans are often used only incidentally as a vehicle for furnishing retirement benefits.

Contributions by Employees—Thrift Plans. Some profit-sharing plans require contributions from employees. Where a plan is designed as a thrift-promotion device or where the basic intent is to use the fund for retirement, disability, or death benefits, it is entirely appropriate to require employees to contribute. In some cases the employee is required to make a specific contribution, such as 3 per cent of salary, whether or not any profits are contributed to the profit-sharing plan in any particular year. Other plans permit some elective latitude in employee contributions, such as 2 to 5 per cent of salary, the employer's contributions of profits to the fund being allocated among employees in proportion to their own rates of contribution. In some cases, employee-contribution rates are varied according to earnings groups. From the standpoint of meeting the requirements of the Internal Revenue Service, thrift plans are classified under the heading of profit-sharing plans. The most commonly found thrift plans call for employees to contribute at a specified rate. Sometimes a minimum rate of contribution is required, the employee being permitted voluntarily to contribute additional amounts up to a specified maximum percentage. The employer agrees to contribute some proportion of the employee's amount, such as to match the employee's contribution or perhaps to match the minimum contribution and contribute some other proportion of the voluntary part. A type of thrift plan that has been recently adopted by several corporations calls for the employer to contribute 25 cents for each $1 the employee contributes, the employee's contributions being used to purchase United States savings bonds and the employer's contributions being used to purchase stock of the company.

Allocation among Employees of Profits Apportioned to Fund. Probably nowhere in the field of profit-sharing plans is there such variety of formulas as in those used to allocate among individual participants the year's profits apportioned to the fund. While it is not required by the current regulations to have a definite formula for determining the portion of profits to be credited to a profit-sharing fund (although it is customary), in order to avoid improper discrimination among employees, it is essential to have a definite formula for allocating to individuals any amounts so contributed.

The amounts allocated are usually credited on the basis of service and earnings. Many plans allocate the profits apportioned to the plan directly according to wages or salary. Others use more involved formulas. The following is an illustration of one method (the figures are for illustrative purposes only and are not necessarily typical):

Each year of service up to 5 years is counted as one; each year in excess of 5 years but less than 10 years, as two; and each year of 10 years and over as three. Each $100 of current annual earnings is counted as three. The total "count" is determined for all employees participating, and the value of a unit share is found by dividing the allocable profits by this total. The individual allocation is then made in proportion to the number of "counts" assigned to each participant.

Another illustration is based on the social-security wage ceiling:

Amounts of annual salary of eligible participants of $4,200 or less are multiplied by two and amounts of annual salary in excess of $4,200 are multiplied by three. These products are totaled and the distributable profits allocated accordingly.

Vesting. Under some profit-sharing plans, the allocated profits are immediately distributable in cash; in such cases, vesting is immediate, and each year (or longer period or "cycle") the participant receives his share of the profits. In plans providing for deferred distribution, it is usual to include some graded vesting scheme. For instance, where the profits are held in trust until an employee dies, becomes permanently disabled, or retires, it is customary to give the employee (or his beneficiary) his full share of the fund either as a lump sum or as an annuity. When employment is terminated earlier, it is not unusual to restrict the employee's benefit to some portion of his full share. For example, the schedule shown in Table 17-1 might be used. Assume that the

TABLE 17-1

Completed years of service	Per cent vesting
Fewer than 2	None
2	20
3	40
4	60
5	80
6 or more	100

total credit of a particular employee in the fund implementing the profit-sharing plan is as shown in Table 17-2. If this participant with-

TABLE 17-2

Completed years of service	Equity in fund
2	$ 200
3	300
4	700
5	900
6	1,000

draws after 3, but fewer than 4, years of service, he receives 40 per cent of $300, or $120. The balance ($180) of the $300 equity he had before withdrawal is then allocated among the remaining participants in the same way as would be an equivalent amount of profits assigned to the fund.

Death Benefits. It is customary to provide that upon death a participant's full equity will be payable to his beneficiary. Under a contributory profit-sharing plan, an amount not less than the employee's aggregate contributions should be payable if death occurs before eligibility for any other distribution.

Disability Benefits. Various provisions are made for total and permanent disability. Sometimes periodic payments in an amount determined according to a schedule set out in the plan will commence and continue as long as the participant's equity permits. In some cases the profit-sharing committee is instructed to determine on an individual basis the amounts and manner of distribution in the event of disability. If the benefit payable at disability exceeds that payable in the event of termination of employment, disability claims should be thoroughly investigated. Otherwise, employees who contemplate terminating employment may find it advantageous to become "disabled."

Distribution of Profit-sharing Funds. Many students of the subject believe that immediate (or frequent) cash distribution of any amounts credited to the profit-sharing fund is productive of greatest return to the employer. It is argued that young employees particularly are spurred to greater efficiency and production by a plan that provides for early distribution than by prospect of later benefits. This practice has drawbacks as well as advantages, since distributions made annually or oftener are usually spent immediately. They are often very small and have little beneficial effect. If reasonably substantial and regularly granted, too frequent distributions may lead recipients to regard them as almost a part of salary. Curtailment or omission because of insufficient profits is likely to engender dissatisfaction. Deferred-distribution methods eliminate many of these objections but may result in the plan's functioning less well as a stimulant to profitable production.

Funds built up by profit allocation are frequently used to provide a form of pension benefit. Although, for reasons mentioned below, a profit-sharing plan is not essentially the best method of providing pension benefits, it has the advantage of assisting the employer to meet his retirement obligations and at the same time of creating the incentive to profitable production that has been cited as a fundamental reason for adopting a profit-sharing plan.

At least initially, a profit-sharing plan cannot by itself provide satisfactory pension benefits, because profit-sharing payments cannot be relied upon to provide definite retirement benefits. It costs about $2\frac{1}{2}$ times as much money to provide a male employee aged sixty with a specified retirement benefit at age sixty-five as one aged thirty. Nevertheless, under an approved plan it is not permitted to allocate profits in relation to this end; i.e., the age of the employee may not be one of the factors entering into the distribution formula.

To illustrate this point, suppose that profits each year are adequate to permit the contribution of an amount equal to 15 per cent of each covered employee's salary to the profit-sharing plan and that the allocation formula for employees under this plan is based entirely upon earnings. The allocation to the employee aged thirty will be adequate, on the basis of present rates, to furnish him with a pension of over three-fourths of his salary at age sixty-five. The man aged sixty (who may have had long years of service) will receive at sixty-five a pension benefit from the profit-sharing plan of only a little over 5 per cent of his salary.

Where a profit-sharing plan uses an allocation formula that introduces service as well as salary, the man aged sixty, if he has substantial past service, will fare somewhat better than in the example set out above, but it is not possible to design a profit-sharing plan to furnish prearranged retirement benefits, as may be done with a regular pension plan.

As mentioned previously, for tax-exemption purposes the Internal Revenue Code limits an employer's contribution to a profit-sharing plan for any year to 15 per cent of the payroll of covered employees. At the same time, it permits a total of 25 per cent (or 30 per cent in certain circumstances) of participating payroll as the allowable tax-exempt cost of a combination of profit-sharing and pension plans. Under such a combination program, while the contributions to the profit-sharing plan may not be diverted to meet the cost of the pension plan, it is possible to design the pension-plan portion of the program so that the contributions thereto will be allocated, at least in the early years of the plan, in such a way as to give greater credit to the older, longer-service employees.[9] Through this combination of profit-sharing and pension plans, if 25 per cent of payroll (or a smaller percentage, if sufficient) is set aside, an adequate pension benefit can usually be provided. The percentage of payroll necessary to sustain the pension plan will tend to decrease as the initial past-service liability is gradually liquidated. Even if annual profits consistently allow 15 per cent of payroll to be set aside for the plan, a deferred-profit-sharing plan by itself will not operate successfully as a vehicle for effecting retirements until at least 15 or 20 years after it has been installed.

Payment of Retirement Benefits under a Profit-sharing Plan. Where a profit-sharing plan has been established primarily to furnish retirement benefits to the participants, consideration must be given to the arrangements to be made for the distribution of the profit-sharing funds at retirement. For the contributions to a profit-sharing plan to be regarded as tax-deductible under regulations of the Internal Revenue Service, the employer must irrevocably relinquish his right to the amounts allocated to the plan. In most instances, this is accomplished through the creation of a trust. This trust may be administered either by a corporate trustee or by one or more individual trustees. When the employee retires, the amount of the periodic (usually monthly) pension payment that can be provided is actuarially determinable from the amount that stands to his credit in the plan at the time he retires. The trustee (or trustees) may disburse the amount from the profit-sharing fund. Alternatively they may turn over to an insurer part or all of the amount of funds held in his account, and the insurer will make the appropriate life-annuity payments.

Some life insurers have adapted their money-purchase group-annuity plans to use in connection with profit-sharing plans. Under the money-purchase type of group annuity, deferred-retirement annuities are established for the participants in amounts determined by the funds turned over periodically to the insurer. This type of group-annuity plan is sometimes termed an *irregular money-purchase plan.*

Some life insurers have made arrangements under which funds may

[9] In some instances a pension plan has been designed to provide the pension benefits based only on the past service of the participants, the profit-sharing plan providing benefits only with respect to current service.

be drawn from a profit-sharing plan and used as premiums for a group-permanent-insurance annuity or for individual-insurance-annuity contracts.[10] Since the amounts distributed to a profit-sharing plan are not determinable in advance, an estimate is made of the probable average amount that will be allocated annually to each particular participant. A portion of this estimated amount (such as one-third) is then used as a premium to purchase an individual-insurance-annuity contract, with the understanding that in those years when the participant's allocation is not adequate to pay this premium recourse may be had to the extra amounts held to his credit in the profit-sharing fund that had not previously been used for premiums. This is one way of utilizing insurance contracts under a profit-sharing plan, but there are many other suitable procedures that could be followed.

Special Plans. Special plans, classified as profit-sharing plans by the Internal Revenue Service, have been developed for the purpose of extending to salaried employees the type of benefit provided wage employees under supplementary-unemployment-compensation arrangements which have been negotiated with several unions.

Under such a plan the employer contributes from current profits or from surplus a fixed amount, such as 5 cents, for each hour worked by a covered employee. These amounts are set aside in individual employee accounts, usually in a trust. During layoffs a covered employee may obtain certain payments from his account. Any amount remaining to the employee's account is payable as a lump sum in the event of death, retirement, or termination of employment.

Profit-sharing Plans and Pension Plans. It is difficult to compare profit-sharing plans with pension plans. They are fundamentally different in principle and are generally designed to accomplish quite different ends, although a form of pension is frequently one of the benefits included in a profit-sharing plan. The impossibility of giving

[10] A profit-sharing trust may also provide death benefits through the investment in (purchase of) ordinary-life-insurance contracts, provided the insurance element is incidental and subordinate to the primary purpose of the plan. This type of plan must provide that the individual contracts are to be converted into annuity benefits at or before retirement and that less than half of the total contribution made to the profit-sharing fund for a particular employee is used as premiums for the life insurance.

adequate recognition to past service under a profit-sharing plan and the requirement that any system under which retirement benefits may be definitely determinable in advance renders the plan a pension plan make it difficult to furnish satisfactory retirement benefits solely under a profit-sharing plan.

If a survey were made to determine the attitudes of large groups of employees toward profit-sharing plans and pension plans, it would probably be found that the younger employee preferred a profit-sharing plan providing for immediate distribution of funds over a pension plan (or over a deferred-distribution type of profit-sharing plan). On the other hand, the older employee, being more concerned about his imminent retirement, would prefer a pension plan. This desire for immediate cash payment on the part of the younger employee in lieu of deferred distribution has been made evident in certain cases where the younger employees have agitated for immediate distribution of funds accumulated in profit-sharing plans that provided for deferred distribution. This situation is similar to those where employees have been given the choice of accepting an increase in pay or the deferred-pension benefits that could be provided in lieu thereof. Where such a choice is permitted, the younger employees frequently favor an increase in pay and the older ones usually favor pension-plan benefits.

A sizable number of profit-sharing plans adopted years ago have been abandoned. Some of them, including a few established many years ago, were discontinued because under the terms of the plan so many employees became eligible that the amount allocated to each participant was small—a form of dilution that tends to nullify the incentive element. For others, termination was the natural result of a period of years when there were few or no distributable profits.[11]

Notwithstanding the fact that some profit-sharing plans have not fulfilled expectations, the profit-sharing movement has spread dramatically in recent years. According to data prepared by the Internal Revenue Service, as of the end of 1956 there were almost 35,000 quali-

---

[11] According to a recent requirement of the Internal Revenue Service, discontinuance of contributions to a deferred-distribution profit-sharing plan, or termination of the plan, requires that full vesting of the interests of all participants must take place. This requirement also applies to a pension plan, although some postponement of the application of full vesting may be permitted.

fied pension and profit-sharing plans combined, an increase of nearly 5,000 such plans in a year. Of the plans which were qualified with the Service during 1956 about two out of five were profit-sharing plans. Some industrialists take the position that a well-designed plan will furnish adequate incentives to stimulate all employees to much greater efficiency and satisfaction. Others believe that for most organizations a modest pension plan is the principal consideration but that this might be supplemented by both a deferred-distribution profit-sharing plan and a system of currently paid cash bonuses.

A recent development in the profit-sharing field was the organization of the Council of Profit-sharing Industries, whose aims are "to promote profit-sharing as a means of preserving the American System of Free Private Enterprise" and to compile and disseminate information on profit-sharing plans. The membership of this organization—employers with profit-sharing plans in effect—has been growing steadily.

The attitude of organized labor toward the profit-sharing movement is changing. At one time labor unions took a dim view of profit sharing, apparently feeling that it was a device for stimulating production with relatively little reward. Currently this antagonism may be weakening, and in some instances, particularly where the workers have a high degree of confidence in management, unions are viewing profit-sharing plans more favorably. In fact, where a pension plan is already in existence there are indications that the unions may even agitate for some sort of profit-sharing plan in addition.

While pensions have now become acceptable—indeed, a must—to labor and labor is generally more amenable to profit-sharing plans, the profit-sharing arrangement still meets some opposition. For one thing, profit-sharing plans, by their very nature, are not susceptible to union participation, short of "codetermination" (the German *mitbestimmung*, "participation of labor in management affairs"). A quotation from a labor report of several years ago will illustrate this point: [12]

The G.E.B. has no objection to a plan which while gearing profit sharing to increased productivity provides for the employees receiving their genuine proportionate share of the profits resulting from such increased productivity. Generally, however, the Union has no voice in determining the premises

[12] Attitude in Regard to Profit-sharing, General Executive Board's Report at 27th Annual Convention, Upholsterers' Union–AFL.

upon which a profit sharing scheme is based. In such cases, the Union must accept the employer's "facts and figures" without having an opportunity of making its own examination and evaluation of them in determining whether such facts and figures are genuine and bona-fide. In these circumstances, the Union must unilaterally oppose such employer schemes.

A perusal of these plans indicates that the duties and obligations of our members are always clearly and unmistakably set forth in definite and precise terms. Conversely, it is noted that the employers' duties and obligations are virtually indefinable and usually vague and that fundamentally no adequate methods are provided by which our members can be assured that they will participate equitably in increased profits. These plans seldom, if ever, provide adequate methods by which the employees and the Union may objectively ascertain the actual profits made by an employer since the Union is not given the right of review of the employer's financial records and the employer by the simple and expedient technique of draining off excess profits by "loading" contingency reserve and operating accounts, may wipe out on the books a considerable portion of the real profits.

Other objections to profit-sharing plans are raised by the rank and file of workers. The ups and downs of the amounts allocable to them—according to good or bad years—are not likely to be understood. If the plan is all-inclusive, as most union plans are (i.e., no age or service exclusions), the dilution of the allocable profits among so many, especially during the times when employment is high, results in apparently low or trivial benefits. In contrast to immediate-disbursement plans, the deferred-profit-sharing plan, particularly the long-deferred type which often claims the attributes of a retirement system, is frequently not liked by workers who, while having the "profit-sharing" slogan given them, do not find any "profits" coming to hand. This feeling is pronounced under the common type of deferred-profit-sharing plans that impose forfeitures, partial or total, of any accumulated allocations if the employee terminates service before some fixed vesting point based on age, length of service, or both. Finally, the profit-sharing plan does not take the place of a pension plan in protecting the already aged worker. Even the deferred type can only offer the potentiality of protection for the young employees; and unless a supplementary past-service pension plan is established, the profit-sharing plan can do little to produce old-age income for employees already at, or near, retirement age when the plan is set up.

CHAPTER 18

Pension Plans in Canada

When the United States reached a position to export capital, Canada was one of the first countries to benefit therefrom. Previously Canadian development had been financed from English and European sources. At the present time, United States capital investment in Canada is greater than in any other foreign country. In addition, there are nearly 5,000 business enterprises in Canada that are branches or subsidiaries (in whole or in part) of United States parent corporations.

When a business has been acquired or established in Canada, the practice has been to send a manager from the United States who gives the benefit of his knowledge and training to the Canadian employees. This tends to duplicate as nearly as possible the operation as conducted in the United States. The common language, similarity of habits and customs, and favorable laws all combine to make this assimilation easy. Besides their technical and other knowledge, the managers bring with them ideas developed in the United States in the field of employee benefits, and to some extent these ideas have been adopted in Canada. Furthermore, nonresident international-union leaders have stipulated that they must be permitted to bargain in Canada for pension plans whose terms and benefits are tailored to conditions in the United States.

There has been some resistance in Canada to certain features of pension plans developed in the United States which differ from European, and particularly British, practice and which are contrary to basic principles incorporated in the Canadian tax law. As a result there are, among others, two features which can be regarded as repre-

sentative of pensions in Canada that are not present in the United
States. These are the two following provisions in the Canadian Income
Tax Act:

1. Tax relief will be given for contributions made up to certain
stated maximums by both employer and employee. An employee may
contribute and receive tax relief for contributions for both current
service and past service up to a maximum of $1,500 a year for each
type of service. An employer may contribute and claim as a deduction
the cost of a current-service benefit for the year to the extent that it
does not exceed $1,500 for any one employee. The cost of past service,
without limitation, may be charged as an expense if amortized over
not fewer than 10 years.

2. Tax relief will be given only for contributions to a plan accepted
and registered by the Minister of National Revenue with respect to
its constitution and operations for the tax year under consideration.

These provisions are discussed in some detail later on.

Regulation. The wide discretionary power given to the Minister
of National Revenue (who is responsible for the administration of
the income tax laws) to approve and accept plans makes administration flexible. The granting of such power to an executive officer of
the Crown gives him absolute authority over the terms and conditions
of any pension plan, if the contributions to such a plan are to be
tax-free. Provided such power is exercised in a reasonable manner,
it is not subject to review by any board or court. Even if a court held
that the power had not been properly exercised, it would have no
jurisdiction to make a decision in the place of the Minister. It could
merely direct him to make a finding upon a proper exercise of the
power.

The effect of the existence of this discretionary power has been
to preclude regulations as a guide in drafting pension plans in Canada.
The absence of regulations stems from the proposition that as in
theory the Minister must exercise his discretion in every case it is
not possible effectively to regulate the exercise of that discretion.
However, a small booklet was issued in 1950 by the Taxation Division
of the Department of National Revenue which purported to contain
the principles and rules by which the Minister would be guided in

making his decision. In fact, while the principles and rules were used and have left their imprint on the general pattern of pension plans in Canada, they did not, and legally could not, restrict the Minister in the exercise of his discretion. As a result, the Minister has approved plans that did not in every respect comply with the published principles and rules.

Eligibility. Eligibility is limited to *employees,* but this term is interpreted to cover a wide area. It includes officers, directors, and agents who act on a substantially full-time basis for their principals. This interpretation brought within the definition life-insurance and other agents whose status is analogous to that of an employee.

The requirements for coverage are not restrictive, although plans covering only shareholders, higher-paid personnel, or the spouses of partners or proprietors are not acceptable. Inclusion of female employees is required, but special conditions, such as different ages at entry and of retirement, can be set up. Participation as well as contributions may or may not be compulsory, and although discrimination is mentioned as a basis for nonapproval, it is nowhere defined.

Pension Formula. A formula indicating the amount of the proposed pension must be set forth in the plan. Benefits may be provided on an equitable basis, including a money-purchase, unit-benefit, or fixed-benefit basis, or any combination thereof. For example, the past-service pension might be a fixed percentage of salary at the effective date, and the current-service pension might be based on a money-purchase formula. Pensions may also be provided for a surviving widow and/or dependent children, an easing of the restriction that plans are to be set up for employees only.

Benefits for past service may be based on current earnings or on actual earnings during the past-service period or may be granted only for specified years or after attainment of a stated age. In addition to the statutory limitation on the tax-deductible amount of each year's contributions, the principles and rules indicate a further restriction against excessive pensions for past service. Past-service benefits on a higher scale than those for current service are not acceptable.

The Dollar Limitation. The Canadian tax law allows tax deductibility for both employer and employee contributions to approved pension plans, up to certain maximum amounts. Since these provisions are a departure from the main purpose of the income tax laws, they are subject to strict construction in their application. The statute places a limit on the amount which may be deducted from taxable income as the cost of current-service pensions by both the employer and the employee. In the United States there is a comparable close supervision over the maximum amount of employer contribution allowed as a deduction.

The limitations on the amount of pension contribution which could be deducted from taxable income were first imposed in Canada during World War II. By 1941 the income tax rates for a married man started at 37 per cent with a limited marital and dependent exemption. The resulting tax was so high that part of it was designated as "compulsory savings" and was returned tax-free after the end of the war. Certain payments that were in the nature of savings, such as mortgage payments, insurance and annuity premiums, and contributions to pension plans, could be deducted from such compulsory savings. At the same time corporations were subject to a very high rate of regular tax and an excess-profits tax of 100 per cent. Furthermore, wages and salaries were limited to those actually paid during the year 1941.

It was obvious that, unless there was a limitation, both employers and employees could take advantage of the tax laws to purchase pension benefits at the expense of the national revenue. Accordingly, legislation was enacted fixing $300 as the maximum amount of deduction allowed in any one year to any employee for current-service contributions to a pension plan. The employer was restricted to a similar amount for each employee, officer, or director who was covered under a pension plan. At the same time it was decreed that only those superannuation or pension plans that were "approved" by the Minister of National Revenue would be recognized.

The limitation of the deductible amount is applicable to amounts contributed for current service. An employee is allowed to deduct from taxable income an equal amount for past-service pensions. No dollar limitation is imposed on amounts paid by an employer for past service or to make up a deficit in a fund. These costs may be written off over not less than a 10-year period, if approved by the Minister on the advice of the Superintendent of Insurance as being required to meet the obligations of the plan.

The imposition of the limitation during the war period was to reduce the impact of such contributions against the national revenue. This may be the reason that the principle is still retained. However, the dollar limits on employer and employee contributions for current service and on employee contributions for past service were raised to $900, effective January 1, 1946, and to $1,500, effective January 1, 1954.

In the case of group plans, the limitation on cost for each individual created an administrative difficulty if the law was to be strictly enforced. To avoid this, the tax authorities adopted a rather ingenious formula that did not come within the terms of the statute. It operated apparently without difficulty for some years but was finally challenged in 1954, when an appeal was entered against an assessment in which a portion of the cost of current-service pensions under a group-annuity contract was disallowed. This appeal [1] was allowed by the Income Tax Appeal Board, which, in a judgment based entirely on the interpretation of the statute, held that an employer was entitled to deduct for tax purposes the amount actually paid, to the extent that it did not exceed $1,500 multiplied by the number of lives covered under the plan. The judgment was reversed by the Exchequer Court in March, 1958.

In the meantime, in order to clear up the ambiguity, legislation was enacted in 1956 which permitted the Minister to prescribe by regulation the manner in which the deductible costs for current service could be determined. The regulation, the only one issued in connection with pension matters, is designed to retain the formula that has been in effect and is as follows:

(1) For the purpose of subparagraph (ii) of paragraph (g) of subsection (1) of Section 11 of the Act, the amount determined in prescribed manner (hereinafter in this Part referred to as the "prescribed amount") shall be determined as follows:

    (a) determine, in respect of each individual employee on whose behalf the employer's contribution was paid, the amount that is the lesser of

[1] *No. 281 v. Minister of National Revenue*, T.A.B.C. 369 (1955).

(i) the amount paid in the year by the taxpayer as salary or wages to that employee,

or

(ii) that proportion of the total payroll that $1,500 is of the employer's contribution; and

(b) determine, in respect of each individual employee on whose behalf the employer's contribution was paid, the amount that is that proportion of the amount determined under paragraph (a) in respect of that employee that the employer's contribution is of the total payroll; and

(c) determine the amount that is the aggregate of each of the amounts determined under paragraph (b);

and the amount determined under paragraph (c) is the prescribed amount.

(2) In lieu of determining the prescribed amount in accordance with subsection (1), the taxpayer may elect to determine that amount as follows:

(a) determine, in respect of each individual employee on whose behalf the employer's contribution was paid, the amount that is the lesser of

(i) the amount that can be established to be the actual cost to the taxpayer of benefits under the registered pension fund or plan in respect of services rendered by that employee in the year,

or

(ii) $1,500; and

(b) determine the amount that is the aggregate of each of the amounts determined under paragraph (a);

and the amount determined under paragraph (b) is the prescribed amount.

(3) In this section,

(a) "employer's contribution" means the amount paid by the taxpayer in the year or within 60 days from the end of the year to or under a registered pension fund or plan in respect of services rendered by employees of the taxpayer in the year; and

(b) "total payroll" means the aggregate of all amounts paid in the year by the taxpayer as salary or wages to employees of the taxpayer who are included in the fund or plan.

Employer Contributions for Past Service. Past-service costs are deemed to be a payment for an "enduring benefit" and are therefore of a capital nature in so far as tax treatment is concerned. When legislation was enacted in Canada permitting such costs to be deducted, the practice of both Great Britain and the United States was followed, and the total amount of past-service costs is permitted to be written off for tax purposes over a period of not fewer than 10 years.[2] The language used [3] was sufficiently broad to include actuarial deficits as well as past-service costs, and the two are given identical treatment.

Thus there is no limitation on the amount that can be paid in by an employer for past service or for a deficit in the plan if such amounts are approved by the Minister. This nullifies, to some extent, the limitation on the current-service contribution, particularly as there is no obligation or requirement to pay every year the full current-pension cost. The deficiency can later be treated as a "deficit."

Past-service costs include those for service with a predecessor company, provided it has been taken over or purchased by the present employer. Here again considerable latitude is allowed.

All past-service costs are subject to scrutiny, as regards magnitude, by the Superintendent of Insurance. In checking such costs the factors used by the actuary for the plan are accepted unless they are clearly unreasonable. The costs must be irrevocably charged for the purposes of the plan, but a definite funding formula is not always insisted upon. However, under the discretionary powers of the Minister, complete control can be exercised over this, as well as other, features of a plan, if it is deemed necessary.

Employee Contributions. 1. *Current Service.* A distinctive feature of the Canadian income tax law relating to pensions is the granting of tax deferment on employee contributions to such plans. By ministerial

[2] In the United States the limitation is expressed as 10 per cent per year; the necessity of paying interest on the unfunded balances requires a longer amortization period than 10 years.

[3] "Where a taxpayer is an employer and has made a special payment (or payments) on account of an employees' superannuation or pension fund or plan in respect of the past services of employees pursuant to a recommendation by a qualified actuary in whose opinion the resources of the fund or plan required to be augmented by the amount of one or more special payments to ensure that all the obligations of the fund or plan to the employees may be discharged in full and has made the payment so that it is irrevocably vested in or for the fund or plan and the payment has been approved by the Minister on the advice of the Superintendent of Insurance, there may be deducted in computing the income for the taxation year . . . 1/10 of the whole amount so recommended to be paid. . . ." Income Tax Act, sec. 76.

ruling the maximum statutory allowance of $1,500 has been further limited to the amount required to be paid in accordance with the terms of the plan. Plans that require excessive contributions from employees will not be approved.

The effect of tax deferment on employee contributions has made contributory plans the general rule. Until the introduction of union-negotiated plans, there were few, if any, noncontributory plans established after the start of World War II. This may have been because of the right to deduct such contributions from compulsory savings as well as a desire to produce larger pensions than the employer was prepared, or able, to provide.

The attitude of labor unions in Canada toward contributory plans has been dictated by the general policy in the United States, which has not favored such plans. There is reason to believe that this policy is not always approved by labor-union leaders in Canada, who realize the advantage of contributions on a tax-deferred basis but who nevertheless accede to the policies laid down by the international unions. Certain representatives of labor urged the enactment of social legislation similar to the OASDI sections of the Social Security Act to provide benefits based on service in covered industries on a contributory basis. This approach of tying old-age benefits to covered employment was rejected by a joint committee of Parliament in the report recommending the establishment of a national old-age-pension system.[4] The issue is now (1958) again being raised in Parliament.

All employee contributions for current service must be made by payroll deductions. They need not be equalized over the pay period as long as the total is withheld within the calendar year. The employer is required to report the amounts withheld on a salary-information slip, which gives the tax authorities sufficient information to allow the claim for tax deduction. This system works without friction.

2. *Past Service.* In addition to contributions for future service the Income Tax Act permits an employee to deduct contributions for past service up to an amount of $1,500 a year, in effect permitting, under certain circumstances, a total employee tax deduction of $3,000 a year.

4 See p. 378.

The legislation under which this deduction is permitted is quite ambiguous.[5]

In applying this section of the act, certain limitations were imposed, which were possible only under the system of approval at ministerial discretion. Under the principles and rules a contribution for past service could be made by an employee only if it was permissible under the terms of the plan, and such terms limited the total amount that could be paid in to that ascertained by "applying the minimum percentage of contribution for future service to the total earnings received by the employee from the employer during the years in which he was not a contributor." Service for which the contribution could be made included that with a predecessor of the present employer, but not with a stranger, and excluded any service as a partner or proprietor. The amount so ascertained could be paid over in a lump sum and written off at the rate of $1,500 a year or paid in from time to time and allowed as a tax deduction to the extent that it did not exceed $1,500 a year. To meet cases where pay records were not complete, a table of percentages based upon age at entry into the plan was set up to give a roughly equivalent tax benefit.

The intent behind the legislation was to give an employee the same tax benefits he would have received if the pension plan had been in effect from the time he entered the employment. It is not used by the low-income employee but does offer an advantage to those in higher income tax brackets. In spite of the ambiguities, it has not caused any administrative difficulties—partly owing to the fact that so few take advantage of it.

Unlike the contributions of an employee for current service, which may only be deducted from pay, those for past service may be paid

---

[5] ". . . the following amounts may be deducted in computing the income of a taxpayer for a taxation year: . . .

"(i) . . . amounts contributed by the taxpayer to or under an approved superannuation fund or plan, . . .

"(ii) not exceeding in the aggregate $1,500 paid in the year into or under the fund or plan by the taxpayer in respect of services rendered by him previous to the year while he was not a contributor; . . ."

Income Tax Act, sec. 11, subsec. (1)

over directly or may be deducted from pay. In either case a special receipt is required to support a claim for tax relief.

Under all pension plans registered in Canada the employee may not receive a return of his contributions while he remains employed. This is in line with the policy that the tax deferment is an incentive to provide a pension at retirement and that a fund is not to be used as a form of savings plan.

Vesting. The economic concept of a pension as essentially a deferred payment for services rendered was accepted and recognized in the report of The Royal Commission on The Taxation of Annuities and Family Corporations.[6]

Before 1956 the right of the employee to such payments was recognized by the general requirement that the benefit arising from employer contributions must be vested in the employee and that this vested right must be acquired by an employee after having completed 20 years' service and having attained age fifty.

There is always a full and immediate vesting in the employee of his own contributions or any benefits arising from them, but before 1956 vesting of employer-contributed benefits extended only to a right to the pension benefits. In the event that anything happened to frustrate the payment of a pension, such as the death of the employee, the necessity of using the pension contributions as a death benefit was avoided.

In 1956 the Minister reviewed the previous requirements as regards vesting and gave notice that in the future vesting of employer-purchased benefits could be at the sole option of the employer, but in any event vesting must take place upon retirement. This rule is in effect at the present time.

Financing. In Canada, financing mediums are essentially the same as in the United States, the one notable exception being the contracts issued by the Annuities Branch of the Federal Department of Labour. These contracts were first issued about 1906 and were primarily designed as an inexpensive means of providing income for old age to

---

[6] "There can be little doubt that the contributions made by an employer to employees' pensions, irrespective of how such contributions are made, are essentially a reward for services." Report of The Royal Commission on The Taxation of Annuities and Family Corporations, Ottawa, 1945, p. 36.

low-income individuals. They were sold at low cost based on a high interest rate, and all administrative expenses were borne by the government. The maximum amount of annual annuity that could be purchased was $1,200. To meet the demand for pension contracts arising at the outbreak of war in 1939, the government issued both individual and group contracts at favorable rates. As a result, of the employees covered under insured plans at the end of the war about one-half were under government-annuity contracts.

After the war, when inflation became pronounced, it was necessary to seek other mediums to provide for the excess of pensions over $1,200 a year. The government contracts were based, to a large extent, upon the money-purchase principle, and difficulties were encountered in getting private-insurance contracts on the same basis. While this demand was met in part and some insurers issued group contracts on a money-purchase basis, many employers were forced into trusteed funds or group contracts providing a unit-benefit type of pension.

It was some years after the war before trust companies made any special effort to develop the trusteed fund as a medium for providing pension benefits. They have now actively entered the field and have met with some success, assisted by the increased use of this medium for plans negotiated as a part of labor-union contracts. In Canada the trust-company business, like that of banking, is limited to a few companies. As of 1955, there were only 54 such companies. Some larger trust companies have introduced common-trust and diversified-trust funds, and in addition to larger pension plans they are attracting small but growing accounts. Investments have been limited to those authorized for insurers, but a recent announcement indicates that this requirement no longer exists, and the trustee is free to choose any investment, except obligations of the employer.

Recently the deposit-administration type of contract has been made available by several insurers and is being adopted for the financing of an increasing number of pension plans. The Annuities Branch of the Department of Labour, while not refusing such business, is not actively promoting the sale of group annuities, on the ground that sales efforts are too expensive and that they do not wish to compete with the trust companies or insurers for this business. As a result, this medium is being bypassed in large measure, and it may be assumed that in the future the funding of pension plans will follow a pattern similar to that found in the United States.

Actuarial Considerations. A *qualified actuary* in Canada is defined to mean one who is a fellow of one of the actuarial societies of England, Scotland, or the United States. For income tax purposes the past-service costs or unfunded deficiency in a plan must be certified by a qualified actuary and approved by the Superintendent of Insurance.

As yet, no purely Canadian tables of mortality have been developed for valuing pension-plan liabilities, but use has been made of tables compiled in both Great Britain and the United States, and it is likely that this practice will continue. The one actuarial factor that is significantly different is the interest rate, which is recognized as at least $\frac{1}{2}$ per cent higher in Canada than in the United States. The lower interest rates used in the United States may be accepted to give a more conservative funding basis.

The general rule is that the assumptions of a qualified actuary are accepted unless they are obviously inappropriate.

Discrimination. While nowhere defined, *discrimination* has been held to be unacceptable in pension plans in Canada. Discrimination was at one time deemed to include a variation in benefits between hourly-paid and salaried employees. Since the introduction of labor-union–negotiated plans, the pension-benefit coverage of these two groups has tended to differ. Presently the position is that only two groups are recognized, hourly-paid employees and salaried employees. Within each group no distinction in treatment is permitted (although there may be differences between the benefits for the two groups).

Profit Sharing. Profit sharing and plans embodying the profit-sharing principle have been adopted by many employers in the United States. The development of such plans has been well publicized in Canada, and some have been established there, following the usual pattern. The current tax treatment in Canada does not favor the development of deferred-profit-sharing plans although attempts have been made to induce the government to enact legislation affording the same tax deferment as is available in the case of approved pension plans.

Where the profit-sharing plan provides for an immediate distribution, no great problem exists, the payments to each employee being treated as a bonus or addition to salary or wages and taxed accordingly. In the case of a deferred plan, where contributions are paid to a trustee for future distribution, the tax situation is different from that in the United States. Before the enactment of specific legislation in 1953, all contributions by an employer to a profit-sharing trust, as well as the earnings thereon, were taxed against either the employee or the trustee. In 1953 legislation [7] was passed under which amounts paid over under a profit-sharing plan are subject to tax against the employees among whom allocation is made, irrespective of whether the right of the employee to such amounts is contingent or absolute. Any gain from the fund is taxed against the employees to whom it is allocated, except that any capital gains are excluded therefrom, and the dividend credit of 20 per cent, permitted under the tax law, is allowed where applicable. The effect of this legislation has been to limit deferred-profit-sharing plans to a small number, probably not more than a handful in the whole country.

To offset the effect of the restrictive legislation on deferred-profit-sharing plans, the government announced that it would recognize and give approval to a pension plan under which the employer's contribution would be dependent upon profits. Under the system of ministerial approval of pension plans there is a measure of control, since the total contribution of the employer may not exceed the lesser of 20 per cent of the profits or 15 per cent of the covered payroll. The dollar limitation on pension-plan contributions, discussed earlier, prevents a too discriminatory distribution formula. A definite commitment on the amount or percentage of profits is not required; an employer may contribute any amount up to the maximum limitations.

As in any conventional pension plan, employees may contribute within prescribed limits. Under a contributory plan, in a loss year the employer is required to make a minimum token contribution, which may be as low as 1 per cent of the covered payroll.

While the amounts contributed to the plan may vest in the employees, they are not permitted to withdraw any amount while remaining in employment nor to pledge or borrow against it. Upon separation from employment before retirement, settlement may be made on the

[7] Income Tax Act, sec. 79.

same bases as under a conventional pension plan. At retirement the amount to the credit of an employee must be applied as a single premium on an annuity contract. The usual options are available in purchasing such a contract, but the annuity must be primarily payable to the employee during his lifetime.

Plans based on this procedure have substantial appeal and are being widely adopted.

Deferred Compensation. Deferred-compensation plans are essentially a United States product and have been suggested in Canada as a means of providing income to an executive after he has been retired. Such plans are of value only in the case of executives or employees in a high-income bracket who are unable, for various reasons, to accumulate a reasonable pension under a general plan. Their chief merit lies in providing a pension for a senior official who is employed at an advanced age.

While there are some plans of this kind, the provisions of the taxing law are such as to prevent their general acceptance. If such a plan were tested in the courts, it might be held that a payment made under the agreement used in establishing these plans would not meet the test of having been made "for the purpose of gaining or producing income from property or a business of the taxpayer." [8] Where the former employee is to be available for advice or for normal duties, the test of "reasonableness" [9] might still prevent the payment by the employer from being deductible for tax purposes.

In 1948 legislation was passed to prevent the operation of such plans where an insurance contract was purchased to provide a secure source from which the future payments could be made.[10] This section of the

---

[8] *Ibid.*, sec. 12, subsec. (1), par. (*a*).

[9] "In computing income, no deduction shall be made in respect of an outlay or expense otherwise deductible except to the extent that the outlay or expense was reasonable in the circumstances." *Ibid.*, sec. 12, subsec. (2) .

[10] "(1) A payment or transfer of money, rights or things made pursuant to the direction of, or with the concurrence of, a taxpayer to some other person for the benefit of the taxpayer or as a benefit that the taxpayer desired to have conferred on the other person shall be included in computing the taxpayer's income to the extent that it would be if the payment or transfer had been made to him.

"(2) For the purpose of this Part, a payment or transfer in a taxation year of money, rights or things made to the taxpayer or some other person for the bene-

law has not yet been tested in the courts, and therefore its effectiveness is not known. It is of interest only as showing that the taxing authorities are not disposed to regard favorably any scheme that provides retirement benefits outside the limitations prescribed and applicable to conventional pension plans.

Old-age Pensions. In 1950, a joint committee of the Canadian Senate and House of Commons considered the advisability of establishing a plan in Canada for the payment of old-age benefits. After consideration of the numerous old-age-benefit systems in effect in the United States and other parts of the world, a proposal was made. It was accepted by the government and was implemented by the enactment in 1951 of old-age-security benefits.

Under this act provision was made to pay a pension to every person in Canada who applies therefor and also fulfills the following requirements:

1. Has attained the age of seventy

2. Has resided in Canada for the 20 years immediately preceding the day on which his application is approved, or, if he has not so resided,

   a. Has been present in Canada before those 20 years for an aggregate period at least equal to twice the aggregate periods of absence from Canada during those 20 years and

   b. Has resided in Canada for at least 1 year immediately preceding the day on which his application is approved

The amount authorized to be paid was $40 a month.[11] Unlike OASDI payments in the United States, it is taxable income to the recipient. It is to be financed (at least in part) by allocating to a separate fund

2 per cent of the 10 per cent general sales tax (i.e., 20 per cent of the sales tax) plus

---

fit of the taxpayer and other persons jointly or a profit made by the taxpayer and other persons jointly in a taxation year shall be deemed to have been received by the taxpayer in the year to the extent of his interest therein notwithstanding that there was no distribution or division thereof in that year." *Ibid.,* sec. 16.

[11] This amount was raised to $46 per month effective July, 1957, and to $55 effective November, 1957.

2 per cent on the income of corporations plus

2 per cent on the income of individuals up to a maximum amount of $60 tax a year

The tax on the income of the individual and the tax on the income of corporations were additional taxes imposed to help meet the cost of the pension.

In the report of the joint committee it was stated: [12]

> The Committee feels that any plan to be considered should not interfere with employee pension plans, the purchase of governmental or private annuities, or private savings. Any scheme conceived under public auspices should be such as to place a floor under these private or collective provisions for retirement security;—this would make possible the development under private initiative of supplemental programs which, taken together with governmental provisions, would result in more adequate retirement security for the largest possible number of Canadians.

The expectation, as expressed by the committee, has been realized in practically all pension plans established by Canadian employers. However, in the case of plans established by employers controlled in the United States, it has been the practice to integrate the old-age pension payable in Canada in the same manner as is done with the primary OASDI benefits in the United States. The fact that the governmental payments are of distinctly different types in the two countries does not appear to have been fully appreciated.

Registered Retirement Savings Plan. In 1957 the government enacted legislation to give tax-deferred pensions to the self-employed. This legislation was incorporated as Section 79B of the Income Tax Act. It uses the term *registered retirement savings plan* to describe the scheme, which is a more accurate name than *pension plan*. In effect, it is a method by which a *self-employed* person may make one or more payments to a licensed insurer or to a trust or corporation, in return for a life annuity. A plan must be "registered"; that is, it must comply with regulations to be issued and the statutory requirements. Monies paid in are to be paid out in the form of a life annuity commencing before age seventy-one. The annuity may not provide

---

[12] Report of the Joint Committee of the Senate and House of Commons on Old Age Security—1950, p. 103.

any benefit before maturity except for refund of premiums, or any benefit after maturity except a life annuity (with a term certain not to exceed 15 years) to the individual or a joint-and-survivor annuity with his spouse, payable in periodic installments of uniform amounts. However, the retirement annuity may be adjoined to another contract providing other benefits, and the contract may provide for dividends after maturity or for the reduction of benefits on account of benefits which may become payable under the Old Age Security Act. Amounts received other than as above are subject to severe penalty.

If the plan is in the trust form, the income of the trust is not subject to tax. Under either insured or trust form, the premium paid by the individual may be deducted in computing his taxable income up to a maximum of the lesser of 10 per cent of his taxable income or $2,500. If the individual is also covered by a plan under which his employer makes contributions on his behalf, the limit becomes the lesser of 10 per cent of income or $1,500 and is applicable to the total payments made by the individual under the employer's plan, if contributory, and under the registered retirement plan. Benefits received by the individual are taxable as income for the year in which received.

No pattern of how this legislation will operate has yet developed. It appears to offer opportunities to insurers and trust companies which are now establishing plans that will be acceptable for registration. Other organizations whose business is the encouragement of personal savings will also participate where it is feasible to do so. There will be means by which individuals can take advantage of the legislation, and associations of professional people, such as doctors and lawyers, can be expected to adopt group plans available to their members.

This legislation was the result of recommendations presented by various professional associations. It is now evident that some members do not wish to have their savings "locked in" under a registered plan and not available either in cash or as collateral in the event of need. To others, the tax advantage is conclusive. It cannot yet be said whether the scheme will meet the full objective of its advocates.

Conditions and Trends. It has often been said that in Canada ideas and trends in employee-benefit plans tend to lag somewhat behind those in the United States. It might be thought that the reason for the time lag is to permit a proper evaluation of the merits of any new

ideas. Actually, the close business relationships and the interchange
of technical literature leads Canadians to have a reasonably good
understanding of the merits and operation of any new developments
in the United States and of how they would fit into Canadian business.
It is probable that the development of such plans in Canada will
correspond to that in the United States, except to the extent that it is
blocked by limitations in the law. The requirements established under
the tax laws have controlled and influenced the growth and development of such plans, and it may be expected that this very strong
influence will continue.

Government policy to date has indicated a noticeable reluctance to
extend the principle of tax deferment beyond that already granted
to contributors to recognized conventional pension plans. The tremendous growth in insured and trusteed funds in the United States
does not fit in with the Canadian economy. Canada needs risk capital,
and benefit funds, where security of principal is the important factor,
are a rather poor source.[13] There will, therefore, tend to be little
further governmental incentive offered to the development of schemes
that will remove capital from the risk market.

At present a typical Canadian plan might be one requiring a contribution from employees of not more than 5 per cent to provide a
benefit of 1½ per cent of career-average earnings per year of credited
service. This is being changed by the introduction of noncontributory
plans, demanded by international unions, that provide a fixed benefit
or, alternatively, a contribution of x cents per hour. The latter types
have not been generally adopted by Canadian-owned or -controlled
employers, nor demanded by Canadian employees or unions.

Salaried groups, except those under influence of unions with headquarters in the United States, are usually covered under plans with
a required contribution of up to 5 per cent of earnings. It may be
expected that a further group, the executives, including employees in
salary brackets over $10,000, will be recognized in the future and that
separate plans will be available for them.

The present dollar limitation on the amount of the deductible
yearly contribution may be increased from time to time. These in-

[13] Except perhaps for pension plans based on the variable-annuity principle
utilizing investment in equities.

creases, however, will be slow in coming and only if they are necessary to overcome the consequences of inflation and a corresponding rise in the wage and salary scale.

In the 1956 legislation affecting pension plans, one amendment removed from the Income Tax Act the word "approved" in connection with pension plans. Instead there was substituted the requirement that a plan must be "registered." [14] The reason for this change was to remove any possible impression that by having a plan "approved" the government accepted any responsibility or liability thereunder. While there apparently never was any legal liability, the "approval" by the government was misconstrued by some persons. In effect, the amendment does not alter the discretionary control by the Minister over the "constitution" and "operation" of a plan. If he wishes to do so, he may refuse to register a plan or take off the register one that has previously been accepted.

The great stimulus for the growth of pension plans in Canada derived from the high taxes imposed during the war. This situation is a little different from that in the United States, where the stimulus came initially from the enactment of social-security legislation some years before the entry of the United States into the war.

A country at war and under such strict economic controls as existed in Canada does not offer the best field in which to develop social schemes. There is good reason to believe that the great increase in pension plans during the war was actuated perhaps as much by the desire to reduce taxes as by the desire to establish sound retirement schemes for employees. A further obstacle was the attitude of the taxing authorities who in time of war and high taxes were inclined to place a strict construction on any relief or exemption from the general tax burden. The result was the adoption and retention of certain principles and concepts which have hindered the full development of pension schemes.

Former restrictions are being relaxed, and this tendency may be expected to continue. For example, the government has recently an-

---

[14] " 'Registered pension fund or plan' means an employees' superannuation or pension fund or plan accepted by the Minister for registration for the purposes of this Act in respect of its constitution and operations for the taxation year under consideration." Income Tax Act, sec. 139, subsec. (1), par. (*ahh*).

nounced that a pension plan need not require vesting of employer-paid benefits except at retirement. The limitation on the investment of funds in trusteed plans to those authorized for insurers has been removed altogether except as regards investments in obligations of the employer. Discrimination as an element bearing on the acceptance (registration) of a pension plan has been under severe criticism as an improper exercise of the discretionary power of the Minister. The grounds for objection are that this regulates the business of the employer, who should be free to act for his own best interests.

No elaborate statistical data are available in Canada regarding pension plans, their coverage, and operation. The growth of plans was discussed in a report issued in 1955 as follows: [15]

In 1936–37, a survey by the National Employment Commission found that 8 per cent of Canadian establishments had a pension plan. Shortly after the war, in 1947, the Dominion Bureau of Statistics estimated the proportion to be almost 25 per cent. By 1951, according to the Economics and Research Branch survey, the proportion had risen to 37 per cent, and in 1954 to 45 per cent.

The Taxation Branch, reporting on the taxation year 1955, stated that companies filing tax returns claimed pension contributions of $132,400,000. For the same year, individuals claimed exemption for contributions to pension plans amounting to $177,590,000.

[15] "Industrial Pension Plans in Canada," Department of Labour, Economics and Research Branch, Ottawa, 1955, p. 21.

CHAPTER 19

Trends

Growth and Development. The gradual decrease in mortality rates in past years has resulted in an increase both in the number of older persons and in their proportion to the total population. With relatively fewer younger persons to contribute to the support of the aged, the need for annuities provided out of funds accumulated during working years has become more pronounced. The development of pension and profit-sharing plans was, however, fairly slow until the early 1940s. Several factors in the economy since that time have implemented the formation of such plans, and their growth since then has been phenomenal. These factors include wartime controls, growth of unions, high business profits, heavy taxes, and labor scarcity coupled with keen competition among organizations for well-qualified employees.

The roster of larger firms and organizations having employee pension plans is now so complete that almost the only area left uncovered is found among small or less coherent concerns and individual workers, entrepreneurs, or professional men. Various bills aimed toward assisting these individuals have been presented in Congress. These bills would permit the individual to treat as deductible from personal income tax amounts allocated to the provision of pensions up to a defined limit each year. These amounts would be set aside in approved financing vehicles to provide pensions in old age. Since no bill of this type has ever been enacted in the United States, it is not possible to foresee what the future in this particular area will be.[1]

---

[1] Canada enacted a bill in 1957 allowing deductions from current income of sums set aside under a registered retirement savings plan. See pp. 379–380.

As regards the small concerns, particularly the numerous very small ones, only those that are established as corporations may, under existing laws, establish approved pension plans (where the employer's contributions are tax-deductible) designed to include employed proprietors among the covered participants.

It would seem, therefore, that under existing laws further expansion of the pension movement will lie largely in increasing benefits for employees already covered. Many of the existing plans have now been in operation for a number of years, and those under which past-service costs have been funded fairly rapidly may soon experience a drop in the level of annual contributions. If favorable business profits are the rule and taxes are high, it is to be expected that at least some of the contributions formerly applied toward the liquidation of past-service costs will be channeled into providing increased benefits, such as higher benefits for each year of service, more complete and earlier vesting, adoption of pensions based on final-average pay, disability benefits, or widows' coverage.

If business profits drop substantially, a quite different situation may result—reduced or suspended contributions, increases in unfunded past-service liabilities, and even the curtailment or termination of some plans. The future growth of the pension movement will be closely related to economic conditions.

However, many forces would probably operate to make a downgrading of benefits take a much slower course in periods of business recession than the corresponding growth of pension plans during periods of high business prosperity. Such forces would be union pressure to maintain benefits at their previous level (although a program aimed at 100 per cent funding might be temporarily set aside) and employer efforts to maintain high employee morale.

Responsibilities Resulting from Growth. The vast increase in the number and magnitude of pension plans has brought with it certain responsibilities. The establishment of a plan and the setting aside of great sums of money to meet prospective pension disbursements mean that investment mediums (insurers, trust companies, and individuals acting as trustees) must exercise careful stewardship to avoid the loss of funds entrusted to their safekeeping.

Recent criticisms of employee benefit plans have been directed largely at those employee welfare plans which provide benefits upon illness and death rather than at pension plans. In some instances trustees of such welfare funds have misappropriated money in their safekeeping, and a few insurance-company representatives have resorted to highly questionable practices in dealing with insurance coverage under these plans. Several investigations of the administration of these welfare plans and of pension plans have recently been made, notably by the Ives, Douglas, and Kennedy committees of the United States Senate and by the New York insurance and banking departments.

It is virtually certain that periodic reports will be required on all pension plans and employee-welfare funds attesting to the status of the fund implementing the plan at the end of each reporting period and making full disclosure of the income and disbursements of the fund during the interval between reports. Several states have recently enacted "disclosure" laws. New York State, for example, under the Mitchell-Hollinger law (enacted April 18, 1956) requires that employee welfare funds (including pension plans) jointly established by an employer and a union must be registered with either the New York banking department or the insurance department (the banking department if the plan is in the hands of a corporate trustee, otherwise the insurance department).

The administrative work and expense required under pension and other employee benefit plans will increase. In addition to the periodic tax returns required under Section 404(a) of the Internal Revenue Code, there was imposed in 1954, under this code, the requirement that each trustee must prepare and submit an additional form, 990-P, for each tax-exempt trust, containing specified data relative to the trust and information on transactions between the trust and the business or organization which created the trust that were not of an arm's-length character. An additional requirement is to file the Form 990-T where a trust engages in an unrelated business. Certain information regarding pension plans in connection with the stockholder proxies of corporations is required to be reported to the SEC. Other various requirements of the Internal Revenue Service have been described. Many authorities feel that some of these special reports would be unnecessary if full-disclosure statements on the operation of the funds were made public annually. Pressure of public opinion might then be adequate to police the plans.

Growth of Funds Implementing Pension Plans. If only the pension plans now in existence are continued and if reasonable efforts are carried out to fund them on a sound actuarial basis, there will be large continuing increases in the assets of these plans for quite some time into the future.

It is estimated that in 1957 there were about 30 billion dollars held by trustees or insurers to provide pension benefits; this amount was held in plans which, on the average, had had only a short existence. As time goes on and the funds increase for 20, 30, or 40 years or even longer periods, they should attain a reasonably stable position (where the annual normal-cost contributions plus interest on the accumulated funds become equal to the pension-benefit disbursements), and there might be accumulated funds amounting to several times the 30-billion-dollar figure. During the 6-year period ending December 31, 1955, the funds accumulated for private pension purposes more than doubled. Indeed, the pension fund of one corporation and its subsidiaries exceeds $2\frac{1}{2}$ billion dollars. In the case of several companies the funds exceed $\frac{1}{2}$ billion dollars. It is questionable whether a pension fund of this dimension needs to be increased. Regardless of the actuarial basis of such a plan and its present funding program, it may be desirable to slow down or to forgo any substantial amount of additional funding, but careful account must be kept of the growth in the liabilities under the plan.

The setting aside into a trust or under an insurance contract of these vast amounts of money has had some impact on the economy of the country. The current trend toward inclusion of more common stocks in the pension-plan portfolios of trusteed plans has undoubtedly had some effect in the direction of stabilizing prices in the stock market. The impact of huge amounts of equity investments resulting from a greater utilization of variable-annuity plans can only be guessed.

The channeling of these funds into the equity market, while attended by a certain amount of risk of capital loss, has served to answer one criticism frequently leveled at the traditional procedures for making pension-fund investments: that such funds were in the past largely invested in bonds and other evidences of indebtedness and therefore did not assist in meeting sound needs for new risk capital. Suggestions have been made that a part of these funds might be invested in residential mortgages at times when such financing is tight.

The question whether to invest part of the assets of the pension fund in the stocks or obligations of the employer has received considerable attention recently. The 1954 code and the relevant regulations of the Internal Revenue Service have imposed certain restrictions on the income tax–deductible status of contributions to an approved pension plan if debentures of the employer are used as an investment of the pension fund. Oddly enough, equity-type securities of the same company are not subject to this scrutiny if purchased competitively (e.g., on the open market) and not in preponderant amounts (legislation in 1958 may relax the restrictions on debentures).

Employee Relationships. A pension plan or a profit-sharing plan can favorably affect employee-employer relationships to such a degree and can be such an important element in attracting and holding employees that, to an increasing extent, employees are kept informed of their rights and interests under the plan. The existence of pension or profit-sharing plans has been widely mentioned in advertisements by employers competing for well-qualified employees, and publicity about the plans has been used as a device for holding present employees.

There is a trend toward counseling employees before retirement. More and more employers are providing their employees with information on post-retirement activities and with data on the relative merits of, and living costs in, various geographical areas. In some instances counseling in anticipation of retirement is commenced either by the employers or by unions well before that date arrives.

Growth of Consulting Firms, Insurers, and Related Service Agencies. The rapid increase in the pension-plan movement has been attended by considerable growth in agencies which assist in establishing such plans. The services offered by these organizations involve design and development of pension plans, determination of liabilities under such plans, investment of funds and their later distribution, and administration.

Rarely does a meeting of actuaries, attorneys, accountants, investment people, life-insurance underwriters, or employee-relations counselors take place but that some phase of pension planning is a topic, and frequently a major topic, for discussion. Several associations have been formed largely for the purpose of disseminating information about one or more aspects of pension plans.

Pension-plan Design. Pension-plan design is constantly changing to reflect changing conditions. The trend seems to be toward noncontributory plans, occasioned in large degree by high tax rates, both corporate and personal. To some extent it also reflects the tendency to simplification in the funding structure of pension plans. Greater emphasis is being placed on true bulk methods (deposit administration and trust fund) in lieu of the methods involving more extensive individual record keeping. If the federal government should ever enact a bill permitting employee contributions to a pension plan to be treated as deductible from personal income (as was proposed in 1956 as an amendment to the Railroad Retirement Act but rejected as class legislation,[2] or as is permitted in Canada) there might well be some reversal of the trend toward noncontributory plans.

There is growing emphasis on final-pay plans—where the pension is based on compensation levels shortly before retirement—and many employers have recently redesigned their plans accordingly. The final-pay plan may be expected to work better as an employee-relations instrument, because it is generally conceded that it is more readily comprehended by employees. The drawback usually cited for this type of plan—that it is not possible to forecast costs with any reasonable degree of reliability—is also a criticism of unit-benefit or career-average plans. The fact that during a period of inflation it is necessary to adjust periodically the accrued benefit under the career-average plan in order to keep the benefits in line with the inflationary trend has raised the question which of the benefit structures enables more accurate cost predictions to be made. In some instances a combination plan provides for determination of part of the benefit on career-average salary and the balance on final-average salary.

The variable-annuity concept is being adopted in an increasing number of pension plans in order that the retired employee's pension payments may be related to some degree to the future inflationary (or

[2] A bill was reintroduced in 1957.

deflationary) trend. A variable annuity is now optionally available to state employees in Wisconsin, and at least one other state is now considering a similar provision. A few pension plans accomplish somewhat the same result by including a provision which gears the pension payments to a cost-of-living index, and some unions have expressed interest in this principle.

The changes made in the Social Security Act in 1956, including the provision for the disability-insurance benefit, have served to emphasize total-and-permanent-disability benefits. Just as the passage of the original Social Security Act stimulated interest in pensions for retired employees, so may the adoption of the disability-insurance benefit under OASDI result in the inclusion of some form of total-and-permanent-disability benefits in plans that do not now contain them. On the other hand, where pension plans already have generous disability benefits, it is to be expected that steps will be taken to treat the federal benefit as a total or partial offset to such benefits.

While these new federal disability benefits will have to be considered in relation to a plan's disability benefits, the earlier prevalence of provisions adjusting the old-age pension by deducting all or one-half of the federal OASDI benefit has been diminishing. New pension plans seldom adopt this offset method for age retirements, and many previously established plans with the offset feature have changed to benefit formulas independent of OASDI. This is not to say that OASDI is being ignored in establishing the pension formula but only that the offset approach is not used so much as formerly, though it is frequently retained for disability retirements. For example, the pension arising from the first $4,200 of earnings is usually at a lower rate than the part deriving from earnings in excess of $4,200; the resulting total pension is thus payable in addition to federal old-age benefits, but the latter are taken into account automatically.

There is a trend toward eliminating or increasing maximum benefits. In many salaried plans the dollar-maximum amounts have been increased recently or removed entirely (in some instances minority groups of stockholders have opposed these changes). The limit on the number of years for which service is credited is being extended or removed. The eligibility conditions requiring, for example, the attainment of age thirty-five with 5 years of service before benefits will accrue under the plan are being made less severe, and in many plans, particularly in noncontributory types, employees are permitted to include all years of continuous service for credit.[3]

A provision for vesting of benefits attributable to employee contributions is generally found in new contributory plans. The trend toward the inclusion of some form of vesting of employer contributions and the liberalization of existing vesting provisions have been stimulated by the inclusion of such provisions in many recently negotiated pension plans. In some plans where extremely generous vesting provisions were included earlier (e.g., in plans designed during the period of wage and salary stabilization where one of the features of the plan was the provision of a separation allowance in the guise of a vesting provision), the vesting provision has been tightened up. Employers who had experienced heavy outlays, in the form of either cash or deferred benefits, by reason of short-term employees leaving employment with vested rights, have taken steps to curtail this frittering away of pension funds by requiring more stringent age and length-of-service requirements to be met before vesting becomes effective.

In the area of negotiated pension plans some of the unions have indicated that their next objectives will be (1) improving benefit levels to bring pension payments (inclusive of OASDI) closer to the pay received shortly before retirement, (2) improving the vesting provision with a view to ultimately attaining full and immediate vesting of employer contributions, (3) increasing the total-and-permanent-disability benefits and easing the eligibility requirements for receiving such benefits, and (4) including some form of pension payment to widows of deceased pensioners.

Some union officials favor investment of a substantial portion of funds implementing negotiated pension plans in housing for active and retired members and in medical centers.

Termination and Combination of Plans. The burgeoning of the pension-plan movement over the last two decades and the unusual business situation that persisted during this period (and to some extent still persists) has resulted in the installation of a number of plans that were ill-conceived and sometimes devised primarily for purposes

---

[3] Sometimes, however, the benefit-accrual rate selected may be reduced somewhat from what it would have been if credited service had been limited.

other than meeting future pension obligations. A few employers, growing rapidly and making large profits, adopted overly generous pension plans which became difficult to continue when business conditions became more competitive. Some of these plans came to the position where termination, in whole or in part, became desirable if not necessary.

Recent years have witnessed the frequent combining of corporations by merger or purchase. Often each corporation has its own pension plan, and it becomes necessary to redesign one of the plans to accommodate it to the other or to develop an entirely new plan which will, in so far as possible, reflect the benefit provisions of the plans of each corporation. This can be an extremely difficult and complex procedure, not only because of the need for preserving the equities of the participants in each plan, as far as is practicable, but also because of the natural tendency to select the most liberal provisions of each plan so that the pension-benefit status of all the employees will be improved (or at least not worsened). Frequently, too, quite diverse funding methods and financing mediums will have to be reconciled.

Financing. Since the late 1940s there has been a well-defined trend toward using trust funds for financing medium- and large-sized pension plans. Before that time most pension benefits were financed through insurance contracts either of the group-annuity form or of the individual-policy form. The statutory restrictions on investments of life-insurance companies, precluding all but a relatively small investment in common stocks, and the flexibility possible under a trust-fund plan are factors promoting this trend.

The generally higher rates of interest return of trust funds (sometimes substantially higher but on occasion lower, especially where the assets of the trust funds were invested almost entirely in government bonds) as compared with insurers and the capital gains, realized and unrealized, of those trusts that included a substantial amount of stock in their pension-fund portfolios influenced the movement toward trust funds. To some extent the favorable tax position of an exempt trust as against an insured plan was a contributing factor. Whether this trend toward the trust-fund financing arrangement will continue is impossible to forecast accurately. With a view to making their product more competitive with trust-fund plans, the insurance companies have developed plans which utilize types of funding commonly used under trust funds, have streamlined administration procedures, and have increased flexibility in other areas.[4]

The split-funding approach [5] has become increasingly popular within the last few years, especially for large pension plans. Both an insurance contract and a trust fund are utilized, with part of the contributions under the plan going to one and part to the other. Under one split-funding approach the trust fund is used substantially for the accumulation of funds up to retirement, funds then being transferred to the insurer, which acts both as investment medium and as disbursing agency. The indicated advantage of the split-funding approach is that it offers a middle course between the trust fund and the insurer and thereby serves to reduce the risk of complete reliance on either financing vehicle.

Small Employers. The almost complete coverage by pension plans, in one form or another, of the employees of medium and large corporations has produced increased emphasis on meeting the pension problems of the small concern. Until recently most small employers establishing pension plans based them on individual-insurance contracts of the insurance-annuity or retirement-annuity type, with a custodian trustee holding the policies. One of the disadvantages of a trust fund as the financing medium for a small pension plan has been the inability of the trust to diversify its investments and the added expense when relatively small units of securities were purchased. To alleviate this condition the use of common trusts [6] by pension plans has been promoted and, subject to appropriate provisions, has been accepted as a suitable arrangement by the Internal Revenue Service. Some common trusts have a stipulated dollar limit on the amount of investments which can be made, after which a new common trust is established and similarly succeeding ones. Other common trusts are

---

[4] There are other considerations besides financing. For example, some authorities in the pension field point out that insurers are in a favorable position to disburse pension payments because of their extensive facilities for tracing and making payment to annuitants and beneficiaries.

[5] See p. 185.

[6] Wherein the assets of more than one pension fund are commingled for investment purposes.

not restricted in this manner. Trust companies have established different forms of common trusts. One may invest only in common stocks, another only in bonds, and still another in a mixture of stocks and bonds. By offering these several types of common trusts, greater choice is permitted in the type of investment that may be utilized for a pension fund. For example, if an employer installed a pension plan that included a variable annuity as well as a fixed type of benefit, the common trust utilizing equities only might be used to finance the variable annuity and the mixed trust, or the 100 per cent bond trust, might be used to finance the balance of the benefit. The pension-trust fund could then "buy into" such a common trust and become the "owner" of a fractional part of it. Similarly, it could invest in a number of common trusts. Small funds may also secure investment averages, although not mortality averages, through investment in mutual funds.

Conclusion. While some social planners point with pride to the widespread adoption of private pension plans and the seemingly continual "improvement" in the social-security and other governmental benefits payable during old age and disability, others express concern over this trend. It is a moot question whether or not the increased mechanization of industry and business, accompanied by emphasis on bigness in private enterprise, has tended to make it more difficult for individuals to provide for their old age themselves. It is also by no means apparent that the existence of pension plans tends to reduce individual initiative and mobility, although arguments to this effect are frequently presented.

Certainly the scarcity of qualified personnel in almost all categories, caused by the prosperous conditions of the last decade, and the favorable tax treatment afforded pension plans have greatly stimulated their development. The effect of future business cycles on the pension-plan movement is not possible to foresee, but large numbers of the working people of this country are placing great reliance on the continuation of these plans. It is not unlikely that, in the recent growth of the pension-plan movement, a major shift in the social and economic structure has taken place.

Index